PEARSON English Learning System

Anna Uhl Chamot

John De Mado

Sharroky Hollie

PEARSON

Upper Saddle River, New Jersey • Boston, Massachusetts • Chandler, Arizona • Glenview, Illinois

PEARSON LONGMAN
KEYSTONE A

PEARSON English Learning System

Staff credits: The people who made up the *Longman Keystone team,* representing editorial, production, design, manufacturing, and marketing, are John Ade, Rhea Banker, Liz Barker, Danielle Belfiore, Virginia Bernard, Kenna Bourke, Anne Boynton-Trigg, Johnnie Farmer, Patrice Fraccio, Geraldine Geniusas, Charles Green, Henry Hild, Lucille M. Kennedy, Ed Lamprich, Emily Lippincott, Tara Maceyak, Maria Pia Marrella, Linda Moser, Laurie Neaman, Sherri Pemberton, Liza Pleva, Edie Pullman, Monica Rodriguez, Tania Saiz-Sousa, Chris Siley, Lynn Sobotta, Heather St. Clair, Jennifer Stem, Jane Townsend, Marian Wassner, Lauren Weidenman, and Adina Zoltan.

Smithsonian American Art Museum contributors: Project director and writer: Elizabeth K. Eder, Ph.D.; Writer: Mary Collins; Image research assistants: Laurel Fehrenbach, Katherine G. Stilwill, and Sally Otis; Rights and reproductions: Richard H. Sorensen and Leslie G. Green; Building photograph by Tim Hursley.

Text design and composition: Kirchoff/Wohlberg, Inc., TSI Graphics, Quarasan

Text font: 11.5/14 Minion
Acknowledgments: See page 468.
Illustration and Photo credits appear on page 469, which constitute an extension of this copyright page.

Library of Congress Cataloging-in-Publication Data
Chamot, Anna Uhl.
    Longman Keystone / Anna Uhl Chamot, John De Mado, Sharroky Hollie.
        p. cm. — (Longman Keystone)
    Includes index.
    ISBN 1-42-843490-9 (v. 6)
    1. Language arts (Middle school)—United States. 2. Language arts (Middle school)—Activity programs. 3. Language arts (Secondary)—United States. 4. English language—Study and teaching. I. Demado, John II. Hollie, Sharroky III. Title.
LB1631.C4466 2008
428.0071'2—dc22
                                                2007049279

ISBN-13: 978-1-4284-3490-5
ISBN-10: 1-4284-3490-9

Printed in the United States of America
1 2 3 4 5 6 7 8 9 10 V064 16 15 14 13 12

About the Authors

Anna Uhl Chamot is a professor of secondary education and a faculty advisor for ESL in George Washington University's Department of Teacher Preparation. She has been a researcher and teacher trainer in content-based second-language learning and language-learning strategies. She co-designed and has written extensively about the Cognitive Academic Language Learning Approach (CALLA) and spent seven years implementing the CALLA model in the Arlington Public Schools in Virginia.

John De Mado has been an energetic force in the field of Language Acquisition for several years. He is founder and president of John De Mado Language Seminars, Inc., an educational consulting firm devoted exclusively to language acquisition and literacy issues. John, who speaks a variety of languages, has authored several textbook programs and produced a series of music CD/DVDs designed to help students acquire other languages. John is recognized nationally, as well as internationally, for his insightful workshops, motivating keynote addresses, and humor-filled delivery style.

Sharroky Hollie is an assistant professor in teacher education at California State University, Dominguez Hills. His expertise is in the field of professional development, African-American education, and second-language methodology. He is an urban literacy visiting professor at Webster University, St. Louis. Sharroky is the Executive Director of the Center for Culturally Responsive Teaching and Learning (CCRTL) and the co-founding director of the nationally acclaimed Culture and Language Academy of Success (CLAS).

Reviewers

Sharena Adebiyi
Fulton County Schools
Stone City, GA

Jennifer Benavides
Garland ISD
Garland, TX

Tracy Bunker
Shearer Charter School
Napa, CA

Dan Fichtner
UCLA Ed. Ext. TESOL Program
Redondo Beach, CA

Trudy Freer-Alvarez
Houston ISD
Houston, TX

Helena K. Gandell
Duval County
Jacksonville, FL

Glenda Harrell
Johnston County School Dist.
Smithfield, NC

Michelle Land
Randolph Middle School
Randolph, NJ

Joseph E. Leaf
Norristown Area High School
Norristown, PA

Ilona Olancin
Collier County Schools
Naples, FL

Jeanne Perrin
Boston Unified School Dist.
Boston, MA

Cheryl Quadrelli-Jones
Anaheim Union High School Dist.
Fullerton, CA

Mary Schmidt
Riverwood High School
Atlanta, GA

Daniel Thatcher
Garland ISD
Garland, TX

Denise Tiffany
West High School
Iowa City, IA

Lisa Troute
Palm Beach County School Dist.
West Palm, FL

Dear Student,

Welcome to **LONGMAN KEYSTONE**

Longman Keystone has been specially designed to help you succeed in all areas of your school studies. This program will help you develop the English language skills you need for language arts, social studies, math, and science. You will discover new ways to use and build upon your language skills through your interactions with classmates, friends, teachers, and family members.

Keystone includes a mix of many subjects. Each unit has four different reading selections that include literary excerpts, poems, and nonfiction articles about science, math, and social studies. These selections will help you understand the vocabulary and organization of different types of texts. They will also give you the tools you need to approach the content of the different subjects you take in school.

As you use this program, you will discover new words, use your background knowledge of the subjects presented, relate your knowledge to the new information, and take part in creative activities. You will learn strategies to help you understand readings better. You will work on activities that help you improve your English skills in grammar, word study, and spelling. Finally, you will be asked to demonstrate the listening, speaking, and writing skills you have learned through fun projects that are incorporated throughout the program.

Learning a language takes time, but just like learning to skateboard or learning to swim, it is fun! Whether you are learning English for the first time, or increasing your knowledge of English by adding academic or literary language to your vocabulary, you are giving yourself new choices for the future, and a better chance of succeeding in both your studies and in everyday life.

We hope you enjoy *Longman Keystone* as much as we enjoyed writing it for you!

Good luck!

Anna Uhl Chamot
John De Mado
Sharroky Hollie

v

Smithsonian American Art Museum

Dear Student,

At the end of each unit in this book, you will learn about some artists and artworks that relate to the theme you have just read about. These artworks are all in the Smithsonian American Art Museum in Washington, D.C. That means they belong to you, because the Smithsonian is America's collection. The artworks were created over a period of 300 years by artists who responded to their experiences in personal ways. Their world lives on through their artworks and, as viewers, we can understand them and ourselves in new ways. We discover that many of the things that concerned these artists still engage us today.

Looking at an artwork is different from reading a written history. Artists present few facts or dates. Instead, they offer emotional insights that come from their own lives and experiences. They make their own decisions about what matters, without worrying if others agree or disagree. This is a rare and useful kind of knowledge that we can all learn from. Artists inspire us to respond to our own lives with deeper insight.

There are two ways to approach art. One way is through the mind—studying the artist, learning about the subject, exploring the context in which the artwork was made, and forming a personal view. This way is deeply rewarding and expands your understanding of the world. The second way is through the senses—letting your imagination roam as you look at an artwork, losing yourself in colors and shapes, absorbing the meaning through your eyes. This way is called "aesthetic." The great thing about art is that an artwork may have many different meanings. You can decide what it means to you.

This brief introduction to American art will, I hope, lead to a lifetime of enjoyment and appreciation of art.

Elizabeth Broun
The Margaret and Terry Stent Director
Smithsonian American Art Museum

Glossary of Terms

You will find the following words useful when reading, writing, and talking about art.

abstract a style of art that does not represent things, animals, or people realistically

acrylic a type of paint that is made from ground pigments and certain chemicals

background part of the artwork that looks furthest away from the viewer

brushstroke the paint or ink left on the surface of an artwork by the paintbrush

canvas a type of heavy woven fabric used as a support for painting; another word for a painting

composition the way in which the different parts of an artwork are arranged

detail a small part of an artwork

evoke to produce a strong feeling or memory

figure the representation of a person or animal in an artwork

foreground part of the artwork that looks closest to the viewer

geometric a type of pattern that has straight lines or shapes such as squares, circles, etc.

mixed media different kinds of materials such as paint, fabric, objects, etc. that are used in a single artwork

oil a type of paint that is made from ground pigments and linseed oil

paintbrush a special brush used for painting

perception the way you understand something you see

pigment a finely powdered material (natural or man-made) that gives color to paint, ink, or dye

portrait an artwork that shows a specific person, group of people, or animal

print an artwork that has been made from a sheet of metal or a block of wood covered with a wet color and then pressed onto a flat surface like paper. Types of prints include lithographs, etchings, aquatints, etc.

symbol an image, shape, or object in an artwork that represents an idea

texture the way that a surface or material feels and how smooth or rough it looks

tone the shade of a particular color; the effect of light and shade with color

watercolor a type of paint that is made from ground pigments, gum, and glycerin and/or honey; another word for a painting done with this medium

Contents

Can all mysteries be solved? **2**

UNIT 2

Contents

How does growing up change us?

Contents

Contents

UNIT 4

Contents

UNIT 5

Contents

THE BIG QUESTION

Can all mysteries be solved?

This unit is about real-life and make-believe mysteries. You'll read about strange events, unusual number patterns, mysterious cities, and monster-like creatures. Exploring these mysteries will help you become a better reader. It will also help you practice the academic and literary language you need to use in school.

Reading

1 Social Studies	2 Short Stories	3 Math/Science

"Fact or Fiction?"	*Teenage Detectives* by Carol Farley and Hy Conrad	From *G Is for Googol* by David M. Schwartz
Reading Strategy: Preview	**Reading Strategy: Draw conclusions**	**Reading Strategy: Use visuals 1**

Listening and Speaking—Descriptive

At the end of this unit, you and your classmates will play a **description guessing game**.

Writing—Descriptive

In this unit you will practice **descriptive writing**. This type of writing tells what things look, sound, feel, smell, or taste like. After each reading you will learn a skill to help you write a descriptive paragraph. At the end of the unit, you will use these skills to help you write a descriptive essay.

Quick Write

In your notebook, write the words *look, sound,* and *feel.* Look around your classroom. What do you see, hear, and feel? Write for five minutes.

---

4   Short Story

"The Haunted Yacht Club" by Ellen Fusz

Reading Strategy:
Predict

DVD   VIEW AND RESPOND
Watch the DVD for Unit 1 and answer the questions at
www.LongmanKeystone.com.

3

What You Will Learn

Reading
- Vocabulary building: *Context, dictionary skills, word study*
- Reading strategy: *Preview*
- Text type: *Informational text (social studies)*

Grammar
Parts of speech and parts of the sentence

Writing
Describe a place

► 🔍 THE BIG QUESTION

Can all mysteries be solved? You are going to read about a series of real-life mysteries. The first concerns the Egyptian pyramids. Work with a partner. Use your prior knowledge to explore everything you know about pyramids. What do they look like? Where, when, and how were they built? In your notebook, record what you already know.

Now look at the picture below. Read the facts about the Great Pyramid at Giza in Egypt. Discuss the picture and facts with your partner.

LEARNING STRATEGY

Use your prior knowledge. Relating what you already know to a new topic will make it easier to understand new meanings in English.

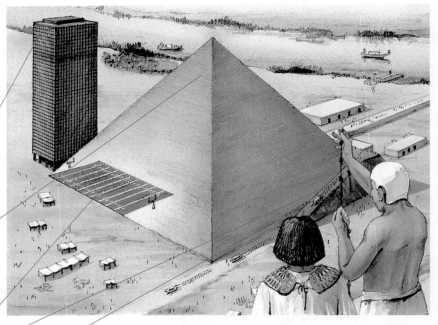

The pyramid is as tall as a forty-story building. It took 20,000 workers twenty years to build it.

It is made up of more than 2 million blocks of stone. Each block weighs about 2,200 kilograms (5,000 lb.).

The bottom of the pyramid is as big as eight football fields.

Workers used a knotted string as a measurement tool.

Workers used logs and ramps.

► BUILD BACKGROUND

"Fact or Fiction?" explores mysterious places, creatures, and events from the past. First, this nonfiction article focuses on the pyramids of Egypt, one of the most puzzling of mysteries. Then it goes on to explore other historical puzzles: *What happened to the people of Machu Picchu? Is there really a curse on King Tutankhamen's tomb? What mysterious creatures live in the depths of the sea? Is there a monster in a lake in Scotland?* As you read, think about how you would try to solve one of these mysteries.

➤ VOCABULARY

Listening and Speaking: Key Words

Key words are important topic-related vocabulary used routinely in written classroom materials and other texts you will read. Read aloud and listen to these sentences with a partner. Use the context to figure out the meaning of the highlighted words. Use a dictionary to check your answers. Then write each word and its meaning in your notebook.

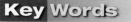

Key Words

archaeologist
clues
creature
disappeared
fantasy
sacred

1. The archaeologist tried to understand the past by digging through the ruins of old buildings.

2. To understand the mysterious ruins, scientists used clues from the soil, statues, and ancient scrolls.

3. A mysterious creature lived in the forest. People believed it was part human and part horse.

4. The first English colony in America disappeared mysteriously. One day, all the people were gone.

5. The unicorn is a fantasy. It is an unreal animal that lives only in the imagination.

6. A church, a temple, and a mosque are three kinds of sacred buildings.

Practice  Workbook Page 1

Work with a partner to answer these questions. Try to include the key word in your answer. Write the sentences in your notebook.

1. What does an archaeologist do?

2. What clues would the police use to track a bank robber?

3. Which creature scares you the most? Why?

4. Why do you think dinosaurs disappeared millions of years ago?

5. Why do people sometimes like fantasy better than reality?

6. What is something that is sacred to you or someone you know?

▲ The unicorn was a popular fantasy during the middle ages.

Listening and Speaking: Academic Words

Academic words are important words used routinely in written classroom materials and other texts you will read. Study the red words and their meanings. You will find these words useful when talking and writing about informational texts. Write each word and its meaning in your notebook, then say the words aloud with a partner. After you read "Fact or Fiction?" try to use these words to respond to the text.

accurate = correct or exact	➡	Archaeologists must collect **accurate** information when they try to solve mysteries from the past.
create = make something exist	➡	The scientist wanted to **create** a model pyramid to see how it was made.
evidence = facts, objects, or signs that make you believe that something exists or is true	➡	The scientist looked for **evidence** to prove when the building had been constructed.
survive = continue to live or exist	➡	No one knows why the animals did not **survive** after the storm; all of them died.

Audio

Practice

Workbook
Page 2

Work with a partner to answer these questions. Try to include the red word in your answer. Write the answers in your notebook.

1. Where could you find accurate information about ancient Egypt?

2. How could you create a model of a pyramid? What materials would you use to make the model?

3. What types of evidence might archaeologists use to figure out why a group of people suddenly died out or vanished?

4. What kinds of things do human beings need in order to survive?

▲ Although the Inca people died out, they left behind evidence of what their culture was like. One example is this counting necklace.

Word Study: Same Sound, Different Spellings

In English, sometimes the same sound can be spelled in different ways. The only way to figure out the correct spelling is to check the word in a dictionary and memorize it. When you read "Fact or Fiction?" you will come across the words *calendar, together, calculator*. Say each word aloud with a partner. What sound do you hear in the final syllable of each word? Notice that the final sound /ər/ is the same, though the spellings are different.

The sound /ər/ can be spelled in different ways when it comes at the end of a word in an unstressed syllable. Study the chart for more examples.

ar	er	or
sug**ar**	feath**er**	auth**or**
cell**ar**	Decemb**er**	mirr**or**
regul**ar**	pitch**er**	neighb**or**

Practice  Workbook Page 3

Work with a partner. Copy the chart above into your notebook. Say a word from the chart, and ask your partner to spell it aloud. Then have your partner say the next word. Continue until you can spell all of these words correctly. Then work with your partner to spell the following words: *beggar, cracker, doctor, dollar, hammer,* and *tractor*. Add them to the chart under the correct headings.

READING STRATEGY | PREVIEW

Previewing a text enhances your comprehension of it. When you preview a text, you prepare yourself for the information you are about to learn. To preview, follow these steps:

- Read the title and headings (section titles).
- Try to turn the headings into questions.
- Look at the visuals and read the captions or labels.
- Think about what you already know about the subject.

Before you read "Fact or Fiction?" look at the title, headings, visuals, and captions. Think about what you already know about these subjects. What more would you like to know?

 Workbook Page 4

Set a purpose for reading Preview the text. What kinds of mysteries do you think the text will present? Read to find out why some mysteries are so hard to solve.

Fact or Fiction?

Path to the Stars?

About 4,500 years ago, the **pharaoh** Cheops and his son and grandson built the three Pyramids of Giza in Egypt. These pyramids were tombs, or places to bury the dead. For thousands of years, people didn't understand why these three pyramids were grouped together.

Then Belgian **engineer** Robert Bauval noticed that the shape of the three pyramids was the same as part of a group of stars in the sky called Orion's Belt. The whole group of stars—Orion—was sacred to the Egyptians. When Cheops died, he was buried in the Great Pyramid of Giza. The Egyptians made a shaft—or hole—in this pyramid. The shaft led from Cheops's tomb to the sky and the three stars of Orion's Belt. Scientists believe that the Egyptians built this shaft so that Cheops could fly from the pyramid to Orion. There, he would become a god.

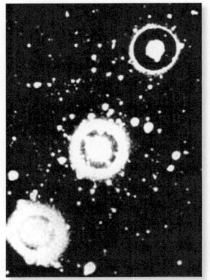
▲ The three stars in Orion's belt

---

pharaoh, ancient Egyptian ruler
engineer, person who plans how to build machines, roads, and so on

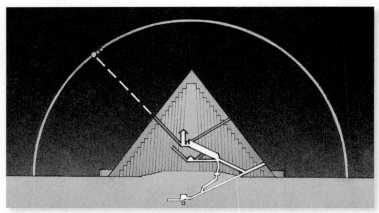
▲ This diagram shows the shaft in the pyramid.

▲ The three Pyramids of Giza from high above

The Secret of the Great Sphinx

A huge **statue** with the head of a man and the body of a lion stands in Giza, Egypt. Known as the Great Sphinx, it seems to defend the pyramids behind it. Like the pyramids, the Sphinx is made from **limestone**, which is very common in Egypt. The exact age of the Sphinx remains one of the world's great mysteries. For thousands of years, wind and sand have **eroded** this enormous sculpture. Some archaeologists believe that water also damaged the Sphinx many **centuries** ago. Was the Sphinx once buried at the bottom of the sea? No one knows for sure.

Mysterious Cities

Some ancient cities were **abandoned** and no one knows why. One of these cities is Machu Picchu, located about 2,440 meters (8,000 ft.) high in the Andes Mountains of Peru. The Inca built Machu Picchu from about 1460 to 1470 C.E. They lived in parts of South America, including what is now Peru. They used stone blocks to make most of the buildings. The blocks fit together perfectly.

In the early 1500s, everyone left the city. No one knows why. Perhaps people died or left because of smallpox, a deadly disease that was brought to the Americas by European explorers and **colonists**. Machu Picchu was forgotten for hundreds of years. Then, in 1911, the American explorer Hiram Bingham rediscovered it. Today, tourists from all over the world visit this unique city.

▲ The Sphinx has the head of a man and the body of a lion.

---

statue, shape of a person or animal made of stone, metal, or wood
limestone, a type of rock that contains calcium, often used to make buildings
eroded, slowly destroyed
centuries, periods of 100 years
abandoned, left completely behind and not used anymore
colonists, people who settle in a new country or area

▼ The abandoned city of Machu Picchu— clues of an ancient civilization

BEFORE YOU GO ON

1. Why do scientists think that the Egyptians made a shaft in the Great Pyramid?

2. What has happened to the Sphinx over time?

On Your Own
Why do you think people might leave a city forever?

Stonehenge

Stonehenge is a mysterious **monument** of huge stones in England. Ancient peoples built Stonehenge about 5,000 years ago. No one really knows who these people were or why they built this strange circle of rocks.

Some people believe that Stonehenge was a **temple** to the sun. Other people believe that Stonehenge was a great stone calendar or **calculator**. They think that the stones were arranged to measure the sun's movements. For example, the stones may have been used to measure the summer and winter solstices—the longest and shortest days of the year. Perhaps Stonehenge was created to mark the rise of the sun and moon throughout the centuries. How will we ever know for sure?

▲ Some stones at Stonehenge came from 480 kilometers (300 mi.) away. How people moved them is a mystery.

Island of Giants

Easter Island is a tiny island in the Pacific Ocean, 3,620 kilometers (2,250 mi.) off the coast of Chile. It was named by Dutch explorers who arrived there on **Easter Sunday**, 1722. The island is covered with nearly 900 large statues, called "moai." Scientists believe the statues are the gods of the ancient people of Easter Island—the Rapa Nui people. But no one knows for sure. Another mystery is how the Rapa Nui people moved the heavy stones as far as 23 kilometers (14 mi.).

Archaeologists have found wooden tablets with the ancient language of the Rapa Nui people on them. No one knows how to read this language today. So the history of the Rapa Nui people is still a puzzle. Only the great stone statues remain to watch over the island.

▲ The Moai have an average height of 4 meters (13 ft.).

---

monument, something that is built to help people to remember an important person or event
temple, holy building
calculator, instrument used to figure out mathematical problems
Easter Sunday, a special Sunday in March or April when Christians remember Christ's death and his return to life

Curse of the Pharaoh

Tutankhamen was a pharaoh in ancient Egypt from 1333 to 1324 B.C.E. When he died, Tutankhamen was buried in a tomb with gold and other treasures.

In 1922, a group led by British archaeologists Howard Carter and Lord Carnarvon opened the tomb of Tutankhamen. They found many treasures, including a beautiful gold mask. Some people believed that a **message** carved in the tomb wall said, "Death will **slay** with his wings whoever disturbs the peace of the pharaoh." Lord Carnarvon died soon after opening the tomb. According to one story, Carnarvon's dog died at the same time at his home in England. Then, five months after Carnarvon died, his younger brother died suddenly.

According to one report, six of the twenty-six people at the opening of Tutankhamen's tomb died within ten years. However, many other people who were there when the tomb was opened lived to be very old. Was there really a **curse**? What do you think?

▲ Tutankhamen's mask

---

message, piece of information that is communicated in words or signals
slay, kill
curse, wish that something bad would happen to someone

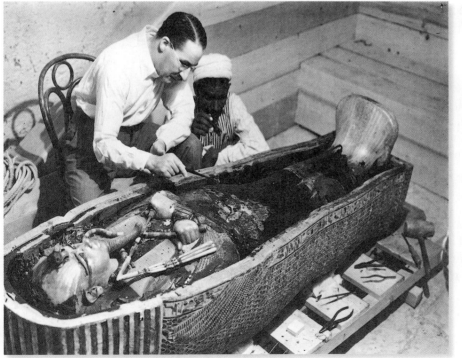

◀ Howard Carter and Tutankhamen's mummy

BEFORE YOU GO ON

1 What is mysterious about Stonehenge and Easter Island?

2 What is the "curse of the pharaoh"?

On Your Own
How do you think Howard Carter and Lord Carnarvon felt when they opened the tomb of Tutankhamen? Would you have liked to be there? Why or why not?

Reading 1 **11**

Terrifying Tentacles

Scientists say that we know more about Mars than we do about the mysteries at the bottom of the ocean. For instance, little is known about giant octopuses and squid. These sea creatures are usually only about 60 to 90 centimeters (2–3 ft.) long. However, there have been reports of giant octopuses and squid with **tentacles** long enough to pull a ship underwater. In 1753, a man in Norway described seeing a huge sea monster "full of arms." The man said that the monster looked big enough to crush a large ship. More recently, giant squid have been discovered with tentacles 10 meters (33 ft.) long. Imagine eating **calamari rings** the size of truck tires!

Scary Monsters

Most people believe that dinosaurs disappeared millions of years ago. However, a few dinosaurs may have survived. The famous Loch Ness monster may be a living dinosaur-like **reptile** called a plesiosaur.

People first reported seeing the Loch Ness monster in April 1933 when a new road was built on the north shore of Loch Ness, a lake in Scotland. A man and woman saw a huge creature with two black **humps** swimming across the lake. Then two more people saw a strange animal crossing the road with a sheep in its mouth. There is now a Loch Ness Investigation Bureau, but most scientists believe that the Loch Ness monster is a creature of **fantasy**.

▲ A giant octopus

---

tentacles, long, thin arm-like parts
calamari rings, sliced squid, often served fried or in a salad
reptile, type of animal, such as a snake or lizard, whose blood
    changes temperature according to the temperature around it
humps, raised parts on the back of an animal

This famous photograph of the Loch Ness monster is not authentic. The photographer tied a plastic head to a toy submarine. ▶

Bigfoot (above) and the Yeti (below) look like giant apes. ▼

Bigfoot and the Yeti

In **various** parts of the world, people have told stories about seeing large ape-like creatures. Different cultures give the creature different names. In the United States, for example, this creature is called Bigfoot or Sasquatch. In Tibet, it is called the yeti.

The first reports of Bigfoot date back to 1811. At that time, a man reported seeing footprints 36 centimeters (14 in.) long. In 1924, another man claimed that Bigfoot had kidnapped him. Each year many people in the United States claim to see Bigfoot. They often report seeing the creature in the forests of the Northwest.

Reports of a huge creature frightened the first European travelers in Tibet. (In Tibet, the word *yeti* means "man-like creature.") In 1951, a Mount Everest explorer found giant footprints in the snow.

Do creatures like the yeti and Bigfoot really exist, or are they **figments of the imagination**? Bernard Heuvelmans (1916–2001), a famous **zoologist**, believed that the world is full of creatures still unknown to science. What do you think?

---

various, different
figments of the imagination, things imagined to be real that do not exist
zoologist, scientist who studies animals

BEFORE YOU GO ON

1 Do most scientists believe that the Loch Ness monster is real or a fantasy?

2 In the United States, where is Bigfoot usually seen?

On Your Own
Do you believe that mysterious animals like the yeti or the Loch Ness monster exist? What is your opinion?

Reading 1 **13**

➤ **COMPREHENSION** 📖 Workbook Page 5

Did you understand the article? If not, reread it with a partner. Then answer the questions below.

Recall

1. Who built the three Pyramids of Giza?
2. What did the ancient people of Easter Island **create?**

Comprehend

3. In what ways are the pyramids and the Sphinx different?
4. How are the mysteries of Machu Picchu and Easter Island similar?

Analyze

5. Do you think that the author believes in the Loch Ness monster or Bigfoot? Explain.
6. How do you think the author feels about the mysteries described in "Fact or Fiction?" Give examples that reveal the author's feelings about four of the subjects.

Connect

7. Would you like to be part of the Loch Ness Investigation Bureau? Why?
8. Do you believe that there are still many creatures unknown to science? Why or why not?

> **Reading** **Skill**
>
> Make sure you understand different types of sentences. Questions are used routinely in speaking and in written classroom materials to ask for information. They often include words such as *who, what, where, why, when,* or *how.*

The dragon shown in this tile is a creature of fantasy. Or is it? ▶

IN YOUR OWN WORDS

Work with a partner. Imagine that you are telling a younger student about "Fact or Fiction?" First make a list of the key topics and main ideas in the article. You may want to use the headings in the article as a guide. Then take turns explaining the information you remember from the article. Try to use some of these words: *pharaoh, engineer, centuries, eroded,* survive, *disappeared, sacred, temple, clues, statues, archaeologists, message, unique, accurate, evidence, humps, creature,* and *fantasy.*

DISCUSSION

Discuss in pairs or small groups.

1. What might have caused the people of Machu Picchu to disappear?
2. Which place described in "Fact or Fiction?" would you most like to visit? Explain.
Q **Can all mysteries be solved?** Which of the mysteries in the selection do you predict will be solved first? Explain.

READ FOR FLUENCY

Reading with feeling helps make what you read more interesting. Work with a partner. Choose a paragraph from the reading. Read the paragraph to yourselves. Ask each other how you felt after reading the paragraph. Did you feel happy or sad?

Take turns reading the paragraph aloud to each other with a tone of voice that represents how you felt when you read it the first time. Give each other feedback.

EXTENSION  Workbook Page 5

Utilize Archaeologists and scientists examine information, data, and other evidence to learn more about mysteries. Imagine that you are an archaeologist. Go to the library or do research on the Internet to find more information about one of the mysteries from "Fact or Fiction?" Then present the new information to the class.

Grammar

Parts of Speech and Parts of the Sentence

A complete sentence has a subject and a predicate. The subject is what or whom the sentence is about. The subject can be a noun, pronoun, or noun phrase. The predicate tells something about the subject. It contains either an action verb or a linking verb. Sometimes an action verb is followed by another noun. It is called the object. A linking verb is followed by either a predicate noun or predicate adjective, which describes the subject.

Subject	Action Verb	Object
Everyone	left	the city.

Subject	Linking Verb	Word to Describe Subject
He	became	a God. *(predicate noun)*
The monster	looked	big. *(predicate adjective)*

An adjective describes a noun. It often follows a linking verb, as above, but an adjective can also come before the noun it describes. An adjective can describe any noun in a sentence.

> The **famous Loch Ness Monster** is a living dinosaur. [describes subject]
> A man and a woman saw a **huge creature**. [describes object]

An adverb can describe the action of a sentence. It can appear in various places in a sentence. Some adverbs end in *-ly*; many do not.

> His younger brother died **suddenly**. [describes how he died]

Many sentences also contain prepositional phrases. These can show time or location. A preposition, such as *in*, *at*, *on*, *from*, and *for*, is followed by a noun or noun phrase, which is called the object of the preposition.

Prepositions Showing Time

In 1911, Hiram Bingham rediscovered it.
Dutch explorers arrived there **on Easter Sunday, 1722**.

Prepositions Showing Location

Easter Island is a tiny island **in the Pacific Ocean**.
Carnarvon's dog died at the same time **at his home**.

Grammar SKILL

If the subject of a sentence is singular, the noun following the linking verb will also be singular: *The **creature** looked like **a giant ape***. If the subject is plural, the noun will also be plural: *The **creatures** looked like **giant apes***.

A sentence is a group of words that expresses a complete thought. A simple sentence must contain a subject and a verb. The verb must agree in number with the subject. If the subject is singular, the verb must be singular. If the subject is plural, the verb must be plural. A simple sentence may also contain an object, predicate adjective or predicate noun, prepositional phrases, or adjectives.

```
                                  predicate noun
                          ┌─────────────────────────────────────┐
                              prepositional phrase
                          ┌───────────────────────┐
              linking
  subject      verb                adjective              prepositional phrase
┌────────┐  ┌──────┐          ┌──────────────┐      ┌───────────────────────┐
Tutankhamen was a pharaoh in ancient Egypt from 1333 to 1324 B.C.E.
```

Practice

Workbook Pages 6–7

Work with a partner. Copy the sentences below into your notebook. Label the parts of speech and parts of the sentence.

GRAMMAR CHECK
What must a *simple sentence* contain?

```
                              prepositional phrase
                            ┌──────────────────────┐
        subject    verb          adjective
      ┌─────────┐ ┌────┐       ┌──────────┐
Example: The rocks lay in a big field.
```

1. They found beautiful treasures.
2. At that time, a man saw footprints.
3. He opened the tomb in 1922.
4. They built the Pyramids in Egypt.
5. Dutch explorers named Easter Island.
6. Six people at the tomb died.
7. A huge statue stands in Giza.
8. In the 1500s, everyone quickly left the city.
9. The research was accurate.
10. Tourists from all over the world visit Machu Picchu.

Apply

Work with a partner. Find five sentences from the reading. Copy them into your notebook. Then label the parts of speech and the parts of the sentence.

Writing

Describe a Place

At the end of this unit, you will write a descriptive essay. To do this, you will need to learn some of the skills used in descriptive writing. When writers describe a place, they choose specific details to help readers picture it in their minds. Writers also arrange details in a logical order. For example, details might be arranged from *near to far* or *top to bottom* or *front to back*. This is called *spatial order*.

Writing Prompt

Write a paragraph that describes a mysterious place. Use spatial order to arrange your details. Include signal words and phrases such as *above, below, close up* or *in the distance* to guide your readers through your place. Be sure to use complete sentences and use the parts of speech and parts of the sentence correctly.

---

1 PREWRITE Begin by choosing a mysterious place.

- Ask yourself which details best describe this place.

- Think about the best way to arrange these details.

- List your ideas in a graphic organizer.

Workbook Page 8

A student named Angelina created this graphic organizer. She plans to describe a pyramid located in Mexico.

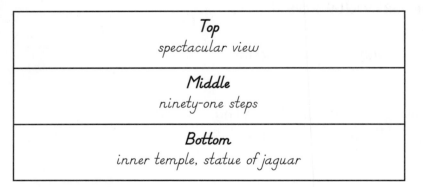

Top
spectacular view

Middle
ninety-one steps

Bottom
inner temple, statue of jaguar

2 **DRAFT** Use your organizer to help you write a first draft.

- Keep in mind your purpose—to describe a place.
- Include details that will help readers picture this place in their minds.
- Use spatial order to arrange details.

3 **REVISE** Read over your draft. Look for places where the writing is unclear or needs improvement. Use the Writing Checklist to help you identify problems. Then revise your draft, using the editing and proofreading marks listed on page 456.

4 **EDIT** Check your work for errors in grammar, usage, mechanics, and spelling. Trade papers with a partner to obtain feedback. Use the Peer Review Checklist on Workbook page 8. Edit your final draft in response to feedback from your partner and your teacher.

5 **PUBLISH** Prepare a clean copy of your final draft. Share your descriptive paragraph with the class. Save your work. You'll need to refer to it in the Writing Workshop at the end of the unit.

ORGANIZATION:
☑ I used spatial order to arrange details.

WORD CHOICE:
☑ I included signal words such as *inside, outside, near,* or *far* in my description.

Here is Angelina's paragraph about a place that seems mysterious to her. Notice how she arranges details to show clearly what is outside the pyramid and what is inside it.

Angelina Xing

Chichén Itzá

The ruins of Chichén Itzá are located on the Yucatan Peninsula of Mexico. As you approach the site, the tallest pyramid, Kukulkan, looks intimidating. It is seventy-nine feet high. When you get closer, you can see the ninety-one original steps that you must climb to get to the top. Before climbing, you can enter an inner temple through a narrow passageway on the north side of the pyramid. Inside is a statue of a scarlet jaguar with eyes made of jade that glow green. Then you can go outside and climb up to the top for a spectacular view of the surrounding ruins. When there is an equinox, crowds of people gather below to see a serpent crawling down the pyramid, an illusion created by the shadow of the sun.

What You Will Learn

Reading

■ Vocabulary building: *Literary terms, word study, dictionary skills*

■ Reading strategy: *Draw conclusions*

■ Text type: *Literature (short stories)*

Grammar

Possessive nouns, adjectives, and pronouns; Indefinite pronouns

Writing

Describe an event

➤ THE BIG QUESTION

Can all mysteries be solved? A detective is someone who solves mysteries for a living. A detective's most important tool is his or her brain. That's because detectives are problem solvers. But what other tools do they use? Work with a partner. Use your prior knowledge to answer the following questions: How do detectives solve crimes? In your opinion, what is the most important tool they use? Share what you know with the class.

➤ BUILD BACKGROUND

Teenage Detectives contains two short stories about two young detectives who are cousins. Their names are Max and Nina. These characters are fictional, or make-believe, but they act like real detectives. They use realistic tools and clues to solve mysteries.

People read mystery stories like these because they enjoy trying to figure out the mystery. Mystery stories are often called "whodunit" stories. *Whodunit* is a made-up word. Look at it carefully. It really says, "Who done it?" It means, "Who did the crime?" Readers want to find out who committed the crime. How did the detectives solve the mystery? What clues did they use? Read *Teenage Detectives* to discover "whodunit"!

▲ Tools detectives use to find fingerprints

► VOCABULARY

Learn Literary Words

Literary Words

idioms

puns

Audio

Writers often use words in new and exciting ways. The authors of *Teenage Detectives* use idioms and puns to make their stories funny and interesting to read. Idioms are expressions that have a meaning that is different from the meanings of the individual words that make them up.

In one of the mystery stories in *Teenage Detectives*, the writer says that a character "mopped his brow." The word *brow* means a person's forehead, the part of the head immediately above the eyes. The character didn't really wipe his forehead with a mop. The writer uses this idiom to create a picture.

Like many writers, the authors of *Teenage Detectives* also make jokes with words. To do this, they use a literary tool called a pun. Puns can be formed in two ways. First, a writer can make a pun by using a word that has two meanings. Second, a writer can make a pun by using words that have the same sound but different meanings.

Here's an example of a pun from one of the stories in *Teenage Detectives*. It's the last line of the first story: "'I had *concrete* evidence,' Nina answered." The pun is on the word *concrete*. The word has two meanings. As a noun, *concrete* refers to the material used to make sidewalks. As an adjective, *concrete* means "real." As you read *Teenage Detectives*, look for puns.

LEARNING STRATEGY

Idioms are expressions. As you read, be sure to analyze, or study, any expressions that you find. Understanding the meanings of expressions is important; it helps you comprehend text.

Practice Workbook Page 9

Take turns reading and analyzing these idioms and puns with a partner. Identify what each idiom means. Explain the humor in the puns.

Idioms	Puns
Bees in her bonnet	What did the triangle say to the circle? You're so pointless.
Flew off the handle	The baker stopped making donuts after he got tired of the hole thing.
It's a whole new ballgame	When a clock is hungry, it goes back for seconds.

▲ What does the idiom "a fork in the road" mean?

Reading 2   **21**

Listening and Speaking: Academic Words

Study the red words and their meanings. You will find these words useful when talking and writing about literature. Write each word and its meaning in your notebook, then say the words aloud with a partner. After you read *Teenage Detectives*, try to use these words to respond to the text.

Academic **Words**

aware
intelligent
motive
pursue

aware = realizing that something is true, exists, or is happening	➡	Detectives are **aware** of how criminals act, and they know which clues will help them solve a case.
intelligent = having a high ability to learn, understand, and think about things	➡	Detectives are **intelligent**, which makes them good problem-solvers.
motive = the reason that makes someone do something, especially when this reason is kept hidden	➡	The man's **motive** for stealing was that he didn't have any money for food.
pursue = chase or follow someone or something to catch him, her, or it	➡	The detective had to **pursue** the criminal from one city to another in order to catch him.

Practice

Work with a partner to answer these questions. Try to include the red word in your answer. Write the answers in your notebook.

1. How do you become aware of world events?
2. Why do archaeologists and detectives both have to be intelligent?
3. What motive could a criminal have for committing a murder?
4. Is it easier for the police to pursue a suspect by car or on foot? Why?

▲ What motive might this man have for hiding in the shadows?

Word Study: Compound Nouns

A compound noun is made up of more than one word. Some are written as one word, as in *airplane* or *courthouse*. Some are written as two words, as in *bubble bath*. Some are written with hyphens between the words, as in *sister-in-law*. Study the examples in the chart below.

One Word	With a Hyphen (-)	Two Words
footprints	take-off	tree house
shortcut	mix-up	boarding pass

New compound nouns are formed in English all the time. Knowing how to divide compound words into their parts helps you spell them and understand what they mean. If you are not sure how to spell a compound noun, check a dictionary. If the compound noun you are looking for is not in a large dictionary, it is spelled as two words.

Practice  Workbook Page 11

Work with a partner. Write two headings in your notebook: *Nouns* and *Compound Nouns*. Copy these words into the Nouns column: *fire*, *sun*, *eye*, *news*. See how many compound words you can form using these nouns (for example, *firefly*, *sunshine*, *eyelash*, *newspaper*). Write them in the Compound Noun column.

READING STRATEGY | DRAW CONCLUSIONS

Drawing conclusions expands your reading skills by helping you figure out the meanings of clues and events in a text. Good readers are like detectives. They put together the clues until they can draw a conclusion. To draw a conclusion, follow these steps:

- Read until you come to a passage that is hard to understand.
- Ask yourself, "What do I think the author means?"
- Look for clues in the text, and think about what you already know from similar situations that you have read about or experienced.
- Add the clues and what you know together, in order to draw a conclusion about what is happening in the text.

Read the first part of "The Case of the Defaced Sidewalk" on pages 48–49. Stop before you come to the heading "How did Nina figure it out?" Draw a conclusion. Finish reading the story. Was your conclusion correct?

Workbook Page 12

Set a purpose for reading How do Max and Nina solve two detective cases? Look for the types of detective tools they use.

Teenage Detectives

The Case of the Defaced Sidewalk

Carol Farley

Teenage cousins Max and Nina love solving crimes in their town, Harborville. In these short stories, they solve two different cases. See if you notice the same clues the detectives do.

One Saturday morning, Nina saw the **three musketeers** in the mall. Jenny, Brittany, and Mitzi called themselves the three musketeers because they were always together.

"I've been shopping for **sandals**," Jenny told Nina. "But I have such a wide foot nothing seems to fit. We've been looking everywhere."

"And it's been **slow going**," Mitzi added. "On account of Brittany's—"

"I know," Nina said, looking at Brittany. "I heard you **sprained** your ankle in gym yesterday. Does it still hurt a lot?"

"It's okay as long as I move really slowly," Brittany told her. "We're going to get ice cream at the Just Desserts Shop now. Want to join us?"

"Better not. Max is meeting me at home. See you later."

Nina was taking a shortcut through Harborville's city park when she saw Mr. Hansen kneeling beside a new sidewalk. The city **maintenance man** frowned as she drew closer.

---

three musketeers, characters from the novel *The Three Musketeers* about a group of adventurous young soldiers
sandals, open shoes worn in warm weather
slow going, not happening quickly
sprained, hurt but didn't break
maintenance man, man who fixes and cleans things

"Somebody jumped right in the middle here while the cement was still wet," he said, pointing at two narrow footprints embedded in the concrete. "Now I'll have to rip out this section and redo it. I sure can't leave the sidewalk looking like this!"

"Any idea of who did it?" Nina asked.

"A kid over there on the slide said that three girls named Brittany, Mitzi, and Jenny were the only ones near here. But he doesn't know which one ruined my sidewalk."

"I know who did it," Nina declared.

How did Nina figure it out?

The footprints were narrow. Jenny has wide feet. Brittany couldn't have jumped because of her sprained ankle. So Mitzi had to be the guilty one.

"You were able to walk into a quick solution for this case," Max told Nina later. "I sure am glad that I'm on your side."

"I had concrete evidence," Nina answered.

BEFORE YOU GO ON

1 What happened to Brittany in gym class?

2 Why is Mr. Hansen frowning?

On Your Own
What conclusion did you draw about the three girls and "whodunit"?

The Case of the Disappearing Signs

Hy Conrad

Nina was eating cold pizza for lunch at Max's house one hot July day. Max's mom, Mrs. Decker, a **real-estate agent**, came in looking warm and weary.

"I'm so **disgusted**," she said. "Remember that old house over on Norton Drive that I **listed**? I put a FOR SALE sign up in the yard early this morning. I just drove by now and it's gone. This is the third sign this month that has disappeared."

"Why would anyone steal a **realtor's signs**?" Nina asked. "What would anybody do with them?"

"Who knows?" Mrs. Decker poured herself a glass of lemonade. "Probably some kids with nothing better to do. I suppose they could use the signs to build something. They were the wooden ones."

Max **nudged** Nina. "Want to bike over and see what we can find out?"

"Not much there to see," his mother told him. "Only two houses on that whole street. An old lady—Mrs. Stearns—lives in the house next to the empty one."

"Maybe she saw something," Nina said. "Let's go ask."

Half an hour later, the two were biking toward the end of Norton Drive. A **pick-up truck** was parked in front of the empty house. A man was standing on the sidewalk looking in all directions.

---

real-estate agent, person who sells houses
disgusted, upset or angry
listed, advertised; put on a list of items for sale
realtor's signs, signs that advertise that a house is for sale
nudged, pushed someone in a gentle way, using your elbow
pick-up truck, vehicle with an open part at the back, used for carrying things

"Do you kids know anything about this place?" he asked. "I'm from out of town, and my nephew, Paul, has been checking houses for me this past month. He thought I might like the one at the end of Norton Drive, so he let me borrow his truck to drive over here. But I don't know if this is the house he meant. There aren't any signs."

"This house is for sale," Max told him. "My mom is the real-estate agent."

"Great! Then can you tell me her name and company? I'd like to ask about this property. Paul tells me that houses in this part of town sell fast. He says this one has been **on the market** for quite some time. I'm glad I got here before it was sold! I just couldn't get over here any sooner."

As soon as Max gave him the information, the man drove off.

Nina stared after the truck. "Know what? His nephew, Paul, might have taken the signs. Maybe he didn't want people to see that the house was for sale until his uncle had a chance to look at it. You can put lots of things in the back of a truck."

Max nodded. "Let's ask Mrs. Stearns if she saw anything this morning."

Mrs. Stearns came to the door as soon as they knocked. She was gray-haired, but she stood straight and tall. "Oh, I think I know who might have taken those signs," she told them. "Freddie Swanson. He lives a block away, and he's always up to **mischief**."

---

on the market, for sale
mischief, bad behavior, especially by children

BEFORE YOU GO ON

1 Who does Mrs. Decker think stole the signs?

2 Why does Nina think that Paul might have stolen the signs?

On Your Own
What motive do you think someone might have for stealing a FOR SALE sign?

Reading 2 **27**

    She held the door open as she talked, and Nina peeked inside. She liked the cozy living room. The sofa and chairs were velvet-covered **antiques**. Lace **doilies** covered the end tables. A large painting hung over the intricately carved fireplace mantel, and a cheerful fire **crackled** below.

    "I know Freddie," Max said. "And I know where he lives. Let's go see him."

    Freddie was putting a lawn mower in the garage when they reached his house. He mopped his brow as he talked to them. "Why would I take a dumb old sign?" he asked. "Besides, I've been out here doing yard work all morning."

---

antiques, very old, valuable objects
doilies, small circular mats or napkins
crackled, made popping sounds

Nina stared past him at the garage. Her parents could hardly get their car in her garage at home because of all the stuff in it, but this one was **practically bare**. Then she noticed a **crudely built** tree house in the yard. The boards were gray and weather-beaten.

She and Max talked as they biked back to his house. Mrs. Decker was washing the lunch dishes when they ran into the house.

"We think we know who took the signs," Nina told her.

How did Nina and Max figure it out?

There was no evidence to show that Paul had used his truck to **transport** the signs. The boards in Freddie's tree house were too old and worn to have been made with the signs. Mrs. Stearns had a fire in her fireplace on a hot July day. She didn't want neighbors moving in next door, so she took the signs and burned them in her fireplace so nobody would know the house was for sale.

"That fire was **a hot tip**," Nina said later as she joined Max and Mrs. Decker for a cold drink of lemonade.

✔ LITERARY CHECK

In this story, why is the phrase "a hot tip" a pun?

practically bare, nearly empty
crudely built, not carefully made
transport, move or carry goods or people from one place to another
a hot tip, a good clue

ABOUT THE **AUTHORS**

Carol Farley has always loved mysteries. Her first book, *Mystery of the Fog Man*, came from an idea she had in the sixth grade. She has written many books for children, including *The Case of the Vanishing Villain* and *The Case of the Lost Look-Alike*.

Hy Conrad has written ten books of short mysteries, including *Whodunit Crime Mysteries* and *Historical Whodunits*. His books have been translated into over a dozen languages. He has developed board games for major toy companies and is a writer and producer of the television series *Monk*.

BEFORE YOU GO ON

1 What does Nina like about Mrs. Stearns's house?

2 What does Nina notice about Freddie's garage and backyard?

On Your Own
Do you think that fictional mysteries like these two short stories are easier or harder to solve than real-life mysteries? Explain.

Reading 2 **29**

Review and Practice

► READER'S THEATER

Act out the following scene between Max and Nina.

Nina: Which of our cases did you like the best?

Max: Well, I really enjoyed solving the case of the missing signs. It was fun because the clues were difficult to find. This made the mystery more exciting for me. What about your favorite case?

Nina: I liked that case a lot, too. I like how we figured out that it wasn't Freddie. I wouldn't have wanted him to get the blame for something he didn't do.

Max: Being a detective is a lot of fun, especially when we have a chance to help people.

Nina: I enjoyed figuring out who stepped in the cement. This time, we got to protect property rather than people.

Max: That's true. Now people who visit the city park will have a smooth sidewalk to walk on. Being detectives lets us help people in so many ways.

LEARNING STRATEGY

Use non-verbal cues, such as gestures and facial expressions to help express your character's thoughts and feelings.

Audio

► COMPREHENSION

Workbook
Page 13

Recall

1. Who jumped in the wet concrete?
2. Who stole the FOR SALE signs?

Comprehend

3. What clues did Nina use to solve "The Case of the Defaced Sidewalk"?
4. What **motive** did Mrs. Stearns have for her actions?

Analyze

5. Why does the author present three possible suspects for each crime? Why do mystery writers make readers suspect more than one character?
6. How can you tell that the teenage detectives are **intelligent**? How can you tell that the authors of *Teenage Detectives* have a sense of humor?

Connect

7. Would you like to **pursue** a career as a detective when you grow up? Why or why not?

8. Some people enjoy puns, while other people think they are silly. What is your opinion of puns? Do you find them funny? Explain.

▶ DISCUSSION

Discuss in pairs or small groups.

1. Do you think Mitzi should have to fix the sidewalk? Why?

2. Can you think of a better way that Mrs. Stearns could have prevented people from moving in next door to her?

3. Mrs. Stearns does not want neighbors. A poet once said: "Good fences make good neighbors." He did not think neighbors should be too friendly. Explain what makes someone a good neighbor. Should neighbors be friendly or not?

Q Can all mysteries be solved? Were serious crimes committed in these stories? What is the difference between a minor crime and a serious one? Give examples of each.

Listening SKILL

Do not interrupt your classmates when they are speaking. Save your questions until the speaker is finished.

▶ RESPONSE TO LITERATURE

Workbook Page 13

Utilize Max and Nina solved two mysteries. They used clues and what they already knew. Take one of these stories and change a few of the clues so that the outcome is different. You may want to use a chart like the one below:

Story title:	
Original Clue 1:	New Clue 1:
Original Clue 2:	New Clue 2:
Original Clue 3:	New Clue 3:
Original outcome:	New outcome:

When you are done writing, narrate or tell your story to a partner. Don't share the ending! See if your partner can figure out the new ending.

Grammar

Possessive Nouns, Adjectives, and Pronouns

Possessive nouns show possession, or ownership. An apostrophe (') and an -s are used to show possession. Rules for forming possessive nouns:

A singular possessive noun takes 's.	**Max's** mom; **realtor's** signs
A plural possessive noun takes an apostrophe only.	**neighbors'** houses **detectives'** cases
A proper possessive noun that ends in an -s can take 's or just an apostrophe.	**Mrs. Stearns's** fire OR **Mrs. Stearns'** fire
Irregular plural nouns take 's.	**women's** doilies, **men's** hats,

A possessive adjective refers to a possessive noun. A possessive pronoun refers to the entire phrase (possessive noun or possessive adjective + noun).

Possessive Noun	Possessive Adjective	Possessive Pronoun
	It's **my pick-up truck**.	→ It's **mine**.
	It's **your dog**.	→ It's **yours**.
It's the **realtor's sign**.	It's **his sign**.	→ It's **his**.
It's **Mitzi's footprint**.	It's **her footprint**.	→ It's **hers**.
	It's **our sidewalk**.	→ It's **ours**.
It's the **kids' house**.	It's **their house**.	→ It's **theirs**.

Grammar SKILL

Make sure the possessive pronoun or possessive adjective agrees in gender (*his/her/hers*) and number (singular or plural) with its antecedent, that is, the noun it refers to.

Practice  **Workbook** Page 14

Work with a partner. Copy the sentences below into your notebook. Then circle the correct word to complete each sentence, as in the example.

Example: They saw (his / theirs / hers) footprint.

1. Mr. Smith is aware of the facts. (His / Her / Their) job is to solve mysteries.
2. It's Jim's mother. (Her / Hers / His) job is selling houses.
3. I know Steve. That's (her / hers / his) house.
4. I went to the neighbors' house. (My / Him / Theirs) house was next door to (theirs / his / mine).

Apply

Tell your partner about a person or persons you know. Make sure you use possessive nouns, adjectives, and pronouns correctly.

Indefinite Pronouns

Indefinite pronouns are words that do not name a specific person, place, or thing. Indefinite pronouns are often used to make generalizations.

> Why would **anyone** steal a realtor's signs?
> **Somebody** jumped right in the middle here while the cement was still wet.
> Do you kids know **anything** about this place?

Indefinite pronouns that begin with *every-* and *some-* are for affirmative statements; *any-* is for questions and negatives; *no-* is for negative statements. Here is a list of some common indefinite pronouns.

everyone	someone	anyone	no one
everybody	somebody	anybody	nobody
everything	something	anything	nothing

Grammar SKILL

Indefinite pronouns that begin with *no-* are already negative. Do not use *not* with the verb.

Use a singular pronoun to refer to an indefinite pronoun. In spoken language, you can use a plural pronoun to refer to an indefinite pronoun.

> **Somebody** left **his** footprint in the cement.
> **Somebody** left **their** footprint in the cement. [only in spoken English]

Practice

Workbook
Page 15

Work with a partner. Copy the sentences below into your notebook. Then choose an indefinite pronoun from the box to complete each sentence.

no one	somebody	everything	nothing	anything	anyone

Example: *Somebody* left an umbrella in the classroom.

1. All the stores were closed. _____ was open.
2. We knocked on the door, but _____ was home.
3. There isn't _____ to talk to. Everybody's busy tonight.
4. She finished all her dinner. She ate _____ on her plate.
5. I'm so bored. There isn't _____ to do.

✔ GRAMMAR CHECK

*In writing, is it better to use a singular or plural pronoun to refer to an **indefinite pronoun**?*

Apply

Work with a partner. Retell "The Case of the Disappearing Sign." Use indefinite pronouns instead of names. You partner must guess the persons' names. Then switch roles.

Writing

Ongoing
Writing
Skills
Practice

Describe an Event

In this lesson, you will describe an event. When writers describe an event, they tell what happened in chronological, or time, order. This means that they describe each step of the event in sequence. They begin with the first step, describe the next steps in order, and end with the last step. Writers also use signal words such as *first*, *next*, and *then*, to help readers understand what happened, and when.

> **Writing Prompt**
>
> Write a paragraph that describes a real or made-up event that puzzled you. Try to include some humor, puns, and idioms. Tell each step in sequence. Use possessive nouns, adjectives, pronouns, or indefinite pronouns correctly.

1 **PREWRITE** Begin by brainstorming ideas for your paragraph.

- Choose a mysterious event that will interest your readers.

- Think about the sequence of steps in the event. What happened first, next, and last?

- List your ideas in a graphic organizer.

Workbook
Page 16

A student named Anna created this sequence chart. She plans to describe what happened when she hid her sister's birthday gift.

First: I hid the hula hoop in a shopping bag under a pile of clothes in the closet

↓

Next: Mom asked Sue to take some old clothes to our local thrift shop.

↓

Then: I went to wrap the gift, but the hoop had vanished.

↓

Finally: A week later, I figured out what happened.

---

2 DRAFT Use your organizer to help you write a first draft.

- Keep in mind your purpose—to describe an event.
- Present each step of the event in sequence.
- Use signal words such as *first*, *next*, *then*, and *finally*.

3 REVISE Read over your draft. Look for places where the writing is unclear or needs improvement. Use the Writing Checklist to help you identify problems. Then revise your draft, using the editing and proofreading marks listed on page 456.

4 EDIT Check your work for errors in grammar, usage, mechanics, and spelling. Trade papers with a partner to obtain feedback. Use the Peer Review Checklist on Workbook page 16. Edit your final draft in response to feedback from your partner and your teacher.

5 PUBLISH Prepare a clean copy of your final draft. Share your descriptive paragraph with the class. Save your work. You'll need to refer to it in the Writing Workshop at the end of the unit.

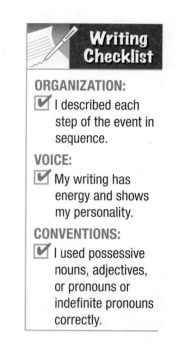

Writing Checklist

ORGANIZATION:
☑ I described each step of the event in sequence.

VOICE:
☑ My writing has energy and shows my personality.

CONVENTIONS:
☑ I used possessive nouns, adjectives, or pronouns or indefinite pronouns correctly.

Here is Anna's paragraph about an event that puzzled her. Notice how her writing voice is strong and lively.

Anna Espínola

The Case of the Missing Hoop

I'm a good detective, but even I had trouble with one case. I bought my sister Sue a striped hula hoop for her birthday this year. First, I hid it in a shopping bag under a pile of old clothes in the closet. Then I decided not to tell anybody because I wanted it to be a big surprise. When Sue's big day came, Mom asked Sue to take some old clothes to our local thrift shop. Finally, I had a chance to wrap the gift, but the hoop had vanished. I looked everywhere but couldn't find it. A week later, I solved the mystery. I was passing the thrift store and saw the hoop in the window for $5. When Sue had dropped off the clothes, she had given away the hoop, too, without knowing it. I bought the hoop again, and gave it to her. Boy did I have to jump through hoops for my sister this year!

What You Will Learn

Reading

■ Vocabulary building:
Context, dictionary skills, word study

■ Reading strategy:
Use visuals 1

■ Text type:
Informational text (math/science)

Grammar
Comparison structures:
Comparative and superlative adjectives

Writing
Describe an object

THE BIG QUESTION

Can all mysteries be solved? Have you ever seen any interesting and unusual patterns in nature? Look at the photograph below of the head of a sunflower. Study it closely. What shapes and patterns do you see? Describe them in your notebook. Now look at the following series of numbers. Can you guess the next number in the series? Can you figure out what the numbers have to do with the sunflower? Don't worry if you can't. This number puzzle will be solved when you read the next selection.

1, 1, 2, 3, 5, 8, 13

The spirals at the center of this sunflower are an example of a mysterious pattern. ▶

BUILD BACKGROUND

People who study numbers are called mathematicians. Many great mathematicians have studied objects in nature in order to develop mathematical ideas. *G Is for Googol* is an informational text about an Italian mathematician named Fibonacci. He discovered a mysterious number pattern through his study of nature. This pattern is called the Fibonacci sequence. It appears in many living things, such as flowers, plants, and snail shells. In fact, the sunflower you just wrote about contains the Fibonacci sequence.

▲ Fibonacci discovered an intriguing pattern in nature.

➤ VOCABULARY

Listening and Speaking: Key Words

Read aloud and listen to these sentences with a partner. Use the context to figure out the meaning of the highlighted words. Use a dictionary to check your answers. Then write each word and its meaning in your notebook.

Key Words

architecture
gradual
infinity
numerals
spirals
steep

Audio

1. The architecture of our city is very varied. All the buildings have different styles and designs.

2. I didn't notice the gradual growth of the oak tree outside. It occurred very slowly.

3. The pattern of numbers continued to infinity. It never ended.

4. Sometimes we use Roman numerals to write numbers: IV (4), X (10), III (3).

5. You can see spirals in the head of a sunflower. Some of these curves go clockwise, and some go counterclockwise.

6. The steps are very steep. Each one is over a foot high.

Practice  Workbook Page 17

Write the sentences in your notebook. Choose a key word to complete each sentence. Then take turns reading the sentences aloud with a partner. Get support from your peers and teacher to develop your ability to use this vocabulary.

1. In class, we use Roman _____ when we make an outline.

   a. spirals   **b.** numerals

2. Many patterns end, while others go on and on to _____.

   a. infinity   **b.** architecture

3. Seashells form _____, not straight lines.

   a. spirals   **b.** numerals

4. A _____ increase occurs bit by bit, and not all at once.

   a. gradual   **b.** steep

5. Because the trail was so _____, it was hard to climb.

   a. gradual   **b.** steep

6. People who study _____ learn all about buildings.

   a. infinity   **b.** architecture

▲ Some clocks and watches use Roman numerals.

Listening and Speaking: Academic Words

Study the red words and their meanings. You will find these words useful when talking and writing about informational texts. Write each word and its meaning in your notebook, then say the words aloud with a partner. After you read the excerpt from *G Is for Googol*, try to use these words to respond to the text.

Academic Words

constant
illustrate
sequence
unique

Audio

constant = happening regularly or all the time	⇒	Light travels at a **constant** speed of 299,792,458 meters (186,282 mi.) per second.
illustrate = explain or make something clear by giving examples	⇒	Photographs of plants help to **illustrate** patterns in nature.
sequence = a series of related events, actions, or numbers that have a particular order	⇒	Fibonacci discovered a **sequence** of numbers with a regular pattern: 1, 1, 2, 3, 5, 8, and so on.
unique = the only one of its type	⇒	Each tiger has a **unique** pattern of stripes on its coat. No two tigers have exactly the same markings.

Audio

◀ Each tiger's coat is unique.

Practice  Workbook Page 18

Write the sentences in your notebook. Choose a red word from the box above to complete each sentence. Then take turns reading the sentences aloud with a partner.

1. Each person has _____ physical traits and character traits.
2. The _____ crying of the baby kept the family awake all night.
3. Each morning I go through the same _____ of steps.
4. The student drew a picture to _____ the shape of a snail.

Word Study: Spelling Words with *ai*, *ay*, *ee*, and *oa*

Learning the relationships between the sounds and letters of English will help you to sound out words as you read. It will also help you learn spelling patterns.

Vowel digraphs, or vowel teams, are two letters that work as a team to stand for one vowel sound. For example, in the word *pail*, the digraph *ai* stands for one sound: the /ā/ sound. In English, the digraphs *ai*, *ay*, *ee*, or *oa* often stand for a long vowel sound. The first letter in these digraphs usually tells you what the long vowel sound will be. Look at the chart below. Take turns reading the words aloud with a partner. Notice the digraphs in each word and the vowel sounds they stand for.

/ā/ spelled *ai*	/ā/ spelled *ay*	/ē/ spelled *ee*	/ō/ spelled *oa*
painter	say	seed	oak
snail	tray	knee	float
aim	spray	feel	soap

Practice

Workbook Page 19

Work with a partner. Copy the chart above into your notebook. Say a word from the chart, and ask your partner to spell it aloud. Then have your partner say the next word. Continue until you can spell all of the words correctly. Now work with your partner to spell these words: *toad, always, steeply, pairs, coast, maintains, okay, needles*. Add them to the chart under the correct headings.

READING STRATEGY USE VISUALS 1

Using visuals enhances and confirms your understanding of written texts. Visuals include art, photographs, diagrams (labeled pictures), and charts. Many informational texts include visuals. To use visuals, follow these steps:

- Look at the visual. Ask yourself, "What does the visual show? How does it help me understand the reading?"
- Read any titles, headings, labels, or captions carefully.

As you read *G Is for Googol*, pay close attention to the visuals. Think about how they help you understand the text.

Workbook Page 20

Set a purpose for reading What **constant** number pattern occurs in pinecones, flowers, and seashells? Read to find out who Fibonacci was and what he discovered about nature.

from

G Is for Googol

David M. Schwartz

Did you know that a googol is a 1 followed by 100 zeros? G Is for Googol is a math alphabet book that explains many unusual mathematical words and facts. Read two sections from this amazing book. Both are about a mysterious number sequence.

F Is for Fibonacci

In the 1200s, an Italian mathematician named Leonardo of Pisa wrote a book about numbers. He signed his name *Fibonacci* (pronounced fee-ba-NAH-chee).

In his book, Fibonacci said that the people of Europe should stop using Roman numerals. He wanted everyone to switch to the numerals used in the Arabic world. Instead of writing LXXVIII, they could write 78. Isn't 78 easier to write than LXXVIII? Well, Fibonacci thought so, and because of him, we use Arabic numerals today.

Fibonacci's book also included story problems. One was about rabbits: How many pairs of rabbits will there be each month if you start with one pair of newborn rabbits, and that pair produces a pair of babies every month? The rabbits start **producing** babies when they are two months old, and their babies also have their first babies when they become two months old.

---

producing, having

1 1 2 3 5 8 13 21 34 55 89

Here's one way to look at it:

After How Long?	How Many Rabbits?
Starting point	1 pair
After 1 month	1 pair
After 2 months	2 pairs
After 3 months	3 pairs
After 4 months	5 pairs
After 5 months	8 pairs
After 6 months	13 pairs
After 7 months	21 pairs
After 8 months	34 pairs
After 9 months	55 pairs
After 10 months	89 pairs
After 11 months	144 pairs

Let's look at the answers another way:

| 1 | 1 | 2 | 3 | 5 | 8 | 13 | 21 | 34 | 55 | 89 | 144 |

These are the first 12 numbers in the famous *Fibonacci sequence* of numbers.

See if you can **figure out** what's so special about the Fibonacci sequence. After the first two numbers, how can the others be made? Think about it before you read on.

Whenever you add one number to the next, you get the following number in the sequence. Try it. Add 2 and 3. What do you get? Now add 5 and 8. Got it? Okay, now what number comes after 144 in the Fibonacci sequence?

Fibonacci numbers are interesting, but what's *amazing* about them is how often they appear. You can find Fibonacci numbers in art, architecture, music, poetry, and nature. Read **N is for Nature**. Get ready to be amazed.

---

figure out, think about a problem or situation until you find the answer or understand what has happened

▼ Within eleven months one pair of rabbits and their offspring will produce 144 pairs of rabbits.

BEFORE YOU GO ON

1 Where and when did Fibonacci live?

2 What number comes after 144 in the Fibonacci sequence?

On Your Own
Where do you think Fibonacci numbers will show up in nature? Use the visuals on pages 42–43 to make predictions about the text.

N Is for Nature

There are numbers in *nature*. Lots.

Do you remember the Fibonacci sequence of numbers? Here are the first twelve numbers of the Fibonacci sequence:

1	1	2	3	5	8	13	21	34	55	89	144

Fibonacci discovered this number sequence, but he did not invent it. Nature invented it. If each page of this book stated one way that Fibonacci numbers appear in nature, we'd need a book so heavy you couldn't lift it. Here are just a few.

The number of **petals** in a flower is usually a Fibonacci number. Some flowers, like daisies, don't have true petals, but petal-like parts called *florets*. Florets come in Fibonacci numbers, too.

---

petals, the brightly colored parts of a flower

Pine needles come in groups, or *bundles*. The bundles almost always have 1, 2, 3, or 5 needles. Do these numbers look familiar?

But pine needles aren't nearly as interesting as pinecones. Find a pinecone. The hard little knobby parts are called *bracts*. (Make sure your pinecone is in good condition, with no missing bracts.) Turn the cone so you're looking at its base. Can you see how the bracts make spirals? There are clockwise spirals, and there are counterclockwise spirals. Follow one spiral as it winds all the way around the cone to the pointy end. Dab a little paint on each bract in that spiral. Now dab a different color on a spiral going in the other direction. You'll see that one spiral winds gradually, and the other one winds more steeply. How many of each type are there? Count them. Remember, it's not the number of bracts that you're counting; it's the number of spirals.

The petal-like parts of a daisy come in Fibonacci numbers. ▶

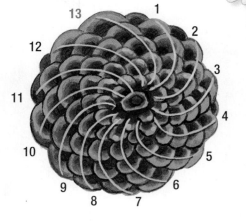

If you count the clockwise or counterclockwise spirals on the bottom of a pinecone, you will get a Fibonacci number. ▼

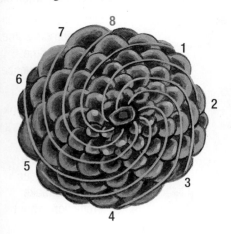

Some pinecones have 3 gradual spirals and 5 steep spirals. Some have 5 gradual and 8 steep. Or 8 and 13. Or 13 and 21. A pinecone's spirals come in Fibonacci numbers. In fact, Fibonacci numbers are sometimes called "pinecone numbers."

Fibonacci numbers could also be called "sunflower numbers," "artichoke numbers," or "pineapple numbers" because you will find the numbers in spirals formed by a sunflower's seeds, an artichoke's leaves, and a pineapple's scales (the diamond-shaped markings on the outside).

Fibonacci strikes again!

No one really understands why Fibonacci numbers show up so much in nature. It's a mystery!

Here's another way that Fibonacci numbers are found in nature: They make a spiral that **maintains** a constant **proportion** all the way to infinity. To find that spiral, take a rectangle that has "Fibonacci" proportions, say 3" x 5", then repeat that same proportioned rectangle, smaller and smaller . . .

---

maintains, continues in the same way
proportion, the amount of something compared to something else

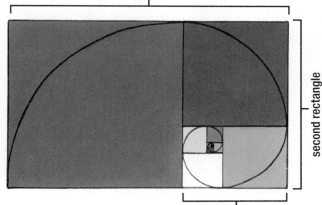

first rectangle

second rectangle

third rectangle, and so on

▲ These seashells have spirals that follow the Fibonacci sequence.

BEFORE YOU GO ON

1 Which part of a pinecone comes in Fibonacci numbers?

2 Where do Fibonacci numbers show up in a sunflower, an artichoke, and a pineapple?

On Your Own
Do you think that scientists will ever be able to explain why Fibonacci numbers show up throughout nature? Explain.

ABOUT THE **AUTHOR**

David M. Schwartz enjoys all things mathematical. In addition to *G Is for Googol*, he has written other award-winning books, including *How Much Is a Million?* and *If You Made a Million*. Each year, Schwartz visits more than fifty schools and conferences to spread his enthusiasm about numbers. He is also fascinated by the stars in the night sky, birds in the rain forest, and other natural wonders.

Review and Practice

➤ COMPREHENSION

Workbook
Page 21

Recall

1. Which type of numerals did Fibonacci want people to use?

2. What are the first twelve numbers in the Fibonacci sequence?

Comprehend

3. What is so special about the Fibonacci sequence?

4. How do the numbers of spirals on the bottom of a pinecone illustrate the Fibonacci sequence?

Analyze

5. Why does the author say that Fibonacci did not invent the Fibonacci sequence?

6. How did the author use visuals to explain the Fibonacci sequence? Did this help you understand the author's ideas? Why?

Connect

7. Think about nature. Have you ever noticed an interesting pattern on an animal or in a plant, flower, or body of water? Describe the pattern and what makes it unique. Why did it attract your attention?

8. Think about what you have learned in your math classes. What is something you find interesting about numbers or number patterns? Why?

▲ This sequence of nine photographs shows different kinds of water patterns.

➤ IN YOUR OWN WORDS

Work with a partner. Imagine that you are teaching a younger student about Fibonacci and his discovery. Tell your partner five important facts that you learned in the reading. You may want to use actual objects or visuals, such as diagrams and photographs, to help explain some of the facts. Take turns telling your partner about Fibonacci and the number sequence he discovered. Then, in your notebook, describe one example of the Fibonacci sequence.

🔊 *Speaking* SKILL

Use words that help your partner visualize and understand facts about Fibonacci and the Fibonacci sequence.

▶ DISCUSSION

Discuss in pairs or small groups. Use suggestions and support from your peers and teacher to enhance and confirm your understanding of the ideas in this article.

1. How do daisies, seashells, and rabbits illustrate the Fibonacci sequence?

2. Fibonacci made life easier by having people use Arabic numerals rather than Roman numerals. What would happen if we suddenly had to use Roman numerals again? How would our lives change?

Q **Can all mysteries be solved?** What is mysterious about the Fibonacci sequence? Does knowing about the Fibonacci sequence help you understand other mysteries in nature? Explain.

▶ READ FOR FLUENCY

It is often easier to read a text if you understand the difficult words and phrases. Work with a partner. Choose a paragraph from the reading. Identify the words and phrases you do not know or have trouble pronouncing. Look up the difficult words in a dictionary.

Take turns pronouncing the words and phrases with your partner. If necessary, ask your teacher to model the correct pronunciation. Then take turns reading the paragraph aloud. Give each other feedback on your reading.

▶ EXTENSION
Workbook
Page 21

Utilize In addition to Fibonacci, many other people made important contributions to mathematics. Go to the library or do research on the Internet to find information about another famous mathematician, for example, Descartes, Pascal, or Pythagoras. Then write a brief report. Explain why the person is important. Tell what you learned about math from your research. Try to use as much academic language as possible. Use this chart to organize your research:

Who?		What?	
Where?		Why?	
When?			

Grammar

Comparison Structures: Comparative Adjectives

A comparative adjective is a type of comparison structure. An adjective is a word that describes a noun. A comparative adjective describes how two things are the same or different. How to form comparative adjectives:

For most one-syllable adjectives not ending in -e, add -er. [small]   This rectangle is **smaller than** the others.
For most one-syllable adjectives ending in -e, add -r. [large]   The petals on sunflowers are **larger than** the petals on daisies.
For most one-syllable adjectives that have a consonant-vowel-consonant pattern, double the final consonant and add -er. [big]   A bear is **bigger than** a cat.
For adjectives ending in -y, change the y to i and add -er. [easy]   Isn't 78 **easier** to write **than** LXXVIII?
For most adjectives with two syllables or more, use *more* before the adjective. [*interesting*]   Pinecones are **more interesting than** pine needles.
For some two-syllable adjectives, you can add -er or use *more*. [*friendly*]   A rabbit is **friendlier / more friendly than** a fox.
Some comparative adjectives are irregular. You must memorize these.   good → **better**   bad → **worse**   far → **farther/further**

Practice
Workbook Page 22

Work with a partner. Copy the sentences below. Then complete each sentence with the correct form of the adjective in parentheses.

Example: Alaska is _larger_ (large) than Kansas.

1. Her class was _____ (interesting) than his.
2. Tea is _____ (healthy) than coffee.
3. This summer is _____ (hot) than last summer.
4. Ryan's jokes are _____ (funny) than Sam's.
5. My sister is a _____ (good) singer than I am.

Apply

Work with a partner. Think of a place and write down some adjectives to describe it. Then describe this place to your partner.

> **Grammar SKILL**
>
> A comparative adjective is usually followed by *than*, but you may omit *than* if the context is clear. *I like ice cream better (than cake).*

Comparison Structures: Superlative Adjectives

Another type of comparison structure is a superlative adjective. These adjectives compare one item in a part of a group to the rest of that group. Look at the chart to learn how to form superlative adjectives.

For most one-syllable adjectives not ending in *-e*, add *-est*. [*steep*]   This mountain is **the steepest** of them all.
For most one-syllable adjectives ending in *-e*, add *-st*. [*large*]   The spirals on the head of that sunflower are **the largest** I've ever seen.
For most one-syllable adjectives that follow a consonant-vowel-consonant pattern, double the final consonant and add *-est*. [*hot*]   This is **the hottest** place in nature.
For most adjectives ending in *-y*, change the *y* to an *i* and add *-est*. [*easy*]   It's not **the easiest** idea to figure out.
For most adjectives with two syllables or more, use *most* before the adjective. [*beautiful*]   This is **the most beautiful** flower I've ever seen.
Some superlative adjectives are irregular. You must memorize these.   good → **the best**   bad → **the worst**   far → **the farthest/furthest**

Practice  **Workbook** Page 23

Work with a partner. Copy the sentences below into your notebook. Then correct the mistake in each sentence.

Example: Her house is ⟨the⟩ biggest on our block.

1. This is the baddest movie ever.
2. She's the prettyest girl in school.
3. I think English is the more difficult subject this year.
4. I always take the most long way home.
5. My sister is the younger person in our family.

Apply

Work with a partner. In your notebook, write five superlative adjectives. Read them to your partner and ask him or her to make a sentence using each one. Then switch roles.

Example: the deepest
The Pacific Ocean is the deepest ocean in the world.

STRENGTHEN YOUR SOCIAL LANGUAGE

Making comparisons means communicating well. Go to www.LongmanKeystone.com and do the activity for this unit. This activity will help you use specific learning strategies to acquire basic vocabulary words necessary for describing people, places, and objects.

Grammar SKILL

A superlative always begins with *the*.

✔ GRAMMAR CHECK

When forming a superlative adjective, when do you use most?

Writing

Describe an Object

You have described a place and an event. In this lesson, you will describe an object. When writers describe something, they choose specific words and details that appeal to the five senses: sight, hearing, touch, taste, and smell. Words and details that appeal to the senses are called sensory details.

> **Writing Prompt**
>
> Write a paragraph that describes a fruit or vegetable. Describe this object with specificity and detail. Try to include a detail for each of the five senses: sight, hearing, touch, taste, and smell. Remember to use comparison structures correctly.

1 **PREWRITE** Begin by choosing your topic.

- Choose a fruit or vegetable that you can describe clearly.

- Ask yourself which sensory details best describe this object.

- Select details that appeal to the five senses.

- List your ideas in a graphic organizer.

Workbook Page 24

A student named Wendy created this graphic organizer.

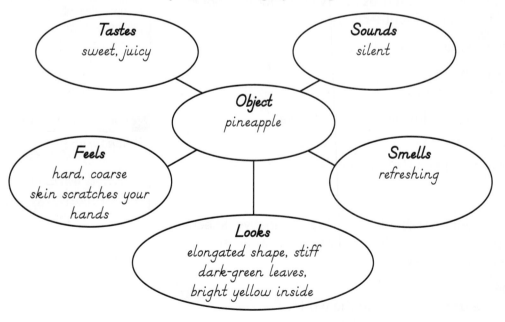

48 Unit 1

2 DRAFT Use your organizer to help you write a first draft.

- Remember your purpose—to describe an object.
- Choose sensory words and details to help readers form an image of the object in their minds.
- Be sure to use comparison structures correctly.

3 REVISE Read over your draft. Look for places where the writing is unclear or needs improvement. Use the Writing Checklist to help you identify problems. Then revise your draft, using the editing and proofreading marks listed on page 456.

4 EDIT Check your work for errors in grammar, usage, mechanics, and spelling. Trade papers with a partner to obtain feedback. Use the Peer Review Checklist on Workbook page 24. Edit your final draft in response to feedback from your partner and your teacher.

5 PUBLISH Prepare a clean copy of your final draft. Share your descriptive paragraph with the class. Save your work. You'll need to refer to it in the Writing Workshop at the end of the unit.

Here is Wendy's paragraph about a pineapple. Notice how she includes sensory details such as *coarse skin* and *liquid gold*.

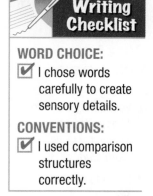

Writing Checklist

WORD CHOICE:
☑ I chose words carefully to create sensory details.

CONVENTIONS:
☑ I used comparison structures correctly.

Wendy Willner

The Pineapple

 The pineapple is dark, hard, and elongated in shape. Its stiff dark-green leaves stand silently on the table. The pineapple seems as if it wants to tell you something, but it doesn't want to tell you too much. When you pick the fruit up, the coarse skin scratches your hands. The scales form three sets of spirals. A set of five spirals goes gradually up to the right. A set of eight spirals goes more steeply down to the left, and a set of thirteen spirals goes very steeply up to the right. These are Fibonacci numbers. When you slice the pineapple open, it is almost brighter and more yellow than the sun at noon. Put a slice in your mouth, and it tastes sweet and juicy. The fresh-cut pineapple fills any room with a refreshing smell. When you eat it with your hands (you shouldn't but I do), it feels as if you are touching liquid gold.

Prepare to Read

What You Will Learn

Reading

- Vocabulary building: *Literary terms, dictionary skills, word study*

- Reading strategy: *Predict*

- Text type: *Literature (short story)*

Grammar

Single-word prepositions of location; Multi-word prepositions of location

Writing

Describe a character

► 💿 THE BIG QUESTION

Can all mysteries be solved? Have you ever heard a ghost story? Do you believe that ghosts are real? Some people do. Often something mysterious happens and legends are created. Legends are old well-known stories often about brave people, adventures, or strange events. What legends do you know about?

► BUILD BACKGROUND

"The Haunted Yacht Club" is a short story about a hotel that is thought to have ghosts. According to one legend, in the 1920s, two hotel guests, Mary and Telly, disappeared from the deck of a yacht. In the short story, three children set out to find Telly and Mary. They want to discover whether ghosts really do exist. In the process, they also learn important things about one another.

▼ Yachts at a dock

➤ VOCABULARY

Learn Literary Words

Novels, short stories, and poems are all types of literature. The people or animals in a novel or short story are called **characters**. Like people in real life, the characters in a story have certain qualities, or **character traits**. You can learn about characters and their traits through what the characters say and do and by what happens to them in the story. You can also get to know the characters' personalities or traits by paying attention to what other characters say about them.

Plot is what happens in a story. Most plots include a problem, the events leading to solving the problem, and the solution to the problem. Usually plots move forward in time. They have a beginning, middle, and end.

The beginning prepares you for what will happen in the story. The middle contains the conflict or a problem. The end of the story shows how the conflict is resolved.

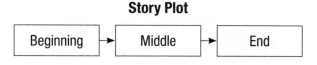

Story Plot

| Beginning | → | Middle | → | End |

Practice

Think of a character from a movie or television show whose character traits you know well. In your notebook, make a copy of the character-traits web below. Fill in the web with traits and examples. Then describe the character to a classmate.

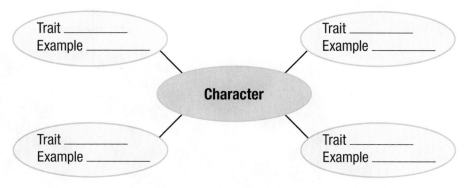

LEARNING STRATEGY

Use words that you already know to learn new and essential language, or words that you must know in order to understand your schoolwork.

Listening and Speaking: Academic Words

Study the red words and their meanings. You will find these words useful when talking and writing about literature. Write each word and its meaning in your notebook, then say the words aloud with a partner. After you read "The Haunted Yacht Club" try using these words to respond to the text.

Academic Words

identify
individual
occur
physical
theory

Audio

identify = recognize and name someone or something	⇒	The children tried to **identify** the ghostly figures that appeared on the deck.
individual = a person, not a group	⇒	Madison is an **individual** in the story. She is one of the characters you will read about.
occur = happen	⇒	The main events in the story **occur** at a haunted hotel.
physical = relating to the body or to other things you can see, touch, smell, feel, or taste	⇒	Telly's and Mary's **physical** presence is one you can see but not touch.
theory = an explanation that may or may not be true	⇒	Everyone has a different **theory** about whether ghosts exist.

Audio

Practice

Workbook Page 26

Work with a partner to answer these questions. Try to include the red word in your answer. Write the answers in your notebook.

1. How would you identify a good place to go for vacation?
2. How could an individual prove that ghosts exist?
3. Where do accidents often occur?
4. What are the benefits of physical activity?
5. What is your theory about why some people believe in ghosts and others don't?

▼ Strange events occur at a haunted house.

Word Study: Prefixes: *un-, dis-*

Affixes are groups of letters that can be added to a word to change its meaning. When the letters are added at the beginning of the word, the word part is called a prefix. Knowing the meanings of prefixes can help you figure out the meanings of many words you read and hear. Learning how to quickly identify and pronounce prefixes will help you as you sound out words.

The prefixes *un-* and *dis-* occur often in English. *Un-* can mean "not" or "the opposite of." *Dis-* can mean "not," "outside of," or "the opposite of." Look at the examples below. Notice how the meaning of the prefix changes the meaning of each base word.

LEARNING STRATEGY

Use a concept map to acquire new vocabulary. Adding words or phrases to a Venn diagram, a timeline, or a chart will help you see the relationships between words and their meanings.

Prefix	Base Word	New Word
un- +	likely	unlikely (not likely)
un- +	afraid	unafraid (not afraid)
dis- +	like	dislike (opposite of like)
dis- +	appear	disappear (opposite of appear)

Practice  Workbook Page 27

Work with a partner. Use what you have learned about prefixes to figure out the meanings of the words below. Then check the meanings in a dictionary. Write the words and definitions in your notebook. Then use each word in a sentence.

disagree	disoriented	unfair	unkind	unknown

READING STRATEGY | PREDICT

You can expand your reading skills by learning to make predictions about texts. Predicting helps you better focus on the text and enhances your comprehension of it. Before you read, predict (or guess) what the story will be about. To predict, follow these steps:

- Stop after each paragraph. Ask yourself, "What will happen next?"
- Look for clues in the story and illustrations. Use the clues from the story and what you already know to predict what will happen.

Read paragraph five of "The Haunted Yacht Club." What prediction can you make about the children seeing ghosts? Explain your answer.

 Workbook Page 28

Set a purpose for reading What kind of individual is Madison? How would you describe her? What is she trying to prove? Read to find out what she is trying to prove to herself.

THE HAUNTED YACHT CLUB

by Ellen Fusz

When Madison Statton's father, Bob, suggested the family vacation at Point Isabel for Spring Break, she fled to her room in tears. Pounding her fists on her pillow, she was **seething** in silent rage. This would be the first vacation with her father's new wife. Madison liked her stepmother, Martha, but she disliked her children. Martha was **vivacious**, upbeat, and always **put a positive spin on** any situation. She was a good match for Madison's father, who often worried and was afraid that the worst would happen.

Hearing a soft tap at the door, she called out, "Who is it?" knowing full well that it was her stepmother. The familiar giggle stopped and Martha's **melodious** voice replied, "Who do you think it is?"

Madison sat up and called for her to come in. "Sorry, Martha. It's just that I thought the three of us could be . . ."

"Alone? You know it's my turn to have the boys stay with me, and I miss them when they're with their father. Besides, they aren't monsters. You just **got off on the wrong foot**. This vacation will put things right. Wait and see," Martha added.

✔ **LITERARY CHECK**

*What **character traits** does Madison admire most about her stepmother?*

---

seething, feeling very angry
vivacious, happy, lively, full of energy; outgoing
put a positive spin on, viewed things optimistically
melodious, musical
got off on the wrong foot, started off badly

Many boats dock at a yacht club. ▶

54 Unit 1

The following week, the family piled into the car and headed for Point Isabel. Trying her best to get her two boys and Madison to become friends, Martha explained, "We're staying at the Haunted Yacht Club. It's a famous hotel built in the 1920s. There's a **rumor** that a couple whose names were Telly and Mary disappeared from a yacht. From time to time, people thought they saw them, but they would then **vanish** from sight," she continued. "Maybe you'll be able to find the ghosts of Telly and Mary."

"Unlikely!" said Danny. "There are no such things as ghosts."

"What happened to them, then? How did they die?" Madison asked.

"Maybe they scared each other to death!" chuckled Jimmie. He was the only one to laugh at his joke.

Madison failed to see the humor in Jimmie's joke. They think girls are always fearful. I'll show them. Girls are as brave as any of the boys I know. I think I'll challenge them to a contest, Madison thought.

"Why don't we look for Telly and Mary?" Madison suggested. The boys hesitated, but then seemed ready to meet the challenge.

Arriving at the Yacht Club, the children wasted no time in heading toward the pier. Large yachts with masts **bobbed** on the water. Moored by the pier, other boats rocked up and down.

---

rumor, information passed from one person to another that may or may not be true
vanish, disappear
bobbed, moved up and down

▼ Sailboats have very tall masts.

BEFORE YOU GO ON

1 Why was Madison upset that her stepbrothers were coming on the vacation?

2 Who are Telly and Mary?

On Your Own
Have you heard any ghost stories? Do you believe them?

Reading 4 55

The children explored the boats along the dock. At dusk, Martha signaled them from the patio of the hotel to come for dinner. The dining room provided a nice **buffet** with meats, breads, and all kinds of vegetables. Danny filled his plate, but he kept his eye on the dessert cart which stood nearby. When Madison finished her dinner, she took a handful of chocolate cookies and called for the boys to follow her.

"Let's go find Telly and Mary," she declared with a confident tone. "I've got some cookies for them. If they are really ghosts, they won't eat them."

They headed for the dock armed with the cookies and a flashlight that Jimmie had asked for at the front desk. The moon cast a silvery light on the yachts moored at the dock. Their **rigid** white railings loomed before them like scary fingers reaching up to grab the sky. Madison shivered, even though the temperature was in the 90s.

"I am unafraid," Madison repeated to herself. "Unafraid!"

The children found a **gangplank** leading to one yacht that was docked further away from the other vessels. "Do you think we should go aboard?" Jimmie asked.

Danny said, "I'll go if both of you go."

Madison nodded and they all crept up the wooden gangplank to the deck of the yacht. Suddenly, they heard a noise. It sounded like people laughing and talking. The children quickly sought a hiding place behind some **crates** and **tarps** piled nearby. Madison froze with fear. Her hand still clutched the cookies she had brought from the hotel. Slowly, she released her grasp and the cookies tumbled onto one of the crates.

LITERARY CHECK

What kind of character is Madison? Describe some of her character traits.

---

buffet, a meal in which people serve themselves
rigid, hard; not moving
gangplank, a board for walking between a boat and a dock
crates, wooden boxes
tarps, plastic or canvas material used to cover something

The full moon made the evening right for ghosts to appear. ▶

"Here, Telly and Mary! Here are some cookies from the hotel," Madison whispered as she scurried to join her stepbrothers. Madison **crouched down** next to Danny and Jimmie behind the crates. The talking grew closer and louder. Peeking out from behind the crates, the children saw two figures approaching. A gloved hand reached over and grabbed the cookies.

Danny, Jimmie, and Madison shrieked and stumbled out from behind the crates. They raced down the gangplank and bolted up the hill to the hotel. They called out to Martha and Bob, but they were nowhere to be found. Finally the children saw them walking hand-in-hand along the dock. Frantically, they screamed:

"We've seen Telly and Mary! We've seen the ghosts of the haunted yacht club!" they shouted.

Bob and Martha looked surprised. "You're safe now. The ghosts won't get you," said Martha as she **consoled** them. Madison threw her arms around her.

"I think Telly and Mary were trying to get us," she gasped.

Martha took Madison's face in her hands and looked her in the eyes. "Maybe they were just having some fun with you. I've heard that ghosts can be playful."

"You were very brave, Madison," Jimmie declared. Danny nodded in agreement.

As Martha brushed some crumbs from the corner of her lips, she whispered, "This is turning out to be a great vacation after all!"

---

crouched down, lowered one's body by bending the knees
consoled, comforted

▲ The children hid behind wooden crates.

✔ **LITERARY CHECK**

*What is the **plot** of the story?*

BEFORE YOU GO ON

1 How does Madison feel when she is on board the yacht?

2 What clue helps us **identify** who ate the cookies?

💡 **On Your Own**
Do you think that the figures on the yacht were really ghosts? Explain.

Reading 4 57

Review and Practice

► READER'S THEATER Audio

Act out the following scene when the children are on the yacht.

Madison: Let's go find Telly and Mary. I've got some cookies for them. If they are really ghosts, they won't eat them.

Jimmie: Let's go down to the dock. I got a flashlight at the front desk. It will light our way.

Danny: The moon is bright. It sheds light on the yachts moored at the dock.

Madison: I am unafraid! Unafraid!

Jimmie: Do you think we should go aboard?

Danny: I'll go if both of you go.

Madison: Me, too!

The children creep on board. Madison puts the cookies on a crate.

Madison: Here, Telly and Mary! Here are some cookies from the hotel.

Madison hides with her stepbrothers. They hear noises, and then get up and run away.

> **Speaking SKILL**
> Speak naturally and with feeling.

► COMPREHENSION

Workbook Page 29

Recall

1. Where do the events of the story **occur**?
2. What does Madison want to discover?

Comprehend

3. Why was Madison against taking the trip to Point Isabel?
4. What is Madison's plan for finding out if the ghosts are real?

Analyze

5. What kind of **individual** was Madison's father?
6. Why do you think Danny and Jimmie went along with Madison?

Connect

7. In your opinion, what character traits make the individuals in the story seem like real people even though they are not?

8. Madison believes that girls are just as brave as boys. Do you think she proves that this is true?

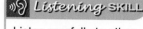

Listening SKILL

Listen carefully to other classmates' ideas. Compare them to your own.

► DISCUSSION

Discuss in pairs or small groups.

1. Do you think Madison will have a better relationship with her stepbrothers after this vacation? Why or why not?

2. What was the importance of cookie crumbs on Martha's mouth at the end of the story?

3. What would make you believe that a ghost story is true? Do you need **physical** evidence to believe something?

Q **Can all mysteries be solved?** Do the cookie crumbs prove that Martha was on the yacht? What other **theory** might explain the cookies being taken from the yacht?

► RESPONSE TO LITERATURE

Workbook
Page 29

Utilize At the beginning of this story, Madison and her stepbrothers do not get along. As the story unfolds, the characters change their opinions of one another. Jimmie realizes that girls are not always afraid and that Madison is really brave. In your notebook, write a paragraph describing how you have changed your opinion about someone. Describe the incident and what made you change your mind.

▲ Not getting along

▲ Getting along

Grammar

Single-Word Prepositions of Location

Many single-word prepositions can be used to show a location or place. A preposition followed by a noun or noun phrase is called a prepositional phrase. It answers the question *Where?* A prepositional phrase of location usually appears at the end of a sentence or clause.

> They didn't live **in Miami**.
> Large vessels with sailing masts bobbed **on the water**.
> Bob suggested the family vacation **at Point Isabel**.

Certain prepositions are used with certain places. Use *in* with a city, state, country, or closed area; use *on* with a surface; use *at* with a specific place.

in	on	at
Miami	the water	Point Isabel
the United States	the table	work
the car	the floor	school
her purse	her pillow	the Haunted Yacht Club

Practice

Workbook Page 30

Work with a partner. Write the sentences in your notebook. Complete each sentence with *in, on,* or *at*.

Example: The book is ___*on*___ the chair.

1. Sue is standing _____ the bus stop.
2. He's sitting _____ the sofa.
3. The picture is hanging _____ the wall.
4. We live _____ New York.
5. His phone is _____ his backpack.

Apply

Write down three things you see in your classroom. Describe them to a partner, telling him or her where they are without saying what they are.

Example: It's green and brown. It's on the table.

Multi-Word Prepositions of Location

There are also many multi-word prepositions that show location.
A multi-word preposition is made up of more than word, but it
has a single meaning. You can use the context of the sentence to
figure out the meaning or look up the main word of the multi-word
preposition in a dictionary.

Madison crouched down **next to** Danny and Jimmie.
The children found a gangplank that was docked **away from** the rest of the vessels.
We got **out of** the car.
Madison sat **in between** the two boys.
The cookies fell **on top of** the crate.
The ghosts were standing right **in front of** them.

Practice

Work with a partner. Write the sentences in your notebook. Figure
out the meaning of the underlined multi-word preposition. Use a
dictionary if necessary. Then circle the correct letter.

Example: The tree is planted <u>next to</u> the fence.
    a. not close to   **(b.)** very close to

1. The bear ran <u>in front of</u> me.
   a. in the direction I wasn't looking   **b.** in the direction I was looking
2. I left my keys <u>on top of</u> the bookshelf.
   a. upper surface   **b.** below
3. The cat slept <u>in between</u> the two dogs.
   a. in the middle of   **b.** nearby
4. She took her wallet <u>out of</u> her purse.
   a. outside   **b.** inside
5. I ran <u>away from</u> the bear as fast as I could.
   a. moved close to   **b.** moved far from

Apply

Work with a partner. Use a dictionary to find other multi-word
prepositions. Use them in sentences.

Writing

Ongoing Writing Skills Practice

Describe a Character

In this lesson, you'll learn how to describe a character. When writers describe a character, they usually include both physical traits and character traits. To describe someone's physical traits, you use words to create a picture of that person's appearance. When you describe someone's character traits, you tell how that individual behaves, thinks, and feels.

Writing Prompt

Write a paragraph describing someone you know. You might describe one of your family members, a friend, or a teacher. Be sure to include his or her physical traits and character traits. Use words to help readers form a clear and vivid image of this person in their minds. Remember to use prepositions of location correctly.

1 PREWRITE Choose someone you can describe clearly.

- Think about that person's physical appearance. What is striking about how he or she looks? For example, does the person have curly hair or straight hair? What color is it?

- Ask yourself what this individual likes to do, and how he or she behaves toward others.

- List your ideas in a graphic organizer.

Workbook Page 32

Here's a graphic organizer created by a student named Bruno. He wanted to describe one of his teachers.

Physical traits	Character traits
red hair	*asks good questions*
tall	*listens carefully*
thin	*great sense of humor*
glasses	*likes teaching a lot*

2 **DRAFT** Use your organizer to help you write a first draft.

- Remember to choose someone you can describe clearly.
- Include both physical and character traits.
- Be sure to use prepositions of location correctly.

3 **REVISE** Read over your draft. Look for places where the writing is unclear or needs improvement. Use the Writing Checklist to help you identify problems. Then revise your draft, using the editing and proofreading marks listed on page 456.

4 **EDIT** Check your work for errors in grammar, usage, mechanics, and spelling. Trade papers with a partner to obtain feedback. Use the Peer Review Checklist on Workbook page 32. Edit your final draft in response to feedback from your partner and your teacher.

5 **PUBLISH** Prepare a clean copy of your final draft. Share your character description with the class. Save your work. You'll need to refer to it in the Writing Workshop at the end of the unit.

Writing Checklist

IDEAS:
☑ I included physical traits and character traits.

WORD CHOICE:
☑ I included precise words and details to create a picture of this person in readers' minds.

Here is Bruno's description of someone he knows. Notice how he uses precise words and details to help readers see and understand Mr. Wayne.

Bruno Martelli

Mr. Wayne is a sixth-grade teacher. He teaches at a middle school in Madison, Wisconsin. He has bright red hair and is very tall and thin. He wears glasses but sometimes pushes them up on top of his head. The books he assigns are really interesting. He asks good questions so everybody gets involved in class discussions. Then he listens carefully to what we have to say. When Mr. Wayne gets excited about a topic, he paces back and forth across the classroom. He has a great sense of humor and a great laugh. Mr. Wayne seems to really like teaching. He makes me think that I might want to be a teacher one day, too.

Link the Readings

Critical Thinking

Look back at the readings in this unit. Think about what they have in common. They all tell about mysteries. Yet they do not all have the same purpose. The purpose of one reading might be to inform, while the purpose of another might be to entertain or persuade. In addition, the content of each reading relates to mysteries differently. Now copy the chart below into your notebook and complete it.

Title of Reading	Purpose	Big Question Link
"Fact or Fiction?"		
Teenage Detectives		The characters solve mysteries.
From *G Is for Googol*	to inform	
"The Haunted Yacht Club"		

Discussion

Discuss in pairs or small groups.

- How does the purpose of *Teenage Detectives* differ from *G Is for Googol*? How do both readings concern mysteries?

- **Q Can all mysteries be solved?** What conclusion can you draw about mysteries in nature, based on what you read in "Fact or Fiction?" and *G Is for Googol*? How are these mysteries the same as fictional mysteries such as the ones in *Teenage Detectives*? How are they different?

Media Literacy & Projects

Work in pairs or small groups. Choose one of these projects.

1 Create a skit based on *Teenage Detectives*. Choose one of the stories and perform it as a play for the class. You may wish to include simple costumes and music, too.

2 Create a scale model of one of the real-life places described in "Fact or Fiction?" For example, you might construct a model of the Great Pyramid at Giza, Stonehenge, or Machu Picchu. Start by establishing your scale (for example, 1 centimeter equals 5 meters or 1 inch equals 10 feet). Then choose a building material and create your model. Write a description of the mystery on an index card to put with the model.

3 Use the Internet to find pictures of the creatures described in "Fact or Fiction?" Make a collage and share it with the class. Ask your classmates if they think the pictures are authentic. Then tell them your opinion.

4 Draw a picture of something from nature that shows the Fibonacci sequence. You may choose a sunflower or pinecone, for instance. Explain the number sequence to your classmates.

Further Reading

Choose from these reading suggestions. Practice reading silently with increased ease for longer and longer periods.

Stranger than Fiction Urban Myths, Phil Healey and Rick Glanvill
This Penguin Reader® is full of strange, funny, and sometimes unbelievable myths.

Chasing Vermeer, Blue Balliett
When a book of unexplainable occurrences brings Petra and Calder together, strange things start to happen.

From the Mixed-Up Files of Mrs. Basil E. Frankweiler,
E.L. Konigsburg
Hiding in New York's Museum of Metropolitan Art, a sister and brother spot a beautiful angel statue. Could it be a work by Michelangelo? Mrs. Frankweiler, the statue's previous owner, holds the key to the mystery.

Put It All Together

LISTENING & SPEAKING WORKSHOP
Description Guessing Game

You will describe an object or place and let your classmates guess what it is.

1 THINK ABOUT IT In this unit, you've learned about all kinds of solved and unsolved mysteries. You've also learned how to write descriptions. Now you are going to play a guessing game in which you will describe an object or place related to a crime. Your classmates will act as detectives and try to guess what your object or place is.

In teams, discuss some of the objects and places discussed in the unit readings. Think of other objects and places that might be related to a crime. Write down your ideas.

Work on your own to make a list of objects and places you could describe in this guessing game. Choose one, and don't tell anyone what it is.

2 GATHER AND ORGANIZE INFORMATION
Brainstorm details about the object or place you have chosen. Organize them in a sensory details web.

Research Go to the library, look at pictures, or use the Internet to get more information about your object or place. Add the new details to your web.

Order Your Notes Think about how you will describe your object or place to the class. Which details will you include? Write them on separate note cards. Do you want to begin with the most important detail and end with the least important one? Do you want to use spatial order, such as top to bottom or left to right? Select the method of organization that works best with your topic. Put your note cards in that order.

Use Visuals Find or draw a picture of your object or place. You will show it to the class after someone guesses your object or place. Do not show it to anyone now!

▲ Alfred Hitchcock was famous for making mysterious movies.

3 PRACTICE AND PRESENT

Use your note cards as an outline, but practice describing your object or place without reading them. Ask a friend or family member to listen to your presentation, or tape-record yourself and listen to the tape. Find the places where you need more work. Keep practicing until you can present your description smoothly and confidently. Try to include enough details so that the audience can guess your object or place, but not so many that you give away the answer too easily. Remember not to let anyone see your visual.

Deliver Your Description Speak loudly enough so that everyone can hear you. Look at people as you speak. Emphasize key details with your voice and gestures. When you're finished, invite students to guess your topic. After someone guesses correctly, or if no one guesses correctly, show your picture of the object or place.

4 EVALUATE THE PRESENTATION

A good way to improve your skills as a speaker and listener is by evaluating each presentation you give and hear. Use this checklist to help you judge your presentation and the presentations of your classmates.

- ☑ Did the description include lots of sensory details?
- ☑ Could you picture the object or place that was being described?
- ☑ Could you hear and understand what the speaker was saying?
- ☑ Did the speaker seem to be having fun?
- ☑ What suggestions do you have for improving the presentation?

))) Speaking SKILLS

Be sure you are speaking slowly and clearly. Ask your listeners for feedback. Can they understand all of your words?

Try to stay relaxed and have fun as you give your description. Remember, this is a game!

))) Listening SKILLS

Listen for clues to the speaker's topic. Try to figure out right away if the topic is an object or a place. Then you can get more specific.

Write down key details as you listen. Think about how they relate to objects and places you know.

STRENGTHEN YOUR SOCIAL LANGUAGE

Providing others with detailed descriptions means communicating well. Go to www.LongmanKeystone. com and do the activity for this unit. This activity will help you expand your vocabulary using high-frequency English words necessary for talking about people, objects, and places.

WRITING WORKSHOP

Write a Descriptive Essay

You have learned how to write a variety of descriptive paragraphs. In this workshop, you will write a descriptive essay. An essay is a group of paragraphs about one topic. Most essays include an introduction, two or more body paragraphs, and a conclusion. In a descriptive essay, the writer uses precise words and sensory details to create a vivid impression of someone or something. Details are arranged in the order that best fits the topic: spatial order, time order, or order of importance.

> **Writing Prompt**
>
> Write a five-paragraph descriptive essay about a mysterious and memorable scene that amazed you. Choose a topic that is full of sensory details. For example, you might describe a dazzling fireworks display, a spectacular dinosaur exhibit, a beautiful sunset, or a powerful storm. Remember to use complete sentences in your essay.

1 **PREWRITE** Review your previous work in this unit. Now brainstorm topics for your essay. In your notebook, answer these questions:

Ongoing Writing Skills Practice

- What mysterious and memorable scene amazed me?

- Which sensory details best describe this topic?

- List your ideas in a graphic organizer.  **Workbook Page 33**

Here's a word web created by a student named Talia. She plans to describe the Carlsbad Caverns.

"The Bottomless Pit"

Bats

Fossils

Carlsbad Caverns

Rock formations

Explorers

Guadalupe Mountains

2 **DRAFT** Use your graphic organizer and the model on page 72 to help you write a first draft.

- Keep your purpose in mind—to describe an amazing scene.
- Choose details that will appeal to a reader's five senses.
- Arrange details in the order that best fits your topic.

3 **REVISE** Read over your draft. Think about how well you have addressed questions of purpose, audience, and form. Your purpose is to describe an amazing scene. Have you chosen a topic that will engage a reader's interest? Does your essay include an introduction and conclusion? Have you described this amazing scene with specificity and detail?

   Keep these questions in mind as you revise your draft. Use the Writing Checklist below to help you identify additional issues that may need revision. Mark your changes on your draft using the editing and proofreading marks listed on page 456.

SIX TRAITS OF WRITING CHECKLIST

- ☑ **IDEAS:** Does my first paragraph introduce my topic?
- ☑ **ORGANIZATION:** Do I present details in a logical order?
- ☑ **VOICE:** Does my writing show energy and enthusiasm?
- ☑ **WORD CHOICE:** Do I use words such as *first* and *next* to signal time order, and words such as far and near to signal spatial order?
- ☑ **SENTENCE FLUENCY:** Do I use complete sentences to express my thoughts?
- ☑ **CONVENTIONS:** Do I use the possessive case correctly?

LEARNING STRATEGY

Monitor your written language production. Using a writing checklist will help you assess your work. Evaluate your essay to make sure that your message is clear and easy to understand.

Here are the revisions Talia plans to make to her first draft.

Carlsbad Caverns

Think about taking an elevator down into another world—a world
where there are stalagmites sticking up in front of you and stalactites
                    Inside this place,   er   er
hanging from above. It's more cold and damp than the world you just
          swoop
left. Bats fly all around and, if you look hard enough, you might even
find the fossil of an ancient sea snail. These are examples of what a
traveler might discover on their trip into Carlsbad Caverns.

Revised to improve word choice and correct an error in grammar.

Although you can find different rock formations in all caves, the
ones in Carlsbad Caverns are particularly special. People have given
very funny-sounding names to these different formations, because
the rocks sometimes look like everyday objects. "Cave Popcorn,"
"Limestone Curtain," and "Bent Straw," are just a few of the oddly
shaped rocks in these caves.

All the different "rooms" of the caves also have unique names,
like "Mystery Room, "Chocolate High," and "Ballroom Bedroom." The
Bottomless Pit got its name when early explorers tossed stones down
                    Since the explorers   ∧they figured the pit didn't have a bottom
the hole to see how deep it was. They never heard a sound. Later
                                                        soft
exploration proved that the pit was only 140 feet deep, but the dirt at
the bottom muffled the sound of the falling rocks.

Revised to add details.

Nowadays, lots of bats live in Carlsbad caverns. In addition to rock formations, there are living things and traces of other living things found in the caves The presence of ocean fossils reveals that around 250 million years ago the area was a coastline that eventually turned into a limestone layer of rock. In fact, there are sixteen species of bats, but most are Mexican Free-tailed bats.

Revised to improve organization.

Carlsbad Caverns are located in the Guadalupe Mountains in Southeast New Mexico. If you are ever in that area, you will definitely want to check out Carlsbad Caverns. They are
as
mysterious
as a strange land in an amazing dream
and memorable.

Revised to add details and include a comparison.

4 **EDIT** Check your work for errors in grammar, usage, mechanics, and spelling. Then trade stories with a partner and use the Peer Review Checklist below to give each other constructive feedback. Edit your final draft in response to feedback from your partner and your teacher.

Workbook
Page 33

PEER REVIEW CHECKLIST

- ☑ Does the essay describe an amazing scene?
- ☑ Does it include precise words and vivid sensory details?
- ☑ Is the writing lively and engaging?
- ☑ Are verbs, tenses, and pronoun/antecedents used correctly?
- ☑ Are comparison structures used correctly?
- ☑ What changes could be made to improve the essay?

Look at the next page to see the changes Talia decided to make to her final draft as a result of her peer review.

Talia Marcus

Carlsbad Caverns

Think about taking an elevator down into another world—a world
where there are stalagmites sticking up in front of you and stalactites
hanging from above. Inside this place, it's colder and damper than the
world you just left. Bats swoop all around and, if you look hard enough,
you might even find the fossil of an ancient sea snail. These are examples
of what a traveler might discover on ~~their~~ his or her trip into Carlsbad Caverns.

Revised to correct an error in grammar.

Although you can find different rock formations in all caves, the
ones in Carlsbad Caverns are particularly special. People have given
very funny-sounding names to these different formations, because
the rocks sometimes look like everyday objects. "Cave Popcorn,"
"Limestone Curtain," and "Bent Straw," are just a few of the oddly
shaped rocks in these caves.

Revised to correct errors in mechanics.

All the different "rooms" of the caves also have unique names,
like "Mystery Room," "Chocolate High," and "Ballroom Bedroom." The
Bottomless Pit got its name when early explorers tossed stones down
the hole to see how deep it was. Since the explorers never heard a
sound, they figured the pit didn't have a bottom. Later exploration
proved that the pit was only 140 feet deep, but the soft dirt at the
bottom muffled the sound of the falling rocks.

In addition to rock formations, there are living things and traces
of other living things found in the caves. The presence of ocean fossils
reveals that around 250 million years ago the area was a coastline
that eventually turned into a limestone layer of rock. Nowadays, lots
of bats live in Carlsbad caverns. In fact, there are sixteen species of
bats, but most are Mexican Free-tailed bats.

Revised to correct errors in mechanics.

Carlsbad Caverns are located in the Guadalupe Mountains in
Southeast New Mexico. If you are ever in that area, you will
definitely want to check out Carlsbad Caverns. They are as mysterious
and memorable as a strange land in an amazing dream.

5 PUBLISH Prepare a clean copy of your final draft. Share your
descriptive essay with the class.

Workbook
Page 34

Test Preparation

PRACTICE

Read the following test sample. Study the tips in the boxes.
Work with a partner to answer the questions.

Vacation Planning

Tania and Jill hike every weekend. They have visited many places
in New Jersey. This weekend they are planning a trip to Ocean
Grove. They want to spend some time at the beach.

City of Origin	Miles to Ocean Grove	Approximate Driving Time
Newark	50	1 hour, 8 minutes
Trenton	46	53 minutes
Edison	37	49 minutes
Camden	77	1 hour, 30 minutes

1 What best describes what Tania and Jill like to do?
    A   Go hiking
    B   Go to the beach
    C   Visit cities
    D   Visit Ocean Grove

2 If Tania and Jill live in Camden, how long will it take them to get
to Ocean Grove?
    F   1 hour
    G   1 hour, 30 minutes
    H   77 minutes
    J   49 minutes

3 What does driving time mean?
    A   The time on the clock
    B   The speed you are driving
    C   How far away something is
    D   How long it takes to get somewhere

Taking Tests
You will often take
tests that help
show what you
know. Study the
tips below to help
you improve your
test-taking skills.

Tip
Think of an answer
to the question
before reading the
choices. Then look
at the answers for
one that matches
your answer.

Tip
Read all of the answer
choices before
choosing one.

Workbook
Pages 35–38

Solving the PUZZLE of Letters and NUMBERS

Most of us have seen movies in which someone must figure out a code. Sometimes the character has to find a treasure. Other times he or she might have to use the code to save a friend. Often the code uses letters. We can recognize the letters but not the words they spell. They make no sense until we figure out the pattern of the code.

Some American artists even hide coded messages or stories in their work. They like to use them because the codes add a little mystery and fun!

Mike Wilkins, *Preamble* (1987)

When you look at them one by one, none of the license plates in Mike Wilkins's *Preamble* makes much sense. The trick is to read the license plates from left to right, starting in the top left corner. By the end of the first line, you realize that Wilkins is composing the preamble to the United States Constitution. The letters on the first two license plates, WE TH and P PUL, stand for the words "We the People . . ." LIBBER is part of the word "Liberty."

The plates are listed in alphabetical order by state, with Alabama first and Wyoming last. Wilkins put the license plates against a large square background.

▲ Mike Wilkins, *Preamble*, 1987, metal, 96 x 96 in., Smithsonian American Art Museum

The background brings all the license plates together into one work of art. It also highlights the differences in color between the plates.

It took a year for Wilkins to get license plates from all fifty states and the District of Columbia. He had to figure out word and number combinations that worked together to form the preamble. Each state has different laws about the number of letters and numbers that could be used on a plate. Eventually, Wilkins put this rebus (a puzzle that uses letters and numbers) together. This artwork celebrates the way the fifty states and the capital work together to form the United States.

Robert Indiana, *Five* (1984)

The artist Robert Indiana based *Five* on a poem called "The Great Figure," which is about a fire truck. He used objects that people had thrown away, like an old wood beam from a house. He also used a wooden dowel (the pole running through the beam) and two metal wheels to make the sculpture. At the top of the beam, he painted a small number 5 and a larger 5 over a red five-point star. They all come together to form one image.

Indiana's color choices seem bright when seen against the dull wood beam. He liked to use letters and numbers to make the printed portions of his work look as though they were part of a commercial sign. The red letter *L* on the very top adds to the idea that there is some mystery or story going on that we must figure out. In the same way that we would read a road sign, we must study how all of the various shapes and colors work with each other to create a "story" or message.

As a boy, Indiana spent a lot of time on the highway. He loved the way road signs play with numbers, letters, and bright colors to capture people's attention. Think about some of the signs you see every day on streets and highways: STOP, 55 MPH, YIELD.

The best codes and rebuses force you to use old images in new ways. They celebrate the mystery and beauty of shapes and the way those shapes work together when placed in unexpected patterns.

▲ Robert Indiana, *Five*, 1984, wood beam, 69⅛ x 26¾ x 18½ in., Smithsonian American Art Museum

Discuss What You Learned

1 How do both Mike Wilkins and Robert Indiana use codes in their artworks?

2 In what way are both of these artworks related to cars and other kinds of vehicles?

Big Question
How would you make artwork with a mystery or puzzle? Would you want viewers to be able to solve the mystery or puzzle? Why?

THE BIG Q QUESTION

How does growing up change us?

This unit is about what happens to people, plants, and animals as they grow and change. You will read about growing up in three ancient cultures, and you'll learn fun facts about plant and animal growth. You will read a novel excerpt and a folk tale about conflicts within families and lessons family members teach one another. As you explore growing up, you will practice the academic and literary language you need to use in school.

Reading

1 Social Studies	2 Novel	3 Science/Folk Tales
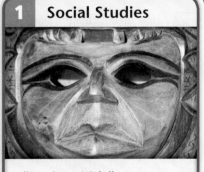		
"Ancient Kids"	From *Becoming Naomi León* by Pam Muñoz Ryan	"Amazing Growth Facts" "The Old Grandfather and His Little Grandson" by Leo Tolstoy
Reading Strategy: Compare and contrast	**Reading Strategy:** Visualize	**Reading Strategy:** Use visuals 2

Listening and Speaking—Narrative

At the end of this unit, you will perform a **skit** about ancient kids.

Writing—Narrative

In this unit you will practice **narrative writing**. This type of writing tells a story. After each reading you will learn a skill to help you write a narrative paragraph. At the end of this unit, you will write a short story.

Quick Write

In your notebook, write several sentences about your first day in school. Who was your teacher? What happened?

4 | **Oral Narrative**

"Thirty Dollars"
Tony Lott's story as told to Alan Govenar

Reading Strategy:
Recognize historical context

DVD

VIEW AND RESPOND
Watch the DVD for Unit 2 and answer the questions at
www.LongmanKeystone.com.

77

Prepare to Read

What You Will Learn

Reading
- Vocabulary building: *Context, dictionary skills, word study*
- Reading strategy: *Compare and contrast*
- Text type: *Informational text (social studies)*

Grammar
Showing contrast: coordinating conjunctions and conjunctive adverbs

Writing
Write a friendly letter

➤ 🔍 **THE BIG QUESTION**

How does growing up change us? What is daily life like for children growing up today? How do children get an education? What sports do they play and watch? What games and toys do they like to play with? Which animals do they keep as pets? Use your prior experiences to answer these questions with a partner. Copy these headings: *Education, Sports, Games,* and *Pets* into your notebook. List your ideas under each heading. Then share your ideas with your peers and teacher.

LEARNING STRATEGY

Compare new information to your prior experiences. This will make the new information more meaningful to you, and it will be easier to understand.

➤ **BUILD BACKGROUND**

"Ancient Kids" describes children's lives thousands of years ago in three different cultures. It tells about growing up among the ancient Greeks, Romans, and Maya. Ancient Greece was a great civilization from around 2000 to 146 B.C.E. The Greeks created beautiful architecture, sculptures, and vase paintings. They also wrote works of literature and philosophy that are still read today.

Rome became powerful after Greece. The Romans made important contributions in the areas of building, medicine, and government.

The ancient Maya established a great civilization in southern Mexico and Central America from 1000 B.C.E. to 1550 C.E. They made accurate studies of the stars, planets, sun, and moon. They had their own calendar, mathematical system, and form of writing. They built remarkable stone temples that are still standing.

Knucklebones was a popular ancient game, played with five small objects made from ankle joints of small animals. ▶

➤ VOCABULARY

Listening and Speaking: Key Words

Read aloud and listen to these sentences with a partner. Use the context to figure out the meaning of the highlighted words. Use a dictionary to check your answers. Then write each word and its meaning in your notebook.

Key Words

ancient
ceremony
citizen   Audio
education
rights
rituals

Audio

1. Studying ancient cultures, or cultures from thousands of years ago, helps us learn about ourselves.

2. At a wedding ceremony, people celebrate a marriage.

3. The girl learned what was expected of her and became a good citizen.

4. Long ago, boys and girls did not get the same type of education. They learned different things.

5. In the past, women did not have many rights. They could not vote or own property.

6. People long ago had rituals, including specific songs and dances, to celebrate important events.

Practice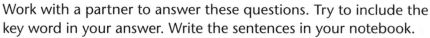

Workbook
Page 41

Work with a partner to answer these questions. Try to include the key word in your answer. Write the sentences in your notebook. Get support from your peers and teacher to develop your ability to use this language.

1. What are three objects that we use today that ancient people didn't have?

2. What would you expect to happen at a graduation ceremony?

3. What are some rules a citizen has to follow in the United States?

4. Which subjects are important to your education at school?

5. What rights do you think are most important? Why?

6. What rituals does your family perform to celebrate a birthday?

This ancient Greek vase shows a ceremony honoring an important man. ▶

Listening and Speaking: Academic Words

Study the **red** words and their meanings. You will find these words useful when talking and writing about informational texts. Write each word and its meaning in your notebook, then say the words aloud with a partner. After you read "Ancient Kids," try to use these words to respond to the text.

classical = belonging to the culture of ancient Greece or ancient Rome	→	**Classical** plays from thousands of years ago are still performed in large, outdoor theaters in Greece and Rome.
cultural = relating to a particular society and its way of life	→	Creating art, music, and literature are **cultural** activities.
feature = quality, element, or characteristic of something that seems important, interesting, or typical	→	A special **feature** of Maya culture is its system of writing.
philosophy = the study of what it means to exist, what good and evil are, what knowledge is, or how people should live	→	People still read ancient Greek **philosophy** today. They learn how people thought and what they valued.

Audio

Practice

Workbook Page 42

Work with a partner to answer these questions. Try to include the **red** word in your answer. Write the sentences in your notebook.

1. Where might you look to see **classical** art from long ago?

2. What part of American **cultural** life do you know most about? Do you know about music, art, or literature?

3. What is a unique **feature** of your school? What makes it different from other schools?

4. Why do you think people study **philosophy**?

Classical plays were performed in theaters like this one. ▼

Socrates taught philosophy in ancient Greece. ▶

Word Study: Spelling Words with Long Vowel Sound /ē/

In English, the long vowel sound /ē/ can be spelled in many different ways. For example, when you read "Ancient Kids," you will read the words in the first row of the chart below. Say each word with a partner. Notice the /ē/ sound and its spelling. Study the rest of the chart for more examples.

e	ee	ea	ie	y	ey
evil	Greece	wreaths	married	baby	journey
he	free	treat	fields	lady	honey
redo	wheels	leave	buried	ceremony	money

Practice
Workbook Page 43

Work with a partner. Copy the chart above into your notebook. Say a word from the chart, and ask your partner to spell it aloud. Then have your partner say the next word. Continue until you can spell all of these words correctly. Now spell the words in the box below and add them to the chart under the correct headings. Circle the letters that stand for /ē/.

bead	families	philosophy	studied	valley
even	geese	response	treat	vary

READING STRATEGY | COMPARE AND CONTRAST

Comparing and contrasting helps you to understand what you read more clearly. When you compare, you see how things are similar. When you contrast, you see how things are different. To compare and contrast, follow these steps:

- Look for words the author uses to show that things are similar, such as *alike, also, too, in the same way,* and *likewise.*
- Look for words the author uses to show that things are different, such as *one main difference, but, however, yet, unlike,* and *opposite.*
- Use a graphic organizer to list your comparisons and contrasts.

As you read "Ancient Kids," compare and contrast the Greek, Roman, and Maya cultures.

Workbook Page 44

Reading 1 **81**

Set a purpose for reading Compare and contrast what it was like growing up among the ancient Greeks, Romans, and Maya. How did each culture treat children differently? What is different about growing up today?

Audio

ANCIENT KIDS

Growing Up in Ancient Greece

ANCIENT GREECE

| 2000 B.C.E. | 146 B.C.E. | 0 | 2000 C.E. |

When a baby was born in ancient Greece, the father performed a ritual. He did a dance, holding the newborn baby. For boy babies, the family **decorated** the house with **wreaths** of olives. For girl babies, the family decorated the house with wreaths made of wool.

There were many differences in the lives of boys and girls as they grew up. One main difference was that girls did not go to school and boys did. Some girls learned to play musical **instruments**.

Mostly, girls helped their mothers with **chores** in the house or in the fields. They didn't leave their houses very often. Sometimes they went to festivals or funerals. They also visited neighbors.

Girls stayed home with their parents until they got married. Girls' fathers usually decided whom the girls would marry.

---

decorated, made it look more attractive by adding things to it
wreaths, circles made from flowers, plants, or leaves
instruments, objects used for making music
chores, small jobs

▲ Some girls learned to read and write at home.

Boys stayed home until they were six or seven years old. They helped grow **crops** in the fields, and they learned to sail boats and to fish.

When boys were about seven years old, they started their **formal education**. They went to school and learned reading, writing, and mathematics. They had to memorize everything because there were no school books! They memorized the poetry of Homer, a famous poet. They also learned to play a musical instrument, such as the **lyre**.

At school, boys learned about the arts and war. They also learned how to be good citizens. At the age of eighteen, boys went to **military school** for two years.

Children played with many toys, such as rattles, clay animals, pull-toys on four wheels, yo-yos, and **terra-cotta** dolls. Children also had pets, such as birds, dogs, goats, **tortoises**, and mice.

▲ A student and his teacher working together

---

crops, wheat, corn, fruit, and so on, that a farmer grows
formal education, education in a subject or skill that you get in school rather than by practical experience
lyre, ancient instrument, similar to a guitar
military school, school where students learn to fight in wars
terra-cotta, baked red clay
tortoises, land animals that move very slowly, with a hard shell covering their bodies

◀ People placed these clay figures in the graves of children to keep them company in the afterlife.

Reading Skill

As you read, identify the words you don't understand and ask your peers or teacher for help with those words.

BEFORE YOU GO ON

1 How were boys' lives different from girls' lives in ancient Greece?

2 What toys did children play with?

On Your Own
Did your family have any special ceremonies when you were born? Describe them.

Growing Up in Ancient Rome

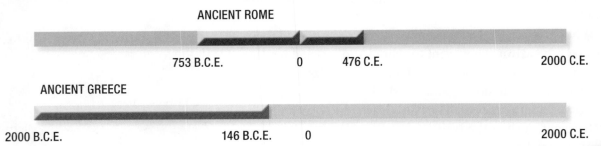

ANCIENT ROME

753 B.C.E.   0   476 C.E.   2000 C.E.

ANCIENT GREECE

2000 B.C.E.   146 B.C.E.   0   2000 C.E.

When a Roman baby was born, a relative put the baby at the feet of the father. The father picked up the baby to accept it into the family. The baby was named nine days after birth.

The oldest man in a family—the father, the grandfather, or an uncle—was the "**head of the family**." However, women were also important to family life. They **managed** the house and household **finances**. In the early years of ancient Rome, women did not have many rights. In later years, they had more rights. They were allowed to own land and to have some types of jobs. They could manage some businesses, but they were still not allowed to hold jobs in the government or to become lawyers or teachers.

Girls and boys wore a special **locket**, called a *bulla*, around their necks. The bulla protected them from evil. A girl wore the bulla until her wedding day. A boy wore the bulla until he became a citizen. A boy became a citizen at age sixteen or seventeen. The family had a big celebration on this day.

Some Greeks lived in southern Italy and Sicily. The ancient Greeks had a cultural **influence** on the Romans. Greek teachers introduced the Romans to the Greek gods and goddesses and to Greek literature and philosophy.

▲ Roman children dressed like their parents. They wore long shirts called tunics.

Marble heads of a
▼ Roman girl and boy

---

head of the family, person who is in charge of the family
managed, controlled or directed
finances, money matters
locket, piece of jewelry like a small round box in which you put a picture of someone
influence, effect

▲ Glass and clay marbles

School was not free. Most children in ancient Rome were not from rich families. They were poor. In poor families, parents taught their children at home. Many poor children did not learn to read or write.

Rich families sent their children to school at age seven to learn basic subjects. Girls did not continue in school after they learned the basic subjects. They stayed at home, where their mothers taught them how to be good wives and mothers.

Boys from rich families continued their education in formal schools or with **tutors**. They became lawyers or worked in government.

What did children do after school? They played with friends, pets, or toys. Toys included balls, hobbyhorses, kites, **models** of people and animals, hoops, **stilts**, marbles, and knucklebones. War games were popular with boys. Girls played with dolls. They also played board games, tic-tac-toe, and ball games.

What kind of pets did children play with in ancient Rome? Dogs were the favorite pets. Roman children also kept birds—pigeons, ducks, **quail**, and geese—as pets. Some children even had pet monkeys.

---

tutors, teachers of one student or a small group of students
models, small copies
stilts, a pair of poles to stand on, used for walking high above the ground
quail, small fat birds that are hunted and shot for food and sport

▲ Dolls were popular toys.

BEFORE YOU GO ON

1 What did Roman girls do when they grew up?

2 What kind of work did Roman boys from rich families do?

On Your Own
How is what you do after school different from what Roman children did?

Reading 1 **85**

Growing Up in the Ancient Maya Culture

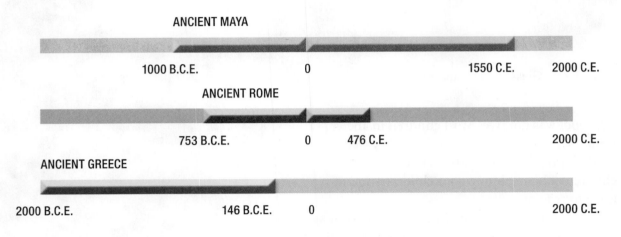

ANCIENT MAYA

| 1000 B.C.E. | 0 | 1550 C.E. | 2000 C.E. |

ANCIENT ROME

| 753 B.C.E. | 0 | 476 C.E. | 2000 C.E. |

ANCIENT GREECE

| 2000 B.C.E. | 146 B.C.E. | 0 | 2000 C.E. |

The Maya lived throughout parts of southern Mexico and Central America, including Belize and Guatemala. They built large cities and created extraordinary art and architecture. You can visit the **ruins** of some ancient Maya cities, such as Chichén Itzá in Mexico's Yucatan region.

In Maya culture, the father was the head of the family. Maya men worked hard to support their families, and they paid **taxes** to the government. Women in Maya society cooked, made cloth, sewed clothing, and took care of the children.

When a boy was about five years old, the Maya tied a small white bead to the top of his head. When a girl was about five, the Maya tied a red shell around her waist. When boys and girls were twelve or thirteen years old, the village had a big ceremony that marked the end of childhood. During the ceremony, a priest cut the beads from the boys' heads. Mothers removed the red shells from the girls' waists. After the ceremony, boys and girls could get married. Young men painted themselves black until they were married.

Maya boys and girls, unlike Roman children, did not have to pay to go to school. They learned from their parents, too. Girls learned

All women did some weaving and spinning. They made things for their families and to sell. ▼

---

ruins, parts of buildings that are left after other
    parts have been destroyed
taxes, money that must be given

◄ This Maya mask shows a jaguar.

how to weave and cook. Boys learned to hunt and fish. Children also learned how to grow crops, such as corn. At age seventeen, boys joined the army to learn about war and fighting.

Children played games and they played with toys. Some of their toys had wheels. Surprisingly, the Maya did not use wheels in their work or transportation. However, toys, such as animal pull-toys, had wheels.

Animals were important in everyday life and religion. The Maya used animals in their art. They decorated various items with pictures of foxes, owls, **jaguars**, hummingbirds, eagles, and other animals. The Maya sometimes ate dogs, but they mainly used dogs for hunting. The Maya thought that dogs could **guide** people on the journey to the **afterlife**. This is why they buried dogs with their owners.

---

jaguars, large wild cats with black spots
guide, show the way to
afterlife, life that some people believe you have after death

BEFORE YOU GO ON

1 What are three modern-day countries where the ancient Maya lived?

2 Why did Maya boys and girls have a special ceremony when they turned twelve or thirteen?

On Your Own
What would you have enjoyed about growing up among the Maya?

Review and Practice

► **COMPREHENSION** 📖 Workbook Page 45

Recall

1. What pets did the children of ancient Greece have?

2. What did Greek teachers introduce to the Romans?

Comprehend

3. Who taught ancient Maya girls how to weave and cook?

4. What did both six-year-old girls and boys in ancient Greece do?

Analyze

5. Why do you think grown-ups in all three cultures had toys for their children?

6. What do you think was the most important **feature** of education in ancient Rome?

Connect

7. Do you think that **cultural** activities are as important today as they were in ancient times? Why?

8. What do you think makes a person well educated? What do you think people should learn in school? Do you think people should learn about **classical** art and literature? Why or why not?

► **IN YOUR OWN WORDS**

Summarize the reading. Use the topics and vocabulary below to tell a partner about growing up among the Greeks, Romans, and Maya.

🔊 *Speaking* SKILL

Present each topic clearly.

Ancient Greeks	Ancient Romans	Ancient Maya
The Birth of a Baby	The Birth of a Baby	Life for Men and Women
Education for Boys	Women's Rights	Ceremonies
Education for Girls	Education for Boys	Education for Boys
Learning to Play Music	Education for Girls	Education for Girls
Toys	Toys	Toys
Pets	Pets	Animals

➤ DISCUSSION

Discuss in pairs or small groups.

1. What are some examples of ceremonies in "Ancient Kids"? What ceremonies are important to family life today?

2. Which ancient society would you have wanted to grow up in—the Greek, Roman, or Maya culture? Why?

3. In your opinion, why is education important for children?

Q How does growing up change us? Compare and contrast what it was like growing up in ancient cultures to growing up today. What is different for kids today? What is similar?

»Ⓖ Listening SKILL

Listen carefully to your classmates. Identify the important ideas. Retell these ideas in your own words to confirm that you have understood them correctly.

➤ READ FOR FLUENCY

When we read aloud to communicate meaning, we group words into phrases, pause or slow down to make important points, and emphasize important words. Pause for a short time when you reach a comma and for a longer time when you reach a period. Pay attention to rising and falling intonation at the end of sentences.

Work with a partner. Choose a paragraph from the reading. Discuss which words seem important for communicating meaning. Practice pronouncing difficult words. Give each other feedback.

➤ EXTENSION  **Workbook Page 45**

Utilize In "Ancient Kids" you learned about growing up long ago. Choose any one of the three cultures you read about. Think about what features of the culture you would like to research. For example, you could read more about ancient Greek games like knucklebones or find out about an ancient Maya ballgame called pok-a-tok. Select a cultural feature to research. Then use encyclopedias, books, and the Internet to find the information. Share the information with your classmates.

▲ The ancient Maya played pok-a-tok on large ball courts.

Grammar

Showing Contrast: Coordinating Conjunctions

A coordinating conjunction is used to connect two ideas in a sentence. The two parts of the sentence are called independent clauses. The coordinating conjunctions *but* and *yet* contrast two ideas. The conjunction usually begins the second independent clause and is preceded by a comma. The second clause shows the contrasting idea.

> The Maya sometimes ate dogs, **but** they used most dogs for hunting.
> Women could manage some businesses, **yet** they were still not allowed to hold jobs in the government.

Practice

Workbook
Page 46

Work with a partner. Copy the sentence starters in Column A into your notebook. Complete the sentences with *but* or *yet* and the contrasting idea in Column B. Be sure to add the proper punctuation.

Example: *The father was the head of the family, yet women had some rights.*

Column A	Column B
1. Animals were kept as pets	a boy learned to hunt and fish.
2. Children worked hard	Roman girls did not.
3. A girl learned to weave and cook	they were also eaten.
4. Roman boys kept going to school	a boy wore the bulla until he became a citizen.
5. A girl wore the bulla until her wedding day	they still had time for fun.

Apply

Work with a partner. In your notebook, write five sentence starters. Switch notebooks with your partner. Take turns reading each other's sentences and finishing them with clauses that begin with *but* or *yet* and show a contrasting idea.

Example: Yesterday I went to a restaurant, but I didn't enjoy the food.

Showing Contrast: Conjunctive Adverbs

A conjunctive adverb, like a coordinating conjunction, also connects two ideas. A conjunctive adverb is used with two complete sentences, each with a complete thought. A conjunctive adverb is a type of transition. Use transitions to help your reader notice a change in thought.

Some examples of conjunctive adverbs are *however, nevertheless,* and *nonetheless*. Like other adverbs, they describe the verb. The conjunctive adverb begins the second sentence and is followed by a comma. The second sentence shows a contrasting idea.

> The oldest man was the "head of the family." **However**, women were also important to family life.
> The Romans' culture was very different from the Greek's. **Nevertheless**, the Greeks introduced them to their philosophy.
> Education was important to Romans. **Nonetheless**, education was not free.

Practice

Workbook
Page 47

Work with a partner. Copy the pairs of sentences below into your notebook. Rewrite the sentences using *however, nevertheless,* or *nonetheless*. Remember to include proper punctuation.

Example: He was angry. He took her to the dance.

He was angry. Nonetheless, he took her to the dance.

1. It was cold. I went swimming.
2. Sue ate a lot for lunch. She was hungry.
3. He was sleepy. He went running.
4. It was raining heavily. We went for a walk.
5. I studied a lot. I failed the test.

Apply

Work with a partner. In your notebook, write five sentences about yourself. Then write a contrasting idea. Read the sentences to your partner, using the transitions above.

Example: I like studying English. *Nevertheless,* it's difficult.

Writing

Ongoing Writing Skills Practice

Write a Friendly Letter

A narrative is a story. It can be told about real people and events or about characters and events that a writer creates. In this lesson, you will write a narrative paragraph in the form of a friendly letter. A friendly letter is written to a friend or family member. In friendly letters, writers often tell about events in their lives. They use a personal and informal voice. A friendly letter includes five parts: date, greeting, body, closing, and signature.

Writing Prompt

Write a friendly letter to an older family member. Tell a story about an event that happened when you were younger. Tell what happened in time order, using signal words such as *then* and *next*. Use connecting words to combine sentences. Be sure to use coordinating conjunctions and conjunctive adverbs correctly.

---

1 **PREWRITE** Choose an interesting event from your past.

- Ask yourself why this event was important to you.

- Think about someone who would enjoy reading about it.

- List your ideas in a graphic organizer.

Workbook Page 48

A student named Tyler created this graphic organizer.

Date: *July 23, 2011*

Greeting: *Dear Grandpa,*

Body: *Being in my school play helped me overcome stage fright.*
Didn't really enjoy performing in front of others—nervous.
Performed well. Amazing sense of accomplishment.

Closing: *Love,*
Signature: *Tyler*

2 DRAFT Use your organizer to help you write a first draft.

- Keep in mind the person who will read your letter.
- Remember to include all five parts of a friendly letter.
- Use coordinating conjunctions and conjunctive adverbs correctly.

3 REVISE Read over your draft. Look for places where the writing is unclear or needs improvement. Use the Writing Checklist to help you identify problems. Then revise your draft, using the editing and proofreading marks listed on page 456.

4 EDIT Check your work for errors in grammar, usage, mechanics, and spelling. Trade papers with a partner to obtain feedback. Use the Peer Review Checklist on Workbook page 48. Edit your final draft in response to feedback from your partner and your teacher.

5 PUBLISH Prepare a clean copy of your final draft. Share your friendly letter with the class. Save your work. You'll need to refer to it in the Writing Workshop at the end of the unit.

Here is Tyler's letter to his grandfather. Notice how Tyler used coordinating conjunctions and conjunctive adverbs to show contrast.

Writing Checklist

VOICE:
☑ My voice was personal and informal.

CONVENTIONS:
☑ I included the five parts of a friendly letter.

☑ I used coordinating conjunctions and conjunctive adverbs to show contrast.

July 23, 2011

Dear Grandpa,

Did I ever tell you how being in my school play helped me overcome stage fright? I was only six years old, and I didn't really enjoy performing in front of others. All week, my class and I practiced hard, but I couldn't get over my fear. Then, on the night of the play, I was so nervous! When I walked on stage, I had the urge to run away. The heat from the stage lighting was almost unbearable. During the performance, I felt as if the eyes of everyone in the audience were glaring at me. However, even though I was really nervous, I performed well. Afterwards, I felt an amazing sense of accomplishment. Since you saw the play, I wanted to share my memory of that night with you.

Love,
Tyler

Prepare to Read

What You Will Learn

Reading

- Vocabulary building: *Literary terms, dictionary skills, word study*

- Reading strategy: *Visualize*

- Text type: *Literature (novel excerpt)*

Grammar
Count and non-count nouns; Quantifiers

Writing
Write about a character and setting

▶ 💿 THE BIG QUESTION

How does growing up change us? What kinds of families do children grow up in? Some grow up in large families; others grow up in small families. Sometimes children are raised by their grandparents, aunts, or uncles.

Work with a partner. Use your prior experiences to talk about the kinds of families you know and those in stories and on TV. In your notebook, draw a picture of a family from a TV show or a book. Label the members of the family using words such as *mother, father, sister, brother, aunt, uncle, grandmother, grandfather, stepmother, or stepfather.* Share your ideas about how our families influence who we become with your peers and teacher.

▶ BUILD BACKGROUND

Becoming Naomi León is a realistic novel—a fictional narrative about events that could happen in everyday life. The main character, Naomi Soledad León Outlaw, lives in Lemon Tree, California. She and her younger brother, Owen, have been cared for by Gram, their great-grandmother, ever since their mother left them seven years ago. Naomi often feels unhappy. To cheer herself up, she writes lists and carves beautiful objects out of soap. In the novel excerpt, you will read about Naomi's reunion with her father in Oaxaca, Mexico.

Oaxaca is a city in southern Mexico. The people there hold a radish-carving festival every year. After reading the novel excerpt, you may want to try carving, too. A how-to piece called "Soap Carving" will tell you how.

A girl carves a radish. ▶

► VOCABULARY

Learn Literary Words

In fiction, you can learn a lot about a character by paying attention to what the character says. **Dialogue** is the exact words spoken by two or more characters. Writers use dialogue to reveal what the characters in a story are like. Often, dialogue makes the characters seem like real people.

Read the examples of dialogue below. They are from *Becoming Naomi León*. Notice that each bit of dialogue begins and ends with quotation marks ("__").

> "I will go with you," said Santiago, and they headed towards the garden.
> "Do not be sad," he whispered.

Another important part of a story is the **setting**—the time and place where the narrative occurs. Identifying the setting will help you better understand what is happening in a story. Sometimes writers state the setting directly. In other cases, you must use clues to figure out where the narrative takes place. Clues might include details about the type of clothing, houses, land, weather, time of day, and transportation.

Practice
Workbook Page 49

Work with a partner to develop your comprehension of literary language. Take turns reading each setting aloud. First, identify the time—past, present, or future—of the setting. Then identify the place.

Type of Literature	Setting
Mystery story	Joe walked down a dark road on the edge of town. It was raining hard and flashes of lightning lit up the deserted house at the end of the street. Joe heard a clock strike midnight and a dog howl in the distance. He took out his cell phone, but the battery was dead.
Science fiction novel	In the year 3050, a strange yellow aircraft landed on Earth. Two huge insect-like creatures stepped out. They waved their many legs in the air but did not speak.
Historical novel	In the 1850s, I met a woman who ran a big cattle ranch in Arizona. She used to ride into town on a palomino pony, wearing a big leather hat and a long cotton skirt.

Listening and Speaking: Academic Words

Study the red words and their meanings. You will find these words useful when talking and writing about literature and informational texts. Write each word and its meaning in your notebook, then say the words aloud with a partner. After you read the excerpt from *Becoming Naomi León*, try to use these words to respond to the text.

Academic Words

assist
bond   Audio
conflict
process

assist = help someone do something	→	Grandparents sometimes **assist** parents with child care.
bond = a feeling or interest that unites two or more people or groups	→	Children usually feel a strong **bond** with their parents.
conflict = disagreement	→	The two friends solved their **conflict** by discussing their disagreement openly.
process = a series of actions that someone does in order to achieve a particular result	→	There are many steps in the **process** of writing a story.

Audio

Practice  Workbook Page 50

Write the sentences in your notebook. Choose a red word from the box above to complete each sentence. Then take turns reading the sentences aloud with a partner.

1. We want this _____ between the two countries to be settled right away. Otherwise, the two countries may go to war.

2. Brothers and sisters often have a close _____. They feel attached to each other.

3. My friend from Oaxaca explained the steps involved in the _____ of carving radishes.

4. I often _____ my aunt when she is caring for her son. I help her make his lunch.

She has a close bond with her younger brother. ▶

Word Study: Suffixes -*ness*, -*tion*, and -*ation*

A suffix is a letter or a group of letters placed at the end of a base word. A suffix can change a word's part of speech and its meaning. Sometimes when a suffix that begins with a vowel is added to a base word that ends in a vowel, the last letter is dropped from the base word. Study the examples in the chart below. The letter *e* in the verb *admire* is dropped before adding the suffix -*ation*.

Word	Suffix	New Word
fierce (adjective)	-ness	fierceness (noun)
admire (verb)	-ation	admiration (noun)
consider (verb)	-ation	consideration (noun)

Practice  Workbook Page 51

Copy the chart below into your notebook. Work with a partner. Add the suffix to the end of the word to create a new word. Check the dictionary to make sure that you have written the word correctly. Write the word in the chart.

Word	Suffix	New Word
good (adjective)	-ness	(noun)
imagine (verb)	-ation	(noun)
transport (verb)	-ation	(noun)

READING STRATEGY | VISUALIZE

Visualizing helps you understand what the author wants you to see. When you visualize, you make pictures in your mind. To visualize what you are reading, follow these steps:

- Read the text, such as these sentences from *Becoming Naomi León*:

  Tied to the branches with transparent fishing line, the carved wooden animals appeared suspended. When a warm breeze tickled the dragons, reptiles, birds, and lions, they twirled and swayed.

- Now, close your eyes and visualize what you read. What do you see?

- As you read, look for descriptive words the author uses.

As you read the excerpt from *Becoming Naomi León*, ask yourself, "What words help me create a picture of what things look like and what is happening?"

Workbook Page 52

Set a purpose for reading Naomi is reunited with her father in Oaxaca after many years. How does the experience change her?

from

Becoming Naomi León

Pam Muñoz Ryan

Life changes when eleven-year-old Naomi's mother, Skyla, comes back and tries to obtain **custody of** *Naomi. Gram and the children flee in their trailer, Baby Beluga, to Oaxaca in search of the children's father, hoping that he will make Gram the children's legal guardian. They arrive just in time for Oaxaca's radish-carving festival. Naomi finally finds her father and discovers that he loves carving, too.*

On Christmas morning Owen and I stood in the yard and looked up. I had to pinch myself to make sure I was not dreaming. A jungle of painted beasts floated beneath the **jacaranda** tree, the leaves and purple flowers like a **canopy** above them. Tied to the branches with **transparent** fishing line, the carved wooden animals appeared suspended. When a warm breeze tickled the dragons, reptiles, birds, and lions, they twirled and swayed.

Owen and I lay down on the ground and watched them. A few minutes later Santiago came out from behind the trailer, where he had been waiting. He lay down next to us and we watched the **spectacle** to the music of Owen's **raspy** laughter.

Later in the afternoon I sat outside, carving with Santiago. He was an expert on wood and had brought some of the special copal branches from the trees in the mountains. I loved watching him carve.

He held up a curved branch. "Each piece has a personality. Sometimes you can look at the wood and see exactly what it might be. The promise

---

custody of, the right to legally care for
jacaranda, type of tropical American tree with purple flowers
canopy, cover attached above a bed or seat, used as decoration or as a shelter
transparent, clear and easy to see through
spectacle, public scene or show that is very impressive
raspy, rough sounding

reveals itself early. Other times you must let your imagination **dictate** what you will find. How do you see your soap today? It is a dog, right?"

I nodded. I had been working on it for several days. "This end will be the tail. And here"—I pointed to the bottom corner—"will be one of its legs, running."

Santiago nodded.

Almost done, I pulled my knife across the soap but dug a little too deep and a large piece crumbled to the ground. With one slip of the knife, I had accidentally carved off the running leg.

I gasped.

"No, do not be sad," said Santiago. "There is still some magic left inside. Let us say that the missing leg is *simbólico* of a **tragedy** or something the dog has lost. Or that its destiny was to be a dog with three legs." He picked up my carving, and with a few strokes of the knife smoothed the ragged piece into a perfect three-legged dog. "You must carve so that what is inside can become what it is meant to be. When you are finished, the magic will show itself for what it really is."

---

dictate, influence or control
simbólico, Spanish for "symbolic"; standing for a particular event, process, or situation
tragedy, event that is extremely sad, especially one that involves death

BEFORE YOU GO ON

1 How do Owen and Naomi spend Christmas morning?

2 What is Naomi carving out of her bar of soap?

On Your Own
Have you ever created something and in the **process** allowed your imagination to "dictate what you find"? Describe the experience.

Reading 2 **99**

Santiago considered an odd-shaped piece of wood. "When the promise does not reveal itself early, your imagination must dictate your intentions. Then the wood, or the soap, it will become what you least expect. Sometimes the wood fools me. I think I am carving a parrot, and when I am finished it has a fish tail. Or I begin a tiger, and in the end it has the body of a dancer."

With the small **machete**, he scraped at the layers of the bark that had built up over time, exposing the **innards** of what used to be a tree branch and revealing the unprotected heart meat. He traded the machete for a knife and chaffed at the wood with quick strokes. Soon he handed me a rough figure.

I held it up in the air. I could see that is was a lion's body with a human's head, maybe that of a girl.

As I turned it around, admiring it, Gram came out of the house and slowly sat down in one of the chairs. She stared at her folded hands and cleared her throat. "I just checked in with [our neighbor] Mrs. Maloney [in Lemon Tree]. The **mediator**, a young woman, showed up at Avocado Acres yesterday to interview her. Imagine showing up on Christmas Eve! The woman asked Mrs. Maloney where we were because she needs to talk to all of us by Friday, January third. Mrs. Maloney told her we'd return from our family vacation in time for the interview, which is what I had told her to say if anybody asked. That's in nine days, and what with four or five days' driving ahead of us . . . I'm sorry, Naomi, but we should leave the day after tomorrow."

---

machete, knife with a broad, heavy blade, used as a cutting tool
innards, inside parts
mediator, person who tries to help two groups to
stop arguing and make an agreement

I took a deep breath and looked around the yard. "Can't we just stay here?" I asked, my hands suddenly **quivering**. "You like it here. You said so yourself." I heard Owen's and Rubén's giggles coming from the garden. "Owen loves it and we could . . . we could go to school here. We're learning Spanish real good. Or . . . or we could go to **Puerto Escondido** and live in the little house and help sell the carvings. . . . I could learn to paint them, like Aunt Teresa . . . and . . ."

Santiago pulled me from my chair to his side on a small wooden bench. He put his arm around me.

"Naomi, I would love for you to come to my house, but right now your life is in California. I have written the letter for the judge. I told the truth about your mother and that my wishes are for you and Owen to live with María [Gram]. I told that I want to be a part of your life and see you . . . maybe in the summer for vacations if that is all right with you and Owen. More, if it is possible."

My lips **trembled**. I stared at the ground.

"I did not fight for you when you were little," said Santiago. "It is something for which I am sorry. I should not have believed your mother when she said I would never be able to see you. If I had been stronger, maybe things could have been different, but maybe they would not have been so different. . . . How will we ever know?"

I looked at him. "But why can't you come with us?"

"For that to happen," he said, "I would have to prepare. Much would need to be done. Sell my house. My boat. Much of my money comes from my carvings, which are sold only in Oaxaca. My work, it is here."

"But what if the judge—"

"Naomi," said Gram, "we are not going to consider the worst that could happen. Thinking that way does not help **self-prophecies**."

Since we'd found Santiago, Gram was wearing her fierceness again. At least on the outside.

"I guess I better tell Owen," said Gram.

"I will go with you," said Santiago, and they headed toward the garden.

Alone, beneath the jacaranda, I stared at the three-legged dog and the lion girl in my lap.

We rode home to Lemon Tree silently. The truck and Baby Beluga seemed to drag along the highway. We traveled with less than we had brought. . . . So why did we seem to plod along? Did the weight of our memories slow us down?

---

quivering, shaking slightly because of nervousness or worry
Puerto Escondido, Spanish for "Hidden Port," a port city in the state of Oaxaca, Mexico
trembled, shook because of fear
self-prophecies, predictions about yourself that could come true

✔ **LITERARY CHECK**
What does the **dialogue** *between Gram and Naomi show about Gram's character?*

BEFORE YOU GO ON

1 What does Santiago carve out of the tree branch?

2 Where does Santiago sell his carvings?

On Your Own
How would you feel if you were Naomi? Would you want to stay in Oaxaca? Why?

For hundreds of kilometers, I held the lion girl and thought about all that I wanted to tell [my friend] Blanca, especially about my father.

On our last days in Oaxaca, Owen and I had gone everywhere with Santiago: to visit Aunt Teresa, to **el zócalo**, to **el Mercado** for pineapple-coconut ice cream. And to admire the statue of Soledad in **la basilica**.

I would never forget that day. The statue with the long robe, a crown of gold, the sparkling stained-glass windows. Our footsteps echoing on the floor. Holding Santiago's hand and listening to his adoration.

"*Our Lady of Solitude* is loved by sailors and fisherman," he said. "She protects us at sea: when our boats are rocking in a storm, when it is foggy and we cannot see the way, when we need to get home and our motor fails us. Then we ask for her assistance. She is part of Oaxaca. And since you have her name and have been here to see the wonder of this city, Oaxaca is part of you."

The morning we left, Santiago came early to help load the last of the luggage. He cut down all the animals hanging from the jacaranda and gave them to Owen and me.

It was a long good-bye . . . the kind of good-bye where everyone hugged and kissed every single person, then stood around talking and looking at each other, then all of a sudden started hugging and kissing everyone again, crying a little each time.

When we were finally ready to climb into the truck, Santiago hugged me and said, "Be brave, Naomi León."

I nodded, but when he took me in his arms one more time and rocked me back and forth, I didn't pretend to be brave.

"Do not be sad," he whispered. "We have found each other. I will write. You will write. We have much for which to be thankful and everything will be the way it was meant to be. You will see. I promise. I promise. Now you must promise."

"I promise." . . .

Oaxaca had long disappeared from our view. I opened my notebook to make a list of all that I hoped to remember, but I closed it. My pen seemed too heavy to lift.

---

el zócalo, a public square/town square
el Mercado, the market
la basilica, the church

Soap Carving

Audio

Here's how you can learn to carve soap like Naomi.

What you will need:

- Newspapers or a tray or a bowl (something to catch the soap shavings)
- Scissors
- Craft sticks
- Tracing paper (optional)

- A bar (or bars) of pure and natural soap that will need to be aired overnight (see steps 2 and 3 below)
- Pencil or ballpoint pen
- Sheet of paper

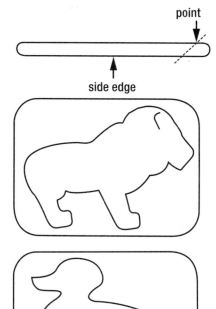

point

side edge

1. Using your scissors, cut off the tip of your craft stick at an angle, creating a point.
2. Unwrap the soap. Using the long edge of a craft stick, scrape the logo from each side of the bar so that you will have a flat surface.
3. Let the soap air out overnight.
4. Draw or trace a design (or create your own) onto a piece of paper such as the ones on the left. Remember, the design should be no larger than your bar of soap. Or you can carve without a pattern and create your own abstract design.
5. Place the piece of paper with the design against the broad, flat side of the soap. Using a ballpoint pen or a pencil, trace the outline of the design, pressing hard so it will leave an impression on your soap.
6. Following the basic rectangular shape of the soap, block out your design. Using the side edge of the angled craft stick, cut away the soap you don't need in thin layers. (Note: Cutting away too much at once will likely cause your soap to crumble apart.)
7. Once the basic angles have been established, start rounding your form. Keep turning your piece, working evenly and from all angles.

ABOUT THE **AUTHOR**

Pam Muñoz Ryan grew up in California's San Joaquin Valley. Her grandparents and many of her aunts and uncles lived nearby. The stories her family told had a big influence on her as she was growing up. Ryan loved reading as a child and became a bilingual teacher before she began writing her own stories for children. Some of her other well-known novels include *Riding Freedom* and *Esperanza Rising,* both of which have won many literary awards. Ryan still lives in southern California with her husband and four teenage children.

BEFORE YOU GO ON

1 Where do Owen and Naomi go on their last days in Oaxaca?

2 What does Santiago give to Owen and Naomi before they leave?

On Your Own
How might creating something in writing, carving, or some other artistic form make an unhappy person feel better?

Reading 2 **103**

➤ **READER'S THEATER**

Audio

Act out the following scene between Naomi and her father.

Santiago: Let me teach you how to carve. Be careful with the tools.

Naomi: I'll try, but the soap gets slippery in my hands.

Santiago: Start by drawing the design you want on the soap. Choose something simple, like a dog or cat.

Naomi: I'll draw a dog. There . . . that looks good. Now I'm ready to start carving. First, I'll carve the outside pieces. This will be the dog's shape.

Santiago: Wonderful, Naomi! Now, be very careful when you start carving the legs. They're more difficult to carve because they are so thin.

Naomi: Oh, no! Look what I've done. I cut off the running leg!

Santiago: Don't worry. We'll make a different kind of dog, one that has lost something. Look now. Isn't this three-legged dog even more lovely?

Naomi: Yes, it's not the dog I planned, but it is beautiful.

> **Speaking SKILL**
>
> Face your partner when you are speaking to him or her. Speak clearly and loudly so that your audience can hear you.

➤ **COMPREHENSION** 📖 Workbook Page 53

Did you understand the story? If not, reread it with a partner. Then answer the questions below.

Recall

1. What does Mrs. Maloney tell the mediator about the Leóns?

2. What wishes does Santiago express in his letter to the judge?

Comprehend

3. What are several reasons why Naomi wants to stay in Oaxaca?

4. Why would it be hard for Santiago to go to California?

Analyze

5. Why does Naomi say, "My pen seemed too heavy to lift"?

6. Will Naomi be allowed to stay with Gram? Predict what will happen.

Connect

7. With what person in your life do you have a strong **bond**? Why?

8. Have you ever loved a place so much that you felt that it was "part of you"? Describe the place and your feelings about it.

▶ DISCUSSION

Discuss in pairs or small groups.

1. In your opinion, should Naomi and Owen live with Santiago, Gram, or Skyla? Give reasons for your answer.

2. Imagine that you could travel anywhere in the United States or Mexico. Where would you go and why?

Q **How does growing up change us?** What sorts of feelings did Naomi have when she had to say good-bye to her father? Describe the **conflict** that she felt. How do you think that kind of experience affects a person her age?

»)⌒ Listening SKILL

Implicit ideas are suggested, but they are not stated directly. Listen to your classmates for implicit ideas. Look for clues, such as facial expressions, word choice, or intonation.

▶ RESPONSE TO LITERATURE

Workbook Page 53

Utilize Think about what you have learned about Oaxaca from *Becoming Naomi León.* Jot down words and phrases that the author uses to describe the setting. Based on what you have learned, write a short travel brochure in which you tell people why Oaxaca would be a nice place to visit. Describe three features of Oaxaca that would attract tourists. Use descriptive words that will make people want to travel there. You may want to find several photographs or make some drawings for your brochure. Share your completed travel brochure with a classmate.

◀ The streets of Oaxaca City

Grammar

Count and Non-count Nouns

There are two kinds of nouns. Count nouns, such as *apples*, are items that can be counted. Non-count nouns, such as *food*, cannot be counted.

Count Nouns			Non-count Nouns		
trees	bubbles	benches	wood	soap	furniture
carvings	apples		art	work	food

A singular count noun may be preceded by *a, an,* or *the*. A plural count noun usually ends in *-s* or *-es* and may be preceded by *the*. A non-count noun will not be preceded by *a* or *an*. It has no plural, so it does not end in *-s* or *-es*. A non-count noun may be preceded by *the*.

Non-count nouns fall in several categories. Look at the following chart.

Grammar SKILL

A or *an* means "one." When *a* or *an* precedes a noun, you know it is a singular count noun.

Whole groups made up of similar items: clothing, fruit, jewelry, money
Fluids, solids, gases, particles: water, dirt, air, rice
Abstractions: love, beauty, grammar, intelligence
Languages: English, French, Spanish
Fields of study: philosophy, biology, math
Recreation, activities: biking, soccer, driving, studying
Natural phenomena: sunshine, rain, fire, darkness, heat

Practice  Workbook Page 54

Work with a partner. Circle the non-count nouns.

Example: (ice) (soda) drink (tea)

1. snowman   snowball   snow   wind
2. lunch   sandwich   milk   apple
3. teacher   geography   test   studying
4. Portuguese   language   verb   dictionary
5. tennis   ball   player   game

Apply

Work with a partner. Decide which categories the non-count nouns in the first chart fall under. Give reasons for your choices.

✔ **GRAMMAR CHECK**

*Are nouns having to do with weather, such as snow, **count** or **non-count**?*

Quantifiers

Quantifiers are words that help you count. Some quantifiers are used with count nouns, some are used with non-count nouns, and some are used with both. Notice that some quantifiers for count nouns always take a singular noun and some always take a plural noun.

Count Nouns	Non-Count Nouns	Count and Non-Count Nouns
each piece **every** vacation **a few** minutes **both** parents **several** days **many** carvings	**a little** fierceness **much** imagination **a great deal of** work	**no** tears/crying **some** branches/magic **any** knives/tea **a lot of/lots of** dogs/food

You can use only certain quantifiers to express a negative quantity or to ask questions. Use the following quantifiers with *not* for negatives. Remember to use the appropriate singular or plural verb.

Grammar SKILL

Don't use *not* with the quantifier *no. There is no water.* NOT *There isn't no water.*

Negatives	Questions
There are**n't many** trees. There is**n't much** wood. There is**n't a great deal of** soap. There is**n't any** money.	Are there **many** trees? Is there **much** wood? Is there **a great deal of** soap? Is there **any** money?

Practice
Workbook Page 55

Work with a partner. Copy the sentences into your notebook. Circle all the possible correct quantifiers in parentheses to complete each sentence.

Example: Is there ((much)/ many /(any)) rice?

1. There isn't (any / several / much) sunshine today.
2. I met (several / many / a great deal of) people.
3. (Some / A few / A little) books came in the mail.
4. He bought (a great deal of / a lot of / every) stamps.
5. (Every / Many / Each) day I go to the gym.

Apply

Work with a partner. In your notebook, make a list of 8–10 nouns. Switch notebooks with your partner. Think of a quantifier for each noun. Then take turns reading each other's quantifiers and nouns.

Writing

Write about a Character and Setting

At the end of this unit, you will write a short story or fictional narrative. To do this, you will need to learn some of the skills used in story writing. A good story has interesting characters and a believable setting. The setting is the time and place of the story.

> **Writing Prompt**
> Write a narrative paragraph about a character you create. Set your story in a real time and place. Start your paragraph with this sentence: *I will never forget the day I met (character's name) in* or *at (real place).* Describe your character's physical and character traits. Use sensory details to describe the setting. Be sure to use count nouns, non-count nouns, or quantifiers correctly.

1 **PREWRITE** Brainstorm ideas for your character and setting.

- Choose a setting that you can describe clearly and vividly.

- Think about the kind of person you might meet there.

- List your ideas in a graphic organizer.

Workbook Page 56

A student named Talia created this graphic organizer.

Character (Who)
Laura very tall, very short hair shy, plays tennis feels homesick, distraught

Setting (Where and When)
Camp Hillcrest on a beautiful hill near a huge lake first day of sleep-away camp

2 DRAFT Use your organizer to help you write a first draft.

- Keep your purpose and audience in mind as you write.
- Describe how your character looks, acts, and thinks.
- Include sensory details to **assist** readers to picture the setting.

3 REVISE Read over your draft. Look for places where the writing is unclear or needs improvement. Use the Writing Checklist to help you identify problems. Then revise your draft, using the editing and proofreading marks listed on page 456.

4 EDIT Check your work for errors in grammar, usage, mechanics, and spelling. Trade papers with a partner to obtain feedback. Use the Peer Review Checklist on Workbook page 56. Edit your final draft in response to feedback from your partner and your teacher.

5 PUBLISH Prepare a clean copy of your final draft. Share your narrative paragraph with the class. Save your work. You'll need to refer to it in the Writing Workshop at the end of the unit.

Writing Checklist

IDEAS:
- ☑ I wrote about an interesting character.
- ☑ I placed my story in a believable setting.

WORD CHOICE:
- ☑ I used precise words to create a vivid setting.

Here is Talia's story about a character she named Laura. Notice how Talia uses precise words to describe both Laura and Hillcrest.

Talia Marcus

At Camp

I will never forget the day I met Laura at Camp Hillcrest. It was Laura's first day at sleep-away camp, but I had been going there for several years and loved Hillcrest. It's located on a beautiful hill near a huge lake and has many great activities. I had just arrived when I noticed her. She's a very tall girl with very short hair, and she was standing all by herself. She seemed shy, so I talked to her and tried to make her feel comfortable. I discovered we both play tennis! For a while, Laura seemed fine. Then, at bedtime, a wave of homesickness suddenly came over her, and she wanted to see her parents. She looked distraught! I told her that everyone feels this way at first and that if she gave Hillcrest a try, she would really like it. After that, Laura calmed down and went to sleep. She ended up loving camp, just like I knew she would.

What You Will Learn

Reading

■ Vocabulary building:
Context, dictionary skills, word study

■ Reading strategy:
Use visuals 2

■ Text type:
Informational text (science article); Literature (folk tale)

Grammar
Simple past: regular and irregular verbs

Writing
Write a story from a different point of view

➤ THE BIG QUESTION

How does growing up change us? How is growing up different for plants and animals than it is for human beings? Some plants and animals are very small when they are fully grown. Others are very big. Which animals are very small even when they are completely grown? What are the largest animals you can name? What are the tallest plants you can name? Use your prior knowledge as you share what you know with the class.

LEARNING STRATEGY

Use your prior knowledge. Relating what you already know to a new topic will make it easier to understand new meanings in English.

➤ BUILD BACKGROUND

"Amazing Growth Facts" and **"The Old Grandfather and His Little Grandson"** are two very different kinds of texts. The first is a science article about physical growth. It presents interesting facts about how living things grow in size. The second text is a folk tale about another kind of growth. It is a narrative about a young child who teaches his parents a lesson. The child's actions help the parents grow as human beings.

Folk tales are old stories that are passed down over the years. They are often told to children to teach them lessons. Some folk tales warn children to stay away from danger. Others teach children to be kind to others.

◀ Giraffes are 1.83 meters (6 ft.) tall when they are born, but they grow to be 5.49 meters (18 ft.) tall.

◀ Giant Sequoias are the tallest trees in the world.

► VOCABULARY

Listening and Speaking: Key Words

Read aloud and listen to these sentences with a partner. Use the context to figure out the meaning of the highlighted words. Use a dictionary to check your answers. Then write each word and its meaning in your notebook.

Key Words

average
conversion
height
length
rate
weight

1. At birth, the average baby weighs about 3.5 kilograms (7 or 8 lbs.).

2. We use a conversion chart to change numbers from one system of measurement to another. For example, we can change centimeters to inches, meters to feet, or kilograms to pounds.

3. The building's height is 30 meters (around 100 ft.) from the bottom to the top.

4. The anaconda is the longest snake in the world. It can grow to more than 10.5 meters (close to 35 ft.) in length.

5. A baby has a very fast rate of growth. It can grow almost 18 centimeters (about 7 in.) in one year!

6. We measure weight to figure out how heavy someone or something is.

Practice Workbook Page 57

Work with a partner to answer these questions. Try to include the key word in your answer. Write the sentences in your notebook.

1. How do you figure out the average of a series of ten numbers?

2. When might you need to use a conversion chart?

3. What tools could you use to measure someone's height?

4. How does the length of your hand compare to the length of your feet?

5. Why do you think that babies grow at such a fast rate?

6. What can people do to lower their weight?

▲ Anacondas are also the world's heaviest snakes, sometimes reaching 200 kilograms (440 lb.) in weight.

Listening and Speaking: Academic Words

Study the red words and their meanings. You will find these words useful when talking and writing about informational texts and literature. Write each word and its meaning in your notebook, then say the words aloud with a partner. After you read "Amazing Growth Facts" and "The Old Grandfather and His Little Grandson," try to use these words to respond to the text.

benefit = something that gives you an advantage, that helps you, or that has a good effect	Growing fast is a great **benefit** to animals. It helps them live on their own sooner.
category = group of people or things that have related characteristcs	Bears and deer belong to the **category** of warm-blooded animals. Snakes and lizards belong to a different group.
enormous = extremely large in size or amount	The elephant is **enormous**! It is a huge animal.
percent = equal to a particular amount in every hundred	About 75 **percent** of the eggs hatched. The rest of the eggs did not hatch.

Audio

Practice  Workbook Page 58

Work with a partner to answer these questions. Try to include the red word in your answer. Write the sentences in your notebook.

1. What is a benefit of living in your city or town?

2. What category would you use to group cars, trucks, boats, and trains?

3. What are some of the most enormous animals you have seen in pictures or at a nature preserve?

4. Why do students feel good when they get 100 percent on a test?

▲ Bears are in the category of warm-blooded animals.

Word Study: Spelling Words with Long Vowel Sound /ō/

Learning the relationships between the sounds and letters of English will help you read and spell words correctly. The long vowel sound /ō/ can be spelled in many ways. Four common spellings are *o* as in *cold*, *o_e* as in *bone*, *oa* as in roast, and *ow* as in *snow*. Look at the chart below. Take turns reading the words aloud with a partner. Notice the different spellings for the sound /ō/.

/ō/ spelled *o*	/ō/ spelled *o_e*	/ō/ spelled *oa*	/ō/ spelled *ow*
sc**o**ld	st**o**ne	t**oa**st	gr**ow**n
s**o**	cl**o**se	l**oa**f	sl**ow**
kil**o**	st**o**ve	c**oa**st	bel**ow**

Practice
Workbook
Page 59

Work with a partner. Copy the chart above into your notebook. Say a word from the chart, and ask your partner to spell it aloud. Then have your partner say the next word. Continue until you can spell all of the words correctly. Now work with your partner to spell these words: *jumbo, soap, tone, bowl, home, gold, show, oak*. Add them to the chart under the correct headings.

READING STRATEGY | USE VISUALS 2

Using visuals enhances and confirms your understanding of written texts. Visuals include photographs, art, diagrams, charts, and maps. Informational texts often have visuals. Sometimes visuals give you information that is not in the text. To use visuals, follow these steps:

- Look at the visual. Ask yourself, "What does it show? How does it help me understand what I am reading?"
- Read the titles, headings, labels, or captions carefully.
- Think about how the visual helps you understand what is in the text. Does the visual give you extra information? In what way?

As you read "Amazing Growth Facts," pay close attention to the visuals. What do they show? How do they help you understand the text better?

Workbook
Page 60

Set a purpose for reading How do different plants and animals grow? As you read the article, think about how all living things change when they grow up.

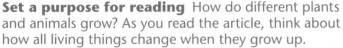

AMAZING GROWTH FACTS

It is one of the wonders of nature that all living things **increase** in size. Think about how a tiny acorn can grow into an enormous oak tree. Growth occurs at different rates. Sometimes growth is very fast. Other times it is very slow.

The average newborn baby is 50 centimeters long and weighs 3.4 kilograms. When the baby grows up and becomes an adult, he or she increases on average to 3.4 times that length and 21 times that weight. Girls and boys are about the same height and weight until early adulthood. Then boys usually grow taller and weigh more than girls.

Bamboo can grow 90 centimeters in one day—the height of an average three-year-old child. Pacific giant kelp (a kind of seaweed) can grow as much as 45 centimeters in one day.

An ant can lift more than 100 times its weight. One hundred times the weight of a 64-kilogram person would be the same weight as three cars!

A baby kangaroo is the size and weight of a paper clip (1 gram). An adult kangaroo is 30,000 times heavier (30 kilograms). If a human grew at this rate, a 3.4-kilogram baby would weigh 102,000 kilograms as an adult—that's as much as

▲ If we were as strong as ants, we could lift three cars!

Pacific giant kelp: 60 m

Bamboo: 30 m

Average man: 1.75 m

---

increase, become bigger

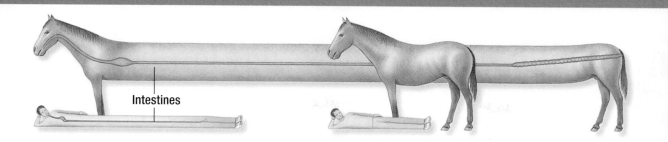

Intestines

a large whale! An average man weighs about 80 kilograms.

The egg of a golden eagle and the egg of a Nile crocodile are both 8 centimeters long. But look how much bigger the crocodile grows!

A 26-centimeter baby crocodile can grow into a 5-meter adult crocodile. If humans grew at the same rate as Nile crocodiles, a 50-centimeter baby would grow into a 9.5-meter adult—more than 5 times as tall as the average person!

Clams are among the longest living and slowest growing of all creatures. A deep-sea clam takes 100 years to grow 8 millimeters. That's as big as your fingernail!

In the average human life of 70 years, a heart pumps enough blood around the body to fill the fuel tanks of 700 **jumbo jets.** The food that we eat in our lifetime is equal in weight to the weight of six elephants! A horse's **intestines** are about 27 meters long. A human's intestines are about 7.5 meters long. Luckily, the intestines are curled up inside the body. Otherwise, people and horses would look very strange!

---

jumbo jets, very large airplanes
intestines, tubes that take food from the stomach out of the body

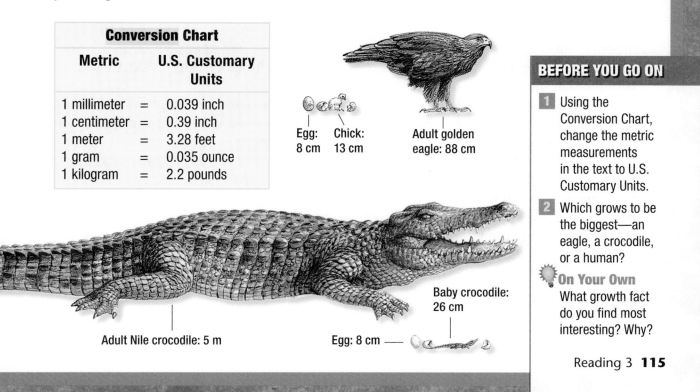

Conversion Chart

Metric		U.S. Customary Units
1 millimeter	=	0.039 inch
1 centimeter	=	0.39 inch
1 meter	=	3.28 feet
1 gram	=	0.035 ounce
1 kilogram	=	2.2 pounds

Egg: 8 cm   Chick: 13 cm   Adult golden eagle: 88 cm

Adult Nile crocodile: 5 m

Egg: 8 cm

Baby crocodile: 26 cm

BEFORE YOU GO ON

1. Using the Conversion Chart, change the metric measurements in the text to U.S. Customary Units.

2. Which grows to be the biggest—an eagle, a crocodile, or a human?

On Your Own
What growth fact do you find most interesting? Why?

Reading 3 **115**

Set a purpose for reading How can a young boy help his parents grow up? As you read this folk tale, think about how Misha's actions help his parents grow and change.

The Old Grandfather and His Little Grandson

An adapted folk tale by Leo Tolstoy

The grandfather had become very old. His legs would not carry him. His eyes could not see and his ears could not hear. He had no teeth. Sometimes when he ate, bits of food dropped out of his mouth. His son and his son's wife no longer let him eat with them at the table. He had to eat his meals in the corner near the stove.

One day they gave the grandfather his food in a bowl. He tried to move the bowl closer. It fell to the floor and broke. His daughter-in-law **scolded** him. She told him that he **spoiled** everything in the house and broke their dishes. She said that from now on, he would get his food in a wooden dish.

The old man sighed and said nothing.

A few days later, the old man's son and his wife were in their hut, resting. They watched their little boy playing on the floor. He was making something out of small pieces of wood. His father said, "What are you making, Misha?"

The little grandson said, "I'm making a wooden bucket. When you and Mama get old, I'll feed you out of this wooden dish."

The young man and his wife looked at each other. Tears filled their eyes. They were **ashamed** they had treated the old grandfather so badly. From that day on, they let the old man eat at the table with them, and they took better care of him.

---

scolded, spoke angrily to
spoiled, ruined

---

ashamed, embarrassed or guilty

ABOUT THE **AUTHOR**

Leo Tolstoy was born in 1828 in Russia. A writer, dramatist, and philosopher, he is considered by many to be the founder of realistic fiction. Tolstoy is most famous for his novel *War and Peace*. Many literary critics consider this book to be one of the greatest books ever written.

BEFORE YOU GO ON

1 Why do the man and his wife make the grandfather eat his meals in the corner?

2 Why does Misha's bowl make his parents feel ashamed?

💡 **On Your Own**
What **benefits** can children gain from living with their grandparents?

Review and Practice

► COMPREHENSION

Workbook
Page 61

Recall

1. According to the article, how long does it take a clam to grow 8 millimeters?

2. In the folk tale, what object does Misha make for his parents?

Comprehend

3. Based on "Amazing Growth Facts," what category would you use to group bamboo and Pacific giant kelp together?

4. In the folk tale, why are the man and his wife angry with the grandfather?

Analyze

5. In what ways is "Amazing Growth Facts" both informative and entertaining?

6. What lesson does Misha teach his parents?

Connect

7. What advantages do enormous animals have?

8. What can children learn from their parents? What can parents learn from their children?

▲ How does this artwork help you visualize the size of a slow-growing clam?

► IN YOUR OWN WORDS

Demonstrate your understanding of the readings by summarizing each one. Copy the following chart into your notebook. Use it to help you organize your summaries. Then share your summaries with a partner.

Speaking SKILL

Use notes and pictures to help you remember important facts.

"Amazing Growth Facts"	"The Old Grandfather and His Little Grandson"
Fact 1:	Beginning:
Fact 2:	Middle:
Fact 3:	End:
Overall summary:	Overall plot summary:

➤ DISCUSSION

Discuss in pairs or small groups.

1. Why do you think the two readings were paired? How are they similar? How are they different?

2. What other information would you like to learn about growth? Give at least two examples.

3. Are you more interested in very large animals or very small ones? Why?

Q How does growing up change us? What do you think your life will be like sixty-five years from now? Describe what you think you will be like. Will you want to be with people your own age, with younger people, or both? Why?

»)) Listening SKILL

Listen carefully to your classmates. Identify the most important ideas. Retell or summarize these ideas in your own words. Use complete sentences.

➤ READ FOR FLUENCY

Reading with feeling helps make what you read more interesting. Work with a partner. Choose a paragraph from the folk tale. Read the paragraph to yourselves. Ask each other how you felt after reading the paragraph. Did you feel happy or sad?

Take turns reading the paragraph aloud to each other with a tone of voice that represents how you felt when you read it the first time. Give each other feedback.

▲ You can track your growth by measuring yourself against a wall every few months.

➤ EXTENSION

Workbook Page 61

Utilize "Amazing Growth Facts" presents interesting information about how certain living things grow. Learn more about the growth of other plants and animals. Use encyclopedias, reference books, and the Internet. Summarize your findings in a short report. Use as much academic language as possible. Then share your findings with your classmates.

LEARNING STRATEGY

To better acquire and understand new academic language, use and reuse these words in meaningful ways in your writing.

Grammar

Simple Past: Regular Verbs

Use the simple past to talk about actions that began and ended in the past. There are rules for forming the simple past of regular verbs.

Rule	Base Form	Simple Past
If base form ends in more than one consonant or ends in vowel + *y*, add *-ed*.	watch scold play	They **watched** him playing. She **scolded** him. He **played** on the floor.
If base form ends in *-e*, add *-d*.	increase live	The tree **increased** in size. He **lived** for many years.
If consonant + vowel + consonant pattern, double final consonant and add *-ed*.	drop stop sip	Bits of food **dropped** out of his mouth. He **stopped** eating. The old man **sipped** his soup.
If base form ends in *-y*, change *y* to *i* and add *-ed*.	try cry	He **tried** to move the bowl closer. The daughter-in-law **cried**.

Grammar SKILL

The base form of a verb is also called the simple form. There are no endings (*-s, -es, -d, -ed*) on the base form.

Grammar SKILL

In the simple past, the form of the verb is the same for all persons:
I / you / he / she / we / they slept.

Form questions in the simple past with the auxiliary verb *did* and the base form of the verb. Form the negative with *did not* or the contraction *didn't* and the base form.

> **QUESTION: Did** they **look** at each other?
> **NEGATIVE:** He **didn't look** at his family.

Practice

Workbook
Page 62

Work with a partner. Copy the sentences below into your notebook. Choose the correct form of the verb in parentheses.

Example: He (lookd/looked) very tired.

1. It (raind/rained) all afternoon.
2. Meg (finished/finish) her homework early.
3. We (worked/works) all weekend.
4. When I was a baby, I (likeed/liked) milk.
5. He (sliped/slipped) on the ice this morning.

✔ **GRAMMAR CHECK**

*When do you add -d to form the **past** of a regular verb?*

Apply

Work with a partner. In your notebook, write the rules from the chart above. Think of as many regular verbs as you can for each rule.

120 Unit 2

Simple Past: Irregular Verbs

Many verbs have an irregular form in the simple past. Their simple past form is not made by adding *-d* or *-ed*. You will need to memorize simple past forms that are irregular.

Base Form	Simple Past
have	He **had** a grandson.
give	One day they **gave** the grandfather his food in a bowl.
say	The old man sighed and **said** nothing.
be	The old man **was not** happy. / They **were** in bed.
let	They **let** the old man eat at the table with them.

Form questions in the simple past with *did* and form negative statements with *did not* or the contraction *didn't*, the same as with regular verbs.

QUESTION: Did he **say** anything?
NEGATIVE: She **didn't let** him sit at the table.

Grammar SKILL

Remember that the negative form of *be* in the past is *wasn't* and *weren't*, as in *He wasn't happy*. Form questions by switching the verb *was* or *were* with the subject, as in *Was he happy?*

Practice  Workbook Page 63

Work with a partner. Copy the sentences into your notebook. Complete the sentences with the simple past of the verb in parentheses. Use a dictionary if necessary.

Example: The old man _felt_ (feel) very sad.

1. My birthday _____ (be) yesterday.
2. _____ Pat _____ (forget) his coat?
3. We _____ (say) goodbye.
4. My sister _____ (not give) me a present.
5. _____ you _____ (get) a hundred percent on the test?

Apply

In your notebook, write five regular or irregular verbs. Work with a partner. Take turns using your verbs to tell a story.

Example: It was a cold and dark night . . .

Writing

Write a Story from a Different Point of View

A story's point of view is the perspective from which it is told. A story can be told, or narrated, by someone outside the story, such as the writer. It can also be told by a character in the story. A character who tells the story uses the pronouns *I* and *me* to refer to himself or herself. Changing the point of view changes the story. That's because different narrators will tell the story differently.

Writing Prompt

Write a narrative paragraph retelling a familiar story from a different point of view. Be sure your narrator is not the story's original narrator. Choose a particular character to tell about events. For example, you could retell the story of Cinderella from her point of view, her stepmother's point of view, or the prince's point of view.

---

1 **PREWRITE** Choose the story that you want to retell.

- Ask yourself which character would be a good narrator.

- Ask yourself how your narrator's point of view will be different from the original narrator's.

- List your ideas in a graphic organizer.
  Workbook
  Page 64

A student named Dan created this graphic organizer. He used it to organize his ideas about changing the point of view to retell the excerpt from *Becoming Naomi León* on pages 98–102.

Naomi's Point of View	Santiago's Point of View
When I was carving soap, I accidentally cut off one of the dog's legs.	The dog made of soap was destined to have three legs.
I want to stay in Oaxaca with Santiago.	Naomi must go home to California.
I want Santiago to come to California.	I have to stay here in Oaxaca.
I was sad to leave Oaxaca.	I was thankful to have met Naomi.

2 DRAFT Use your organizer to help you write a first draft.

- Keep in mind your narrator's point of view.

- Make sure your narrator uses the pronouns *I* and *me* to talk about himself or herself.

- Remember to spell the simple past of verbs correctly.

3 REVISE Read over your draft. Look for places where the writing is unclear or needs improvement. Use the Writing Checklist to help you identify problems. Then revise your draft, using the editing and proofreading marks listed on page 456.

4 EDIT Check your work for errors in grammar, usage, mechanics, and spelling. Trade papers with a partner to obtain feedback. Use the Peer Review Checklist on Workbook page 64. Edit your final draft in response to feedback from your partner and your teacher.

5 PUBLISH Prepare a clean copy of your final draft. Share your narrative paragraph with the class. Save your work. You'll need to refer to it in the Writing Workshop at the end of the unit.

Here is Dan's retelling of *Becoming Naomi León* from Santiago's point of view. Notice Dan's use of the pronouns *I*, *me*, and *my*.

Dan Comstock

My daughter, Naomi

I spent Christmas afternoon with my daughter Naomi. We carved animals out of soap. She was making a dog and accidentally cut off one of its legs. I taught her not to be sad because that dog might have been destined to have three legs. Naomi wants to stay here in Oaxaca with me, but her life is in California and she must go back there. I would move to California to be with her, but I can sell my carvings only in Oaxaca. I was sad when she left, but I am so happy to have met her. I have much to be thankful for. Everything will turn out just fine.

Prepare to Read

▼ After emancipation, enslaved African Americans stayed on ranches to work as cowboys.

🔍 THE BIG QUESTION

How does growing up change us? We all have memories of things that happened to us when we were growing up. Some memories are happy; other memories are sad. Some memories are about small things, such as a birthday party or losing a tooth. Other memories are about important events, such as the birth of a baby brother or the death of a grandparent.

Think about your earliest memories. Try to recall a smell, a sound, a person, a place, or an event. How old were you? Did it change the way you think or feel about something today?

▶ BUILD BACKGROUND

"Thirty Dollars" is an oral narrative told to Alan Govenar by Tony Lott, an African American who grew up in southeast Texas. Tony Lott describes his memories of the time when he worked as a ranch hand and cotton baler. During the early twentieth century, ranch hands were hired to tend cattle. Herding thousands of cows weighing over 1,500 pounds was no easy task. These men worked hard.

An oral narrative gives us an added perspective on history. We can better understand history and culture from the memories of ordinary people. Alan Govenar has devoted his life to collecting and preserving those memories for future generations.

► VOCABULARY

Learn Literary Words

Point of view is the position from which a story is told. Some stories are told from the point of view of one of the characters. The character tells the events as they are happening to him or her. This is called *first-person point* of view. The person telling the story uses the pronouns *I, me, my,* and *we.* Other stories are told from the *third-person point* of view. The **narrator**, or person telling the story, uses the pronouns *she, he,* and *they.* The narrator can be one of the characters in the story, or just someone telling the story from the outside. Read the examples below and notice the pronouns.

Literary Words

narrator
point of view

Audio

> **First-person point of view:** In 1919, I left the Powell Ranch.
>
> **Third-person point of view:** But when he was working, he was a different man altogether.

Practice

Workbook
Page 65

Work with a partner. Read the first three paragraphs of "Thirty Dollars" on page 128. Then answer the questions below in your notebook.

1. Is the narrator Tony Lott, James Welder, or Alan Govenar? How can you tell?

2. Which words in the paragraphs would be different if it were told from James Welder's point of view?

3. Which words in the paragraph would be different if it were told from James Welder's point of view?

Listening and Speaking: Academic Words

Study the red words and their meanings. You will find these words useful when talking and writing about literature. Write each word and its meaning in your notebook, then say the words aloud with a partner. After you read the excerpt from "Thirty Dollars," try to use these words to respond to the text.

affect = do something that produces a change in someone or something	⇒	Events that happen during childhood can **affect** the way people feel when they get older.
document = to collect written evidence	⇒	He hoped to **document** the events of the last ten years.
effect = a result, or a reaction to something or someone	⇒	Working for thirty dollars had a big **effect** on Tony's life.
perspective = a way of thinking about something that is influenced by the type of person you are or what you do	⇒	The story you will read is told from the **perspective** of a ranch hand.

Note: People often confuse the words *affect* and *effect*. Use the verb *affect* to talk about making changes, and use the noun *effect* to talk about the results of changes. Remember, *effect* is almost always a noun that means "result."

Practice

Workbook
Page 66

Work with your partner to answer these questions. Try to include the red word in you answer. Write the sentences in your notebook.

1. How does lack of food **affect** a person?
2. What could you do to **document** your family history?
3. What **effect** can unemployment have on a person?
4. Whose **perspective** is *Becoming Naomi León* told from?

Unemployment has a serious effect on a family. ▼

Word Study: Sound-Letter Relationships

In English, the letter *s* has two different sounds. It can sound like a hissing snake /sss/. Listen to the sound the letter *s* makes in these words: *stop, sunny,* and *singing.* Notice that the letter *s* comes at the beginning of those words.

Sometimes when the letter *s* comes at the end of a word, it has a different sound. It sounds like a buzzing bee /zzz/. Listen to the sound the letter *s* makes in these words: *coins, years,* and *cars.*

Practice

Think about which is the proper sound for *s* in each of the bold words.

> They put **six** on a trailer. **So** I rode at night. And the first week, I made thirty **dollars.** Three **tens,** I will never forget it.

Then make a T-chart in your notebook. Label one column *s makes the /sss/ sound.* Label the other column *s makes the /zzz/ sound.* Work with a partner. Write the words in the correct column. Then find six more words in the reading beginning or ending with the letter *s* and write them in the correct column.

READING STRATEGY | RECOGNIZE HISTORICAL CONTEXT

Analyzing the historical context of a story helps you understand it better. Historical context includes the culture, politics, and social setting for a particular group of people. It also includes the conditions in which they live. To analyze historical context, follow these steps:

- Think about the people's role in society. In what ways are the roles important to the story?
- How do the people live? What are their houses, food, and clothing like? What do they believe?
- Think about what you know about African-American history. How does this help you understand the story?

As you read the story, try to think about the people and events in their historical context.

Set a purpose for reading How might Tony's point of view be different from that of Mr. James Welder and Mr. Johnny Simpson? Read to find out if business owners had the same experiences as Tony.

Thirty Dollars

Audio

Tony Lott's story, as told to Alan Govenar

Tony Lott was born on November 4, 1906. He grew up on the Powell Ranch in southeast Texas, where his parents and grandparents had labored before him. His grandfather, Isaiah Weathers, was a slave who stayed on the ranch after he was emancipated. Lott started working as a cowboy when he was eight years old, "throwing calves all day long." In this excerpt, Lott recounts his experiences as a ranch hand in the early part of the twentieth century.

In 1919, I left the Powell Ranch and started work for Mr. James Welder. One time, Mr. James had a horse name Squito. And old Squito was a good horse. I used to ride old Squito myself and he'd take me with him. And the boss tell me, "You take that old Squito."

Well, Squito's a good horse, a good **cuttin' horse,** he's a good cuttin' horse, but he'd get hot and he'd get **riled** and walk out of the **herd.** And Mr. James would carry him out there and give him a good whooping, hoping to put him back in the herd. And Mr. James Welder was a businessman when he wasn't working. He **whooped** old Squito out there and made him go back to the herd and stop him before he went into the herd. He'd be just like one of us boys when we were working. He'd laugh and joke with us, something like that. But when he was working he was all a different man altogether.

---

cuttin' horse, horse that separates cows from a herd
riled, extremely angry
herd, group of animals
whooped, beaten badly

Reading Skill

To help you understand the reading, study the title and headings. This will help you identify the most important ideas.

▼ Tony Lott

In 1924 came a great big freeze, great big freeze. We had a **bunkhouse** about 200 yards from the kitchen and we got up in the morning and it was sunny. And he (Mr. Welder) was already up. We didn't get up early that morning. I don't know, we slept a little late. We'd all dressed and walked on that ice to the camp house and he was waiting on us. He said, "I want a **volunteer** to go to deliver something for me." That's twenty miles, everything was froze over, ice everywhere. He said, "I want a volunteer," and the third time he said, "I want a volunteer."

I said, "I'll go, Mr. Welder."

He said, "Come on in the house."

Where they lived was a big white house. He said, "Come on in the house." So, I went on in the house. And he put a **soldier suit** on me, wrapped my legs good, put a little short coat on me and then put a big old coat on me. Then he give me some gloves and he said, "Take that **sorrel** horse."

So I got on that horse, walked that horse two miles, just walking, couldn't ride. The slopes were too icy. You'd slip up. Just walked him. I got to the gate and had to unlock the gate. I got off that horse, my hands was like near froze. I got off the gate, run down the fence. That horse run. Got back on that horse again and just walk on that solid ice. Then I come to a creek. I knew it was coming because, oh, I remember this creek. So I got off the horse, that horse was sliding. That creek was icy, and I wanted to help that horse some. Then I got back on the horse, and all along that side of the fence that cattle was piled up frozen. So I walked on, 'til I went to where I was supposed to go.

He had a big farm. Some went this away, some went that away, and we drift all the cows to the bottom. I stayed all night. Slept on some hay, put hay all over me, and that man give me an old quilt. Got up the next morning, ate breakfast, and had to go back to the ranch, some twenty miles away.

---

bunkhouse, building where ranch hands sleep
volunteer, one who offers to do something
soldier suit, military uniform
sorrel, reddish-colored

◀ Sorrel horses

✔ LITERARY CHECK

*Is this narrative told from the **first-person point of view** or the **third-person point of view**? How can you tell?*

▼ Ranch hands lived in the bunkhouse when they were not out with cattle.

BEFORE YOU GO ON

1️⃣ Why did Mr. Welder want old Squito to go back to the herd?

2️⃣ What did Tony volunteer to do?

On Your Own
Why do you think Mr. Welder put Tony in a soldier suit?

Reading 4 **129**

When I got back to the ranch, a boy there named Boone, me and him **hitched up** his horses, that had the camp wagon, and we had to go work together cutting trees down. We take our axe, we didn't have no chain saw, we take our axe and we cut. We cut up about fifteen, twenty trees a day. Because everything was covered with ice. We had another cow, and we had to put hay down in the tent. We put the hay down on top of the ice about four or five days; then, when we moved camp, and that ice was still **underneath.** We had hay on top of it, we didn't know.

So **bossman** come down there, Mr. James come down there, and said, "You boys come in this evening."

So we **saddled up** and got all the stuff together and put it in the wagon and go on back to the ranch. That was a pretty big ranch.

When came time for **dippin'** the cattle, we'd be two days at this ranch. Then we go to Taylor Ranch, about two, three days over there. Then we come back and go to Angelino. That's sixty miles. At Angelino we'd dip down there, and by the time we get through dipping down there, it'd be time to start over. Just ten to fourteen days over there, and we have to start somewhere else.

We never did sing much for songs. We told jokes mostly around the camp. But Mr. James make us sing one song he liked. That's a long time ago. I'm eighty-seven years old, that was a long time ago.

*In what ways do you think the story would be different if the **narrator** was James Welder?*

When my life's work is ended and I cross that
swimming tide
In that bright and getting' up mornin'
I shall see, I shall see,
I shall know my Redeemer when I reach the
other side

---

hitched up, attached
underneath, below
bossman, supervisor, manager
saddled up, got a horse ready to ride
dippin', killing ticks on

Longhorn cattle ▶

I left Mr. Welder in 1924. I said, "Mr. James, I want to go to Corpus Christi to see my sister, I'll be back Monday."

He said, "All right, Tony," says, "That'd be a good thing, there ain't much to do now, that'd be good."

So, he probably give me three or four dollars, I don't know. I went home, taken a bath, wrapped up a shirt, a pair of pants, underwear in a paper bag, and tied a string around it, and went down there to Corpus, got on the railroad track. Twelve o'clock, if the train's coming, you had to flag the train down. You step right there next to the track, toot-toot, he stop. You get on. And I went into Corpus and stayed.

Back then, in 1927, I had a meeting with my brothers and sisters.

That was on Saturday. On Saturday night, my brother-in-law said, "Tony, why don't you stay down here and go to work at the **compress**?" But I didn't want to do that.

He said, "Yeah, they hiring over there. You can get a job. I'll carry you there in the morning."

So Sunday morning he carried me over to the ranch, over to the compress. A man named Johnny Simpson, he just died about two years ago. "Mr. Simpson, here's a boy that want to work."

"What can you do, boy?"

I said, "Nothin'."

He said, "You the man I want."

Compress is where they bale cotton. Where they make big bales and they bale cotton. They bale the cotton and tie it and **bale** it. And had folks come into the compress and ...

So, I went to work at the compress, **trucking** cotton. He showed me how to catch the **bale**. So I caught the bale as he pulled the bale, and I'm trucking and dumping. Then the man give me a hook to pull cotton down. I pulled cotton down. Then he give me a job riding a trailer to the docks. They put six on a trailer. So I rode at night. And the first week, I made thirty dollars. Three tens, I never will forget it. Open the envelope and Oh! three tens, good night! Three tens, I was gettin' seven dollars out there on the ranch, seven dollars.

Cotton was picked by hand and bundled at the compress. ▼

---

compress, place where cotton is baled
bale (verb), compress and package
trucking, moving or hauling
bale (noun), compressed package
    of cotton or hay

BEFORE YOU GO ON

1 What does Tony mean when he says, "We never did sing much for songs"?

2 Why did Tony stay in Corpus?

On Your Own
How does what you're paid change your feelings about doing a job?

Reading 4　**131**

Three tens, I said, "That's too much." So, I backed off, my number was 360. Six hundred men working there. I'll never forget it. I backed off, and he paid all the other people off. This is true. I went to him and said, "Mr. Simpson, you make a mistake in my money?"

"Let me see, Brother Lott, let me see, Brother Lott." He said, "Monday night you went to the dock with Charlie Dean. Tuesday you went to the dock with Ezra. Wednesday night you went to the dock with Ted."

I said, "Oh, yeah, yeah, yeah." He thought I wanted some more money, but I wanted to give some of that back. Thirty dollars.

Where I lived was about two miles from compress, and I broke into a run. I broke into a run. I says, "Sister," I said, "I made thirty dollars!"

"Well," she said, "you take your bath and we'll carry you downtown to get you a suit."

So, I take me a bath in the number three tub. And she carried me downtown to this **tailor.** I never had a suit before. He measured me up, said, "The suit would be ready soon."

I paid him fifteen dollars, that suit was thirty dollars. I paid him fifteen dollars down on that suit. I never will forget it. I paid him fifteen dollars down on that suit. Gray finished, **gabardine, double-breasted.**

I asked, "When will it be ready?"

He said, "It'll be ready next Saturday, Tony."

He called me Tony.

I said, "Okay."

Next Saturday, I went down there. I owed fifteen dollars. Next door there was a store that sold Thom McCan Shoes, cheap shoes. Get a good pair of shoes for five dollars, eight dollars, they didn't have no name, just shoes. I bought me **two-toned,** black-and-white **spat shoes.** Sunday morning I put them shoes and that gray suit and went to church. I was all dressed up.

▼ Tony Lott

---

tailor, suit-maker
gabardine, heavy fabric
double-breasted, coat style with one part of the front covering the other
two-toned, with two colors
spat shoes, (spats) shoes that cover the ankle

I worked at the compress about seven, eight years. Then I went back to the ranch. I went back to the ranch on a Monday. I been in **soup lines** four or five blocks long. It was the Depression. I went back on a Monday. It was seven years (from the time I left) I went back on the ranch in the spring. And they looked up to see me get off the bus out there on the highway.

"That look like Tony, old boy. That look like Tony coming **yonder**."

I had a suitcase then. I had some clothes, I had a suitcase, and Mr. James, he met me and he said, "Tony, you said you was coming back Monday, but you didn't say what Monday!"

I said, "No, I didn't say what Monday."

He said, "Get in that **pickup** there."

They had a little old country store down there. "Go down to the store and get a roll of rope." So I got in the pickup went down and got a ball of rope. And I worked there back at the ranch about another three years. Then I come back to Corpus. I was a **chauffeur** for a man who raised **quarter horses**. He hired me because I knowed horses. Then I started cutting grass, doing yard work, and I still do a little yard work.

---

soup lines, lines of people waiting for food during the Depression
yonder, in the distance
pickup, truck with an open bed
chauffeur, driver
quarter horses, small, fast race or ranch horses

ABOUT THE AUTHOR

ALAN GOVENAR is the founder of Documentary Arts, Inc., a nonprofit organization dedicated to preserving the thoughts and ideas of people as part of our cultural heritage. Govenar has written numerous books on many subjects, including *Untold Glory: African Americans and the Pursuit of Freedom, Stompin' at the Savoy, Extraordinary Ordinary People,* and  *Texas Blues.* In addition to writing, Govenar is a photographer and filmmaker. His musical *Blind Lemon Blues,* which he created with Akin Babatunde, appeared off-Broadway in New York City.

BEFORE YOU GO ON

1 Why was Tony so surprised by the thirty dollars?

2 What jobs did Tony do at the compress?

On Your Own
What would you buy with your first paycheck from a job?

> **READER'S THEATER** Audio

Act out the following scene between Tony, his sister, Mr. Simpson, and the tailor.

Tony: Three tens. That's too much. Mr. Simpson you make a mistake in my money?

Mr. Simpson: Let me see, Brother Lott, let me see, Brother Lott. Monday, you went to the dock. Tuesday, you went to the dock, and Wednesday you went to the dock.

Tony: Oh, yeah, yeah, yeah.

Tony realizes there is no mistake and runs to his sister's house.

Tony: Sister, I made thirty dollars!

Sister: Well, you take your bath and we'll take you downtown to get a suit.

Tailor: Your suit will be ready soon.

Tony: When will it be ready?

Tailor: It'll be ready next Saturday, Tony.

Tony: Okay.

> **COMPREHENSION**   Workbook
Page 69

Recall

1. Where did Tony sleep while at the ranch?
2. How soon after the great freeze did Tony leave Mr. Welder?

Comprehend

3. How did the ice **affect** Tony's journey to the farm by horse?
4. Why was Mr. Welder so surprised to see Tony on that Monday?

Analyze

5. Why do you think Mr. Simpson would hire a man who couldn't do anything?

6. What does Tony say to document the hard times of the Depression?

Connect

7. What thoughts do you now have about ranch life after reading Tony's story?

8. How would the story be different if it was told from Alan Govenar's **perspective** instead of Tony's?

▶DISCUSSION

Discuss in pairs or small groups.

1. Think about Tony's relationship with his bosses. Why do you think he isn't angry at Mr. Welder for paying him so little money?

2. What memories do you think had the greatest **effect** on Tony's future?

Q **How does growing up change us?** What effect do you think Tony's time on the ranch had on his later life?

▶ RESPONSE TO LITERATURE

Workbook
Page 69

Utilize This story is an oral narrative. It tells about certain events in Tony's life. Work with a partner and come up with an oral narrative to describe an event that was important in your childhood. Be sure to say it in the first person. Remember to tell how the event changed you. Then share your narrative with the class.

▲ Moving to a new place is a life-changing event.

Grammar

Direct Quotations: Statements

A direct quotation is enclosed in quotation marks (" "). Quotation marks always come in pairs. Be sure to use them at the beginning and at the end of the direct quotation. A direct quotation is usually introduced with a phrase identifying the speaker. The phrase includes a reporting verb such as *said*. The first letter of the quotation is capitalized.

   The phrase identifying the speaker may begin the sentence. The phrase must begin with the speaker and a comma comes after *said*. A period comes after the quotation, followed by the final quotation mark. When the direct quotation begins the sentence, a comma follows the quotation and a period ends the sentence.

> He said, "Come on in the house."
> "Come on in the house," he said.

When a direct quotation is interrupted by the phrase identifying the speaker, quotations marks enclose both parts of the quotation. Do not capitalize the second part of the quotation. Commas come after the first part of the quotation and after the phrase.

> "Well," she said, "we'll carry you downtown to get you a suit."

Grammar SKILL

When you use a pronoun in the phrase identifying the speaker, the pronoun should begin the phrase.

Practice Workbook Page 70

Work with a partner. Copy the sentences below into your notebook. Add commas and quotation marks.

Example: "All right," she said, "we can go."

1. My mother said She is coming to dinner tonight.
2. The teacher said Our test is tomorrow.
3. I will take you to the airport my brother said.
4. I'll try it she said but I won't like it.
5. My friend said We can go to the movies.

Apply

Work with a partner. Rewrite the quotations in the Practice exercise, putting the phrase identifying the speaker in a different place.

Direct Quotations: Questions

When quoting a question directly in your writing, use the reporting verb *ask* in the phrase identifying the speaker. When the phrase identifying the speaker begins the sentence, use a comma after the phrase. The question begins with a capital letter and ends with a question mark (?). The final quotation marks come after the question mark.

> I asked, "When will it be ready?"

When the phrase identifying the speaker comes after the question, a question mark still ends the question, but the phrase is followed by a period.

> "When will it be ready?" I asked.

The reporting verb *ask* is often followed by an object or object pronoun.

> "When will it be ready?" I asked **him**.

Practice  Workbook Page 71

Work with a partner. Copy the sentences below into your notebook. Add question marks, quotation marks, periods, and correct capitalization.

Example: *"Are you ready?"* she asked.

1. Maria asked him did you like it
2. can you see it Teresa asked
3. what's for lunch he asked
4. Aggie asked me do you speak French
5. where is it Bert asked

Apply

Work with a partner. Ask and answer questions about the reading. Then write five direct quotations from your discussion.

Writing

Write a Personal Narrative

A personal narrative is a story about something memorable that happened in the writer's own life. Tony Lott's account of his experiences as a young ranch hand could be called a personal narrative. In a personal narrative, the writer uses specific details to describe the people and setting involved. Events are told in time order. The narrative is organized to have a beginning, middle, and end.

Writing Prompt

Write a personal narrative about an experience you had when you were growing up. Be sure your narrative has a beginning, middle and end. Use direct quotations in your narrative. Remember to punctuate statements, questions, and exclamations correctly.

1 **PREWRITE** Choose a meaningful experience from your past.

- Ask yourself why you remember this experience.
- Think about how it began, what happened in the middle, and how it ended.
- List your ideas in a graphic organizer.  **Workbook** Page 72

A student named Brandon created this sequence chart. He planned to write about an experience he had shared with his grandfather.

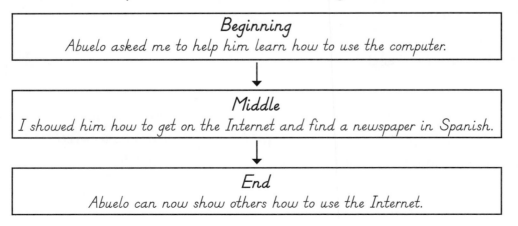

> *Beginning*
> *Abuelo asked me to help him learn how to use the computer.*
>
> ↓
>
> *Middle*
> *I showed him how to get on the Internet and find a newspaper in Spanish.*
>
> ↓
>
> *End*
> *Abuelo can now show others how to use the Internet.*

2 **DRAFT** Use your organizer to help you write a first draft.

- Remember to present events in time order.

- Narrate events with specificity and detail.

- Tell what happened in your own voice and from your own point of view.

3 **REVISE** Read over your draft. Look for places where the writing is unclear or needs improvement. Use the Writing Checklist to help you identify problems. Then revise your draft, using the editing and proofreading marks listed on page 456.

4 **EDIT** Check your work for errors in grammar, usage, mechanics, and spelling. Trade papers with a partner to obtain feedback. Use the Peer Review Checklist on Workbook page 72. Edit your final draft in response to feedback from your partner and your teacher.

5 **PUBLISH** Prepare a clean copy of your final draft. Share your personal narrative with the class. Save your work. You'll need to refer to it in the Writing Workshop at the end of the unit.

Writing Checklist

ORGANIZATION:
☑ I told events in time order.

IDEAS:
☑ I narrated events with specificity and detail.

CONVENTIONS:
☑ I used direct quotations in my narrative.

Here is Brandon's personal narrative. Notice how he uses words such as *then* and *finally* to signal the correct time order of events.

Brandon Saiz

My Abuelo

One day I went to my abuelo's house to visit. Abuelo said, "Do you want to help me learn how to use the computer?" He is kind and has helped me with many things, so I was happy that I could help him this time. We sat down in the kitchen, where he had set up the computer on the counter. He said, "Show me how to get on the Internet." I automatically clicked the browser because that is what I do on my computer at home. I could see Abuelo was pleased because his eyes opened wider as he studied the screen through his reading glasses. Then he asked me if I could find a newspaper in Spanish for him on the Internet, which I did. Finally, I showed him how to turn off the computer. He liked that. Abuelo can now show other people how to use the Internet.

Link the Readings

Critical Thinking

Look back at the readings in this unit. Think about what they have in common. They all tell about growing up. Yet they do not all have the same purpose. The purpose of one reading might be to inform, while the purpose of another might be to entertain or persuade. In addition, the content of each reading relates to growing up differently. Now copy the chart below into your notebook and complete it.

Title of Reading	Purpose	Big Question Link
"Ancient Kids"	to inform	tells about kids in ancient times
From *Becoming Naomi León*		
"Amazing Growth Facts," "The Old Grandfather and His Little Grandson"		
"Thirty Dollars"		

Discussion

Discuss in pairs or small groups.

- What similarities can you see between *Becoming Naomi León* and "The Old Grandfather and His Little Grandson"?

- **Q How does growing up change us?** What conclusions can you draw about growing up, based on what you learned in each of the readings?

Media Literacy & Projects

1 What do you think happens at the end of *Becoming Naomi León*? Share your ideas with a classmate. Then read the book to see if your prediction is correct.

2 Use the Internet to find a museum near you that displays art and objects from ancient cultures. Visit the museum. Prepare an oral report about what you saw and what you learned.

3 Make a soap carving. Ask a classmate to read the directions in "Soap Carving" on page 103. Follow each direction as it is read aloud. You may want to make an animal, as Naomi does. Or you can make something else. Write a title for the figure on an index card to put with it. Have your classmates place their carved figures next to yours to make a class art display.

4 Share a folk tale with your class. You can retell "The Old Grandfather and His Little Grandson" in your own words. Or you can choose another folk tale to tell.

Further Reading

Choose from these reading suggestions. Practice reading silently with increased ease for longer and longer periods.

Rip Van Winkle and the Legend of Sleepy Hollow,
Washington Irving
This Penguin Reader® includes adaptations of Irving's two beloved classics.

The Barefoot Book of Heroic Children, Rebecca Hazel
This book presents inspiring stories of some of the most amazing young people in history.

Just Juice, Karen Hesse
A family in Appalachia faces many challenges and, together, overcomes them.

Put It All Together

LISTENING & SPEAKING WORKSHOP

Skit

You will write and perform a skit about growing up in ancient times.

1 THINK ABOUT IT Work in teams. Choose one of the ancient cultures you read about in "Ancient Kids": Greek, Roman, or Maya. Talk about growing up in that time and place. Focus on topics such as school, families, ceremonies, gifts, toys, and foods. Also, discuss how girls and boys were treated and how brothers and sisters might have felt about each other. Think of a situation in your ancient culture that you could present as a skit, or short play. Talk with your team members. Listen to their ideas. Then identify points of agreement and disagreement. Write down your shared ideas.

2 GATHER AND ORGANIZE INFORMATION Work with your team to plan your skit. Choose a team member to be the director. He or she will decide which role each of the remaining team members will play.

Research Go to the library or use the Internet to gather more information about your ancient culture. Take notes on what you find.

Order Your Notes Write these headings in your notebook: *Characters, Setting, Plot*. Make notes under each heading.

Prepare a Script Use your notes to write a script for your skit. The dialogue should look like this:

Jason:	I don't want to go to school today. I want to stay home and play.
Jacinda:	You should be grateful that you can go to school! Girls like me have to stay home all the time.
Jason:	That sounds like fun.
Jacinda:	Well, you're wrong! I hardly ever have time to play. Mother keeps me busy doing chores all day.

Include important details about the setting, props, and action:

Jason stops playing and frowns. Then he starts to get ready for school.

Use Visuals Make or find the costumes and props you need for your skit.

3 **PRACTICE AND PRESENT** As a team, practice your skit until you can perform it without looking at the script. To make your skit richer and more interesting, use a variety of grammatical structures, sentence lengths and types, and connecting words. The director will provide you with instructions about how to improve your performance. Listen to and follow these directions. The director will also serve as *prompter* while you practice. (A prompter watches the skit and follows along in the script. If someone forgets what to say or do, the prompter quietly reminds him or her.) Practice with your props and costumes.

Perform Your Skit Speak loudly enough so that everyone in the class can hear you. Say each word carefully so that it is clear. Be sure to face the audience as you speak, even if your body is pointing in another direction. Pay attention to the other actors, and be ready when it's your turn!

4 **EVALUATE THE PRESENTATION**
A good way to improve your speaking and listening skills is to evaluate your own performance and the performances of your classmates. Use this checklist to help you judge your group's skit and the skits of your classmates.

- ☑ Could you understand the plot?
- ☑ Did the skit show what it was like to grow up in an ancient time?
- ☑ Were the costumes and props helpful and appropriate?
- ☑ Could you hear and understand the actors?
- ☑ What suggestions do you have for improving the skit?

Speaking SKILL

Learning Strategy: As you speak, employ non-verbal cues, such as gestures and facial expressions. Doing this will help you convey your character's actions and emotions to the audience.

Listening SKILLS

Listen carefully to the other actors so that you know when to say your lines. Learn your *cues*—words or actions that signal when it is your turn to speak.

When you watch a skit, listen to the words a speaker uses. Watch his or her facial expressions and gestures. Use both verbal and nonverbal cues to understand a speaker's message.

STRENGTHEN YOUR SOCIAL LANGUAGE

Writing a script helps you learn basic vocabulary and language structures. Go to www.LongmanKeystone.com and do the activity for this unit. This activity will require you to use and reuse basic language in other meaningful writing activities.

WRITING WORKSHOP

Write a Short Story

You have learned how to write a variety of narrative paragraphs. Now you will use your skills to write a longer fictional narrative. A fictional narrative is a story a writer creates. It includes interesting characters, a believable setting, and a plot. The plot is the series of events in the story. Usually these events involve a conflict. The plot builds to a climax, or high point. By the end of the story, the conflict is resolved.

Writing Prompt

Write a short story about jealousy between two friends or family members. Tell your story from the point of view of one of the characters. Include dialogue to show how the characters think and feel. Remember to describe a believable setting. Narrate events with specificity and detail. Be sure to include a conflict and tell how it is resolved.

1 PREWRITE Review your previous work in this unit. Now brainstorm ideas for your story. Why might someone feel jealous of a friend or family member? In your notebook, answer these questions:

Ongoing Writing Skills Practice

- Which of my characters is jealous and why?

- What is the conflict about? How is it resolved?

- List your ideas in a graphic organizer.

Workbook Page 73

Here's a graphic organizer created by a student named Wendy. She used it to organize her ideas about her characters, setting, and plot.

CHARACTERS Who?	SETTING Where?	PROBLEM What is the conflict?	SOLUTION What is the resolution?
Max Joni their parents	their home	Joni gets all the family's attention. Max is jealous.	Max tells about volunteering. Parents are proud of him.

2 **DRAFT** Use your graphic organizer and the model on pages 147–148 to help you write a first draft.

- Include interesting characters and a believable setting.
- Organize the events of the plot in time order.
- Use dialogue to help bring your characters to life.

3 **REVISE** Read over your draft. Think about how well you have addressed questions of purpose, audience, and form. Will your story engage and entertain your readers? Does it include interesting characters, a believable setting, and a good plot?

Keep these questions in mind as you revise your draft. Use the Writing Checklist below to help you identify additional issues that may need revision. Mark your changes on your draft using the editing and proofreading marks listed on page 456.

SIX TRAITS OF WRITING CHECKLIST

☑ **IDEAS:** Is my story focused on jealousy between two characters?

☑ **ORGANIZATION:** Do I tell events in chronological order?

☑ **VOICE:** Does my story have a clear point of view?

☑ **WORD CHOICE:** Do I include realistic dialogue?

☑ **SENTENCE FLUENCY:** Do I use connecting words to combine sentences?

☑ **CONVENTIONS:** Do I punctuate dialogue correctly?

LEARNING STRATEGY

Monitor your written language production. Using a writing checklist will help you assess your work. Evaluate your essay to make sure that your message is clear and easy to understand.

Here are the revisions Wendy plans to make to her first draft.

Max Learns a Lesson

For a long time,
I thought my sister was better than I was at everything. I worked

so hard for a B average. Joni ~~got~~ *just breezed through with* an A in every class My parents

weren't upset with my grades; they just paid a lot more attention

to Joni. My sister also is a ~~good~~ *terrific* athlete.

Last month,
I helped rebuild homes damaged by a flood in a nearby community.

I ~~liked~~ *was excited about* making a difference in other people's lives. *Even so,* Every afternoon,

the only thing Joni and my parents talked about was Joni!

One night, *as we were having dinner* I got sick and tired of the world revolving around her.

"Doesn't anybody ever want to hear about <u>me</u>?" *I demanded.* "I'm working with a

family whose house was really messed up by the flood."

My parents looked ~~at me.~~ *surprised* "Of course we want to hear about you,"

my father said. "You don't always seem to <u>want</u> to tell us anything.

Usually, when we ask, you just shrug." I had to admit to myself that

was true.

"I knew the school asked you to volunteer," my mother said slowly.

"But I wasn't sure exactly what you were doing." So I ~~telled~~ *told* them

~~about working hard.~~ *to repair soggy floors and repaint water-stained walls.*

Just then, joni spoke up. I figured she was about to say something

even wonderful~~er~~ *more* about herself. *, but instead* She said, "Max, did you tell Mom and

Dad you made the debate team." I was stu*n*ed she cared!

<table>
<tr><td>*Revised to clarify sequence and improve word choice.*</td></tr>
<tr><td>*Revised to clarify sequence and improve word choice and sentence fluency.*</td></tr>
<tr><td>*Revised to add details.*</td></tr>
<tr><td>*Revised to improve word choice, add details, and correct an error in grammar.*</td></tr>
<tr><td>*Revised to correct errors in grammar and spelling and improve sentence fluency.*</td></tr>
</table>

ˇSince then, I try to ~~talk~~ share more about my interests and activities. My parents congratulated me on volunteering and making the team. I'm no longer jealous of Joni because my parents seemed just as proud of me. They know that we are each special in our own way.

Revised to improve word choice, sentence fluency, and organization.

4 **EDIT** Check your work for errors in grammar, usage, mechanics, and spelling. Then trade stories with a partner and use the Peer Review Checklist below to give each other constructive feedback. Edit your final draft in response to feedback from your partner and your teacher.

Workbook
Page 73

PEER REVIEW CHECKLIST

- ☑ Does the story build to a climax?
- ☑ Do precise words tell how the characters look, act, and feel?
- ☑ Is the setting believable?
- ☑ Are verbs, tenses, and pronoun/antecedents used correctly?
- ☑ Do sentences vary in length and pattern?
- ☑ What changes could be made to improve the essay?

Here are the changes Wendy decided to make to her final draft as a result of her peer review.

Wendy Willner

Max Learns a Lesson

For a long time, I thought my sister was better than I was at everything. I ~~worked so hard~~ struggled for a B average. Yet Joni just breezed through with an A in every class. My parents weren't upset with my grades; they just paid a lot more attention to Joni. My sister also is a terrific athlete.

Revised to correct an error in mechanics and improve word choice and sentence fluency.

Last month, I helped rebuild homes damaged by a flood in a nearby community. I was excited about making a difference in other people's lives. Even so, every afternoon, the only thing Joni and my parents talked about was Joni!

One night as we were having dinner, I got sick and tired of the world revolving around her. Doesn't anybody ever want to hear about me?" I demanded. "I'm working with a family whose house was really messed up by the flood."

Revised to correct an error in mechanics.

My parents looked surprised. "Of course we want to hear about you," my father said. "You don't always seem to <u>want</u> to tell us anything. Usually, when we ask, you just shrug." I had to admit to myself that was true.

"I knew the school asked you to volunteer," my mother said slowly. "But I wasn't sure exactly what you were doing." So I told them about working hard to repair soggy floors and repaint water-stained walls.

Just then, joni spoke up. I figured she was about to say something even more wonderful about herself, but instead she said, "Max, did you tell Mom and Dad you made the debate team." I was stunned she cared!

Revised to correct errors in mechanics.

My parents congratulated me on volunteering and making the team. Since then, I try to share more about my interests and activities. I'm no longer jealous of Joni because my parents seem just as proud of me. They know that we are each special in our own way.

5 **PUBLISH** Prepare a clean copy of your final draft. Share your short story with the class.

Workbook
Page 74

Test Preparation

PRACTICE

Read the following test sample. Study the tips in the boxes. Work with a partner to answer the questions.

Quinceañera

1   Almost every culture in the world has coming of age ceremonies. These ceremonies mark the time when children are recognized as adults. In Latin American countries, girls have a ceremony called the quinceañera. The ceremony is held on or near the girl's 15th birthday.

2   If the girl's family is religious, her special day will begin with a religious service. The family's religious leader will often be involved in some part of the ceremony. The girl may receive gifts of religious items, such as a rosary.

3   After the religious ceremony, the girl's family holds a celebration in their home or in another location such as a banquet hall. The girl will often carry a doll, which represents the last doll of her childhood. The girl's father will exchange her flat shoes for heels, at which time the girl will give her doll to her father. She then dances with her father and godfather. Soon the other guests dance as well. The event ends with everyone making toasts and eating cake.

1 The subject of this passage is _____.
  - A   weddings
  - B   quinceañera
  - C   national holidays
  - D   religious ceremonies

2 Why does the girl put on heels?
  - F   To dress like an adult
  - G   To dance with her father
  - H   She likes high heels.
  - J   To please her grandmother

Taking Tests
You will often take tests that help show what you know. Study the tips below to help you improve your test-taking skills.

Tip
Use context clues to help you figure out the meanings of words you don't know.

Tip
Even if you don't know the answer to the question, you can almost always eliminate answer choices that make no sense.

Workbook
Pages 75–78

Capturing Childhood

Artists have used many methods to try to capture how people grow up. Many use photographs and paintings. Sometimes families hand these images down over the years, from generation to generation. The clothes and the favorite toys in the images may change over time. Usually, though, there's something familiar in the parade of family faces.

Albert Bisbee, *Child on a Rocking Horse* (about 1855)

This little girl with curly hair stares out at you. She looks a bit uncertain about sitting on the rocking horse. Albert Bisbee, who took a lot of family portraits, once said that he liked to photograph children as soon as they sat on the horse. If he missed his early chance, he felt it got more difficult with each passing minute because the child would get restless.

It took a lot more time to create a photograph in 1855 than it does today. The child had to sit very still. This was because Bisbee used an early photographic process called a daguerreotype. The image was printed directly on a sheet of silver-plated copper. If someone moved even a little bit, the photograph would be blurry.

Photographs were expensive over 150 years ago. Many families had only one or two pictures taken of their children as they grew up. Most of them wanted their child's photograph to be taken on a toy horse. The rocking horse was a very popular toy in nineteenth-century America. The little girl's face in this photograph shows how serious it was to have your picture taken. She wears a checkered dress trimmed with lace. She also wears fancy shoes. She is all dressed up for this important event.

▲ Albert Bisbee, *Child on a Rocking Horse*, about 1855, daguerreotype, 4¼ × 4½ in., Smithsonian American Art Museum

William Holbrook Beard, *The Lost Balloon* (1882)

The balloon off in the distance in William Holbrook Beard's painting *The Lost Balloon* is not a toy. It is a hot-air balloon floating beneath the clouds. A group of nine children and a dog are on the edge of a great ledge, watching the balloon as it moves through the sunlight.

An enormous rock face, which rises to their right, is partly hidden by stormy clouds. The children stand very close to the rim of a sharp drop-off in the landscape. Oddly, there are no adults with them. Perhaps Beard was trying to capture the quickly changing nature of childhood. In the painting, he seems to be saying that childhood is like the lovely balloon hanging on the edge of a storm. The children certainly seem very small against the wilderness.

Both of these artists captured an instant in childhood that's temporary, but somehow timeless. Each of us must move on from being ten or twelve or fourteen and face the next stage in life.

◀ William Holbrook Beard, *The Lost Balloon*, 1882, oil, 47¾ x 33¾ in., Smithsonian American Art Museum

Discuss What You Learned

1 In what way does each of these artworks capture a moment in childhood?

2 Which medium do you feel is better at capturing the feelings of childhood—photography or painting? Explain.

Big Question
Why do you think that many artworks are about childhood and change?

Workbook
Pages 79–80

THE BIG QUESTION

How does helping others help us all?

This unit is about living creatures helping one another. You'll read about an Apache boy who receives help from a farm family and biographies about people who devoted their lives to helping others. You'll read a girl's diary entries that ask for peace in her war-torn country, and you'll read about the impact of urban expansion on wildlife. As you read, you'll practice the academic and literary language you need to use in school.

Reading

1 Novel	2 Social Studies	3 Diary
	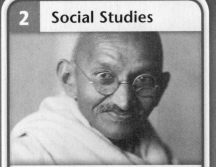	
From *Run Away Home* by Patricia C. McKissack	"Extraordinary People: Serving Others"	From *Zlata's Diary* by Zlata Filipovic
Reading Strategy: Make inferences	**Reading Strategy:** Identify problems and solutions	**Reading Strategy:** Distinguish fact from opinion

Listening and Speaking—Persuasive

At the end of this unit, you'll present a **TV talk show** about a person you admire.

Writing—Persuasive

In this unit you will practice **persuasive writing**. This type of writing tries to get the reader to do something or to agree with a viewpoint. After each reading, you will learn a skill to help you write a persuasive paragraph. At the end of the unit, you will write a persuasive speech.

Quick Write

Make a list of places you have been to or places you would like to visit.

---

4 | **Science**

"Friendship and Cooperation in the Animal Kingdom"

Reading Strategy:
Identify main idea and details

DVD **VIEW AND RESPOND**
Watch the DVD for Unit 3 and answer the questions at
www.LongmanKeystone.com.

What You Will Learn

Reading
- Vocabulary building: *Literary terms, word study*
- Reading strategy: *Make inferences*
- Text type: *Literature (novel excerpt)*

Grammar
Agreement in simple and compound sentences

Writing
Write a book review

➤ THE BIG QUESTION

How does helping others help us all?

Everyone needs help sometimes. Sometimes we need help because of a big problem or a small problem. Use your prior experiences to think about a time when you needed help. What was the situation? How did that person help you? Think about a time when you helped someone else. What happened? How did you feel? Discuss with a partner.

➤ BUILD BACKGROUND

Run Away Home takes place on a farm in Alabama in 1888. Novels that take place in a real time and place in the past are called historical fiction. In *Run Away Home*, the main characters are an African-American farm family and an Apache boy. The main characters and plot are imaginary, but certain people and events mentioned in the novel are real.

In 1888, many Apaches were forced to move onto reservations in Alabama. A reservation is land set aside for Native Americans by the U.S. government. Living conditions on the reservations were poor, and many Native Americans became sick.

Some Native American children were sent from reservations to schools far away. At school, they had to stop speaking their native languages and speak only English. They had to eat, dress, and act like whites. The Apache boy in *Run Away Home* doesn't want to be sent to the Carlisle Indian School. This was a real school for Native Americans in Carlisle, Pennsylvania, near Harrisburg.

▲ An 1880 class photo from the Carlisle Indian School

➤ VOCABULARY

Learn Literary Words

To make stories realistic, writers sometimes use **dialect** when they write dialogue. Dialect is the way people speak in a specific region. For example, in the southern part of the United States, people use different expressions and may say words differently from the way people do in other parts of the country. Read the examples of dialect. How are these examples of dialect different from the English you are asked to use in school?

> I **might can't** save him. (I may not be able to save him.)
> He's **fixin'** to leave. (He's getting ready to leave.)

Usually, writers create a **mood**, or feeling, in a narrative. For example, they might create a funny, sad, hopeful, or tense mood. One mood that many writers create is a feeling of **suspense**, or uncertainty about what will happen. Suspense keeps readers interested and makes them want to read on to find out what will happen. Read the example below. What mood does the writer create?

> It was a dark moonless night outside the cabin. My father and I were alone for the weekend and were about to go to bed. Suddenly, we heard the sound of heavy footsteps coming closer. We stayed very still and listened. The footsteps sounded like a steady heartbeat getting louder and louder. I shivered.

Practice  Workbook Page 81

Work with a partner. Take turns reading the examples of dialect from *Run Away Home*. Discuss how the dialect might be different from the English you hear at school.

> "What are you thinkin' 'bout, Georgianne? How could you bring trouble to our front door like this? Mr. Wratten was just here lookin' for this boy, and here we got him in our house, takin' care of him."
>
> "Aine it enough 'round here to do, besides taking on a sick boy, somebody we don't even-now know. What business is it of ours?"

Now read these sentences aloud in the English you hear at school. There might be many ways to say the same sentence.

Listening and Speaking: Academic Words

Study the red words and their meanings. You will find these words useful when talking and writing about literature. Write each word and its meaning in your notebook, then say the words aloud with a partner. After you read the excerpt from *Run Away Home*, try to use these words to respond to the text.

Academic Words

appropriate
communicate
period
precise

appropriate = suitable for a particular time, situation, or purpose	⇒	It is **appropriate** to say "thank you" when someone helps you.
communicate = express your thoughts and feelings so that others understand them	⇒	Some people **communicate** their ideas by writing fiction.
period = a particular length of time in history or in a person's life	⇒	Some novels take place during a specific **period** in history. For example, historical fiction might be set in the nineteenth century.
precise = exact and correct in every detail	⇒	Directions must be **precise** so that students know exactly what to do.

Audio

Practice  Workbook Page 82

Work with a partner to answer these questions. Try to include the red word in your answer. Write the sentences in your notebook.

1. What is appropriate to say to someone after he or she has helped you?
2. What might you do to communicate that you need help?
3. Which period in history do you like to read about? Why?
4. Why is it important for travelers to get precise directions?

Apache "burden baskets" were used to carry loads during the 1800s—a period of great change for the Apache people. ▶

Word Study: Uses of the Apostrophe

A contraction is a word that is made up of two words that have been shortened into one. An apostrophe is a mark of punctuation that shows where letters have been left out in contractions. Read the examples below.

Two Words	Contraction
is not	isn't
do not	don't

An apostrophe is also used in dialect to show that letters are missing. Read the examples below. What letters does the apostrophe replace in each example of dialect?

Word	Dialect
thinking	thinkin'
children	chil'en or chill'un

▲ The sun is shining. There isn't a cloud in the sky.

Practice
Workbook Page 83

Write these contractions and examples of dialect in your notebook: *I'll, he'd, shouldn't, 'cause, 'round, 'til*. Work with a partner to identify the letter or letters each apostrophe replaces. Then rewrite the words by replacing apostrophes with the letters that are missing.

READING STRATEGY | MAKE INFERENCES

You can expand your skills by making inferences or figuring out information that authors do not state directly. To make inferences, follow the steps in this example:

- Read the sentence: *By then, the boy was shaking with chills.*
- Think about your own experiences. Ask yourself: "What are chills? How do I feel when I shake with chills?"
- Use the information in the text and your own experiences to make an inference. You can infer (or make the inference) that the boy is probably shaking with chills because he is sick.

As you read the excerpt from *Run Away Home*, make inferences. Think about what the author means but does not say directly.

Workbook Page 84

Set a purpose for reading Does it take courage to help someone who is very ill? Read to find out what happens to the sick boy that Sarah and her mother find in their barn. Who is he, and why does he need their help?

from

Run Away Home

Patricia C. McKissack

It is 1888 in Alabama when eleven-year-old Sarah Crossman sees an Apache boy escape from a train taking him to a reservation. Later Sarah and her mother find the boy dying of swamp fever in their barn.

When we pulled the shirt over Sky's head, Mama sucked in her breath and clicked her teeth. I covered my mouth to keep from screaming. He was covered with what looked like hundreds and hundreds of mosquito bites. He had scratched them and they had formed sores.

"Swamp fever," Mama whispered. By then, the boy was shaking with chills. We covered him with quilts, and wrapped his hands with strips of cloth so he couldn't scratch and **infect** himself more.

---

infect, spread disease throughout

"Boil water for sassafras tea," Mama snapped an order. "We've got to drive the **impurities** out of his body."

Mama began humming, the way she did when she was deep thinking, worried, or unsure. "I need **quinine**," she said. "Run get yo' daddy."

Turning around, I ran right into Mr. Wratten, who looked **larger than life**, framing the doorway. "I have some quinine in my saddlebag," he said. Right away, I guessed Mr. Wratten had not gone back to Mount Vernon, but had hung around, **suspecting** maybe that Sky was hiding out at our place, or we were hiding him. He'd probably seen us carry Sky into the house and come to get him. Seeing how sick Sky was, Mr. Wratten's face softened with concern. "Looks bad," he said. "If I try to take him back to Mount Vernon, he'll never make it."

"Leave him here, then." I said, knowing I was speaking out of place, getting deeper and deeper into trouble with Mama. But I couldn't help myself. I went right on talking. "Mama knows Indian ways; she can help him."

Mr. Wratten looked to Mama for her **consent**. Sky coughed and moaned. She mopped his forehead with a cool cloth. "I might can't save him," she said. "But I can try."

Mr. Wratten studied on the idea, shifting his weight from foot to foot. "So many Apaches died in Florida," he said, looking beyond Mama to some place in his past. "They're a mountain people, used to dry, cool weather." He mumbled something about the damp climate that seemed to **sap** the life right out of the Apaches. He was talking more to himself than us.

"Can the boy speak English?" Mama asked. "That might make things a whole lot easier later on."

"Sky speaks Apache and Spanish," he answered. "But he can manage English better than most. He learned it mostly by listening and from a few nuns who used to come several times a week to teach those who were interested. Sky is interested in everything."

---

impurities, poisons, or unclean substances that cause sickness
quinine, a drug used for treating fevers
larger than life, important and exciting
suspecting, thinking that
consent, permission
sap, drain

»)) **Listening** SKILL

Take turns reading aloud with a partner. As you listen, look at the illustrations on pages 158–162. Use these visuals to help you understand the people and events described in the reading.

✔ **LITERARY CHECK**
*What is the **mood** of the story at this point? Do you feel any **suspense**? Why?*

BEFORE YOU GO ON

1 Why does Mama ask Sarah to boil sassafras tea for Sky?

2 Why did many Apaches die in Florida?

On Your Own
Have you or someone close to you ever nursed someone who was very sick? What was it like?

Reading 1 **159**

Mr. Wratten sighed deeply. "Sky will be better off here **for the time being**," he said. "I guess I'll just say I couldn't find him."

I felt relieved. "If he doesn't make it," he added, "wire me that *the quilt is torn*. If he makes it, wire me that *the quilt is ready*, and I'll come get him. Don't let Sky know I've been here or he'll run again." Mama agreed.

Following Mr. Wratten out to his horse to get the quinine, I asked, "Why did Sky run?"

"Sky is the first Apache who has run away. I don't think he wants to go to Carlisle School for Indians up in Pennsylvania. And I can't say as I blame him. Most Apaches who go there come back home in a coffin. As many of them die of **homesickness** as they do from **diseases**."

I had many more questions, but it was not the time to ask. Mr. Wratten was gone by the time Papa came in from the fields for noontime meal.

When Papa didn't smell anything cooking and saw who we had made the sickroom for, he **commenced to** fussing. "What are you thinkin' 'bout, Georgianne? How could you bring trouble to our front door like this? Mr. Wratten was just here lookin' for this boy, and here we got him in our house, takin' care of him."

"He's sick and needs our help," Mama said. "And besides," she added, "Mr. Wratten knows he's here and asked me to care for him 'til he gets better."

"Aine it enough 'round here to do, besides taking on a sick boy, somebody we don't even-now know. What **business** is it of ours?"

Mama had started a pot to boil some rice. But she stopped and raised the wooden spoon as if she planned to use it as a weapon. "Lee Andy, you the one always talkin' 'bout how you s'posed to love yo' neighbor as yo'self. What meaning is in them words?" Mama asked.

Right away, Papa fled to the barn. Within the half hour he came back, Bible story in hand.

"I'm reminded here of the parable of the Good Samaritan who took care of a stranger he found 'side the road. It is right that we should take care of this poor soul who is in need. I've made up my mind, now. So, don't try to talk me out of it."

"Yes, you're right, Lee Andy," Mama said.

I turned away so Papa wouldn't see me smiling as I spooned hot tea into Sky's mouth.

---

for the time being, for now
homesickness, feelings of sadness when away from home
diseases, illnesses
commenced to, began
business, personal responsibility or task

Reading Skill

Identify the words you don't understand as you read and ask your teacher or peers for help with those words.

✔ LITERARY CHECK
*How do the examples of **dialect** on this page help to communicate what Mama and Papa are like?*

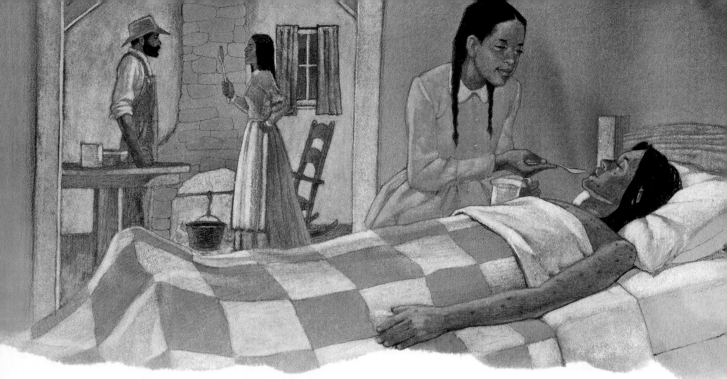

Getting Sky through the night took a powerful lot of doctoring. I sat by his bedside, hoping some and praying some, always helping Mama by fetching and carrying whatever was needed. Sky tossed and turned, and yelled out in his feverish sleep, calling **Geronimo**'s name, and mumbling words in Apache. "Fight," I whispered to him. "Fight to stay alive. Don't give up."

Mama burned herbs and called upon her grandmother for **guidance**. And then she rattled her bag of bones over his body and sang a song her father had taught her. . . .

All through the night I rubbed Sky's arms and legs with a soothing paste Mama'd made from dried roots. . . .

Sky's fever broke early the next morning, shortly before the southbound rumbled through Quincy. But he wasn't **out of the woods** yet—far from it. On the third day, his breathing settled into a steady rhythm as his body stayed cool. "He'll make it," said Mama, giving her head a quick nod, the way she did when she felt **triumphant**. Strengthened by her success, Mama stopped humming and sang a happy tune while preparing breakfast.

But I was **bone tired** because I hadn't slept more than a few hours in days. Now that it looked like Sky would live, I yawned and stretched and dragged into the kitchen. "Put a little life in your step," Mama said in a lively way. "You're too young to know what tired is."

Geronimo, a famous Apache chief who fought to protect his people's lands
guidance, help and advice
out of the woods, out of trouble
triumphant, victorious
bone tired, extremely tired

BEFORE YOU GO ON

1 What does Mama say to convince Papa to help Sky?

2 Why is Sarah bone tired?

On Your Own
What does it mean "to love yo' neighbor as yo'self"? Is this a good saying? Why?

Yes I do, I wanted to say, but dared not be that sassy. I was forever getting my legs switched for talking back, talking out of turn, or just plain talking too much. When I'm all grown up, I thought, I'm going to say what's on my mind. But that was a ways off. As far as I knew I was still on the wrong side of Mama, even though she hadn't mentioned anything to Papa about my part in Sky's escape. I decided it was best not to **rile** her. So I kept my mouth shut and took joy in knowing we would not have to wire Mr. Wratten that *the quilt is torn*.

Buster met me at the door, yelping all kinds of questions. I explained everything to him, putting in all the details about how we'd saved Sky's life. He listened, head cocked to one side as if he understood everything I was saying. "Buster, I'm so glad I've got you to talk to," I said. "You're a good dog, no matter what Papa thinks."

The smells of Mama's kitchen must have awakened Sky. He was sitting bolt straight in the bed, looking wild-eyed and frightened when I brought a plate of food to him. He asked something in Apache. When I shook my head to show I didn't understand, he switched to English. "Where is this place?" he asked, trying to get up, but he was too weak.

Putting my hand on his shoulder, I smiled, saying, "Here, lie back down, before you . . . "

Sky pulled away and his first words to me were, "I don't know you!" He snapped at me in very clear English, "I don't know you." This time, I snatched my hands away like I'd touched a sleeping alligator by accident. He tried to sit up, but once more he flopped back down on his pallet.

"I was just trying to help," I said, feeling **put out**. The past few days, I'd imagined a lot of things about Sky, but I never expected him to be an Un-person. In my way of thinking, an Un-person was one who was unkind, ungrateful, unpleasant, unfair, unanything.

The **patient** wasn't any nicer to Mama. When she tried to get him to eat, he shoved it away. "No pig meat," he said, looking down in disgust.

---

rile, anger or upset
put out, hurt or unfairly treated
patient, person getting medical care

Maybe the fever had **addled his brain**, I thought.

"Eat a few **grits**, then," Mama insisted. "You need to build up your strength again. You're still sick."

"I am not sick!" he scoffed. Sky would have nothing to do with us. He pulled the sheet up to his chin, and refused everything we offered him. By then I was close to tossing the food on his head. Just then Papa came in.

Papa introduced everybody by name, including himself. "This is my family." Sky shook his head, never taking his eyes off Mama, who stood at the foot of the bed. "Son, you're 'mongst the living this morning, 'cause of the Good Lord working through my wife and daughter." Sky seemed to be **hanging on every word** Papa said. "Now, let's get this understanding," Papa went on. "As long as you're in this house, you'll treat them with respect or I'm gon' know why. Clear?"

It took me back when Sky's whole attitude changed in a hurry—I mean, right now. He commenced to eating, shoving down three helpings of grits, eggs, and biscuits—but he still wouldn't touch the pork.

He was still an Un-person, I decided—ungrateful! But I remembered one of Papa's favorite sayings. "**Tote** the load of another person 'fore you pass judgment." So I **put myself in Sky's shoes**. He had awakened in a strange man's house and bed with that man's family **attending to** him in a very **personal** way. Maybe he wasn't being rude, but waiting until he had been welcomed by the head of the household—Papa. Somehow Sky had gotten a welcome in Papa's words—the permission he needed to feel comfortable with us. I may have been all wrong, but my reason made good sense to me.

---

addled his brain, confused him
grits, crushed dried corn that is cooked and eaten for breakfast
hanging on every word, listening closely to every word
tote, carry
put myself in Sky's shoes, put myself in his place
attending to, taking care of
personal, private

ABOUT THE **AUTHOR**

Patricia C. McKissack based *Run Away Home* in part on a family story her great-uncle told about her great-great-great-great-grandfather, who was a Native American. She has written numerous award-winning novels and nonfiction books. McKissack sometimes writes biographies and nonfiction books with her husband, and she has also written one book, *Black Diamond: The Story of the Negro Baseball Leagues*, with her son.

BEFORE YOU GO ON

1 Why does Sarah snatch her hands away as if she had touched an alligator?

2 What does Sarah mean when she calls Sky an Un-person?

On Your Own
What do you think of the Crossmans? What kind of people are they?

Reading 1 **163**

► READER'S THEATER

Act out this scene between Sarah and her mother.

Sarah: Mama, how sick is Sky? All those sores look pretty bad.

Mama: He is very sick, Sarah. He has a bad disease. Sky might die.

Sarah: Oh, no! Can you cure him, Mama? How can you help him?

Mama: I am going to give him a medicine called quinine. It will help lower his fever. If we can get his fever down, he will probably recover. I will wash him with cool water, too.

Sarah: What can I do to help you? Should I get some water?

Mama: Get your father. I need his help, too. Then boil some water for sassafras tea. Sky will need to drink a lot of this tea in order to get the poisons out of his body.

Sarah: Okay, Mama. I really hope that Sky gets better.

Mama: Hurry up now, and get your Papa.

Speaking SKILL

Try to use your voice to communicate your character's traits. For example, Mama would speak in a strong, grown-up way, but Sarah would sound less sure of herself.

► COMPREHENSION

Workbook Page 85

Recall

1. What illness does Sky have?
2. What message is Mama to send if Sky lives? Give the precise words.

Comprehend

3. During what time period does this novel take place?
4. What are some things that Mama does to help Sky get well?

Analyze

5. Why do you think that Sky listens only to Papa?
6. How does the writer create suspense? At what point in the selection did you know that Sky would get better?

Connect

7. Does it help to try to put yourself in someone else's shoes? Why?
8. When have you or someone close to you felt homesick?

▲ Can you tell what this advertisement is for?

➤ DISCUSSION

Discuss in pairs or small groups.

1. How does Mama get Papa to do what she wants? Explain.

2. Papa says, "Tote the load of another person 'fore you pass judgment." What does he mean by this?

3. How do you think Sky knew that he would not like the Carlisle Indian School? What inferences can you make about Sky's character and feelings?

Q **How does helping others help us all?** How do the Crossmans feel when Sky gets better? Do they feel better about themselves for helping him? Why?

»)) *Listening* SKILL

Ask questions if you want more information. If you don't understand what someone is saying, ask the person to repeat or explain his or her answer.

➤ RESPONSE TO LITERATURE

Workbook Page 85

Utilize Imagine that you are in Sky's shoes. Why did you run away? How do you feel about having Mama and Sarah take care of you? Write a journal entry in which you **communicate** your experiences and feelings. Describe the following:

- Why I ran away
- What happened to me
- How I feel about being sick
- How I feel about being cared for by a girl and her mother

When you are done writing, share your journal entry with a partner. Discuss which details in the selection helped you write your journal entry.

Geronimo, the Apache chief who fought to protect Apache lands from settlers ▶

Grammar

Agreement in Simple Sentences

Remember that a simple sentence must contain a subject and verb. The verb must agree in number with the subject.

> **Sky speaks** Apache and Spanish. [singular subject and singular verb]
> **They speak** Apache and Spanish. [plural subject and plural verb]

Be careful when a prepositional phrase comes between the subject and the verb. The verb must still agree in number with the subject.

> subject | prepositional phrase | verb
> **The pots** of rice **were** on the stove.   NOT The pots of rice was on the stove.

The verbs in questions and negative sentences must also agree in number with their subjects. Remember to use *do* and *does* correctly.

> **Doesn't the car need** oil?   NOT Don't the car need oil?
> **The tires** on the bike **don't need** air.   NOT The tires on the bike doesn't need air.

Practice  Workbook Page 86

Work with a partner. Write the sentences in your notebook. Complete each sentence with the correct form of the verb in parentheses.

Example: My friend _____ (lives, live) in Seattle.

1. Our father never _____ (works, work) on weekends.
2. The bag of groceries _____ (was, were) on the table.
3. His parents _____ (is, are) both doctors.
4. Their car _____ (breaks, break) down all the time.
5. The dishes in the kitchen _____ (is, are) dirty.
6. _____ (Don't, Doesn't) they live in the mountains?

Apply

Work with a partner. Find three simple sentences in the reading. Analyze them with your partner, showing how the subject agrees with the verb.

Agreement in Compound Sentences

A compound sentence is two simple sentences or two independent clauses joined with a coordinating conjunction such as *and, but,* or *so.*

When a coordinating conjunction connects two independent clauses, the verb form in both clauses must agree. A comma is usually used before the coordinating conjunction.

> simple past   simple past
> I **had** many more questions, but it **was not** the time to ask.

A pronoun must also agree with its antecedent, the noun that comes before it. Be careful that the person (first person: *I, my, me*) and the gender (male: *he, his*) are in agreement.

> **I** may have been all wrong, but **my** reason made good sense to **me**.
> **He** stayed with us, so **his** homesickness grew.

Grammar SKILL

Remember that *and* shows similarity, *but* shows contrast, and *so* shows a result.

Practice

Work with a partner. Copy the pairs of simple sentences into your notebook. Then, using a coordinating conjunction, combine each pair to make a compound sentence.

Example: I want to buy that video game. I'm saving my money.

> *I want to buy a video game, so I'm saving my money.*

1. Matt studied a lot for the spelling contest. He didn't win.
2. She saw a cat run in front of her. She fell down.
3. It was raining. We still went fishing.
4. It wasn't appropriate to say that. She said it anyway.
5. Jane liked Susan. She didn't like Carlo.

✔ GRAMMAR CHECK

What joins the two simple sentences in a compound sentence?

Apply

Work with a partner. In your notebook, write five simple sentences. Take turns combining your sentences with each other's, using *and, but,* and *so,* to make compound sentences.

Writing

Write a Book Review

In this lesson, you will write a book review. A book review is a form of persuasive writing. In persuasive writing, the writer tries to convince readers to agree with his or her opinion. In a book review, you give your opinion about whether a particular book is worth reading. Then you support your opinion with reasons and examples.

> ### Writing Prompt
>
> Write a review of a book that you like very much. Begin by stating your opinion. Then give reasons and examples to support your opinion. Present your reasons and examples in a logical order. Include both simple and compound sentences in your review.

1 PREWRITE Choose a book that you want to recommend to other readers.

- Ask yourself why you like this book so much.

- Think about examples in the book that show why you like it.

- List your ideas in a graphic organizer.

Workbook Page 88

A student named Danielle created this graphic organizer.

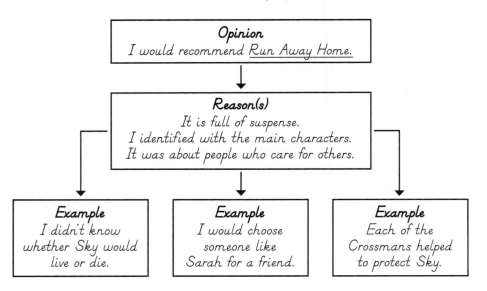

Opinion
I would recommend <u>Run Away Home.</u>

↓

Reason(s)
It is full of suspense.
I identified with the main characters.
It was about people who care for others.

Example
I didn't know whether Sky would live or die.

Example
I would choose someone like Sarah for a friend.

Example
Each of the Crossmans helped to protect Sky.

2 DRAFT Use your organizer to help you write a first draft.

- Keep your purpose and audience in mind as you write.
- State your opinion clearly in your first sentence.
- Choose specific examples to show why you like the book.

3 REVISE Read over your draft. Look for places where the writing is unclear or needs improvement. Use the Writing Checklist to help you identify problems. Then revise your draft, using the editing and proofreading marks listed on page 456.

4 EDIT Check your work for errors in grammar, usage, mechanics, and spelling. Trade papers with a partner to obtain feedback. Use the Peer Review Checklist on Workbook page 88. Edit your final draft in response to feedback from your partner and your teacher.

5 PUBLISH Prepare a clean copy of your final draft. Share your book review with the class. Save your work. You'll need to refer to it in the Writing Workshop at the end of the unit.

Here is Danielle's book review. Notice that she gives reasons for her recommendation. She supports her opinion with examples.

Writing Checklist

IDEAS:
☑ I presented reasons and examples to support my opinion.

SENTENCE FLUENCY:
☑ I accurately used a variety of sentence lengths and patterns.

Danielle Christian

Run Away Home

<u>Run Away Home</u> is the most exciting book I've read in a long time, and I think that many students would feel the same way. It is the story of a runaway Apache boy who is helped by an African-American farm family in Alabama in 1888. I liked the book because it is full of suspense. When the Crossmans find Sky dying of swamp fever, I didn't know whether he would live or die. I had to keep reading until I found out. I also liked the book because I identify with the main characters, most of all with Sarah. She is brave, kind, and rebellious. I would choose someone like Sarah for my friend. In addition, I enjoyed the book because it is about people who care for others. Each of the Crossmans helped to protect Sky. I recommend <u>Run Away Home</u> to anyone who likes suspense, real-life characters, or stories about helping others.

What You Will Learn

Reading

■ Vocabulary building: *Context, dictionary skills, word study*

■ Reading strategy: *Identify problems and solutions*

■ Text type: *Informational text (social studies)*

Grammar

Prepositions of time: *in, on, at*; Prepositional phrases providing details

Writing

Write a persuasive paragraph

➤ 🔍 THE BIG QUESTION

How does helping others help us all? Heroes are people whom we admire and respect because they've helped others. Sometimes people do heroic things because of their work. Firefighters, teachers, doctors, men and women who serve in the military—they can all be heroes. Who are your heroes? How are, or were, they heroic? How do, or did, they help others?

➤ BUILD BACKGROUND

"Extraordinary People: Serving Others" is a series of short biographies of heroic figures from around the world. Many readers will be inspired by the stories of these remarkable people and how they helped change the world. All of these heroic figures are greatly admired for their bravery, strength, and willingness to help others.

Two of the people you will read about also had to face their own physical challenges. Helen Keller became blind and deaf as a young child. Franklin Delano Roosevelt lost the ability to walk when he was thirty-nine years old. Both of these extraordinary people worked hard to conquer their physical challenges. Heroes always face challenges, but they don't give up.

▲ President Roosevelt had to wear leg braces to help him walk.

◄ Anne Sullivan (right) helped Helen Keller (left) learn how to communicate.

➤ VOCABULARY

Listening and Speaking: Key Words

Read aloud and listen to these sentences with a partner. Use the context to figure out the meaning of the highlighted words. Use a dictionary to check your answers. Then write each word and its meaning in your notebook.

1. Sometimes leaders are assassinated. Kings, presidents, and other important people have been killed by surprise attack.

2. The doctor had extraordinary abilities. She saved the lives of three children whose injuries were thought to be beyond hope.

3. The founders of this school wanted to establish a place of learning for students with special needs.

4. The people showed resistance to the law by voting against it.

5. The superintendent of our group makes all the rules and is in charge.

6. You show tolerance by respecting other people's ideas.

Key Words

assassinated
extraordinary
founders   Audio
resistance
superintendent
tolerance

Audio

Practice   Workbook Page 89

Write the sentences in your notebook. Choose a key word from the box above to complete each sentence. Then take turns reading the sentences aloud with a partner.

1. At first there was much _____ to the new idea, but everyone finally came to accept it.

2. _____ helps people live peacefully because it encourages people to respect one another's ideas.

3. In the 1960s, three important U.S. leaders—John F. Kennedy, Martin Luther King Jr., and Robert F. Kennedy—were all _____ by gunmen.

4. The doctor was one of the three _____ of the hospital in 1938.

5. Tiger Woods is an _____ golfer. He has amazing abilities.

6. The _____ hired all the nurses and was in charge of running the hospital.

▲ Senator Robert F. Kennedy attends the funeral of assassinated civil rights leader Dr. Martin Luther King Jr.

Listening and Speaking: Academic Words

Study the red words and their meanings. You will find these words useful when talking and writing about informational texts. Write each word and its meaning in your notebook, then say the words aloud with a partner. After you read "Extraordinary People: Serving Others," try to use these words to respond to the text.

achieve = succeed in doing or getting something as a result of your actions	→	Some people **achieve** success by getting important things done.
alter = change in some way	→	Many people want to **alter** the health-care system in the United States.
impact = the effect that something or someone has on someone or something	→	Doctors have a big **impact** on the health and well-being of their patients.
role = the position, job, or function someone or something has in a particular situation or activity	→	Nurses play an important **role** in a hospital. They help doctors, and they help sick people get well.

Audio

Practice  Workbook Page 90

Work with a partner to complete these statements. Try to include the red word in your answer. Write the sentences in your notebook.

1. By the time I am a grown-up, I would like to achieve . . .

2. When it rains, I alter my plans by . . .

3. I think my close friends have an impact on my life because . . .

4. First-grade teachers play an important role in a child's life because . . .

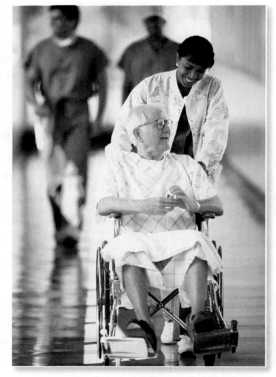

▲ This nurse plays an important role in caring for senior citizens.

172 Unit 3

Word Study: Spelling Words with Silent *gh*

Learning the relationships between the sounds and letters of English will help you to sound out words as you read. It will also help you learn spelling rules. In English, the letters *gh* are often, but not always, silent. Study the words in the chart. You will read some of these words in "Extraordinary People: Serving Others." Notice that in these words, the letters *gh* are silent.

brought	daughter	fought	night	rights	sight

Practice

Say a word from the chart, and ask your partner to spell it aloud. Then have your partner say the next word. Continue until you can spell all of the words correctly. Now think of three more words that contain the silent letters *gh*. Say the words one by one. Ask your partner to spell each word.

READING STRATEGY | **IDENTIFY PROBLEMS AND SOLUTIONS**

Identifying problems and solutions helps you understand a text better. Many texts include a problem that a person, group, or character has to solve (or find a solution to). To identify problems and solutions, ask yourself:

- What problem or problems does the person or group have?
- How does the person or group solve or try to solve the problem?

In "Extraordinary People: Serving Others," heroes face problems and find solutions. As you read the biographies, think about each problem and its possible solutions. Read to find out how the problem was solved.

Reading 2 **173**

Set a purpose for reading What motivates certain people to spend their lives helping others? Read these biographies of extraordinary people to find out.

Extraordinary People: Serving Others

In different places and at different times, people have achieved extraordinary things. In the short biographies that follow, you will read about people from different times in history who helped others in many ways. You will also read about a group of people who continue to do extraordinary things in troubled parts of the world today.

Benito Juárez

Benito Juárez (1806–1872) is a national hero in Mexico. He was the son of poor Zapotec Indian farmers in the state of Oaxaca, Mexico. At age thirteen he couldn't read, write, or speak Spanish. He trained to become a priest, but later he decided to become a lawyer. As a young man, he became interested in **social justice**, especially the rights of native peoples. He was very popular among the native Indian population. In 1847, he was elected governor of Oaxaca.

In 1861, Juárez became the first Zapotec Indian president of Mexico. He improved education. For the first time, it was possible for every child to go to school. He stopped the French from **colonizing** Mexico. His many **reforms** made Mexico a fairer, more modern society.

▲ Benito Juárez fought for the rights of all people in Mexico.

---

social justice, fairness for all people
colonizing, controlling a country and sending your own people to live there
reforms, changes that improve a system

Florence Nightingale

Florence Nightingale (1820–1910) came from a **wealthy** English family. Against her parents' wishes, she became a nurse.

In 1853, she became superintendent of a hospital for women in London. In 1854, Britain, France, and Turkey fought against Russia in the Crimean War. Nightingale volunteered to go to Turkey to help. She took thirty-eight nurses with her. They helped many wounded soldiers recover. Nightingale often visited the soldiers at night, carrying a lamp. Soldiers called her "the lady with the lamp."

When Nightingale returned to England, she started a school for nurses. The school still exists today.

Mohandas Gandhi

Mohandas Gandhi (1869–1948) was born in the coastal city of Porbandar, in the western part of India. At that time, India was a British colony. Gandhi went to England in 1888 and studied law. He returned to India and worked as a lawyer in Bombay (Mumbai).

In 1893, Gandhi traveled to South Africa. The government of South Africa had a system of racial separation, called **apartheid**. A group of white South Africans attacked Gandhi and beat him. After this experience, he encouraged people to practice passive resistance against the South African authorities and apartheid.

After he returned to India in 1915, Gandhi became a leader in India's struggle for independence. He became the international symbol of nonviolent protest. He believed in religious tolerance. In 1947, Britain finally ended its 190-year rule in India. Then, in 1948, Gandhi was assassinated by someone who didn't agree with his beliefs.

Gandhi **inspired** nonviolent movements elsewhere. In the United States, Dr. Martin Luther King Jr. used passive resistance when he became leader of the civil rights movement in the 1950s and 1960s.

---

wealthy, very rich
apartheid, a system in which different races in a country are separated
inspired, caused; influenced people to express interest in

▲ Florence Nightingale worked for many long hours to help the sick and dying men.

▲ Gandhi was imprisoned many times for his beliefs.

BEFORE YOU GO ON

1 What **role** did Florence Nightingale play during the Crimean War?

2 What system was Mohandas Gandhi trying to **alter** through passive resistance?

On Your Own
Why do you think Benito Juárez wanted to stop the French from colonizing Mexico?

Reading 2 **175**

Franklin Delano Roosevelt

Franklin Delano Roosevelt (1882–1945) was elected as the thirty-second president of the United States in 1932. During the 1930s, the country was experiencing deep **economic** troubles. This period in American history is called the Great Depression. Banks shut down, workers lost their jobs, and farms failed. Roosevelt declared that Americans had "nothing to fear but fear itself." He put into place a series of new government programs that brought hope to the American people. Many people returned to work.

Roosevelt soon faced another challenge. The Second World War in Europe and the Pacific began in 1939. Great Britain, France, Russia, and other countries (the Allies) fought against Germany and Japan. In 1941, the Japanese bombed Pearl Harbor in Hawaii. Roosevelt asked for and received a declaration of war on Japan, and the United States entered the war. The United States and the Allies fought many brave battles and eventually won the war in 1945.

Roosevelt faced personal challenges as well. He came down with **polio** at the age of thirty-nine, and lost the use of his legs. However, Roosevelt did not allow his physical condition to prevent him from contributing to society. Roosevelt is now considered by many historians to be one of the greatest U.S. presidents.

▲ President Roosevelt overcame polio to lead the United States through two of its most difficult times: the Great Depression and World War II.

Helen Keller

Helen Keller (1880–1968) was nineteen months old when she became sick with a fever. The sickness left her without sight or hearing. Because she was so young when this happened, it was hard for her to learn to communicate. Because she could not see, she was unable to use sign language—the language of hearing-**impaired** people. She also couldn't "read lips," as many hearing-impaired people do. Although these challenges made young Helen very **frustrated**, she was also extremely intelligent. With the help of a skilled teacher, named Anne Sullivan, she learned that everything had a name and that these names were words. Because of the help of others and her own determination, she was eventually able to learn different ways to communicate. For instance, she learned to "hear" and understand speech by touching a speaker's lips and throat.

▲ Helen Keller was the first sight- and hearing-impaired person to graduate from college.

---

economic, relating to business, industry, and managing money
polio, an infectious disease of the nerves in the spine that can
 cause paralysis
impaired, damaged, or less strong, or less good
frustrated, upset because you can't do something

Keller gave lectures (with her teacher's help) and wrote a number of books. Her public talks and her writings inspired countless people with hearing, sight, and other physical problems. She inspired others to not give up in the face of **adversity**. Keller also toured the world. She raised funds for programs to help people with impaired hearing and sight. To this day, Helen Keller remains a figure of inspiration.

Doctors Without Borders

Doctors Without **Borders** is an international organization whose members believe that every person in every country has the right to medical care. It helps victims of war, disease, and natural disasters. A small group of French doctors started Doctors Without Borders (Médecins Sans Frontières) in 1971. Each year, thousands of volunteer doctors, nurses, and **administrators** from countries all over the world provide medical aid to people in more than seventy countries. They provide health care, perform surgery, organize **nutrition** and **sanitation** programs, train local medical staff, and provide mental health care.

Doctors Without Borders works with the United Nations, governments, and the media to tell the world about their patients' suffering and concerns. For example, Doctors Without Borders volunteers told the media about the **atrocities** they saw in Chechnya, Angola, and Kosovo.

Doctors Without Borders won the Nobel Peace Prize in 1999. Accepting the award, one of the organization's founders, Bernard Kouchner, said, "I'm deeply moved, and I'm thinking of all the people who died without aid, of all those who died waiting for someone to knock on their door."

▲ A doctor helps a child in Angola, where many children die of starvation or disease.

---

adversity, difficulties or problems
borders, official lines that separate two countries
administrators, people who manage businesses or organizations
nutrition, food for good health and growth
sanitation, hygiene; cleanliness
atrocities, extremely violent actions

BEFORE YOU GO ON

1 How did Franklin Delano Roosevelt help pull the United States out of the Depression?

2 Why did Helen Keller have trouble communicating?

On Your Own
Would you like to work for Doctors Without Borders? Why or why not?

Review and Practice

► **COMPREHENSION**   📖 Workbook Page 93

Recall

1. What happened to Benito Juárez in 1861?
2. Franklin Delano Roosevelt was president during which war?

Comprehend

3. Why was Helen Keller's childhood so difficult?
4. What North American leader believed in passive resistance?

Analyze

5. Why do you think the author chose to write about Florence Nightingale?
6. Who do you think had the most lasting **impact** on others? Why?

Connect

7. Why is it important for all children to get an education?
8. Describe someone you think is extraordinary. Why is that person special? What has he or she **achieved**?

► **IN YOUR OWN WORDS**

Imagine that you are telling a small group of friends about "Extraordinary People: Serving Others." Tell your friends about each person or organization in the text. Use the chart to help you summarize the history of each person or organization. Then share your summaries with a classmate. See how they compare.

🔊 *Speaking* SKILLS

Make eye contact with your classmates.

Talk to your audience, not your chart.

Famous People	Summary
Benito Juárez	
Florence Nightingale	
Mohandas Gandhi	
Franklin Delano Roosevelt	
Helen Keller	
Doctors Without Borders	

➤ DISCUSSION

Discuss in pairs or small groups.

1. In what ways did Helen Keller's teacher, Anne Sullivan, help her?

2. How are Benito Juárez and Mohandas Gandhi similar? How are they different?

3. What kind of qualities do you think members of Doctors Without Borders have in common?

Q How does helping others help us all? In what ways did Mohandas Gandhi, Helen Keller, and Doctors Without Borders make the world better for all of us?

➤ READ FOR FLUENCY

When we read aloud to communicate meaning, we group words into phrases, pause or slow down to make important points, and emphasize important words. Pause for a short time when you reach a comma and for a longer time when you reach a period. Pay attention to rising and falling intonation at the end of sentences.

Work with a partner. Choose a paragraph from the reading. Discuss which words seem important for communicating meaning. Practice pronouncing difficult words. Take turns reading the paragraph aloud and give each other feedback.

➤ EXTENSION
Workbook Page 93

Utilize Learn more about the people and organization described in "Extraordinary People: Helping Others." Choose any subject described in the text. Use encyclopedias, reference books, and reliable websites to do research. Write a short report that summarizes your findings. Use as much academic language as possible. Then share your findings with a classmate.

▲ Helen Keller had to rely on her sense of touch and smell.

Grammar

Prepositions of Time: *in, on,* and *at*

The prepositions *in, on,* and *at* can be used to show a point in time. A preposition is followed by a noun or noun phrase. This group of words is called a prepositional phrase. A prepositional phrase of time can appear at the beginning or at the end of a sentence. When a prepositional phrase begins a sentence, it is followed by a comma.

> **In 1893,** Mohandas Gandhi traveled to South Africa.
> **On Friday,** Helen Keller started to study with her teacher.
> Florence Nightingale took care of her patients **at night**.

Certain prepositions are used with certain time words and phrases. Use *in* for months, years, and centuries; use *on* for days and exact dates; use *at* for times of day.

in	on	at
October	April 19	twelve o'clock
2012	Friday	noon
a month	Friday morning	midnight
the summer	a winter day	dawn
the morning	my birthday	sunset

Practice

Workbook
Page 94

Work with a partner. Write the sentences in your notebook. Complete each sentence with the correct preposition.

Example: The doctor got a call for help __*at*__ night.

1. _____ 1861, Benito Juarez became president.
2. Congress declared war _____ December 8, 1941.
3. Florence Nightingale visited her patients _____ the morning.
4. _____ December 17, the doctors accepted the award.
5. Gandhi met with the government of South Africa _____ five o'clock.

Apply

Work with a partner. Write down five time expressions. Take turns making sentences with each other's expressions.

Grammar SKILL

Note that the preposition *in* is used with *in the morning* and *in the evening*, but *at* is used with *at night / at midnight*.

✔ **GRAMMAR CHECK**

*What punctuation follows a **prepositional phrase** when it begins the sentence?*

Prepositional Phrases Providing Details

Prepositional phrases can add details to a sentence. Here are some common prepositions.

about after among before by for from in near on out to under up with

A prepositional phrase can function as an adjective, meaning it describes a noun.

> He was elected governor **of Oaxaca**. [describes the noun *governor*]

A prepositional phrase can also function as an adverb, meaning it describes a verb (the action in the sentence) or an adjective.

> **In 1861**, he became president. [describes when he *became* president]
> He was popular **among the native peoples**. [describes the adjective *popular*]

Workbook
Page 95

Grammar SKILL

A prepositional phrase usually appears next to the word it describes, but not when it describes the action of a sentence. Then it appears at the beginning or end of the sentence.

Practice

Work with a partner. Copy the sentences into your notebook. Then underline each prepositional phrase and circle the noun, verb, or adjective that the prepositional phrase describes.

Example: (The book) is <u>by Richards</u>.

1. Mike talked about his summer plans.
2. The cat jumped in the box.
3. They were angry with the neighbors.
4. He was leader of the soccer team.
5. Sharon walked out the door.

Apply

Work with a partner. Find sentences with prepositional phrases in the reading. Decide what the prepositional phrase describes.

Writing

Write a Persuasive Paragraph

At the end of this unit, you will write a persuasive speech. One way to organize a piece of persuasive writing is to ask a question and to answer it in a persuasive way. First, you pose the question. Then you give an answer that states your opinion. You explain your answer by giving facts, details, and examples. You include strong, persuasive words to convince readers to agree with your opinion.

> ### Writing Prompt
>
> Choose someone you think is truly extraordinary. Write a paragraph that answers the question: *What extraordinary things did this person do?* Support your opinion about this individual with at least three reasons. Include facts and examples to explain your reasons with specificity and detail. Remember to use prepositions of time and prepositional phrases correctly.

1 PREWRITE Choose someone you admire very much.

- Ask yourself why you admire this individual.
- Think about what this person achieved or changed.
- List your ideas in a graphic organizer.

Workbook
Page 96

A student named Tamar created this graphic organizer.

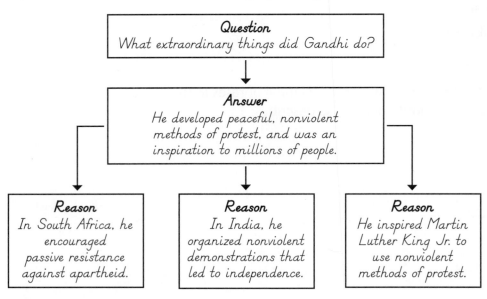

Question
What extraordinary things did Gandhi do?

Answer
He developed peaceful, nonviolent methods of protest, and was an inspiration to millions of people.

Reason
In South Africa, he encouraged passive resistance against apartheid.

Reason
In India, he organized nonviolent demonstrations that led to independence.

Reason
He inspired Martin Luther King Jr. to use nonviolent methods of protest.

2 DRAFT Use your organizer to help you write a first draft.

- Keep in mind your purpose—to persuade.
- Remember to pose a question and answer it.
- Give facts, details, and examples to support your opinion.
- Try to use newly-acquired vocabulary in your answer.

3 REVISE Read over your draft. Look for places where the writing is unclear or needs improvement. Use the Writing Checklist to help you identify problems. Then revise your draft, using the editing and proofreading marks listed on page 456.

4 EDIT Check your work for errors in grammar, usage, mechanics, and spelling. Trade papers with a partner to obtain feedback. Use the Peer Review Checklist on Workbook page 96. Edit your final draft in response to feedback from your partner and your teacher.

5 PUBLISH Prepare a clean copy of your final draft. Share your persuasive paragraph with the class. Save your work. You'll need to refer to it in the Writing Workshop at the end of the unit.

Here is Tamar's persuasive paragraph. Notice how she accurately uses the newly-acquired and content-based words *extraordinary* and *assassinated.*

Tamar Honig

Mohandas Gandhi

What extraordinary things did Gandhi do that set him apart from other people of his time? He developed peaceful, nonviolent methods of protest in the face of violence and injustice, and he was an inspiration to millions of people around the world. While in South Africa, he encouraged people to practice passive resistance against apartheid. In India, he played a major role in the country's struggle for independence by organizing nonviolent demonstrations. Lastly, Gandhi inspired others, including leaders of the U.S. civil rights movement, to use nonviolent methods of protest. Tragically, this man of peace was assassinated on January 30, 1948.

What You Will Learn

Reading
- Vocabulary building: *Literary terms, word study, dictionary skills*
- Reading strategy: *Distinguish fact from opinion*
- Text type: *Literature (diary excerpt)*

Grammar
Placement of adjectives

Writing
Write a diary entry

THE BIG QUESTION

How does helping others help us all? Have you ever kept or wanted to keep a diary? People who keep a diary write about their experiences, observations, and feelings. How could keeping a diary help someone get through a difficult time? What can others learn from that diary if they read it? Discuss with a partner.

BUILD BACKGROUND

Zlata Filipović, an eleven-year-old Bosnian girl, wrote ***Zlata's Diary*** in 1992, during the Bosnian War. Zlata lived in Sarajevo, the capital of Bosnia and Herzegovina, where some of the worst fighting occurred. She used her diary to write about her daily experiences during the war.

Look at the map. It shows the borders of the former Yugoslavia in 1991, just before the Bosnian War. It also shows the six republics that once had been part of the Yugoslav Federation: Bosnia and Herzegovina, Croatia, Macedonia, Montenegro, Slovenia, and Serbia. During the 1980s and 1990s, long-standing national and ethnic conflicts caused war among citizens of Yugoslavia. Before the war, Bosnia and Herzegovina had been a republic within Yugoslavia. As a result of the war, Bosnia and Herzegovina and other republics within Yugoslavia broke away and declared their independence. During this time, much blood was shed.

▲ The six republics of the former Yugoslav Federation

Reading Skill

To help you understand the events described above, look at the map of the former Yugoslav Federation. Name and point to each of the republics that were once part of Yugoslavia. Find Sarajevo on the map.

➤ VOCABULARY

Learn Literary Words

People often use words in ways that do not match the literal, or basic, dictionary definitions of the words. For example, when we say that someone is *driving us crazy*, we do not mean this literally. We are trying to express a feeling of frustration.

A group of words that is used in a different way from the usual meanings of the words is called a figure of speech. Here are some examples.

Literary Words
figure of speech
hyperbole
Audio

> The girl **jumped out of her skin** when she heard a blast.
> The man's **head was spinning** after hearing all the bad news.

The girl can't really jump out of her skin. This figure of speech means that the girl was very frightened. Likewise, the man's head does not go around and around. This is another way of saying that the man was confused and upset.

A figure of speech that uses exaggeration, or overstatement, is called hyperbole. Many everyday expressions are examples of hyperbole. For example, when we are hungry, we say: *I could eat a horse.*

Writers use hyperbole to create an effect, emphasize something, or express a feeling. Here are two examples of hyperbole. What do these figures of speech mean to you?

LEARNING STRATEGY

Earlier in this book you developed the ability to analyze expressions as you read (see Learn Literary Words on page 21). Expand your use of this strategy. Analyze figures of speech and hyperbole by using context clues, or figure out what each expression means based on how it is used in a sentence or paragraph.

> Her laughter was **like a meteor shower** brightening up the dark room.
> It would **take a thousand years** to figure out what happened.

Practice  Workbook Page 97

Take turns reading these everyday figures of speech with a partner. Rephrase each one in your own words.

1. I've told you **a million times** to be more careful.

2. Her love for her parents was **deeper than the ocean**.

3. During the war, she and her friends didn't know what would happen. They were all **in the same boat**.

In your notebook, list several other everyday examples of hyperbole. Then try to create two exaggerated statements of your own.

Listening and Speaking: Academic Words

Study the red words and their meanings. You will find these words useful when talking and writing about literature. Write each word and its meaning in your notebook, then say the words aloud with a partner. After you read this excerpt from *Zlata's Diary*, try to use these words to respond to the text.

consist = are made up of or contain particular things or people	⇒	Diaries **consist** of a writer's feelings and observations. They are made up of daily entries.
establish = create; organize	⇒	Concerned people in our community want to **establish** a neighborhood cleanup project.
method = a planned way of doing something	⇒	The girl had her own **method** of keeping her house safe during bombings. Many of the neighbors liked her way of doing this.
stress = continuous feelings of worry caused by difficulties in your life	⇒	People in wars are under a lot of **stress**. They feel great anxiety and worry.

Audio

Practice  Workbook Page 98

Work with a partner to answer these questions. Try to include the red word in your answer. Write the sentences in your notebook. Get support from your peers and teacher to develop your ability to use his vocabulary.

1. In your opinion, what does a perfect graduation party **consist** of? What things or people would it include?

2. How can countries **establish** peace after a war? What can be done to make people put down their weapons and live peacefully together?

3. What is your **method** of getting to school in the morning? What is your way of getting there on time?

4. How do you deal with **stress**? What do you do to relax?

▲ It is important to take breaks from your work if you are under a lot of stress.

Word Study: Synonyms and Antonyms

Use context clues to figure out the meanings of unfamiliar words. Look for definitions, synonyms, and antonyms. Synonyms are words with the same or nearly the same meanings. Antonyms are words with the opposite or nearly the opposite meanings. Read the examples. Clues to the meanings of the boldfaced words are underlined.

> The war made people go **berserk**, or act <u>crazy</u>. (synonym clue)
> I was filled with <u>sadness</u>. He felt a similar **sorrow.** (synonym clue)
> This war is <u>madness</u>. We have lost our **sanity**. (antonym clue)

Practice  Workbook Page 99

Copy the sentences into your notebook. Work with a partner to figure out the meanings of the boldfaced words. Circle words or phrases that are clues to meaning. Then write your own definition of each boldfaced term. Check your definitions in a dictionary.

1. We saw the worst **massacre**, or killing of many helpless people.
2. During the war, we never lost hope. We never gave in to **despair**.
3. People who were welcomed before are now being **expelled**.
4. The warring groups need to talk and come to an agreement. When will they begin to **negotiate** a settlement?

▲ *Tragedy* is the antonym of *comedy*.

READING STRATEGY | DISTINGUISH FACT FROM OPINION

Distinguishing a fact from an opinion will help you evaluate what you read. A fact is something that can be proven through evidence. An opinion is what someone believes or thinks. Opinions express a point of view, but aren't necessarily wrong. They just can't be proven. To distinguish facts from opinions, follow these steps:

- Read the text. Then ask yourself: "Can I check this information in a reliable source?" If you can, it's probably a fact.
- Look for words that signal opinions, such as *I think* and *to me*.
- Ask yourself: "Is this what someone thinks or believes? Can it be proven?" If it cannot be proven, it's probably an opinion.

As you read *Zlata's Diary*, distinguish between the facts and opinions.

 Workbook Page 100

Set a purpose for reading How does Zlata use her diary to help herself and others? Read this important account of the Bosnian War to find out.

from ZLATA'S DIARY

Zlata Filipović

When Zlata Filipović wrote her diary, which she calls "Mimmy," she was eleven years old and living in Sarajevo. The people of Sarajevo, including Zlata's family and friends, were caught in the middle of a war.

Saturday, May 23, 1992

Dear Mimmy,

I'm not writing to you about me anymore. I'm writing to you about war, death, injuries, **shells**, sadness and sorrow. Almost all my friends have left. Even if they were here, who knows whether we'd be able to see one another. The phones aren't working, we couldn't even talk to one another. Vanja and Andrej have gone to join Srdjan in Dubrovnik. The war has stopped there. They're lucky. I was so unhappy because of that war in Dubrovnik. I never dreamed it would move to Sarajevo. . . .

I now spend all my time with Bojana and Maja. They're my best friends now. Bojana is a year-and-a-half older than me, she's finished seventh grade and we have a lot in common. Maja is in her last year of school. She's much older than I am, but she's wonderful. I'm lucky to have them, otherwise I'd be all alone among the **grown-ups**.

▲ Zlata Filipović

---

shells, bombs
grown-ups, adults

On the news they reported the death of Silva Rizvanbegović, a doctor at the **Emergency Clinic**, who's Mommy's friend. She was in an ambulance. They were driving a wounded man to get him help. Lots of people Mommy and Daddy know have been killed. Oh, God, what is happening here???

Love, Zlata

Tuesday, May 26, 1992

Dear Mimmy,

I keep thinking about Mirna; May 13 was her birthday. I would love to see her so much. I keep asking Mommy and Daddy to take me to her. She left Mojmilo with her mother and father to go to her grandparents' place. Their apartment was shelled and they had to leave it.

There's no shooting, the past few days have been quiet. I asked Daddy to take me to Mirna's because I made her a little birthday present. I miss her. I wish I could see her.

I was such a **nag** that Daddy decided to take me to her. We went there, but the downstairs door was locked. We couldn't call out to them and I came home feeling disappointed. The present is waiting for her, so am I. I suppose we'll see each other.

Love, Zlata

Emergency Clinic, place to go for emergency medical attention

nag, person who asks for something again and again

United Nations peacekeepers arrive. ▶

BEFORE YOU GO ON

1 What fact do you learn about Silva Rizvanbegović?

2 Why is Zlata disappointed when she goes to visit Mirna?

On Your Own
How do you think you would feel if you were living in Sarajevo in 1992?

Reading 3 **189**

Wednesday, May 27, 1992

Dear Mimmy,

SLAUGHTER! MASSACRE! HORROR! CRIME! BLOOD! SCREAMS! TEARS! DESPAIR!

That's what Vaso Miskin Street looks like today. Two shells exploded in the street and one in the market. Mommy was nearby at the time. She ran to Grandma and Granddad's. Daddy and I were **beside ourselves** because she hadn't come home. I saw some of it on TV but still can't believe what I actually saw. It's unbelievable. **I've got a lump in my throat** and a **knot in my tummy**. HORRIBLE! They're taking the wounded to the hospital. It's a **madhouse**. We kept going to the window hoping to see Mommy, but she wasn't back. They released a list of the dead and wounded. Daddy and I were **tearing our hair out**.

✔ LITERARY CHECK
What figures of speech does Zlata use to express her feelings of fear and horror?

We didn't know what had happened to her. Was she alive? At 4:00 Daddy decided to go and check the hospital. He got dressed, and I got ready to go to the Bobars', so as not to stay home alone. I looked out the window one more time and . . . I SAW MOMMY RUNNING ACROSS THE BRIDGE. As she came into the house she started shaking and crying. Through her tears she told us how she had seen **dismembered bodies**. All the neighbors came because they had been afraid for her. Thank God, Mommy is with us. Thank God.

A HORRIBLE DAY. UNFORGETTABLE. HORRIBLE! HORRIBLE!

▲ An injured woman is taken to the hospital.

Your Zlata

---

beside ourselves, very worried
I've got a lump in my throat, I feel like crying
knot in my tummy, bad feeling about something
madhouse, place where everyone seems crazy
tearing our hair out, feeling very worried
dismembered bodies, bodies with missing arms or legs

Thursday, October 1, 1992

Dear Mimmy,

Spring has been and gone, summer has been and gone, and now it's autumn. October has started. And the war is still on. The days are getting shorter and colder. Soon we'll move the stove upstairs to the apartment. But how will we keep warm? God, is anyone thinking of us here in Sarajevo? Are we going to start winter without electricity, water or gas, and with a war going on?

The "kids" are negotiating. Will they finally negotiate something? Are they thinking about us when they negotiate, or are they just trying to **outwit** each other, and leave us to our fate?

Daddy has been checking the attic and cellar for wood. It looks to me as though part of the furniture is going to **wind up** in the stove if this keeps up until winter. It seems that nobody is thinking of us, that this madness is going to go on and on. We have no choice, we have to rely on ourselves, to take care of ourselves and find a way to fight off the oncoming winter.

Mommy came home from work in a state of shock today. Two of her **colleagues** came from Grbavica. It really is true that people are being expelled from there. There's no sign of Mommy's and Nedo's relatives or of Lalo. Nedo is going berserk.

Your Zlata

▲ Cooking is quite an achievement without electricity.

---

the "kids," Zlata's slang for the politicians
outwit, be more clever than; trick
wind up, end up; finally be
colleagues, fellow workers

Reading Skill

To understand the bold words, read the definitions at the bottom of the page. Later, use the words in your own sentences.

BEFORE YOU GO ON

1 How do Zlata and her father feel after the massacre on Vaso Miskin Street? Why?

2 What is the "madness" that Zlata refers to?

On Your Own
What would you do if you were in Zlata's family?

Monday, December 28, 1992

Dear Mimmy,

I've been **walking my feet off** these past few days.

I'm at home today. I had my first piano lesson. My teacher and I kissed and hugged, we hadn't seen each other since March. Then we moved on to **Czerny, Bach, Mozart, and Chopin**, to the étude, the invention, the sonata and the "piece." It's not going to be easy. But I'm not going to school now and I'll give it my all. It makes me happy. Mimmy, I'm now in my fifth year of music.

You know, Mimmy, we've had no water or electricity **for ages**. When I go out and when there's no shooting it's as if the war were over, but this business with the electricity and water, this darkness, this winter, the **shortage** of wood and food, brings me **back to earth** and then I realize that the war is still on. Why? Why on earth don't those "kids" come to some agreement? They really are playing games. And it's us they're playing with.

✔ **LITERARY CHECK**

What does the figure of speech "I'll give it my all" mean?

As I sit writing to you, my dear Mimmy, I look over at Mommy and Daddy. They are reading. They lift their eyes from the page and think about something. What are they thinking about? About the book they are reading or are they trying to put together the **scattered** pieces of this war puzzle? I think it must be the **latter**. Somehow they look even sadder to me in the light of the oil lamp (we have no more wax candles, so we make our own oil lamps). I look at Daddy. He really has lost a lot of weight. The scales say 25 kilos, but looking at him I think it must be more. I think

▲ Zlata expresses her concern about her family in her diary.

---

walking my feet off, walking a lot
Czerny, Bach, Mozart, and Chopin, composers who wrote
   piano music
for ages, for a long time
shortage, lack
back to earth, back to reality
scattered, spread out
latter, the second of two things or people

▲ Sarejevo

even his glasses are too big for him. Mommy has lost weight too. She's shrunk somehow, the war has given her **wrinkles**. God, what is this war doing to my parents? They don't look like my old Mommy and Daddy anymore. Will this ever stop? Will our suffering stop so that my parents can be what they used to be—cheerful, smiling, nice-looking?

This stupid war is destroying my childhood, it's destroying my parents' lives. WHY? STOP THE WAR! PEACE! I NEED PEACE!

I'm going to play a game of cards with them!

Love from your Zlata

---

wrinkles, lines on the face or skin that people get as they age

✔ **LITERARY CHECK**
*Why do you think that Zlata uses **hyperbole** to describe how her parents look?*

ABOUT THE **AUTHOR**

Zlata Filipović escaped to Paris in December 1993, where she began to study at the International School. Her diary has been translated into more than twenty languages. With the money from her book, Zlata helped to start a charity for victims of the Bosnian War. Zlata was awarded the Special Child of Courage Award. She is also co-editor of *Stolen Voices: Young People's Diaries from World War I to Iraq.*

BEFORE YOU GO ON

1 What has Zlata begun studying again?

2 Why is Zlata worried about her parents?

On Your Own
How can a diary like Zlata's help people today?

Reading 3 **193**

Review and Practice

▶ READER'S THEATER

Act out this scene between Zlata and her mother.

Zlata: MOMMY! I am so glad to see you! When the shells exploded in the market and you did not come home, I was so so worried. Are you okay?

Mother: Yes, Zlata, dear. I'm all right. When I heard the explosion, I ran to Grandma and Granddad's home. I am safe and not harmed, but I saw the most terrible things.

Zlata: What happened? What did you see?

Mother: I saw people lying wounded on the ground. Some had lost limbs. It was the most horrible thing I have ever seen. I couldn't stop crying and shaking!

Zlata: Mommy, how awful. Why is this happening in Sarajevo?

Mother: I don't know, but this war must stop. We need peace in our country. We have been torn apart by fighting for too long.

▶ COMPREHENSION

Workbook
Page 101

Recall

1. Zlata says that she does not write about herself anymore. What does she write about now?

2. What happened on Vaso Miskin Street?

Comprehend

3. How have Zlata's parents changed since the war began?

4. What is Zlata's **method** for coping with the **stress** of war?

Analyze

5. How does Zlata think life in Sarajevo has changed since the war started? Support your answer by evaluating information in the text.

6. What does Zlata think about the "kids'" ability to **establish** peace? Support your answer by evaluating information in the text.

Speaking SKILL

Use your voice to express the emotions Zlata and her mother are feeling.

▲ The historic Stari Most bridge in Bosnia was nearly destroyed during the war in 1993.

▲ After being rebuilt to look as it did originally, the bridge was reopened in July 2004.

Connect

7. Do you think that a diary could influence people to be more tolerant and less likely to go to war? Explain.

8. If you kept a diary, would you want it to be published and read by others? Or would you want it to be only for yourself? Explain.

► DISCUSSION

Discuss in pairs or small groups.

1. What do you predict will happen to Zlata and her family when the war finally ends?

2. What kinds of information do the entries in Zlata's diary **consist** of? How is Zlata's diary a clear account of the Bosnian War? How is it not? Discuss some of the facts Zlata presents about the war. Then discuss some of her opinions.

3. Do you think people who live in a country that is at war feel helpless? Why or why not?

Q **How does helping others help us all?** What are some other difficult experiences that a person might go through? What can a person do to help him or herself and others get through these events?

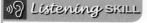

When you listen to your classmates debate an issue, take notes. This will help you evaluate other people's points of view.

Zlata writes at her desk, as the sound of guns echoes from the hills. ►

► RESPONSE TO LITERATURE

Workbook
Page 101

Utilize Reread the excerpt from *Zlata's Diary.* In your notebook, write the dates of the five days she writes about. Then write something important that happened to Zlata on each of these days. Use as much academic language as possible. Compare what you write in pairs or small groups.

Grammar

Placement of Adjectives

Using well-chosen adjectives to describe observations and feelings helps to make writing more precise and interesting. It also helps writers persuade readers to agree with their point of view.

An adjective describes a noun or noun phrase. An adjective + noun or noun phrase can be the subject or object, but the adjective is usually close to the noun it describes.

An adjective often comes right before the noun it describes.

> They were driving **a wounded man** to get him help.
> She told us how she had seen **dismembered bodies**.
> We are fighting off **the oncoming winter**.

An adjective can also appear after a linking verb. A linking verb describes a state of being rather than an action. The linking verb *be* connects the subject of the sentence to additional information about that subject.

> I **am lucky** to have them. [describes *I*]
> The days **are shorter** and **colder**. [describes *the days*]
> My parents **were cheerful**, **smiling**, and **nice-looking**. [describes *my parents*]

Verbs that describe the senses are also types of linking verbs. They are verbs such as *feel, taste, hear, smell,* and *look.*

> I **felt disappointed**.
> Somehow they **looked sadder**.

Other types of linking verbs include *get, become, seem,* and *appear.*

> It **seems worse** than before.

Grammar **SKILL**

When a noun has an article (*a, an, the*), the adjective comes between the article and the noun.

You can use a possessive noun, such as *Zlata's*, or a possessive adjective, such as *my, your, their,* etc., before an adjective.

> **Zlata's best friends** are Bojana and Maja.
> I'm now in **my fifth year** of music.

You can also use the demonstrative adjectives *this, that, these,* or *those* before an adjective.

> **This stupid war** is destroying my childhood.

Practice  Workbook Pages 102–103

Workbook Pages 102–103

Work with a partner. The adjective in each sentence is misplaced. Rewrite the sentences correctly in your notebook.

Example: He found a ring beautiful.   *He found a beautiful ring.*

1. The horrible war was.
2. I was by the violence upset.
3. Confused he seems about it.
4. They cooked food delicious.
5. His mother happy was.
6. Sleepy became the cat.
7. Grown-ups angry get.
8. These pants tight are uncomfortable.

Apply

Work with a partner. Take turns describing famous people or other students in the room using adjectives. Try to guess who the people are.

Example: He is tall. He is wearing a green shirt. . . .

✔ GRAMMAR CHECK

When do you use a, an, *or the* before an adjective?

Writing

Write a Diary Entry

In this lesson, you'll write a persuasive paragraph in the form of a diary entry. In diaries, writers often explore their feelings about issues, and they express opinions. In persuasive writing, it's important to examine both sides of an issue. That way, you can give a good answer to anyone whose opinion is different from yours.

> ### Writing Prompt
>
> Write a diary entry about an important issue. Remember to date your diary entry. Examine both sides of the issue and then come to a conclusion of your own. State your opinion clearly. Use strong adjectives to make your points. Be sure to place adjectives correctly.

1 PREWRITE Choose an issue that matters to you.

- Think about your opinion on the issue.
- Ask yourself why someone might have a different opinion.
- List your ideas in a graphic organizer.

Workbook Page 104

A student named Talia created this graphic organizer.

ISSUE	
Is nonviolence a better way to solve problems than violence?	
For Nonviolence	Against Nonviolence
Innocent people like Zlata and her family suffer during war. Peaceful protest sends a powerful message and is less likely to harm others.	The only way to confront violence is with more violence.

2 DRAFT Use your organizer to help you write a first draft.

- Be sure to look at both sides of the issue.
- State your own opinion clearly.
- Use strong adjectives and place them correctly.

3 REVISE Read over your draft. Look for places where the writing is unclear or needs improvement. Use the Writing Checklist to help you identify problems. Then revise your draft, using the editing and proofreading marks listed on page 456.

4 EDIT Check your work for errors in grammar, usage, mechanics, and spelling. Trade papers with a partner to obtain feedback. Use the Peer Review Checklist on Workbook page 104. Edit your final draft in response to feedback from your partner and your teacher.

5 PUBLISH Prepare a clean copy of your final draft. Share your diary entry with the class. Save your work. You'll need to refer to it in the Writing Workshop at the end of the unit.

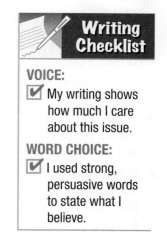

Writing Checklist

VOICE:
☑ My writing shows how much I care about this issue.

WORD CHOICE:
☑ I used strong, persuasive words to state what I believe.

Here is Talia's diary entry. Notice how she presents both sides of the issue. She also states her own opinion clearly.

September 20, 2011

Dear Diary,

Zlata's Diary and "Extraordinary People" show clearly that violence and war have a negative effect on people's lives. Zlata wrote her diary during the war in Sarajevo. She rarely left her house because of the violence. Her family lived in fear and didn't have electricity, water, or gas. In war, innocent people, like Zlata and her family, suffer. Gandhi understood the senselessness of violence and showed how passive resistance was a better way to solve problems. In my opinion, it is much smarter to follow Gandhi's example than to try to solve problems with violence. The people who fought in Sarajevo couldn't solve their problems peacefully and resorted to violence. They thought the only way to respond to violence was with more violence. However, violence hurts everybody. Peaceful protest sends a powerful message and is less likely to harm others.

▲ What is the message of this poster?

What You Will Learn

Reading
- Vocabulary building: *Context, dictionary skills, word study*
- Reading strategy: *Identify main idea and details*
- Text type: *Informational text (science)*

Grammar
Participial adjectives; Prepositions of location

Writing
Write a critical evaluation

➤ 🔍 THE BIG QUESTION

How does helping others help us all? What do you know about animal friendships? Which animals help each other? Are they usually in the same family group, such as monkeys and gorillas? Are they in packs or herds, such as wolves or horses?

Work with a partner to see what you know about animal friendship and cooperation. In your notebook, make a T-chart with two headings: *Kind of Animal* and *How They Act Together.* Complete the chart with the facts you know. Then share what you know with the class.

➤ BUILD BACKGROUND

"Friendship and Cooperation in the Animal Kingdom" is a science article. It describes how certain animals rely on one another, often in unusual ways.

Symbiosis means "living together." When two living things help each other, we say that they have a *symbiotic relationship*. One example of a symbiotic relationship is that between the tickbird and the rhinoceros. The tickbird picks insects called ticks off the rhino. Both animals are helped by this relationship. The tickbird gets food and protection (other animals don't attack the tickbird because it is sitting on the rhino!), and the rhino is not bothered by ticks.

Animals can be friends, too. Like people, animals can enjoy one another's company. Perhaps you have a cat and a dog. They may fight a lot— or they may be best friends.

▲ The rhino and the tickbird have a symbiotic relationship.

► VOCABULARY

Listening and Speaking: Key Words

Read these sentences aloud with a partner. Use the context to figure out the meaning of the highlighted words. Use a dictionary to check your answers. Then write each word and its meaning in your notebook.

Key Words

arrangement
cooperate
damage   Audio
gigantic
intruder
tsunami

1. Lions have an arrangement. The females hunt in a group. The males eat first.

2. Some animals, such as buffalo, cooperate with one another. They work together to help the whole herd.

3. A strong wind can do a lot of damage to trees. It can tear off branches and blow the trees down.

4. The blue whale is a gigantic mammal—the biggest in the world.

5. An intruder broke into the herd of zebras. The unwelcome creature was a hungry lion.

6. After the earthquake, a tsunami crashed into the shore. This series of huge waves destroyed many houses and trees.

▲ Blue whales are gigantic compared to humans.

Practice

Workbook Page 105

Write the sentences in your notebook. Choose a highlighted word from the box above to complete each sentence. Then take turns reading the sentences aloud with a partner.

1. A hippo is a _____ animal. Even a baby hippo weighs 272 kilograms (or 600 lb.).

2. A _____ looks like a huge wall of water. It is often caused by an earthquake.

3. Sometimes my three cats _____. They work together to chase mice.

4. I made an _____ with my best friend to take care of my pets while I'm away.

5. The storm caused a lot of _____. The town was destroyed.

6. The _____ broke into the nature preserve at night. He knew he wasn't supposed to be there, but he loved watching the seals.

Listening and Speaking: Academic Words

Study the **red** words and their meanings. You will find these words useful when talking and writing about informational texts. Write each word and its meaning in your notebook, then say the words aloud with a partner. After you read "Friendship and Cooperation in the Animal Kingdom," try to use these words to respond to the text.

attitude = the opinions and feelings that you usually have about someone or something	➡	After she fell off her horse, she developed a negative **attitude** about horses.
comment = a stated opinion made about someone or something	➡	The speaker made a short **comment** about the hippo. Then he went on to speak about birds.
concept = an idea of how something is or how something should be done	➡	We learned the **concept** of animal cooperation. It was fun to know that they helped each other.
rely on = trust or depend on someone or something	➡	Some animals **rely on** one another for safety.

Audio

Practice  **Workbook** Page 106

Write the sentences in your notebook. Choose a **red** word from the box above to complete each sentence. Then take turns reading the sentences aloud with a partner.

1. The boy began to understand the _____ of two animals working together. He listened as the scientist talked about how it happens.

2. The cub will _____ his mother for care. The cub needs her to help find food.

3. The girl's _____ toward crocodiles changed when she saw the movie about them.

4. The vet made an important _____ about pets and their need for attention. The pet owner listened to his opinion.

▲ Crocodiles in Long Xuyen, Vietnam

Word Study: Greek and Latin Roots

English has borrowed many words from other languages. Many English words come from ancient Greek or Latin word parts, called roots. For example, the word *disaster* contains a Greek root (*aster*), meaning "star." In ancient times, people who suffered disasters were thought to be living under a "bad star." Study the chart below. Notice the relationships between the roots, their meanings, and the English words that contain them.

Root	Meaning	Origin	English Words
anima	breath, life, spirit	Latin	animal animation
aster/astro	star	Greek	aster astrology
bios	life	Greek	biology symbiosis

▲ The aster is a star-shaped flower.

Practice  Workbook Page 107

Work with a partner. Use a large dictionary to look up each of the English words in the chart above. Discuss how the meaning of each Greek or Latin root is related to the meaning of each English word.

READING STRATEGY | IDENTIFY MAIN IDEA AND DETAILS

Identifying the main idea and details in a reading helps you see the key points the author is making. The main idea is the most important idea about a topic. Details are small pieces of information that support the main idea. To identify the main idea and details, follow these steps.

- Look at the title. Ask yourself: "What is the topic of this text?"
- As you read each paragraph, identify the author's main idea about the topic. Sometimes the author will state the main idea in a sentence. Other times you will have to put the main idea into your own words.
- As you read, look for examples, facts, dates, and sentences that tell more about the main idea. These are the supporting details.

As you read "Friendship and Cooperation in the Animal Kingdom," identify the main idea of each paragraph and of the whole article. Then find details that support the author's main idea about the topic.

 Workbook Page 108

Set a purpose for reading Can animals really cooperate and form friendships? As you read, think about the friendships animals develop. Why do you think animals help each other?

Friendship and Cooperation in the Animal Kingdom

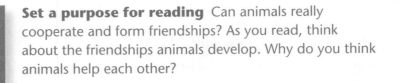

You know that people help other people, but do animals help other animals? It's a **"dog-eat-dog"** world out there, isn't it? Not always! It's true that animals often fight. However, at other times, they help each other out.

Life in the wild can be very difficult for animals. It is not easy for them to find food and water and stay safe. Animals struggle every day to survive.

That's why animals of the same species, or group, such as lions or blue jays, sometimes cooperate. By helping one another, they help their group survive.

Some animals become partners with other kinds of animals. The two types of animals depend on each other for survival.

_____

"dog-eat-dog," very competitive

This is called symbiosis, and animals who depend on each other are said to be in a symbiotic relationship. Sometimes the two animals would die without each other. Other times, they might be able to live, but they would not be as healthy.

One example of symbiosis is the relationship between the plover and the crocodile. The plover is a small wading bird. It helps pick clean the Nile crocodile's body and even its teeth. The crocodile will open its jaws and let the bird enter its mouth safely. Amazingly, the crocodile will not snap its jaws shut. Instead, it patiently allows the plover to eat the small, harmful animals on the crocodile's teeth. The crocodile gets its teeth cleaned, and the plover gets an easy meal!

◀ A Nile crocodile keeps its jaws open while a plover is in its mouth.

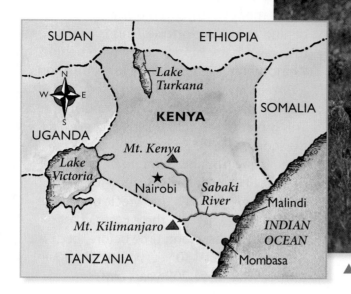

▲ A hippopotamus grazing among cattle egrets

Symbiosis is a working relationship. Many animal species have worked out this arrangement with other animal species. Sometimes, however, animals simply become friends with other animals. There may not be an obvious reason. Perhaps they just like the companionship.

Animals can find friends in the strangest places. For an example, take Owen, a baby hippopotamus. It is hard to believe, but Owen actually became best friends with a 318-kilogram (700-lb.) tortoise named Mzee (mm-ZAY).

Owen, the hippo, lived in the country of Kenya on the east coast of Africa. He was just one year old, and he already weighed 272 kilograms (600 lb.). He lived happily with his mother in a group of about twenty hippos. They grazed on the grass along the Sabaki River near the small village of Malindi.

On December 26, 2004, a disaster struck. There was a huge earthquake under the ocean floor near Indonesia. This caused a gigantic tsunami. The tsunami wiped out towns and villages throughout Asia. Around 230,000 people died. By the time the tsunami reached the east coast of Africa, the waves had lost a great deal of power. However, they still caused flooding and widespread damage. Owen had been swimming in the river with his mother when the tsunami hit. The enormous waves separated Owen from his mother and swept him out to sea.

The next day, the people of Malindi saw the struggling baby hippo, without its mother, stranded on a **coral reef**. It was Owen. He was tired and frightened. Owen could not reach the shore on his own. It took hours for the villagers to rescue Owen from the coral reef.

---

coral reef, line of hard material formed by the skeletons of small ocean creatures that live in warm water

BEFORE YOU GO ON

1 What is the main idea of the second paragraph on page 180?

2 How do plovers help Nile crocodiles?

 On Your Own
What do you think the villagers will do to help Owen?

But what should they do with a 272-kilogram (600-lb.) baby hippo? The people could not return him to the wild. Owen had not yet learned to take care of himself. Another hippo group would not accept him. Other hippos would think Owen was an intruder and probably attack him.

Luckily for Owen, there was an animal shelter nearby named Haller Park. The workers prepared a perfect home for Owen. It had a pond, a mud hole, tall trees, and lots of grass. This seemed perfect for a hippo, but Owen's new home was not empty. Some monkeys and the 318-kilogram tortoise Mzee already lived in Haller Park.

It took hours for the people of Malindi to load Owen into a pickup truck. Owen was very angry, and he was also very frightened. He had lost his mother and his friends. He did not know where he was or where he was going.

When Owen arrived at Haller Park, he quickly left the pickup truck and ran right to Mzee. The workers looked in amazement when Owen quickly hid behind the giant tortoise. This is exactly the way a baby hippo would hide behind its mother if it felt the need for protection.

Mzee was shocked and surprised. He had originally come from Aldabra Island. This is part of the country of Seychelles in the Indian Ocean. Sailors had probably taken Mzee from his home to be used for food. He must have escaped from the ship, maybe during a shipwreck, and come ashore somewhere on the eastern coast of Africa. That was a long time before, because Mzee was about 130 years old. (Some giant tortoises live to be 200 years old!)

Mzee must have seen a lot in his long life. Like most giant tortoises, he was not very friendly. He preferred to be left alone. So, at first, Mzee tried to crawl away from Owen. However, as you know, tortoises cannot move very quickly. Owen just watched where Mzee went and then followed him around. For some reason, Mzee began to like his new companion.

◀ Owen following Mzee

▲ Owen and Mzee nuzzling

Over the next few days, the two giant animals became good friends. Then they became great friends. In fact, Owen and Mzee soon refused to be separated. They would spend all their time together, eating, swimming, sleeping, and playing. Mzee would stretch out his neck and Owen would **tickle** it. At night, the two huge animals would cuddle up next to each other. Mzee and Owen even developed their own way of "talking" with each other.

It is a bit of a mystery why Owen and Mzee became such good friends. After all, Owen is a mammal and Mzee is a reptile. Perhaps Mzee's coloring and round shape reminded Owen of his mother. Maybe

Owen looked like another tortoise to Mzee. For whatever reason, they surprised scientists with the strength of their friendship.

Mzee's name means "wise man" in Swahili (one of the main languages of Kenya). It turned out that Mzee's name was well chosen. When Owen the hippo needed a friend, Mzee was there for him. Owen suffered a tremendous loss, but he never gave up. He kept trying and now has a happy life.

---

tickle, touch a person or animal lightly, often in order to make him or her laugh

BEFORE YOU GO ON

1 Why is Owen upset when the people of Malindi put him into the truck?

2 What does Mzee's name mean in Swahili?

On Your Own
What do you think about the friendship between Owen and Mzee?

Review and Practice

► COMPREHENSION

Workbook
Page 109

Recall

1. Why can't Owen be returned to the wild?
2. Where was Owen born?

Comprehend

3. How does Mzee's attitude toward Owen change?
4. How is symbiosis similar to friendship? How is it different?

Analyze

5. What helps the writer infer that Mzee and Owen have become great friends?
6. What main idea, or overall concept, does "Friendship and Cooperation in the Animal Kingdom" present?

Connect

7. Why do you think the author says, "It's a 'dog-eat-dog' world out there"? What do you think the author means?
8. What examples can you think of in which animals help people survive?

▲ Some dogs and cats get along well together.

► IN YOUR OWN WORDS

Imagine that you are telling a classmate about "Friendship and Cooperation in the Animal Kingdom." Use a chart like the one below to help you organize your ideas. Then share your summary with a classmate.

Main Idea about Symbiosis	Main Idea about Friendship
Definition of *symbiosis*:	Definition of *friendship*:
Examples:	Examples:

🔊 Speaking TIP

Write your main ideas on note cards. Put just a few words in big letters on each card. Use the cards to help you remember your main ideas.

► DISCUSSION

Listening TIP
Respect each speaker. Listen politely, even if you disagree with the speaker's ideas.

Discuss in pairs or small groups.

1. Which do you think is more common in the animal kingdom—symbiosis or friendship? Why?

2. Owen and Mzee live in Haller Park, an animal shelter. Do you think animals should live in shelters and nature preserves? Or should they be allowed to live in the wild? Explain.

Q **How does helping others help us all?** You have thought about how animals can help people. Now describe some specific examples in which people can help animals.

► READ FOR FLUENCY

Reading with feeling helps make what you read more interesting. Work with a partner. Choose a paragraph from the reading. Read the paragraph. Ask each other how you felt after reading the paragraph. Did you feel happy or sad?

Take turns reading the paragraph aloud to each other with a tone of voice that represents how you felt when you read it the first time. Give each other feedback.

EXTENSION   Workbook Page 109

In "Friendship and Cooperation in the Animal Kingdom," you learned about different kinds of animals. Learn more about one of the animals described in the article. Use encyclopedias, reference books, and reliable websites. Copy the chart below into your notebook. Use it to organize the information you find. Add more columns if necessary. Share your findings with the class.

Animal	Habitat (where the animal lives)	Size	Life Span	Foods

Grammar

Participial Adjectives

The present participle, the -*ing* form of a verb, and the past participle, often formed with -*ed*, can be used as adjectives. Like other adjectives, they appear before the noun they describe or after a linking verb, such as *be*.

> The plover is a small **wading** bird.
> The hippo was **tired** and **frightened.**

A present participial adjective modifies the noun that performs an action; it describes the cause of a feeling. A past participial adjective can be restated with a *by* phrase; it describes the receiver of a feeling.

> Animal friendships are **amazing.**
> I am **amazed** by animal friendships.

Grammar SKILL

Don't confuse a present participial adjective with a progressive verb. The participle must describe a noun.

Practice

Workbook
Page 110

Work with a partner. Write the sentences in your notebook. Complete each sentence with the correct participial adjective in parentheses.

Example: I was really *frustrated* by the test. (frustrated / frustrating)

1. The play was really _____. (bored / boring)
2. He's _____ about the new mall in town. (excited / exciting)
3. The news was _____. (surprised / surprising)
4 Do you think that the instructions are _____? (confused / confusing)
5. I felt _____ by the situation. (embarrassed / embarrassing)

Apply

Find other examples of participial adjectives in the reading. Write them in your notebook. Compare your list with a partner's. Write sentences with your partner's participial adjectives.

Prepositions of Location

Remember that a preposition is a word that shows location or time. Using the correct preposition in your persuasive writing helps you be specific when giving information.

Here are some common prepositions of location: *above, across, behind, below, beside, between, in, near, on, outside,* and *under.* Read the example sentences below. Notice the prepositions.

> There was a huge earthquake **under** the ocean floor **near** Indonesia.
> Owen quickly hid **behind** the giant tortoise.
> The hippo cuddled up **beside** the tortoise.
> The plover picked clean the area **between** the crocodile's teeth.
> Owen, the hippo, lived **in** the country of Kenya **on** the east coast of Africa.

Practice

Choose five prepositions from the example sentences above. Write a sentence in your notebook using each preposition. Compare your sentences with a partner's.

▲ Koko the gorilla holds a visiting kitty in her arms.

Writing

Write a Critical Evaluation

In this lesson, you'll write a critical evaluation. When you evaluate a topic critically, you examine it against a set of standards. You then make a judgment about whether the individual, issue, object, place, event, or idea meets those standards. The ability to evaluate someone or something critically helps you identify what you care about in people and life

Writing Prompt

Write a critical evaluation of a person or issue. First, present your standards for judging the topic. Then make a judgment and support it with examples. Use comparisons with *less* and *least* correctly.

1 PREWRITE Begin by choosing a topic.

- Think about the standards you want to apply to this topic.

- Brainstorm examples that show why your topic does or does not meet your standards.

- List your ideas in a graphic organizer.  **Workbook Page 112**

Here's a graphic organizer created by a student named Tyler. Tyler wanted to write about the traits that make a good student.

I. **Introduce Standards** Good students need to have certain traits.
   A. They need to be smart.
   B. They need to be dedicated, proud, and confident.
   C. They need to be willing to share what they know.
II. **Judge Topic** Michaela is a student with these traits.
   A. She is very smart.
   B. She studies hard, takes pride in her work, and has a relaxed and friendly attitude.

2 **DRAFT** Use your organizer to help you write a first draft.

- Remember to introduce your topic.
- Be sure to include a set of standards for judging the topic.
- Give examples that support your judgment.

3 **REVISE** Read over your draft. Look for places where the writing is unclear or needs improvement. Use the Writing Checklist to help you identify problems. Then revise your draft, using the editing and proofreading marks listed on page 456.

4 **EDIT** Check your work for errors in grammar, usage, mechanics, and spelling. Trade papers with a partner to obtain feedback. Use the Peer Review Checklist on Workbook page 112. Edit your final draft in response to feedback from your partner and your teacher.

5 **PUBLISH** Prepare a clean copy of your final draft. Share your critical evaluation with the class. Save your work. You'll need to refer to it in the Writing Workshop at the end of the unit.

Here is Tyler's evaluation. Notice how he presents the topic and a set of standards to judge it against.

> **Writing Checklist**
>
> **IDEAS:**
> ☑ I presented a set of standards for judging my topic.
> ☑ I included strong examples supporting my judgment.
>
> **CONVENTIONS:**
> ☑ I used comparisons with *less* or *least* correctly.

Tyler Welsh

The Perfect Student

Good students need to have certain traits. They must be smart. They also must be dedicated, proud, confident, and willing to share what they know. Many students possess one or two of these traits, but very few possess them all. Michaela, a classmate who sits next to me, is an exception. She is very smart. She reads everything, from science to historical fiction. She studies hard and does well in school. Michaela takes pride in her work. She has a relaxed and friendly attitude in class. When she gives an oral report, she speaks clearly and with confidence. In addition, she is the least selfish person I know. She is always very willing to take the time to help others. This year, she helped me when I was having trouble in one of my classes. To me, Michaela is the perfect example of a good student.

Link the Readings

Critical Thinking

Look back at the readings in this unit. Think about what they have in common. They all tell about helping others. Yet they do not all have the same purpose. The purpose of one reading might be to inform, while the purpose of another might be to entertain or persuade. In addition, the content of each reading relates to helping others differently. Now copy the chart below into your notebook and complete it.

Title of Reading	Purpose	Big Question Link
From *Run Away Home*		
"Extraordinary People: Serving Others"		*Famous people helping others throughout history.*
From *Zlata's Diary*	*to persuade*	
"Friendship and Cooperation in the Animal Kingdom"		

Discussion

Discuss in pairs or small groups.

- How does the purpose of *Run Away Home* differ from the purpose of "Friendship and Cooperation in the Animal Kingdom"?

- **Q** **How does helping others help us all?** Compare and contrast the readings in this unit. In your opinion, which reading best expresses the importance of helping others? Why? Based on the readings, do you think it's more important to help others or to help yourself? Explain.

Media Literacy & Projects

Work in pairs or small groups. Choose one of these projects.

1 Work in small groups to think of some ways in which people help others. You might research a recycling project or volunteers who take food to homebound people.

2 What do you think happens at the end of *Run Away Home*? Write a summary of what you think will happen at the end. Then read the entire book to see if your prediction is correct.

3 Think about a time when you helped a friend. Write a diary entry about what you did and how you felt about the experience. Then share your entry with a classmate.

4 Prepare an oral report about Sarajevo today. The war has ended, but has the country been rebuilt? Do research on the Internet. Look for visuals to use in your presentation. Be sure to use reliable sources for your report.

Further Reading

Choose from these reading suggestions. Practice reading silently with increased ease for longer and longer periods.

Gandhi, Jane Rollason
This Penguin Reader® biography describes the life of Mohandas Gandhi, whose message of peaceful resistance changed the world.

Anne Frank: The Diary of a Young Girl, Anne Frank
To escape Nazi persecution in Holland, Anne Frank and her family hid for two years in a secret warehouse annex. There, Anne wrote her extraordinary diary.

Free At Last, The Story of Martin Luther King Jr., Angela Bull
Civil rights leader Martin Luther King Jr. dreamed of an America where people would be judged by "the content of their character, not the color of their skin."

Put It All Together

LISTENING & SPEAKING WORKSHOP

TV Talk Show

Working in a team, you will present a TV talk show about a person you admire for his or her efforts to help others.

1 THINK ABOUT IT As a team, discuss the selection "Extraordinary People: Serving Others." Discuss how you would introduce the person on your own TV talk show and what questions you would ask him or her.

Work together to develop a list of other people, living or dead, who have done a lot to help others. For example:

- Eleanor Roosevelt
- Bono
- Jonas Salk

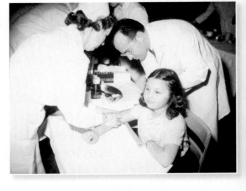

Jonas Salk, developer of the polio vaccine ▶

2 GATHER AND ORGANIZE INFORMATION With your team members, choose a person from your list. Write down what you already know and what you want to find out about the person. Decide who will play the talk show host and the special guest. Then decide what parts the other team members will play (for example, a coworker or someone the person helped).

Research Go to the library or use the Internet to gather information about your person's efforts to help others. Look for facts, details, and examples that show why the person is great. Take notes on what you find.

Order Your Notes Use your notes to make an outline for your TV show. Choose which information the host will include in the introduction and what questions he or she will ask each guest. Decide the order in which the guests will appear, and create a list of main points for each one to discuss.

Also think about the kind of language you will use during your interview. If you are speaking to a person you have not met before or if the interview occurs in a serious setting, use formal language. Formal language includes complete sentences, more formal grammar, and few contractions. If you are speaking to someone you know well, use informal language. Informal language includes more conversational words, simple sentences and phrases, and contractions.

3 PRACTICE AND PRESENT With your team members, practice your TV talk show. Keep your outline handy for reference, but try to speak naturally, without reading. Place your chairs at an angle so that the host and guests can make eye contact with each other and the audience. Keep practicing until you can present your show confidently, with smooth transitions between speakers.

Deliver Your TV Talk Show Speak clearly and loudly enough so that everyone in the class can hear you. Emphasize key ideas by pausing or slowing down. Use natural hand and body movements, too. For example, lean forward and reach out when you are making an important point.

4 EVALUATE THE PRESENTATION
You can improve your skills as a speaker and a listener by evaluating each presentation you give and hear. Use this checklist to help you judge your group's TV talk show and the talk shows of other groups.

- ☑ What was the host's topic?
- ☑ Did the group clearly show how this person has helped others and why he or she is admirable?
- ☑ Did the host give a persuasive introduction?
- ☑ Did the guests provide interesting facts, details, and examples?
- ☑ Did you understand each speaker's relationship to the special guest?
- ☑ Did the host use formal or informal language? Was it appropriate?
- ☑ What suggestions do you have for improving the talk show?

Speaking SKILL

Learning Strategy: Request assistance. Ask a friend or classmate to listen and give feedback as your team practices. Or record your rehearsal, if possible. Listen to the recording together, and find the places where you can improve your presentation.

Listening SKILLS

What more would you like to know about this person? Request or ask for more information about the guest. When responding, provide as many new details as possible.

As you listen, identify the speaker's topic. Listen for the general meaning, main ideas, and important details. After each presentation, exchange this information with a partner to confirm that you have understood it correctly.

STRENGTHEN YOUR SOCIAL LANGUAGE

In social contexts as well as in some of your content-area classes, you will need to ask for and give information. Go to www.LongmanKeystone.com and do the activity for this unit. This activity will help you acquire key structures, expressions, and words needed during extended speaking assignments and in everyday academic and social contexts.

WRITING WORKSHOP
Persuasive Speech

Write a Persuasive Speech

You have learned how to write a variety of persuasive paragraphs. Now you will use your skills to write a persuasive speech. In a persuasive speech, you try to convince listeners to agree with your opinion on an issue. A good persuasive speech begins with an introduction presenting both sides of the issue. The introduction clearly states the writer's opinion. Body paragraphs explain the writer's position with specificity and detail. A conclusion restates the writer's position in a new way.

> **Writing Prompt**
>
> Write a five-paragraph speech that tries to persuade listeners to agree with your opinion on an issue you care about. Focus on the theme of helping others. For example, you might write about why your friends should take part in a particular volunteer activity. You could also write about why an inspiring leader deserves admiration and respect. Use phrases such as *I believe* or *I think* to signal an opinion.

1 **PREWRITE** Review your previous work in this unit. Now brainstorm ideas for an issue. What person or group has helped others and made a difference in the world? In your notebook, answer these questions:

Ongoing Writing Skills Practice

- What issue do I care about?

- What reasons can I give to support my opinion on this issue?

- List your ideas in a graphic organizer. **Workbook Page 113**

Here's a graphic organizer created by a student named Tyler.

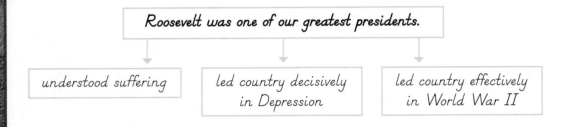

Roosevelt was one of our greatest presidents.

| understood suffering | led country decisively in Depression | led country effectively in World War II |

2 DRAFT Use your graphic organizer and the model on page 222 to help you write a first draft

- Keep your purpose in mind—to persuade.

- Remember to present both sides of the issue.

- Use strong, persuasive words to state your opinion.

3 REVISE Read over your draft. Think about how well you have addressed questions of purpose, audience, and form. Will your speech persuade readers and listeners to agree with your opinion? Does your speech include an introduction and conclusion?

   Keep these questions in mind as you revise your draft. Use the Writing Checklist below to help you identify additional issues that may need revision. Mark your changes on your draft using the editing and proofreading marks listed on page 456.

SIX TRAITS OF WRITING CHECKLIST

☑ **IDEAS:** Do I present both sides of the issue?

☑ **ORGANIZATION:** Do I explain my opinion by giving persuasive reasons, facts, and examples?

☑ **VOICE:** Does my writing show my feelings on the issue?

☑ **WORD CHOICE:** Do I use strong words that will appeal to listeners?

☑ **SENTENCE FLUENCY:** Do I vary my use of sentence lengths and patterns?

☑ **CONVENTIONS:** Do I place adjectives in the correct order?

Here are the revisions Tyler plans to make to his first draft.

A Great President

Franklin Delano Roosevelt, the 32nd President of the United States,
is known for overcoming hardships. He became president at a time
of world and national crisis ~~on~~ *in* 1933. Some people believe Roosevelt
created even more problems by increasing the government's powers. ∧ *but*
I believe he used the government's powers in new ways to help people
In my opinion,
∧Roosevelt was one of the greatest presidents in U.S. history.

Revised to correct an error in grammar, improve sentence fluency, and strengthen word choice.

Roosevelt himself understood human suffering, in part because he
had experienced tragedy. He was born on January 30 1882, in Hyde
Park, New York. ~~On~~ *In* 1921, at age 39, he was diagnosed with polio. The
disease left him partially paralyzed. He felt despair at first. ∧ *but* Then he
fought with all his strength to regain use of his legs. Although he
never was able to walk again without assistance he went on to a
brilliant political career.

Revised to correct an error in grammar and improve sentence fluency.

Elected president during the Great Depression, Roosevelt was a
(leader) decisive and passionate, ∧ who wanted to get the country back on
also
its feet. His administration ∧ worked to create jobs for the unemployed
to assist struggling farmers, to feed the hungry, and to provide for the
elderly. During his presidency, laws were passed to regulate the stock
market. Roosevelt cared about everyone!

Revised to correct an error in grammar and improve organization.

Roosevelt was equally effective during wartime. In World War II, he showed tremendous leadership in preparing the way for an Allied victory. In addition, he thought about the future of peace. ∧and ∕∧ He supported the idea of a global peacekeeping organization. Today, that organization is called the United Nations.

Revised to improve sentence fluency.

Roosevelt died suddenly during his fourth term in office. His death caused sorrow ᵃᶜʳᵒˢˢ∕∧ to the country. Roosevelt was a great president. He inspired hope, introduced important social programs, and led the nation brilliantly during wartime. Without his decisiveness and passion, the United states would not be the country it is today.

Revised to improve word choice.

4 EDIT Check your work for errors in grammar, usage, mechanics, and spelling. Then trade stories with a partner and use the Peer Review Checklist below to give each other constructive feedback. Edit your final draft in response to feedback from your partner and your teacher.

Workbook Page 113

PEER REVIEW CHECKLIST

- ☑ Does the speech have an introduction and conclusion?
- ☑ Does it include signal words such as *I believe* and *I think*?
- ☑ Are reasons and examples presented in an order that makes sense?
- ☑ Does the writing have energy and show the writer's personality?
- ☑ Are prepositions of time used correctly?
- ☑ What changes could be made to improve the essay?

Look at the next page to see the changes Tyler decided to make to his final draft as a result of his peer review.

Tyler Welsh

A Great President

Franklin Delano Roosevelt, the 32nd President of the United States, is known for overcoming hardships. He became president at a time of world and national crisis in 1933. Some people believe Roosevelt created even more problems by increasing the government's powers, but I believe he used the government's powers in *exciting* new ways to help people⊙ In my opinion, Roosevelt was one of the greatest presidents in U.S. history.

Revised to correct an error in mechanics and improve word choice.

Roosevelt himself understood human suffering, in part because he had experienced tragedy. He was born on January 30, 1882, in Hyde Park, New York. In 1921, at age 39, he was diagnosed with polio. The disease left him partially paralyzed. He felt despair at first, but then he fought with all his strength to regain use of his legs. Although he never was able to walk again without assistance, he went on to a brilliant political career.

Elected president during the Great Depression, Roosevelt was a decisive and passionate leader who wanted to get the country back on its feet. During his presidency, laws were passed to regulate the stock market. His administration also worked to create jobs for the unemployed, to assist struggling farmers, to feed the hungry, and to provide for the elderly. Roosevelt cared about everyone!

Revised to correct errors in mechanics.

Roosevelt was equally effective during wartime. In World War II, he showed tremendous leadership in preparing the way for an Allied victory. In addition, he thought about the future of peace, and he supported the idea of a global peacekeeping organization. Today, that organization is called the United Nations.

At age 63, Roosevelt died suddenly during his fourth term in office. His death caused sorrow across the country. Roosevelt was a great president, He inspired hope, introduced important social programs, and led the nation brilliantly during wartime. Without his decisiveness and passion, the United states would not be the country it is today.

Revised to add a detail and correct an error in mechanics.

5 PUBLISH Prepare a clean copy of your final draft. Share your persuasive speech with the class.

Workbook
Page 114

Test Preparation

PRACTICE

Read the following test sample. Study the tips in the boxes. Work with a partner to choose the missing words and answer the questions.

Taking Tests
You will often take tests that help show what you know. Study the tips below to help you improve your test-taking skills.

Helping Pets When Disaster Hits

1   When a disaster like <u>Hurricane</u> Katrina hits, many people have to leave their pets behind. This is always a difficult decision. Pets are lonely and __1__ without their owners. Sometimes they are injured or killed when the disaster hits. Or, they may starve to death when they run out of food and water.

2   Even before Katrina hit, the ASPCA was on the scene trying to help. Many __2__ worked 20-hour days without pay rescuing pets that had been trapped or stranded by the floodwaters. They stayed long after the hurricane was over to help reunite families with their beloved pets and to find new homes for animals that were left homeless. In all, the ASPCA helped more than 8,000 pets.

1 A purebred
   B playful
   C frightened
   D happy

2 F volunteers
   G musicians
   H celebrities
   J prisoners

3 In paragraph 1, <u>hurricane</u> means —
   A a dangerous tornado
   B a type of earthquake
   C a large tropical storm
   D a major winter storm

Tip
Substitute each answer choice in the blank to find the one that makes the most sense.

Tip
Notice the word <u>hurricane</u> in Question 3. You are looking for a definition. Choose the answer choice that makes the most sense.

Workbook Pages 115–118

Sometimes the best way to help someone else is to listen. When you are silent and just listen, you show that you care and respect the person you are listening to. Caring about someone and respecting that person are all important pieces of a larger feeling we call love. Many American artists try to show this emotion in their work.

Jesse Treviño, *Mis Hermanos* (1976)

In this painting, Mexican-born Jesse Treviño uses a large canvas to capture the daily life of Mexican Americans in San Antonio, Texas, the city where he lives. The title of the painting, *Mis Hermanos,* is Spanish for "My Brothers." But the title refers to both members of the Mexican-American community, as well as Treviño's actual family. The sunlight shines across the shirts of his six brothers and the artist himself (center, in striped shirt). The sunlight brings the men together like a strong emotion. Treviño shows the men standing or sitting in different positions against a fence. He captures the crinkles in their shirts and the liquid in the glasses that several of them hold in their hands. Treviño uses a painting style that creates an image almost as realistic as a photograph.

Treviño showed great promise as an artist when he was a young man. Then he lost his right arm when he served as a soldier in the Vietnam War. When he returned to the

▲ Jesse Treviño, *Mis Hermanos,* 1976, acrylic, 48 × 70 in., Smithsonian American Art Museum

United States, he had to teach himself to paint all over again with his left hand. His family and friends helped him as he recovered from his war injury. In *Mis Hermanos*, Treviño captures the respect and support the brothers give each other. Notice the hand of the brother in the back row resting on Treviño's shoulder. Each of the men touches another in some fashion, which adds to the warmth of the portrait.

Jacob Lawrence, *"Men exist for the sake of one another . . ."* (1958)

In *"Men exist for the sake of one another . . . ,"* an adult sits among four children. The man, though very large, bends gently toward the children. He holds a small tree that still has its roots. This means that the tree can be replanted. The older children, two girls, look sad and in need of comfort. The blue background mirrors their unhappy mood. But the child in the center smiles up at the man. The man's long fingers seem to touch her face, and her hand touches his leg. The warmth they show each other also envelops the smallest child, who looks up at the adult with a happy expression. Flowers bloom at their feet.

Jacob Lawrence had a difficult childhood. His father left when Lawrence was young, and his mother moved many times to find work. Lawrence lived in foster care—where another family takes you in until your own family can support you again. Fortunately, like the girls in this painting, Lawrence got support from adults in his community who cared for him.

Lawrence and other artists were hired by a company to create paintings that matched quotations from famous works in Western literature. Lawrence based his painting on a quotation from the Roman emperor Marcus Aurelius Antoninus. The emperor's statement (the title of Lawrence's painting) tells people that they should respect one another.

Respecting others strengthens our sense of community and the quality of our own lives. Both of these artists' works celebrate this give and take.

▲ Jacob Lawrence, *"Men exist for the sake of one another . . . ,"* 1958, oil, 20¾ x 16¾ in., Smithsonian American Art Museum

Discuss What You Learned

1 In what ways are these two paintings similar? How are they different?

2 Why do you think that Jacob Lawrence showed a tree that could be replanted in his painting? What do you think this tree stands for?

Big Question
In what ways are helping people and having respect for them related?

Workbook
Pages 119–120

THE BIG QUESTION

What do we learn through winning and losing?

This unit is about winning and losing. You'll read about winning a race and about different kinds of loss. You'll learn about sportsmanship and how "it's not whether you win or lose, it's how you play the game." As you read, you'll practice the academic and literary language you need to use in school.

Reading

1 Poems

"Casey at the Bat" by Ernest Lawrence Thayer, "Swift Things Are Beautiful" by Elizabeth Coatsworth, "Buffalo Dusk" by Carl Sandburg

Reading Strategy:
Read for engagment

2 Science

- "Going, Going, Gone?"
- "Ivory-Billed Woodpeckers Make Noise" by Jill Egan

Reading Strategy:
Recognize cause and effect

3 Fable and Myth

- "The Hare and the Tortoise" by Aesop
- "Orpheus and Eurydice"

Reading Strategy:
Identify author's purpose

Listening and Speaking—Expository

At the end of this unit, you'll present a **TV sports report** as if you were a newscaster.

Writing—Expository

In this unit you will practice **expository writing**, or writing that explains a topic. You'll write an expository paragraph after each reading and an expository essay at the end of the unit.

Quick **Write**

Write several sentences about a time when you lost a contest, game, or object.

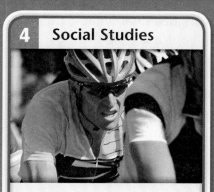

4	Social Studies

"The Biggest Winner of All"

Reading Strategy:
Ask questions

DVD **VIEW AND RESPOND**
Watch the DVD for Unit 4 and answer the questions at
www.LongmanKeystone.com.

227

Prepare to Read

What You Will Learn

Reading

- Vocabulary building: *Literary terms, word study*
- Reading strategy: *Read for enjoyment*
- Text type: *Literature (poetry)*

Grammar

Present perfect; More uses of the present perfect

Writing

Write a response to literature

➤ ⓠ THE BIG QUESTION

What do we learn through winning and losing? How do you feel when you lose a game? How is it different from the way you feel when you lose a person, animal, or thing? How could a poem or song help you remember someone or something you have lost? Use your prior experiences to answer these questions with a partner.

What are some of your favorite poems and songs? Why are the words to these poems and songs so easy to remember? Are any of them about some kind of loss? Discuss with your partner. Then take turns reciting a stanza, or group of lines, from a poem or song that you like.

➤ BUILD BACKGROUND

In this section, you will read three poems: **"Casey at the Bat," "Swift Things Are Beautiful,"** and **"Buffalo Dusk."** Some poems tell a story. For example, "Casey at the Bat" is a narrative poem about a mighty baseball player named Casey. It is his turn to hit the ball. Will Casey hit the ball far, so his team wins the game? Or will he strike out? Some poems focus on an idea or an image, but do not tell a story. "Swift Things Are Beautiful" describes things that are fast and things that are slow. "Buffalo Dusk" focuses on the disappearance of huge herds of buffaloes from the United States in the late 1880s.

▲ Once, a million buffaloes lived on the Great Plains of the United States. By the 1800s, only about a thousand were left.

➤ VOCABULARY

Learn Literary Words

Rhythm is the regular repeated pattern of sounds. The rhythm in a poem is like the beat in a piece of music. Read aloud the nursery rhyme below. What words did you stress? How many beats did you hear in each line?

Hickory Dickory Dock.
The mouse ran up the clock.
The clock struck one,
The mouse ran down!
Hickory Dickory Dock.

As you can see and hear in the nursery rhyme, **repetition** is another tool used in poems. Repetition involves repeating the same sound, words, or lines in a poem. Words that rhyme have the same ending sound but different beginning sounds. Many poems contain end-rhymes, or rhyming words at the ends of lines.

The **rhyme scheme** in a poem is the regular pattern of words that end with the same sound. To find the rhyme scheme, look at the end of every line in a poem. Then use the letters *a, b, c* to label the rhyme scheme. Read these lines from the first stanza of "Casey at the Bat." Notice how the rhyme scheme works and is labeled.

▲ This painting is called *Hickory Dickory Dock*.

The outlook wasn't brilliant for the Mudville nine that <u>day</u>;	a
The score stood four to two, with but one inning more to <u>play</u>,	a
And then when Cooney died at first, and Barrows did the <u>same</u>,	b
A sickly silence fell upon the patrons of the <u>game</u>.	b

Practice

Workbook Page 121

Work with a partner to create a rhyming poem in two stanzas. First, think of four pairs of rhyming words, such as *knee/free, light/night, won/fun, toe/slow*. Write the words in your notebook. Then take turns writing a line that ends with one of the rhyming words. Don't worry if the poem is a bit silly. Just play with the rhythm and rhymes. When you have completed your eight-line poem, share it with the class.

Listening and Speaking: Academic Words

Study the **red** words and their meanings. You will find these words useful when talking and writing about literature. Write each word and its meaning in your notebook, then say the words aloud with a partner. After you read "Casey at the Bat," "Swift Things Are Beautiful," and "Buffalo Dusk," try to use these words to respond to the text.

Academic Words

brief
device
final
respond
sphere
structure

Audio

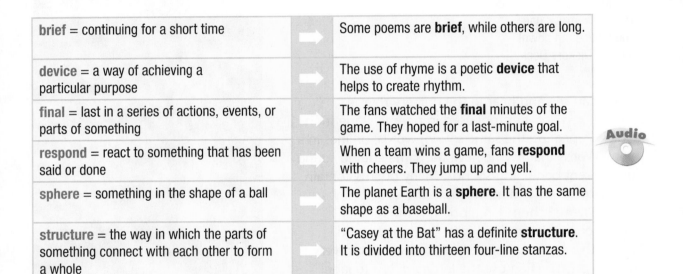

brief = continuing for a short time	⇒	Some poems are **brief**, while others are long.
device = a way of achieving a particular purpose	⇒	The use of rhyme is a poetic **device** that helps to create rhythm.
final = last in a series of actions, events, or parts of something	⇒	The fans watched the **final** minutes of the game. They hoped for a last-minute goal.
respond = react to something that has been said or done	⇒	When a team wins a game, fans **respond** with cheers. They jump up and yell.
sphere = something in the shape of a ball	⇒	The planet Earth is a **sphere**. It has the same shape as a baseball.
structure = the way in which the parts of something connect with each other to form a whole		"Casey at the Bat" has a definite **structure**. It is divided into thirteen four-line stanzas.

Audio

Practice

Workbook Page 122

Write the sentences in your notebook. Choose a **red** word from the box above to complete each sentence. Then take turns reading the sentences aloud with a partner.

1. I didn't know how to _____ when the coach asked me to say yes or no.
2. A _____ is a good shape for a soccer ball because it is easy to kick.
3. All types of writing need some sort of _____ to tie the words together.
4. In the _____ inning of the game, the player hit a home run.
5. Creating suspense is a _____ that many writers use.
6. The chess game was very _____. It lasted for only ten minutes.

▲ A baseball is a sphere, but a football is not.

Word Study: Spelling Long Vowel Sound /ī/

In English, the long vowel sound /ī/ can be spelled in different ways. When you read "Casey at the Bat," you will read the words below.

vi-o-lence	qui-et	nine	pride	style	bright	died

Say each word with a partner. Notice the /ī/ sound and its spellings. Some of the words above contain one syllable; others contain two or three syllables. Notice that when the letter *i* comes at the end of a syllable as in the word *qui-et*, the *i* often stands for /ī/. Study the chart below for more examples.

i	i_e	y	igh	ie
mind	stri**k**e	**try**	fi**gh**t	t**ie**
tiny	fi**v**e	sh**y**	mi**gh**ty	cr**ie**d

Practice

Work with a partner. Copy the chart above into your notebook. Say a word from the chart, and ask your partner to spell it aloud. Then have your partner say the next word. Continue until you can spell all of the words correctly. Then work with your partner to spell the following words: *lightning, smile, kind, pie, fry*. Add them to the chart under the correct headings.

▲ A young man enjoys some quiet time with a good book.

READING STRATEGY | READ FOR ENJOYMENT

Sometimes you read for information. Other times you read for enjoyment. When you read for the fun of it, ask yourself these questions:

- What is enjoyable about the characters, setting, and illustrations?
- Which words help me create images in my mind?
- Which parts of the text do I like best? What makes these parts so enjoyable to read?

As you read "Casey at the Bat," "Swift Things Are Beautiful," and "Buffalo Dusk," ask yourself: "How do the poets make their poems fun, interesting, or exciting to read?"

Set a purpose for reading What will happen when Casey comes up to bat? Is it better to be fast or slow? What happened to the buffaloes? Read the poems to find out what each one has to say about winning, beauty, power, and loss.

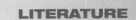

CASEY AT THE BAT

A Ballad of the Republic, Sung in the Year 1888

The outlook wasn't brilliant for the Mudville nine that day;
The score stood four to two, with but one inning more to play,
And then when Cooney **died** at first, and Barrows did the same,
A sickly silence fell upon the **patrons** of the game.

A straggling few got up to go in deep despair. The rest
Clung to that hope which **springs eternal** in the human breast;
They thought, "If only Casey could but get a whack at that —
We'd put up even money now, with Casey at the bat."

But Flynn **preceded** Casey, as did also Jimmy Blake,
And the former was a **lulu** and the latter was a **cake**;
So upon that stricken multitude grim **melancholy** sat;
For there seemed but little chance of Casey's getting to the bat.

Listening SKILL

Follow along in your book as you listen to the Audio CD. Notice the words in bold type. To understand them, read the definitions at the bottom of the page. Knowing the meanings of these words will enhance and confirm your comprehension of the story.

---

died, was "out"
patrons, spectators; fans
springs eternal, flows always
preceded, went before
lulu, person who is extremely stupid, bad, or embarrassing
cake, person who is easy to get out
melancholy, feeling of sadness

But Flynn let drive a single, to the wonderment of all,
And Blake, the much despised, tore the cover off the ball;
And when the dust had lifted, and men saw what had occurred,
There was Jimmy safe at second and Flynn a-hugging third.

Then from 5,000 throats and more there rose a lusty yell;
It rumbled through the valley, it rattled in the **dell**;
It knocked upon the mountain and recoiled upon the flat,
For Casey, mighty Casey, was advancing to the bat.

---

dell, small valley with grass and trees

✔ **LITERARY CHECK**
Is the rhythm of this poem regular or not? How many beats do you hear in each line?

BEFORE YOU GO ON

1 What do Cooney and Barrows do when they come to bat?

2 Who are the two players who come to bat before Casey?

☀ **On Your Own**
Have you ever watched an exciting baseball game? What was it like?

Reading 1 **233**

There was ease in Casey's manner as he stepped into his place;
There was pride in Casey's **bearing** and a smile on Casey's face.
And when, responding to the cheers, he lightly **doffed** his hat,
No stranger in the crowd could doubt 'twas Casey at the bat.

Ten thousand eyes were on him as he rubbed his hands with dirt.
Five thousand tongues applauded when he wiped them on his shirt.
Then while the **writhing** pitcher ground the ball into his hip,
Defiance flashed in Casey's eye, a sneer curled Casey's lip.

And now the leather-covered sphere came hurtling through the air,
And Casey stood a-watching it in haughty grandeur there.
Close by the sturdy batsman the ball unheeded sped—
"That ain't my style," said Casey. "Strike one!" the umpire said.

From the benches, black with people, there went up a muffled roar,
Like the beating of the storm-waves on a stern and distant shore;
"Kill him! Kill the umpire!" shouted someone on the stand;
And it's likely they'd have killed him had not Casey raised his hand.

With a smile of Christian charity great Casey's **visage** shone;
He stilled the rising **tumult**; he bade the game go on;
He signaled to the pitcher, and once more the sphereoid flew;
But Casey still ignored it, and the umpire said "Strike two!"

"Fraud!" cried the maddened thousands, and echo answered "Fraud!"
But one scornful look from Casey and the audience was awed.
They saw his face grow stern and cold, they saw his muscles strain,
And they knew that Casey wouldn't let that ball go by again.

---

bearing, way of moving, standing, or behaving
doffed, took off or tipped
writhing, angry; violently twisting
defiance, bold refusal to obey or give in
visage, face
tumult, noisy and excited situation, often caused by a large crowd

The sneer has fled from Casey's lip, the teeth are **clenched** in hate;
He pounds with cruel violence his bat upon the plate.
And now the pitcher holds the ball, and now he lets it go,
And now the air is shattered by the force of Casey's blow.

Oh, somewhere in this favored land the sun is shining bright,
The band is playing somewhere, and somewhere hearts are light,
And somewhere men are laughing, and little children shout;
But there is no joy in Mudville—mighty Casey has struck out.

—*Ernest Lawrence Thayer*

---

clenched, held together tightly

ABOUT THE POET

Ernest Lawrence Thayer was an American poet who wrote during the 1880s and 1890s. Thayer began his writing career at Harvard, as editor of the school newspaper. He spent most of his career writing humorous pieces for the *San Francisco Examiner*, a paper owned by a fellow Harvard classmate, William Randolph Hearst. "Casey at the Bat" was originally written for the newspaper. However, it didn't become popular until months after it was written, when it was recited on Broadway in front of players from professional baseball teams.

BEFORE YOU GO ON

1 What does Casey do right after he comes to bat?

2 What does the crowd yell at the umpire?

On Your Own
How do you feel about Casey? Is he mighty or not?

Swift Things Are Beautiful

Swift things are beautiful:
Swallows and deer,
And lightning that falls
Bright-veined and clear,
Rivers and **meteors**,
Wind in the wheat,
The strong-**withered** horse,
The runner's **sure** feet.

And slow things are beautiful:
The closing of day,
The pause of the wave
That curves downward to spray,
The **ember** that crumbles,
The opening flower,
And the **ox** that moves on
In the quiet of power.

—*Elizabeth Coatsworth*

---

swift, very fast
meteors, pieces of rock or metal that make a
    bright line in the night sky when they fall
    through Earth's atmosphere
withered, referring to the withers, or ridge
    between a horse's shoulders, the highest
    part of a horse's back
sure, steady; able to walk or run without
    sliding or falling
ember, piece of wood or coal that stays red
    and very hot after a fire stops burning
ox, large bull or cow

Reading Skill

Listen to the way your partner reads this text. If you don't understand an idea or word, ask your partner to clarify or explain. This will help you understand the poem. Then demonstrate your comprehension of the poem by doing the same for your partner.

ABOUT THE POET

Elizabeth Coatsworth was born in Buffalo, New York, in 1893. As a young child, she lived for a time in Europe and Egypt. She began writing when she was twenty years old and continued until she was in her eighties. Coatsworth wrote over ninety books for children and adults, including poetry, novels, and nonfiction. Her 1930 book *The Cat Who Went to Heaven* won the Newbery Medal.

Buffalo Dusk

Audio

The buffaloes are gone.
And those who saw the buffaloes are gone.
Those who saw the buffaloes by thousands and how they
    pawed the **prairie sod** into dust with their great hoofs,
    their great heads down pawing on in a great **pageant**
    of **dusk**,
Those who saw the buffaloes are gone.
And the buffaloes are gone.

—*Carl Sandburg*

---

prairie sod, grass that covers a large, wide-open space
pageant, public show or display
dusk, time just before it gets dark

✔ **LITERARY CHECK**
*How does the **repetition** of the word* gone *make you feel?*

ABOUT THE POET

Carl Sandburg is considered by many to be one of the greatest American writers. Although he is best known for his poetry, Sandburg also wrote nonfiction and folklore. Sandburg won the Pulitzer Prize twice: first in 1926 for a biography titled *Abraham Lincoln: The Prairie Years* and later, in 1951, for *The Complete Poems of Carl Sandburg*.

BEFORE YOU GO ON

1. What slow animal is described in the poem on page 236?

2. What do the buffaloes do at dusk in the poem above?

💡 **On Your Own**
Which of the animals in these two poems have you seen up close? Where did you see them?

Review and Practice

▶ DRAMATIC READING

Work in small groups to reread, discuss, and interpret "Casey at the Bat," "Swift Things Are Beautiful," and "Buffalo Dusk." Describe what you visualize as you read each poem line by line. What poetic devices do the authors use? What images do the poems create in your mind? Then with the rest of the class, read the poems aloud.

One of the best ways to understand a poem is to memorize it, or learn it by heart. Start by saying two lines of the poem you like best. Then memorize the next two lines. Keep going as far into the poem as you can. The part you memorize will be yours forever.

**Workbook
Page 125**

▶ COMPREHENSION

Speaking SKILL

Have fun. The more you enjoy reading the poems aloud, the more your classmates will enjoy the poems, too.

Recall

1. In "Casey at the Bat," what is the score in the baseball game when Casey comes to bat?

2. What swift things are mentioned in "Swift Things Are Beautiful"?

Comprehend

3. In "Casey at the Bat," what happens when Flynn comes to bat? What happens when Jimmy Blake comes to bat?

4. In what ways are the moods of each of the three poems different? Which one contains humor and suspense? Which one expresses a serious and thoughtful mood? Which one expresses sadness?

Analyze

5. How does the structure of "Buffalo Dusk" contribute to its meaning?

6. Why do you think that Ernest Lawrence Thayer chose to write about a baseball player who strikes out? Why does he call Casey "mighty"?

Connect

7. Which fast-moving things do you think are beautiful? Explain.

8. What animal would you like to write a poem about? What three things about that animal would you include in your poem?

► DISCUSSION

Discuss in pairs or small groups.

1. "Casey at the Bat" was written in 1888. Why do you think people still **respond** favorably to this poem?

2. If you were writing a poem about slow things that are beautiful, what five things would you include in your poem?

Q **What do we learn through winning and losing?** What did you learn about winning and losing from each of the three poems? Which poem taught you the most? Why?

► RESPONSE TO LITERATURE

Workbook Page 125

Utilize "Swift Things Are Beautiful" describes both swift and slow things. Write a **brief** poem of your own in which you describe two things that are swift and two things that are slow. Use a graphic organizer like the one below to list your ideas. Share your poem with a partner.

Swift Things	Why They Are Beautiful	Slow Things	Why They Are Beautiful

◄ Cheetahs are very swift.

Grammar

Present Perfect

Use the simple past for actions that happened at a specific time in the past. Use the present perfect for actions that happened in the past but not at a specific time.

> A sickly silence **fell** upon the patrons of the game.
> All the buffalo **have died**. [not a specific time]

Form the present perfect with *has* or *have* and the past participle. Form the negative with *hasn't* or *haven't*. For questions, switch *has* or *have* and the subject.

> **Has** he **thrown** the **sphere** to Casey?   No, he **hasn't**.

For regular past participles, add *-d* or *-ed* to the base form of the verb. Other past participles are irregular. These you must memorize.

Grammar SKILL

Sometimes the past participle is the same as the simple past form. For example, *have / had / had, hear / heard / heard, put / put / put.*

Irregular Past Participles							
be	→ been	go	→ gone	put	→ put	sing	→ sung
eat	→ eaten	have	→ had	see	→ seen	take	→ taken

Practice
Workbook Page 126

Work with a partner. Copy the words into your notebook. Use the words to write sentences in the present perfect.

Example: she / be / to the store / *Has she been to the store?*

1. The game / be / cancelled.
2. you / be / to France?
3. they / eat / dinner?
4. We / not go / shopping.
5. I / finish / my biology homework.

✔ GRAMMAR CHECK

How do you form questions in the present perfect?

Apply

Work with a partner. In your notebook, write three "clues" about something you've done in the past. Take turns asking questions, trying to guess what the other has done.

Example: Mickey Mouse, Florida, hot   "Have you been to Disney World?"

More Uses of the Present Perfect

The present perfect can also be used to express an action that began in the past and continues into the present. You can use the prepositions *for* and *since* to show this. Use *for* to describe the period of time that the action has been going on; use *since* to show the time or date in the past when the action began.

> How long has he played baseball?
> He's played baseball **for six years**. / He's played baseball **since 2006**.

Certain adverbs can be used with the present perfect to indicate general times.

Rule	Adverb
Use *just* for recently finished actions.	Mighty Casey has **just** struck out.
Use *yet* to ask about recent experiences.	Has he struck out **yet**?
Use *already* in affirmative statements.	He's **already** struck out.
Use *yet* in negative statements.	He hasn't struck out **yet**.
Use *ever* to ask about life experiences. For a positive answer, use *before*. For a negative answer, use *never*.	Has he **ever** struck out? Yes, he's struck out **before**. No, he's **never** struck out.

Grammar SKILL

Notice that some adverbs appear midsentence: *just, ever, never*. Some appear at the end: *yet, before*. *Already* can come midsentence or at the end.

Practice

Workbook Page 127

Work with a partner. Copy the sentences into your notebook. Choose the correct word in parentheses to complete each sentence.

Example: Have you gone to the post office __*yet*__ (just, never, yet)?

1. Has he _____ (ever, never, before) been to Italy?
2. We've _____ (yet, just, ever) finished lunch.
3. I've studied English _____ (for, since) two years.
4. Paolo has _____ (ever, never, before) seen snow.
5. They have travelled to Europe _____ (just, before, yet).

Apply

Work with a partner. Interview your partner about his past experiences.

Example: Have you ever seen . . . ?

Writing

Write a Response to Literature

At the end of this unit, you will write an expository essay. To do this, you will need to learn some of the skills used in expository writing. In expository writing, a writer provides information and gives explanations to help readers understand a topic. One type of expository writing is a response to literature. In a response to literature, you give your ideas and opinions about the meaning of a particular story, poem, or other work of literature.

> **Writing Prompt**
> Write a response to "Casey at the Bat." Explain what the poem is about. Describe the impact it had on you and why. Include your ideas, opinions, and feelings. Give specific examples and details to support your ideas and opinions about the poem. Remember to use the present perfect correctly.

1 **PREWRITE** Reread the poem at least twice.

- Think about your ideas and opinions about the poem.

- Ask yourself which specific examples in the poem explain your reaction to it.

- List your ideas in a graphic organizer.  **Workbook Page 128**

A student named Andrew used a word web to plan his response to a poem. His assignment was to write a response to "Buffalo Dusk."

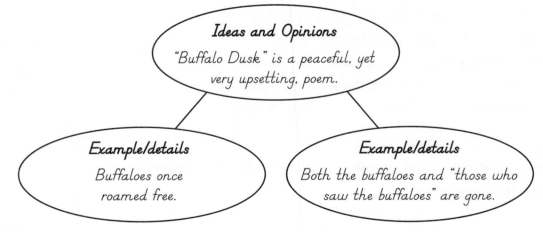

Ideas and Opinions
"Buffalo Dusk" is a peaceful, yet very upsetting, poem.

Example/details
Buffaloes once roamed free.

Example/details
Both the buffaloes and "those who saw the buffaloes" are gone.

242 Unit 4

2 DRAFT Use your organizer to help you write a first draft.

- Include your ideas, opinions, and feelings about the poem.
- Choose details and examples to explain your reaction.
- Check to be sure you have spelled words correctly.

3 REVISE Read over your draft. Look for places where the writing is unclear or needs improvement. Use the Writing Checklist to help you identify problems. Then revise your draft, using the editing and proofreading marks listed on page 456.

4 EDIT Check your work for errors in grammar, usage, mechanics, and spelling. Trade papers with a partner to obtain feedback. Use the Peer Review Checklist on Workbook page 128. Edit your final draft in response to feedback from your partner and your teacher.

5 PUBLISH Prepare a clean copy of your final draft. Share your response to literature with the class. Save your work. You'll need to refer to it in the Writing Workshop at the end of the unit.

Here is Andrew's response to "Buffalo Dusk," the poem he was assigned. Notice his strong voice when he expresses his feelings.

Writing Checklist

IDEAS:
☑ I explained my reaction to the poem by providing good examples from the text.

CONVENTIONS:
☑ I used English spelling rules and patterns to spell words accurately.

Andrew C. Dubin

"Buffalo Dusk"

"Buffalo Dusk," by Carl Sandburg, is a peaceful, yet very upsetting, poem. It is peaceful because Sandburg talks about buffaloes and how they once lived and roamed free on the prairies. He also mentions "those who saw the buffaloes." These are the Native Americans, who also lived freely. The poem is upsetting because Sandburg tells how both the buffaloes and the Native Americans are gone. Reading this has made me angry and upset. The buffaloes were hunted so much, they nearly died out. Without the buffaloes, the Native Americans had no source of food or clothing and began to disappear as well. Some Native Americans and buffaloes did survive, but far fewer of either are alive today compared to 200 years ago. For this reason, the poem is very powerful and also very sad.

What You Will Learn

Reading

- Vocabulary building: *Context, dictionary skills, word study*

- Reading strategy: *Recognize cause and effect*

- Text type: *Informational text (science)*

Grammar

Complex sentences with subordinating conjunctions; Subordinating conjunctions with adverb clauses

Writing

Write a cause-and-effect paragraph

➤ 🄠 THE BIG QUESTION

What do we learn through winning and losing? You are going to read about three kinds of birds that were lost forever. What might cause a type of bird to die out? How would this affect other animals, including humans?

Think about what you know about birds. Make a two-column chart in your notebook with the headings *Birds* and *Facts*. Work in small groups to list the names of birds you know, such as robins, toucans, penguins, and cardinals. Write any facts you know about each bird; for example, robins eat worms. Then share your ideas about what might happen to cause these birds to die out with your peers and teachers. Ask for their feedback in order to develop background knowledge about this topic.

▲ A toucan

➤ BUILD BACKGROUND

"Going, Going, Gone?" and **"Ivory-Billed Woodpeckers Make Noise"** are science articles. The first article explains why three kinds of birds died out. The second suggests that a type of bird once thought to have died out may actually still exist.

In "Buffalo Dusk" you learned that humans were responsible for killing off most of the buffaloes in North America. If laws had not been passed to protect buffaloes, they would have become extinct, or lost forever. Why do specific kinds of animals become extinct? They may not be able to find the food they need. People or other creatures may destroy their habitats. Disease might wipe them out. In the case of dinosaurs, meteors may have struck Earth and killed off these creatures.

▲ A penguin

▲ A cardinal

► VOCABULARY

Listening and Speaking: Key Words

Read aloud and listen to these sentences with a partner. Use the context to figure out the meaning of the highlighted words. Use a dictionary to check your answers. Then write each word and its meaning in your notebook.

Key Words

conservationists
destruction
extinct
habitats
ornithology
predator

1. The conservationists at the park protected the lions by keeping them in a safe area.

2. After the forest was destroyed, the animals had nowhere to live. Their homes had been ruined.

3. Dinosaurs have become extinct. They are all gone now.

4. The birds' habitats in the nature preserve look like their original rain forest homes. There is food to eat, and there are trees to live in.

5. The student took a class in ornithology because he wanted to know all about birds.

6. The cat is a predator that likes to attack birds.

Practice  **Workbook** Page 129

Work with a partner to answer these questions. Try to include the key word in your answer. Write the sentences in your notebook.

1. How do conservationists protect animals?

2. What natural disasters might cause a town to be destroyed?

3. What do you think caused dinosaurs to become extinct?

4. What do you think the habitats of penguins look like?

5. What sort of people would teach classes in ornithology?

6. What animal might be a predator of a cat?

Serious bird-watchers often read
books on ornithology. ►

Listening and Speaking: Academic Words

Study the red words and their meanings. You will find these words useful when talking and writing about informational texts. Write each word and its meaning in your notebook, then say the words aloud with a partner. After you read "Going, Going, Gone?" and "Ivory-Billed Woodpeckers Make Noise," try to use these words to respond to the text.

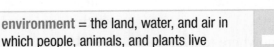

Academic Words

environment
estimate
factors
statistics

environment = the land, water, and air in which people, animals, and plants live	Oil spills and other changes in the **environment** had a bad effect on the birds that lived there.
estimate (verb) = judge the value or size of something	Rico and Li **estimate** that more than 100 birds live in the region. It is a logical guess.
factors = several things that influence or cause a situation	Many **factors** caused the birds to move to a new area. One reason was the weather.
statistics = a collection of numbers that represents facts or measurements	The **statistics** show how the number of birds has gone up and down over the years.

Practice

Workbook
Page 130

Write the sentences in your notebook. Choose a red word from the box above to complete each sentence. Then take turns reading the sentences aloud with a partner.

1. People gather _____ about the number of animals in a certain place.

2. There are many _____ that help to keep an animal safe.

3. Sometimes it's better to _____ than to count every single item.

4. People and other living creatures need a certain _____ in order to survive.

Gentoo penguins like this one live in the cold environment of Antarctica. ▶

Word Study: Homophones

A homophone is a word that sounds the same as another word but has a different meaning and a different spelling, such as *hair* (*hare*). Homophones can be confusing when you read or hear them. To figure out which meaning is being used, check the spelling and use context clues. If you still can't figure out which meaning is correct, look up the word in a dictionary.

Homophone	Meaning
one won	number that comes before two simple past of *win*
prey pray	hunt another animal for food speak to a god
sea see	the ocean use your eyes to notice

Practice  Workbook Page 131

Work with a partner. Define each pair of homophones. Then use each word in a sentence to show its meaning. Check your answers in a dictionary. Write the words and definitions in your notebook.

break/brake	main/mane	tale/tail
hour/our	seen/scene	weather/whether

▲ The sailor could see the sea.

READING STRATEGY | RECOGNIZE CAUSE AND EFFECT

Recognizing cause and effect is a basic reading skill that helps you understand explanations in texts. An effect is "what happened." A cause is "why it happened." To recognize causes and effects, follow the steps in this example:

- Read this sentence: *The bird died because it didn't have food.*
- Look for what happened. (The bird died.) This is the effect.
- Look for the reason why it happened. (It didn't have food.) This is the cause.
- Look for words that signal cause and effect, such as *so, because, because of, therefore,* and *as a result.*

As you read the next two articles, look for the causes and effects. Use a graphic organizer to help you.

 Workbook Page 132

Reading 2 **247**

Set a purpose for reading Why did the birds in these paintings become extinct or almost extinct? Read to find out the causes. Do you think that people learned anything from this loss? Analyze the effects.

Audio

When a species, or kind of animal, becomes extinct, it is lost forever. These online science articles both deal with birds that have become extinct. You will find out the effects that certain events and actions had on the dodo, the passenger pigeon, and the Carolina parakeet. You will also find out why some bird lovers now feel hopeful about a bird that was thought to be extinct. As you read, consider what can be done to prevent other living things from becoming extinct in the future.

More than eighty kinds of birds have died out, or become extinct, in the last 300 years. Some vanished because of natural causes. Humans killed off most of them. They hunted the birds too much and destroyed the birds' habitats. Read on for more details on the search for the ivory-billed woodpecker. (It might not be extinct as once thought.) Then check out the stories behind three extinct birds.

▲ **Ornithology is the study of birds.**

The Ivory-Billed Woodpecker

A team of bird experts is walking through mud and swamps in Louisiana's Pearl River forest. They hope to find the mysterious ivory-billed woodpecker. Experts believed this bird had been extinct for more than fifty years. A college student's sighting of unusual-looking birds sparked hopes that it might still be alive.

Loggers cut down trees in the Pearl River forest during the early 1800s. But some trees have grown back. There are now many old cypress, sweet gum, and oak trees that would serve as a good home for ivory-billed woodpeckers. The birds were known to eat the fat **grubs** that live under the bark of these trees. The researchers have already found trees with areas of bark that have been chipped off, as if by a large woodpecker. Only time will tell if it is an ivory-billed one.

---

loggers, people whose job it is to cut down trees
grubs, insects when they are in the form of small, soft white worms

Adapted from "Going, Going, Gone?" from *Time for Kids*, January 22, 2002. © 2002 TIME for Kids. Reprinted by permission.

The Dodo

The dodo was the first bird to be wiped out by people during modern times. Dodos were large, flightless birds. They were first seen around 1600 on Mauritius, an island in

the Indian Ocean. Less than eighty years later, the dodo was extinct. The dodo's heavy, clumsy body made it an easy target for sailors, who hunted it for food. As forests were destroyed, so was the dodo's food supply. And the cats, rats, pigs, and other predators unleashed by sailors **preyed on** the dodos. Together these factors led to the dodo's extinction.

The Passenger Pigeon

These pigeons once lived in the eastern United States. They flew across this area in flocks so huge that they darkened the sky. In 1808 a single flock in Kentucky was estimated to contain over 2 billion birds. Today the passenger pigeon is extinct because of human activities. Settlers moving West during the nineteenth century cleared huge numbers of eastern chestnut and oak trees to make room for farms and towns. These trees were the passenger pigeon's main source of food. The birds were seen as a threat to crops, so people killed the birds. They were also hunted for food. All of these factors wiped out the passenger pigeon. The last one, which lived in the Cincinnati Zoological Garden, died on September 1, 1914.

preyed on, hunted and ate

The Carolina Parakeet

This colorful bird was the only parrot native to the eastern United States. It had green feathers with a yellow head and orange cheek patches and forehead. The largest Carolina parakeets were 33 centimeters (13 in.) long, including their tail feathers. They once lived throughout the Southeast, as far north as Virginia and as far west as Texas. Parrots are among the smartest of birds. However, farmers thought these fruit-eaters were **pests**. So they shot them from the skies. The Carolina parakeet became extinct in the 1920s. As a result, all that's left are stuffed examples of this bird in museums.

pests, small animals or insects that harm people or destroy things, especially crops or food supplies

BEFORE YOU GO ON

1. What caused the passenger pigeon to become extinct?
2. Why did farmers kill the Carolina parakeet?

On Your Own
Why should we try to prevent species (kinds) of birds from becoming extinct?

Ivory-Billed Woodpeckers Make Noise

Jill Egan

Bird lovers were chirping back in April of 2005. Why? Scientists from Cornell University announced they'd rediscovered the ivory-billed woodpecker. The rare bird was thought to have been extinct since 1944. It was rediscovered at Cache River National **Wildlife Refuge** in eastern Arkansas.

Wildlife Refuge, protective environment for animals

In July, a small group of bird experts said that they weren't sure the ivory-billed woodpecker had really been rediscovered. They said a blurry videotape of the bird wasn't enough evidence. Researchers then decided to send them more proof. They shared a sound recording of the ivory-billed woodpecker's **one-of-a-kind** double-rap.

---

one-of-a-kind, unique, or very special because there is nothing else like it

Adapted from "Ivory-Billed Woodpeckers Make Some Noise" by Jill Egan, from *Time for Kids*, August 5, 2005. © 2005 TIME for Kids. Reprinted by permission.

The ivory-billed woodpecker ▶

The unique sounds made believers out of the bird experts. "The thrilling new sound recordings provide clear and convincing evidence that the ivory-billed woodpecker is not extinct," said Richard Prum, a scientist from Yale University.

The ivorybill is the largest woodpecker in the United States. It has a wingspan of about 91 centimeters (3 ft.). The ivorybill began to disappear because loggers cut down forests across the Southeast between 1880 and the 1940s. Soon after the ivorybill was rediscovered, the U.S. government announced a $10 million plan to protect the rare bird.

Conservationists are trying to help the woodpecker by killing trees. Sound strange? The woodpecker feeds on beetle **larvae** found under the bark of dead trees. When the trees are killed, more beetles will likely be attracted to the trees. With more food for the woodpeckers, the species will have a better chance at recovering.

Only about thirty-five to fifty trees will be cut on four 4-acre sections of land. There are 2,000 to 2,800 trees on each section. In about two or three years, scientists hope the trees will have lots of beetles for the woodpeckers. Then the double-rap of the ivorybill will be a common sound.

---

larvae, young insects with soft, tube-shaped bodies, which will eventually become adult insects with wings

Reading Skill

Take turns rereading paragraphs aloud with a partner. As you read along in the text, listen closely to the way your partner reads. Listen for pauses, stressed words, and rhythm. This will help you understand the reading. Then demonstrate your comprehension of the reading by doing the same for your partner.

BEFORE YOU GO ON

1. What caused bird lovers to be happy?

2. What effect did loggers have on the ivory-billed woodpecker?

On Your Own
How is losing a species different from losing a competition?

Review and Practice

► COMPREHENSION

Workbook
Page 133

Recall

1. About how many kinds of birds do experts **estimate** have become extinct in the last 300 years?
2. Where was the ivory-billed woodpecker rediscovered?

Comprehend

3. What **factors** contributed to the extinction of the passenger pigeon?
4. What two things helped to convince bird experts that the ivory-billed woodpecker was not extinct?

Analyze

5. Why does the author use a question mark rather than a period in the title "Going, Going, Gone?"
6. What could you have said to farmers to protect the Carolina parakeet from becoming extinct?

▲ The green turtle, giant panda, and Bengal tiger are in danger of becoming extinct.

Connect

7. Which animals do you know of that are in danger of becoming extinct? Are changes to the animals' **environment** part of the cause? Explain.
8. How can people help protect animals and plants from extinction?

► IN YOUR OWN WORDS

Imagine that you are telling a classmate about "Going, Going, Gone?" and "Ivory-Billed Woodpeckers Make Noise." For each article, make a three-column chart with these headings in your notebook: *Section, Main Ideas*, and *Important Details*. Use the charts to organize the information in each article. Try to use the academic words. Then share your summaries with a classmate.

> *Speaking* SKILL

Learning Strategy:
Use formal language in class. Use informal language with your family and friends. When you speak, know when to use formal and informal language.

➤ DISCUSSION

Discuss in pairs or small groups.

1. How are the four kinds of birds in "Going, Going, Gone?" similar and different?

2. Do you believe that the ivory-billed woodpecker is extinct or not? Why?

Q **What do we learn through winning and losing?** Imagine that you could bring back the dodo, passenger pigeon, or Carolina parakeet. Which one would you choose? Why? What lessons would people need to learn to make sure the bird didn't die out again?

➤ READ FOR FLUENCY

It is often easier to read a text if you understand the difficult words and phrases. Work with a partner. Choose a paragraph from the reading. Identify the words and phrases you do not know or have trouble pronouncing. Look up the difficult words in a dictionary.

Take turns pronouncing the words and phrases with your partner. If necessary, ask your teacher to model the correct pronunciation. Then take turns reading the paragraph aloud. Give each other feedback on your reading.

➤ EXTENSION

Workbook Page 133

▲ Huge flocks of passenger pigeons used to fill the sky.

Utilize Endangered species are kinds of animals that are in danger of becoming extinct. Learn more about how people around the world are working to protect endangered species. Use encyclopedias, reference books, and reliable websites. Copy the chart below into your notebook. Use it to organize the information you find by writing your notes in the columns. Share your findings with the class.

Ways to Protect Endangered Animals			
Placing Animals in Preserves	Protecting Habitats	Breeding Animals	Passing Protective Laws

Grammar

Complex Sentences with Subordinating Conjunctions

A complex sentence has a main, or independent, clause and one or more subordinate, or dependent, clauses. A subordinate clause "depends" on a main clause. A subordinate clause has a subject and a verb, but it is not a complete sentence. It must be attached to a main clause.

A subordinating conjunction, such as *when*, joins a subordinate clause to a main clause. A subordinate clause can come before or after the main clause. If it comes before the main clause, use a comma after the subordinate clause.

main clause	subordinate clause
A species is lost forever	**when it becomes extinct**.

subordinate clause	main clause
When a species becomes extinct,	it is lost forever.

Practice

Workbook
Page 134

Work with a partner. In your notebook, rewrite the sentences below, switching clauses. Remember to use correct punctuation.

Example: When it began to rain, we went inside.
          We went inside when it began to rain.

1. He works quickly when he has to.
2. When he was in New York, Bob stayed with us.
3. When I saw the statistics, I was surprised.
4. She was afraid of dogs when she was a child.
5. We called you when we were in town.

Apply
Work with a partner. Write three clauses that begin with *when* in your notebook. Take turns finishing each other's clauses.

Grammar **SKILL**

Make sure that all clauses in your writing have a subject and a verb.

✔ GRAMMAR CHECK

What punctuation follows a **subordinate clause** *when it begins a sentence?*

Subordinating Conjunctions with Adverb Clauses

Grammar SKILL

When, *while*, *after*, and *before* show time; *if* shows a condition; *although* shows a contrast; and *because* shows a reason.

As you have learned, a subordinating conjunction introduces a subordinate clause. Often the subordinate clause is an adverb clause. An adverb clause answers the question *Why? When?* or *How?*

Main Clause	Subordinate (Adverb) Clause
Bird experts wanted more proof	**although** they had a videotape.
The ivorybill began to disappear	**because** loggers cut down forests.
The parakeets flew overhead	**while** the farmers shot them.
We can save ivorybills	**if** we cut down more trees.
Experts believed birds existed	**after** they heard the recording.
There were many Carolina parakeets	**before** settlers cleared trees.

Remember that a subordinate clause must always be attached to a main clause. Use a comma after the subordinate clause when it begins a sentence.

Practice  Workbook Page 135

Work with a partner. Copy the sentences into your notebook. Choose the best subordinating conjunction to complete the adverb clause in each sentence.

Example: We stayed (while / after / (although)) the movie was boring.

1. (After / Because / If) we ate dinner, we went shopping.
2. Be sure to read over your tests (if / because / before) you hand them in.
3. (Although / While / If) you want me to call, give me your number.
4. (Before / Because / If) there was a lot of traffic, I was late.
5. Allie phoned (because / if / while) we were talking.

Apply

Work with a partner. Take turns reading the sentences in the chart above, switching the clauses so the subordinate clauses come first.

Writing

Write a Cause-and-Effect Paragraph

You have learned that expository writing presents information. In expository writing, a writer often needs to explain causes and effects. A cause is the reason something happens. An effect is the result of the cause. Writers sometimes use words such as *because, therefore,* and *as a result* to signal cause-and-effect relationships.

> **Writing Prompt**
>
> Write a cause-and-effect paragraph that explains why the ivory-billed woodpecker was nearly wiped out. Show how the causes and effects of this situation are related. Include subordinating conjunctions such as *because* and *so* to signal a cause-and-effect relationship.

1 PREWRITE Reread *Going, Going, Gone?* and *Ivory-Billed Woodpeckers Make Noise.*

- Think about the activities that caused the ivory-billed woodpecker almost to become extinct.

- Ask yourself what specific effects these activities had.

- List your ideas in a graphic organizer. **Workbook Page 136**

A student named Tamar used this graphic organizer. Her assignment was to write about why the passenger pigeon has become extinct.

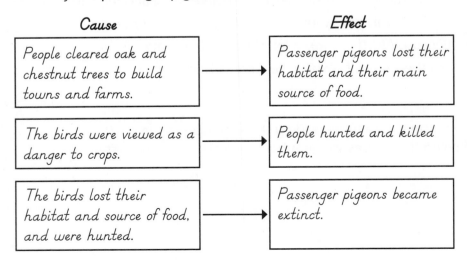

Cause	Effect
People cleared oak and chestnut trees to build towns and farms.	Passenger pigeons lost their habitat and their main source of food.
The birds were viewed as a danger to crops.	People hunted and killed them.
The birds lost their habitat and source of food, and were hunted.	Passenger pigeons became extinct.

2 **DRAFT** Use your organizer to help you write a first draft.

- Remember to state cause-and-effect relationships clearly.
- Use words and phrases such as *because, because of, therefore,* and *so* to signal cause-and-effect relationships.
- Use content-based words and other newly acquired vocabulary correctly.

3 **REVISE** Read over your draft. Look for places where the writing is unclear or needs improvement. Use the Writing Checklist to help you identify problems. Then revise your draft, using the editing and proofreading marks listed on page 456.

4 **EDIT** Check your work for errors in grammar, usage, mechanics, and spelling. Trade papers with a partner to obtain feedback. Use the Peer Review Checklist on Workbook page 136. Edit your final draft in response to feedback from your partner and your teacher.

5 **PUBLISH** Prepare a clean copy of your final draft. Share your expository paragraph with the class. Save your work. You'll need to refer to it in the Writing Workshop at the end of the unit.

Here is Tamar's cause-and-effect paragraph. Notice how she accurately uses the content-based words *extinct* and *habitat*.

Writing Checklist

WORD CHOICE:
☑ I used words such as *because* and *so* to accurately signal cause-and-effect relationships.

SENTENCE FLUENCY:
☑ I used a variety of sentence lengths and patterns.

Tamar Honig

What Happened to the Passenger Pigeon?

At one time, passenger pigeons flew in abundance. Now, they can no longer be found because of human actions. These birds, native to the eastern United States, became extinct in the early 1900s. Several factors caused their extinction. The birds lost their habitat because people cleared a great number of oak and eastern chestnut trees to build towns and farms. In doing so, people wiped out the bird's main source of food. The birds were also viewed as a danger to crops, so people killed them. In addition, passenger pigeons were hunted for food. As a result of these causes, their population gradually decreased until fewer and fewer were left. The last passenger pigeon died in the Cincinnati Zoological Garden in 1914.

What You Will Learn

Reading

■ Vocabulary building: *Literary terms, word study*

■ Reading strategy: *Identify author's purpose*

■ Text type: *Literature (fable and myth)*

Grammar

Adverbs of manner; Placement of adverbs of manner

Writing

Write to compare and contrast

▶ 🔍 **THE BIG QUESTION**

What do we learn through winning and losing? What can ancient stories teach us about winning and losing? Every culture has stories that teach a lesson. Many of these stories have animal characters that talk, think, and act as if they were human. You may know the story "The Grasshopper and the Ant." Who is the winner in this story?

All summer long, Grasshopper relaxed, chirping and singing all day. Ant went by carrying an ear of corn to her nest. "Why work so hard?" Grasshopper said to Ant. "It's summer. Come and relax with me." "I can't," Ant replied. "I'm preparing my nest for winter." Grasshopper laughed and began singing again. "Why worry about winter? We have plenty to eat." When winter came, Grasshopper had nothing to eat and was dying of hunger. He watched the ants eating the food they had gathered in summer. Then Grasshopper realized: It is best to prepare for the future in the present.

Work with a partner. Discuss stories you know that teach a lesson or have animal characters that act like human beings. Compare and contrast them.

▶ **BUILD BACKGROUND**

Almost every culture in the world has fables and myths. These stories are traditionally passed down from one generation to the next. They are wonderful to listen to or read. They often contain wise messages and advice.

"The Hare and the Tortoise" is a fable from ancient Greece about a race between two animals. The main characters are very different from each other. Their character traits lead one to victory and the other to defeat.

"Orpheus and Eurydice" is a myth that is also from ancient Greece. Like many myths, it tells a story and explains how something in nature came into existence.

PACE YOURSELF

◀ According to the road sign, what lesson does the fable "The Hare and the Tortoise" teach?

► VOCABULARY

Learn Literary Words

A **fable** is a brief story that teaches a lesson called a **moral**. The moral is sometimes stated at the end of the fable in a short sentence. At other times, the moral is implied. You, the reader, must figure it out yourself. You may have heard the word *proverb*. The morals at the ends of fables are like proverbs, or short statements of advice. Here are the titles of two other fables and the morals they teach.

Fable	Moral
"The Lion and the Mouse"	A little friend can be a big help.
"The Wolf in Sheep's Clothing"	Don't be fooled by outward appearances.

As you learned earlier, animal characters in a fable talk and act like human beings. When writers create animal characters that have human traits, this is called **personification**. Most fables, such as the one you are about to read, contain examples of personification.

A **myth** is a story from long ago that has been passed on by word of mouth. Myths often try to explain cultural beliefs and why certain things occur in the natural world, such as thunder and lightning. Many myths also tell stories about the actions of gods and heroes.

▲ The little mouse was a big help to the trapped lion.

Place	Myth	What It Explains
Greece	"Poseidon, the God of the Sea"	earthquakes, shipwrecks, storms
Hawaii	"Pele, Goddess of Fire"	fire and volcanoes

Practice

Workbook
Page 137

Work with a partner to discuss these morals and proverbs. Explain what each one means to you. Write your explanations in your notebook.

1. Absence makes the heart grow fonder.
2. Look before you leap.
3. Evil wishes, like chickens, come home to roost.
4. Little by little does the trick.

Listening and Speaking: Academic Words

Study the red words and their meanings. You will find these words useful when talking and writing about literature. Write each word and its meaning in your notebook, then say the words aloud with a partner. After you read "The Hare and the Tortoise" and "Orpheus and Eurydice," try to use these words to respond to the text.

Academic Words

define
instruct
objective
style

define = show or describe what something is or means	One way to **define** a word is to use a synonym, another word that has the same meaning.
instruct = teach someone or show him or her how to do something	The teacher planned to **instruct** the class on how to write a fable. His outline helped him teach the lesson.
objective = something that you are working hard to achieve	The author's **objective** was to entertain. She wanted readers to enjoy the story.
style = a way of doing, making, or painting something that is typical of a particular period	The artist who drew pictures for the fable had a good **style**. He drew funny, colorful characters.

Audio

Practice  **Workbook** Page 138

Work with a partner to answer the questions. Try to include the red word in your answer. Write the sentences in your notebook.

1. What would you say if you were asked to define what a fable is?
2. Who would you ask to instruct you in how to write a short story?
3. What would be your objective if you were running in a race?
4. What kind of writing style do you like best?

This woman is dressed in the style of the Hawaiian goddess Pele. ▶

Word Study: Spellings for r-Controlled Vowels

When a vowel is followed by an r, the vowel stands for a special sound, called an r-controlled vowel. The letters er, ir, and ur all stand for the same r-controlled vowel sound. It is the /ər/ sound you hear in her, bird, and hurt. The letters ar stand for the r-controlled vowel sound you hear in car. The letters or stand for the r-controlled vowel sound you hear in for.

▲ This bird is perching on a fern.

/är/ as in car	/ər/ as in her	/ər/ as in bird	/ôr/ as in for	/ər/ as in hurt
start	fern	third	horse	turn
dark	certain	first	tortoise	burst

Practice  Workbook Page 139

Work with a partner. Copy the chart above into your notebook. Sort the words from the box below by their sound-spelling and add them to the chart. Then add other words with r-controlled vowels.

artist	corner	curve	nerve	short
circle	curled	large	person	thirst

READING STRATEGY | IDENTIFY AUTHOR'S PURPOSE

Identifying an author's purpose (or reason for writing) can make you a better reader because you understand *why* the author wrote the text. Authors can choose to write to inform, to entertain, or to persuade. Sometimes an author has more than one purpose for writing. To identify an author's purpose, ask yourself these questions:

- Is this entertaining? Am I enjoying reading it?
- Am I learning new information? Is something being explained?
- Is the author trying to persuade me about something?

As you read "The Hare and the Tortoise" and "Orpheus and Eurydice," identify the author's purpose.

 Workbook Page 140

Set a purpose for reading Is speed the most important thing in a race? How does the night sky remind us of Orpheus and his loss? Read the classic fable and myth to answer these questions.

The Hare and the Tortoise

Aesop

On a hot, sunny day, Hare saw Tortoise **plodding** along on the road. Hare **teased** Tortoise because she was walking so slowly.

Tortoise laughed. "You can tease me if you like, but I bet I can get to the end of the field before you can. Do you want to race?"

Hare agreed, thinking that he could easily win. He ran off. Tortoise plodded **steadily** after him.

Before long, Hare began to feel hot and tired. "I'll take a short **nap**," he thought. "If Tortoise passes me, I can **catch up to** her." Hare lay down and fell asleep.

Tortoise plodded on steadily, one foot after another.

The day was hot. Hare slept and slept in the heat. He slept for a longer time than he wanted. And Tortoise plodded on, slowly and steadily.

Finally, Hare woke up. He had slept longer than he wanted, but he still felt **confident** that he could reach the **finish line** before Tortoise.

He looked around. Tortoise was nowhere in sight. "Ha! Tortoise isn't even here yet!" he thought.

Hare started to run again. He leaped easily over roots and rocks. As he ran around the last corner and stopped to rest, he was amazed to see Tortoise, still plodding steadily on, one foot after another, nearer and nearer the finish line.

Now Hare ran as fast as he could. He almost flew! But it was too late. He threw himself over the finish line, but Tortoise was there first.

"So what do you say?" asked Tortoise. But Hare was too tired to answer.

MORAL: Slow and steady wins the race.

---

plodding, walking slowly
teased, made jokes and laughed at in order to embarrass
steadily, moving in a continuous, gradual way
nap, short sleep
catch up to, come from behind and reach by going fast
confident, sure
finish line, line at which a race ends

✔ **LITERARY CHECK**

How might the **moral** *of this fable apply to other areas of life besides a race?*

ABOUT THE **AUTHOR**

Aesop was a slave in ancient Greece. He was a great storyteller. In many of his fables, Aesop uses personification to teach people lessons. Some historians believe that Aesop gained his freedom because of his stories. His fables are still popular today.

BEFORE YOU GO ON

1. What kind of character is Hare? Describe Hare's traits.

2. What is Tortoise like? How is she different from Hare?

On Your Own
Who did you want to win the race? Why?

▲ Orpheus leading Eurydice

ORPHEUS AND EURYDICE

In ancient times, no one played more beautiful music or sang more lovely songs than Orpheus. The god **Apollo** gave Orpheus a **lyre** made out of a turtle shell. When Orpheus played on the lyre and sang, everyone—gods, humans, and wild creatures—stopped and listened. The trees and stones danced. Even the rivers stopped flowing to listen to his song.

Orpheus was married to a **wood nymph** named Eurydice. He loved her more than anything else in the world. One day Eurydice was running across a meadow, and failed to notice a poisonous snake. The snake bit her ankle, and she died. Orpheus was left **grief-stricken** and alone. From that time on, Orpheus played such sad songs that gods, nymphs—anyone

> ✔ **LITERARY CHECK**
> *What examples of **personification** can you find in the first paragraph?*

Apollo, Greek god of the sun, medicine, poetry, music, and prophecy
lyre, musical instrument with strings across a U-shaped frame, used especially in ancient Greece
wood nymph, spirit of nature who, according to ancient Greek and Roman stories, appeared as a young girl living in trees, mountains, and streams
grief-stricken, feeling very sad because of something that has happened

who heard the music—felt sorry for him. Soon, Orpheus could not bear his grief any longer. He decided to travel to the Underworld to find his beloved Eurydice. The god Hades and his wife Persephone ruled this underground kingdom of the dead.

As Orpheus came near the secret cave that led to the Underworld, he grew hopeful. He whispered to himself, "I will play such lovely songs that maybe Hades himself will return Eurydice to me."

A fierce three-headed guard dog, called Cerberus, stood in front of the entrance to the cave. Orpheus was determined to find Eurydice. He did not turn back. He played on his lyre until Cerberus fell fast asleep, letting him pass. Next, Orpheus came to the river Styx. Here, the boatman Charon **ferries** dead souls to the Underworld. At first, Charon refused to take Orpheus across the water. But when he heard the lovely music Orpheus made, he was **entranced** and ferried Orpheus to the other side.

At last, Orpheus entered the Underworld and stood before Hades and Persephone. "I beg you, please, let Eurydice come back with me," Orpheus pleaded. The Lord of the Underworld said, "No. I cannot return her to you."

Bold Orpheus did not give up. He played **passionately** on his lyre. Hades softened, and Persephone was moved to tears. Suddenly, the Lord of the Underworld understood Orpheus's grief.

"I will let Eurydice go," Hades said, "on one **condition**. You cannot turn around to look back at her until you reach the light of the living world above."

Orpheus agreed. Eurydice followed Orpheus up the steep path out of the Underworld. They had almost reached the cave entrance, when Orpheus was overwhelmed by a desire to see his wife's face. He glanced back and she cried out. Then Eurydice vanished into the mist. She was caught in the Underworld forever.

Orpheus was **desolate** and remained so for the rest of his life. When he died, the gods hung his lyre in the night sky. To this day, if you look at the night sky, you can see the **constellation** called Lyra. It is a reminder of the sad story of Orpheus and Eurydice.

---

ferries, carries a short distance from one place to another in a boat
entranced, focused so much on something that other things go unnoticed
passionately, with very strong feeling
condition, something that is stated in an agreement that must be done
desolate, very sad and lonely
constellation, group of stars that forms a particular pattern and has a name

▲ The body of a lyre was sometimes made out of a turtle shell.

✔ **LITERARY CHECK**
What aspect of nature does the myth of Orpheus explain?

BEFORE YOU GO ON

1 What great skill does Orpheus have?

2 What is the Underworld? What is the **objective** of Orpheus's trip there?

💡 **On Your Own**
Why is Orpheus desolate at the end of the story?

Reading 3 **265**

Review and Practice

► READER'S THEATER

Audio

Act out this scene between Hare and Tortoise.

Hare: Everyone knows that I am the fastest animal in the forest. No one can run as fast as I can. That's why they call me Speedy.

Tortoise: You think you are so fast. You just like to brag.

Hare: Well, how about having a race to prove that I am the fastest animal of all? I can beat anyone. I can certainly beat you. You are such a slowpoke.

Tortoise: Okay, let's race. But I wouldn't be so sure I'd win if I were you. I may not be so fast, but I am steady.

Hare: Ha! Steady doesn't matter at all. Speed is the only important thing in a race.

Tortoise: We'll just see about that. Let's get some friends to watch us and time us.

Hare: I'll ask Mouse to time us. He's good at keeping time because he likes to run up and down clocks.

Tortoise: Here we go! Let the steadiest animal win!

Hare: Yes, here we go! Let the fastest animal win!

> **Speaking SKILL**
>
> Speak naturally and with feeling. Try to convey the humor of the situation with your voice.

► COMPREHENSION

Workbook Page 141

▲ Hare and Tortoise at the starting line

Recall

1. What is the moral of the fable "The Hare and the Tortoise"?

2. What instrument does Orpheus play in the myth "Orpheus and Eurydice"? Who gave it to him?

Comprehend

3. Why does Hare take a nap and sleep longer than he planned to?

4. How does Orpheus use his music to find Eurydice in the Underworld? What words does the author use to describe the **style** of his music?

Analyze

5. Why does Hare lose the race? Why do you think that Aesop created a character like Hare?

6. Why do you think that Orpheus was unable to obey the instructions he received from Hades?

Connect

7. Why are fables a good way to instruct people on important lessons in life?

8. Why do all cultures have myths that try to explain aspects of nature?

► DISCUSSION

Discuss in pairs or small groups.

1. How does Aesop use personification in "The Hare and the Tortoise"?

2. What did you learn about loss from reading "Orpheus and Eurydice"?

3. How are the fable and myth you read similar? How are they different?

Q **What do we learn through winning and losing?** Why do you think that winning and losing are often themes in traditional stories, such as myths and fables? How are winning and losing experiences that everyone can relate to?

► RESPONSE TO LITERATURE

Workbook
Page 141

Utilize Write a brief fable of your own. Use animals as your main characters and give them human traits. Be sure to use dialogue and personification to make your story lively and appealing.

When you are done writing, read your fable to a small group of classmates. Don't read the moral. See whether your friends can identify the moral on their own.

Orpheus and Eurydice with the messenger of the gods, who guided dead souls to the Underworld ►

Grammar

Adverbs of Manner

An adverb describes a verb, an adjective, or another adverb. Many adverbs answer the question *How?* These are called adverbs of manner. They are used only to describe verbs. Form adverbs of manner by adding -*ly* to an adjective. For example, the adjective *slow* becomes the adverb *slowly*.

Hare teased Tortoise because she was walking **slowly**.	

Follow these spelling rules when forming adverbs of manner.

Rule	Adjective	Adverb
Change -*y* to -*i*	eas**y**	He leaped **easily** over roots and rocks.
Double final consonant	fearfu**l**	Orpheus **fearfully** looked back.
Drop final -*le*	possib**le**	Hare couldn't **possibly** win.
Add -*ally* if ends in -*ic*	trag**ic**	**Tragically**, Orpheus lost Eurydice.

Practice
Workbook Page 142

Work with a partner. Copy the sentences below into your notebook. Complete each sentence with the correct form of the adverb, using the adjective in parentheses.

Example: We walked *quickly* (quick) to the car.

1. The dog _____ (hungry) ate his dinner.
2. Saul plays the piano _____ (beautiful).
3. He **defined** his position _____ (scientific).
4. Josie speaks French _____ (confident)
5. We'll _____ (probable) meet you at the restaurant.

Apply
Work with a partner. Find some adjectives in the reading. Use a dictionary to find the adverb form of each one.

Placement of Adverbs of Manner

An adverb, unlike an adjective, can be placed in many places in a sentence.

After the verb	Tortoise plodded **steadily** after him.
Before the verb	He **sadly** played his lyre.
Between an auxiliary and main verb	Hare agreed, thinking that he could **easily** win.
At the beginning of a sentence or clause	**Suddenly**, he understood Orpheus's grief.
At the end of a sentence or clause	He played on his lyre **passionately**.

Never put an adverb between the verb and the object.

Tortoise crossed the finish line **slowly**.
NOT Tortoise crossed slowly the finish line.

Practice  Workbook Page 143

Work with a partner. Copy the sentences into your notebook. Circle the adverbs. Then rewrite each sentence, moving the adverb to a different place.

Example: (Quietly) he opened the door.

He quietly opened the door.

1. Lilly joyfully opened her presents.
2. The wind blew gently.
3. We walked quickly to the shop.
4. Sally probably will go to Egypt.
5. Gene tapped his fingers nervously.

Apply

Work with a partner. Take turns reading the sentences in the charts above, moving the adverbs to different places.

Writing

Ongoing Writing Skills Practice

Write a Compare-and-Contrast Paragraph

You have learned that expository writing presents information. One type of expository writing explains a topic by comparing and contrasting information. When you compare, you tell how two people, places, events, things, or ideas are alike. When you contrast, you tell how they are different.

> **Writing Prompt**
>
> Write two paragraphs that compare and contrast two people or things. Tell how the two people or things are alike in the first paragraph and how they are different in the second paragraph. Use words such as *similar, too,* and *also* to signal similarities. Use words such as *however* and *although* to signal differences. Be sure to use adverbs of manner correctly.

1 PREWRITE Begin by choosing a story to tell.

- Think about two people or things with clear similarities and differences.

- Ask yourself how these two people or things are alike, and how they are different.

- List your ideas in a graphic organizer.

Workbook Page 144

A student named Wendy used a Venn diagram to compare and contrast "The Hare and the Tortoise" with "Orpheus and Eurydice."

Topic A *"The Hare and the Tortoise"*   Topic B *"Orpheus and Eurydice"*

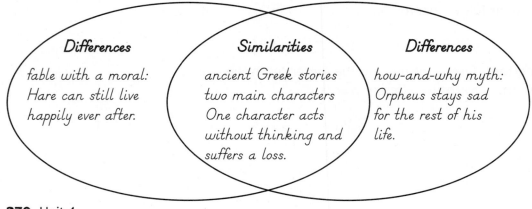

Differences

fable with a moral: Hare can still live happily ever after.

Similarities

ancient Greek stories
two main characters
One character acts without thinking and suffers a loss.

Differences

how-and-why myth: Orpheus stays sad for the rest of his life.

2 DRAFT Use your organizer to help you write a first draft.

- Remember to compare information in the first paragraph.

- Remember to contrast information in the second paragraph.

- Be sure to use adverbs of manner correctly.

3 REVISE Read over your draft. Look for places where the writing is unclear or needs improvement. Use the Writing Checklist to help you identify problems. Then revise your draft, using the editing and proofreading marks listed on page 456.

4 EDIT Check your work for errors in grammar, usage, mechanics, and spelling. Trade papers with a partner to obtain feedback. Use the Peer Review Checklist on Workbook page 144. Edit your final draft in response to feedback from your partner and your teacher.

5 PUBLISH Prepare a clean copy of your final draft. Share your expository paragraph with the class. Save your work. You'll need to refer to it in the Writing Workshop at the end of the unit.

Here is Wendy's compare-and-and contrast paragraph. Notice how she presents similarities in the first paragraph, and differences in the second.

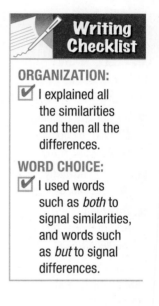

Writing Checklist

ORGANIZATION:
☑ I explained all the similarities and then all the differences.

WORD CHOICE:
☑ I used words such as *both* to signal similarities, and words such as *but* to signal differences.

Wendy Willner

"The Hare and the Tortoise" and "Orpheus and Eurydice"

The fable by Aesop and the myth of Orpheus have several similarities. First, they are both ancient Greek stories about a series of events that occur between two main characters. In each story, one character acts without thinking. Hare does not think deeply before lazily napping. Orpheus does not think when he carelessly looks back at Eurydice. Both characters suffer a loss because of their mistakes.

There are also differences between the two stories. "The Hare and the Tortoise" is a fable with a moral: Slow and steady wins the race. "Orpheus and Eurydice" is a how-and-why myth that explains how Lyra became a constellation. Each story has a very different ending, too. Hare may have lost the race but can still live happily ever after. Orpheus stays madly in love with Eurydice, so he is sad for the rest of his life.

Prepare to Read

What You Will Learn

Reading
- Vocabulary building: *Context, dictionary skills, word study*
- Reading strategy: *Ask questions*
- Text type: *Informational text (social studies)*

Grammar
Past perfect; Past perfect and simple past

Writing
Write a newspaper article

➤ 🔘 THE BIG QUESTION

What do we learn through winning and losing? What are the qualities of a good athlete? What are some traits that most award-winning athletes have in common? Athletes need more than skill to become winners.

Work with a partner. Look at the events listed below. How do you win each activity? Use your prior knowledge to complete the chart. When you are finished, share your ideas with the class.

LEARNING STRATEGY

Use your prior knowledge. Relating what you already know to a new topic will make it easier to understand new meanings in English.

Activity	How to Win
Spelling bee	Spell each word correctly.
Game of chess	
Soccer game	
Marathon race	

➤ BUILD BACKGROUND

▼ Cycling is a popular sport.

In **"The Biggest Winner of All,"** you will read about the cyclist Lance Armstrong. A great athlete, he triumphed on the race course, but his most important victory occurred when he defeated cancer.

The article explains how Armstrong recognized that fighting a disease was more difficult than training for a race. Though the odds were against him, he went on to win the most prestigious cycling race of all—the Tour de France.

➤ VOCABULARY

Listening and Speaking: Key Words

Read aloud and listen to these sentences with a partner. Use the context to figure out the meaning of the highlighted words. Use a dictionary to check your answers. Then write each word and its meaning in your notebook.

1. We studied cancer in science class.
2. Patients in chemotherapy often feel very sick.
3. Cycling is a popular sport in France.
4. The triathlon competition was grueling for the athletes.
5. A Nobel Prize is a prestigious award.
6. When Keesha competed in the triathlon, she liked cycling better than swimming and running.

Key Words

cancer
chemotherapy
cycling
grueling
prestigious
triathlon

Practice

 Workbook Page 145

Write the sentences in your notebook. Choose a key word from the box above to complete each sentence. Then take turns reading the sentences aloud with a partner.

1. The doctor decided that _____ was the best treatment for his cancer.
2. When they went _____ they rode their bikes through the mountains.
3. A _____ consists of swimming, biking, and running.
4. Each year, doctors develop better treatments for _____.
5. Because the Tour de France is so long and difficult, it can be _____.
6. Winning the most admired and important race of all is very _____.

Racing requires endurance. ▶

Listening and Speaking: Academic Words

Study the red words and their meanings. You will find these words useful when talking and writing about informational texts. Write each word and its meaning in your notebook, then say the words aloud with a partner. After you read "The Biggest Winner of All," try to use these words to respond to the text.

Academic Words

element
focus
positive
require

Audio

element = one part of a plan, system, piece of writing, and so on	⇨	Endurance is an important **element** in cycling.
focus = give all your attention to a particular person or thing	⇨	Cyclists must **focus** on the course to avoid accidents with other cyclists.
positive = good or useful	⇨	A good attitude can have a **positive** effect on a competitor in a race.
require = need or must have	⇨	Cyclists **require** physical strength, endurance, and coordination to compete.

Audio

Practice  Workbook Page 146

Work with a partner to answer these questions. Try to include the red word in your answer. Write the sentences in your notebook.

1. What are the three elements of a triathlon?
2. What should a cyclist focus on when competing in a race?
3. Why is a positive attitude helpful when competing in a race?
4. What would a cyclist require to compete in a race?

◀ Swimming is one part of a triathlon.

Word Study: Multiple-Meaning Words

LEARNING STRATEGY

Compare and contrast grade-level vocabulary. You will better remember new words and their meanings by identifying how they are similar to and different from others.

Many English words have more than one meaning. You must figure out which meaning fits the particular context. First, look for any clues to the meaning in the words and sentences surrounding the word. Also, identify the word's part of speech. It may be an important clue to the correct meaning. If you still need help, look up the word in a dictionary. Compare and contrast the words in the chart below.

Sentence	Part of Speech	Word and Meaning
She will **train** for the competition every day.	Verb	**train:** to prepare for a sports event especially by exercising
He saw the **train** jump the track.	Noun	**train:** a connected line of railroad cars
Because there has been so much rain, the **foundation** sank into the ground.	Noun	**foundation:** the base of a building
The **foundation** gave money to help the children go to camp.	Noun	**foundation:** an organization that collects money for a cause
Jane asked if I could **record** the time for the race.	Verb	**record:** to write down information
He won the world's **record** for running.	Noun	**record:** a unique achievement

Practice
Workbook
Page 147

Work with a partner to explore the different meanings of these words: *finish, race, native, award,* and *ride.* Start by looking up each word in a dictionary. Then use each word in two sentences to show two of the word's meanings. Write the sentences in your notebook.

READING STRATEGY ASK QUESTIONS

Asking questions makes you a better reader because you get more information from the text. The five questions you should ask are *Who? Where? When? What?* and *Why?* These questions are sometimes called the 5Ws. They focus on people, places, time, events, and reasons. To ask questions, follow these steps:

- Read a paragraph. Stop and ask yourself one of the five questions.
- Now try to answer the questions from what you've learned in the text.
- Read on and see if your answer was correct. Then ask more questions.

As you read "The Biggest Winner of All," remember to ask yourself the 5Ws.
Workbook
Page 148

Set a purpose for reading What was the most important win of Lance Armstrong's career? Read to find out how he won a battle more challenging than any race. In what ways does Lance continue his fight?

The BIGGEST WINNER of ALL

Audio

Anyone who plays sports knows how important it is to win. Being first is a good thing. All your hard work is recognized. You may get a **trophy,** or at the very least, a ribbon. Think about having all eyes on you as you accept your prize. That's a great feeling. Your picture may even appear in the newspaper. You're the envy of all your friends. If you've broken a record, people will talk about it for a long time.

For one **athlete,** the biggest win of all had nothing to do with sports. Sure, this athlete has broken many records. He's won numerous awards and prizes. His name has appeared in newspapers and magazines hundreds or even thousands of times. You've probably seen him on television. He even has his own official website.

His toughest opponent wasn't another athlete, though. It was something that's even harder to fight. It was a disease— cancer . If you haven't guessed by now, this **famed** athlete is Lance Armstrong. He survived a battle with cancer.

> **Reading Skill**
>
> To help you understand the reading, study the title and headings. This will help you identify the most important ideas.

---

trophy, statue or cup given as a prize
athlete, a person who competes in sports
famed, well known

Lance Armstrong is a determined competitor. ▶

The Winning Begins

Lance Armstrong was born in Plano, Texas. His mother encouraged him to do his best. When Lance was just a little boy, his mom recognized his **talent.** He was strong, **coordinated,** and determined—the elements of a good athlete. By the time he was just thirteen years old, he had won the Kids Triathlon. A triathlon is a sports **competition** with three **events**: swimming (the first event), cycling (the second event), and running (the third event). The distance required for each event is based on the age of the athlete. The cycling part of the competition requires great endurance.

By the time Lance was sixteen, he had become a professional athlete. As he got older he decided to train to be a competitive cyclist. Cycling requires good coordination, because cyclists ride around corners at a fast pace. Serious cyclists must train every day. If they are serious about entering races, they must show **determination.**

---

talent, natural ability
coordinated, not awkward or clumsy
competition, game or sport with a winner
events, activities
determination, quality of trying to do something even when it is difficult

▲ Cyclists need the right equipment in order to stay safe.

BEFORE YOU GO ON

1 What qualities did Lance show as a young child?

2 What event did Lance win at the age of thirteen? What were the elements of that competition?

On Your Own
What types of sports do you like to play? What skills do you need to play those sports?

Reading 4 **277**

A Dangerous Setback

Lance worked hard and earned a place on the U.S. Olympic Team. It seemed as if he had everything he had ever dreamed of. Then, Lance learned that he had cancer. His doctor told him that without treatment, he would die. Even with treatment, he had less than a 50 percent chance to live.

His Biggest Challenge

Lance was determined to fight cancer in much the same way that he would train for a competition. During the repeating pattern of treatments, called chemotherapy, he continued to exercise. He maintained a positive attitude. It was harder than any cycling competition, but Lance was determined to beat cancer and win the race of his life.

After his courageous fight, Lance took up another challenge. He entered one of the most prestigious races of all—the Tour de France. This grueling race requires each competitor to ride 3,600 kilometers (2,237 miles) in 22 days. The course is over plains as well as mountains.

Lance won the Tour de France. This victory inspired him to keep competing. With each win, he scored a **personal** victory for himself and a national victory for the United States. Lance won the famed Tour de France an **unbelievable** seven times!

---

personal, having to do with oneself
unbelievable, hard to imagine

The yellow shirt is worn by the leader in the Tour de France.

His Fight Continues

Lance Armstrong is a **symbol** of hope for cancer patients throughout the world. Anyone suffering from cancer can read about Lance and find inspiration. After he won his battle with cancer, he set up a foundation to help others. The foundation collects money for research to cure and prevent cancer. It also supports community organizations that help people living with this disease.

Though Lance has won his battle, he continues to help others win theirs. This **spirit** makes Lance the biggest winner of all.

symbol, something that stands for a particular idea
spirit, courage, energy, and determination

▲ Like Lance Armstrong, people everywhere stage events to raise money for cancer research.

BEFORE YOU GO ON

1 Why did Lance Armstrong need endurance to compete in the Tour de France?

2 How does Lance Armstrong inspire other cancer patients to fight for survival?

On Your Own
Why do you think Lance Armstrong's story gives hope to cancer patients?

Review and Practice

Speaking SKILL

Use notes and pictures to help you remember and explain the main ideas clearly.

► **COMPREHENSION**  **Workbook Page 149**

Recall

1. Who was first to spot Lance's talent?
2. What and where is the Tour de France?

Comprehend

3. How did Lance focus on his battle with cancer?
4. What experiences in his life enabled Lance to win the Tour de France?

Analyze

5. Why do you think Lance formed a foundation?
6. What are the elements of Lance's successes on and off the racing course?

Connect

7. What would be the most challenging event in a triathlon for you? Why?
8. What positive qualities do you have that could inspire others?

► **IN YOUR OWN WORDS**

Authors of informational texts often use clues to help readers follow the main idea. Section headings, or subheadings, are helpful clues. Imagine that you are telling a classmate about "The Biggest Winner of All." Use subheadings to help you identify the main idea of each section. Complete the chart below to help you organize your ideas. Then share your summaries with a classmate. See how they compare.

Part of the Text	Summary of Main Ideas
Introduction (no subheading)	Winning is not always about sports.
The Winning Begins	
A Dangerous Setback	
His Biggest Challenge	
His Fight Continues	

280 Unit 4

▶ DISCUSSION

Listening SKILL

If you can't hear a classmate who is speaking, you may say, "Excuse me, could you speak louder, please?"

Discuss in pairs or small groups.

1. What role did Lance's mother play in his success as an athlete?
2. Why do you think Lance decided to become a competitive cyclist? Explain.
3. How does a positive attitude help a person with any kind of a challenge? Give some specific examples.

Q What do we learn through winning and losing? Why do you think people like to hear about Lance Armstrong? What can we learn from his way of dealing with winning and losing?

▶ READ FOR FLUENCY

Reading with feeling helps make what you read more interesting. Work with a partner. Choose a paragraph from the reading. Read the paragraph. Ask each other how you felt after reading the paragraph. Did you feel happy or sad?

Take turns reading the paragraph aloud to each other with a tone of voice that represents how you felt when you read it the first time. Give each other feedback.

▶ EXTENSION

Workbook Page 149

Utilize "The Biggest Winner of All" provides a lot of information about one athlete, Lance Armstrong. Go to www.LongmanKeystone.com for links to other types of media on the topic of winning and losing in competition and life. Follow the online instructions to analyze how similar information is conveyed in different media. Study the effect that visual and sound techniques have on these messages. Do they change your reaction to the information? If so, explain how. What effect do editing, sequencing, music, and reaction shots have on the way information is delivered?

Beating cancer will make everyone a winner. ▼

Grammar

Past Perfect

Use the past perfect to describe something that happened before a specific time in the past. You can use time phrases such as *all his life* and *by then* to make reference to the past. You can also use the adverbs *already* and *finally*.

Grammar SKILL

Already can come between *had* and the past participle or at the end. *Yet* usually comes at the end.

All his life, he **had wanted** to ride.	By then, he **had** already **gotten** sick.

Form the past perfect with *had* + the past participle. For regular past participles, add *-d* or *-ed* to the base form of the verb. Other past participles are irregular. These you must memorize.

Irregular Past Participles							
be	→	been	do	→	did	sleep	→	slept
become	→	become	fall	→	fallen	stand	→	stood
catch	→	caught	let	→	let	wake	→	woken

Form the negative with *hadn't* + the past participle. Form questions in the past perfect by switching *had* and the subject. You can use the adverbs *yet* and *already* with negatives and questions in the past perfect.

✔ GRAMMAR CHECK

How do you form the negative of the past perfect?

Before 1996, Armstrong **hadn't been** sick.
Had he already **competed** in the Tour de France?   No, he **hadn't** yet.

Practice
Workbook Page 150

Work with a partner. Write the sentences in your notebook. Complete each sentence with the correct form of the past perfect using the verb in parentheses. **Example:** By September, he *had finished* (finish) his degree.

1. Min _____ already _____ (eat) by the time we got there.
2. Wes _____ (not lock) the door yet.
3. By five o'clock, she _____ (leave) already.
4. All her life, Aimee _____ (want) to go to Paris.
5. _____ they already _____ (arrive) by then?

Apply

Write down three things you did (or didn't do) this morning before nine o'clock. Discuss with a partner. **Example:** By nine o'clock, I had already . . .

Past Perfect and Simple Past

Use the past perfect and the simple past together to show two events that happened in the past. The clause in the past perfect shows the first action; the clause in the simple past shows the action that happened after that. You can use subordinating conjunctions such as *before* with the clause in the simple past and *after* with the clause in past perfect. Subordinating conjunctions connect dependent (subordinate) clauses with independent (main) clauses. You can also use time phrases such as *by the time* with the clause in the simple past.

Lance **had gotten** sick before he **set up** the foundation.
Lance **set up** the foundation after he**'d gotten** sick.
   [First, he got sick. Then he set up the foundation.]
By the time Lance **was** sixteen, he**'d started** doing sports.
   [First, he started doing sports. Then he turned sixteen.]

Practice

Workbook Page 151

Work with a partner. Rewrite the pairs of sentences using the past perfect and simple past, plus the conjunction or phrase in parentheses.

Example: First, she applied to three schools. Then they accepted her. (before)

She had applied to three schools before they accepted her.

1. First, she woke up. Then we arrived. (by the time)
2. First, he studied for hours. Then he fell asleep. (before)
3. First, she packed the car. Then she called me. (by the time)
4. First, she went to the bank. Then she went shopping. (after)
5. First, I finished my lunch. Then my brother started eating. (before)

Apply

Copy the following sentence starters into your notebook. Then complete them using the past perfect or the simple past and your own ideas. Compare with a partner.

1. By the time I got to school, . . .
2. By the time I was ten, . . .
3. Before I went to bed last night, . . .
4. After I had finished my homework, . . .

Writing

Write a Newspaper Article

You have learned that expository writing gives information and explanations. Newspaper articles are one type of expository writing. Newspaper articles tell about recent events of interest to the public. A newspaper article is introduced by a short phrase or title called a *headline*. A newspaper article always answers the questions known as the 5Ws: *Who? What? Where? When? Why?*

> **Writing Prompt**
>
> Write a newspaper article about a sports event or some other competition or game that you found exciting. Be sure to title your article with a headline. Remember to provide information that answers each of the 5Ws. Be sure to use the past perfect tense correctly.

1 **PREWRITE** Begin by choosing a topic.

- Think about an exciting competition that will interest readers.
- Ask yourself which facts about the event your article needs to include.
- List your ideas in a graphic organizer.

Workbook
Page 152

Here's a graphic organizer created by a student named Anna. She decided to write about the FIFA World Cup soccer tournament.

Who?	soccer players from 32 countries

Where?	Germany

When?	June 9 to July 9, 2006

What?	FIFA World Cup soccer tournament

Why?	To compete to be the world champions

2 **DRAFT** Use your organizer to help you write a first draft.

- Remember your purpose—to inform and explain.
- Title your article with a headline.
- Answer the 5Ws clearly and completely.

3 **REVISE** Read over your draft. Look for places where the writing is unclear or needs improvement. Use the Writing Checklist to help you identify problems. Then revise your draft, using the editing and proofreading marks listed on page 456.

4 **EDIT** Check your work for errors in grammar, usage, mechanics, and spelling. Trade papers with a partner to obtain feedback. Use the Peer Review Checklist on Workbook page 152. Edit your final draft in response to feedback from your partner and your teacher.

5 **PUBLISH** Prepare a clean copy of your final draft. Share your newspaper article with the class. Save your work. You'll need to refer to it in the Writing Workshop at the end of the unit.

Here is Anna's article about an exciting sports event. Notice that she answers the five questions: *Who? What? Where? When? Why?*

Writing Checklist

IDEAS:
☑ I included good information about an exciting event.

CONVENTIONS:
☑ I used the past perfect and simple past correctly.

Anna Espínola

The World Cup

Over the past seventy years, the FIFA World Cup tournament has brought countries together, helping them forget their differences as they play soccer and compete to be the world champions. The 2006 Men's World Cup was held in Germany, from June 9 to July 9. Out of 198 countries, 32 countries had qualified to compete in the Cup. To reach the final championship game, teams must first advance past the first round, the quarterfinals, and the semifinals. In 2006, the two finalists were France and Italy. It was a breathtaking game that remained a 0–0 tie after an hour and a half of play. When overtime ended, the teams were still tied. The teams then began a shootout of penalty kicks, the last possible way to determine the winner. In the end, Italy beat France 5–3 and the World Cup was theirs!

Link the Readings

Critical Thinking

Look back at the readings in this unit. Think about what they all have in common. They all have something to do with winning or losing. Yet they do not all have the same purpose. The purpose of one reading might be to inform, while the purpose of another might be to entertain or persuade. In addition, the content of each reading relates to winning or losing in different ways. Copy the chart into your notebook and complete it.

Title of Reading	Purpose	Big Question Link
"Casey at the Bat," "Swift Things Are Beautiful," "Buffalo Dusk"	*to entertain*	
"Going, Going, Gone?" "Ivory-Billed Woodpeckers Make Noise"		*explains what happens when a species is lost*
"The Hare and the Tortoise" "Orpheus and Eurydice"		
"The Biggest Winner of All"		

Discussion

Discuss in pairs or small groups.

- How does the author's purpose in "Ivory-Billed Woodpeckers Make Noise" differ from the author's purpose in "The Hare and the Tortoise"?

- **Q** **What do we learn through winning and losing?** Is it always important to win? What sorts of lessons can you learn from losing? Can you learn as much from winning as you can from losing? Explain.

Media Literacy & Projects

Work in pairs or small groups. Choose one of these projects.

1 Working with some classmates, define what "winning" and "losing" mean to you. Talk about what character traits it takes to be a real winner.

2 Use the Internet to research species that are in danger of becoming extinct. What is putting these species in danger? Make a poster with your findings and present it to the class.

3 Perform "The Hare and the Tortoise" as a play. Work with several classmates. First, rewrite the fable as a script. Then create simple costumes and props. Learn the lines and rehearse the play. When everyone is ready, perform the play for the class.

4 Find out more about buffaloes. Why did they almost become extinct? How did they come back? Research this topic, and write a brief report about buffaloes. Use visuals and present your report to the class. Be sure to mention your sources in your report.

Further Reading

Choose from these reading suggestions. Practice reading silently for longer periods with increased comprehension.

Moby Dick, Herman Melville
In this Penguin Reader® adaptation of the classic novel, Captain Ahab and his men hunt for Moby Dick, the most dangerous whale in the ocean.

Black Star, Bright Dawn, Scott O'Dell
When her father is injured, Bright Dawn takes his place in the Iditarod, a 1,000-mile dogsled race through Alaska's frozen wilderness. She must learn to keep going despite her fears.

Sasha Cohen: Fire on Ice: Autobiography of a Champion Figure Skater, Sasha Cohen
The much admired skater describes the hard work and challenges she faced that made her a National Champion and an Olympic silver medalist.

Put It All Together

LISTENING & SPEAKING WORKSHOP

TV Sports Report

You will explain what happened at a sports event as if you were a TV newscaster on the scene.

1 **THINK ABOUT IT** Think about the baseball game in "Casey at the Bat" and the footrace in "The Hare and the Tortoise." How would a TV sports reporter at the scene tell what happened?

Work in small groups. Discuss what kinds of sports you like to watch in person or on TV. Work together to develop a list of sports events you would like to tell about on TV. For example:

- A championship soccer match
- A World Series baseball game
- An Olympic skating competition

2 **GATHER AND ORGANIZE INFORMATION** Choose a sports event from your group's list. Write down what you would like to find out about it. Think about how a TV sports reporter would describe it. Watch a TV news show and get ideas from the sports reporters.

Research Go to the library and read newspaper articles about your sports event, or look for information about it on the Internet. If possible, watch the event on TV or in person. Take notes on the information you find. Include details that show why the event was exciting, surprising, or special.

Order Your Notes Arrange your notes in a logical way. For example, you could use a timeline to arrange them in time order, from the beginning of the event to the end. Put extra information, such as descriptive details and quotes from players, in a separate section.

Use Visuals TV sports reporters often show video clips of the events they describe. Make or find posters or other visuals to show during your report, such as drawings of team logos or photographs of the star players. Be sure your visuals can be seen from the back of the room.

Prepare a Script Use your notes to write a script for a TV sports report. Include enough details to explain what happened and to convey the excitement or other emotions felt by people at the event.

3 **PRACTICE AND PRESENT** Read your script aloud. To make your report more interesting, use a variety of grammatical structures, sentence lengths and types, and connecting words. Practice giving your sports report and showing your visuals to a friend or family member.

Deliver Your TV Sports Report Remember that a TV sports report is an informal presentation. Use appropriate language. Speak loudly enough so that everyone in the class can hear you. Say each word carefully so that it is clear. Emphasize key ideas by pausing or slowing down. Use natural hand and body movements, too. Make eye contact with the audience as you speak, and don't hide behind your script! Hold up your visuals so that everyone can see them.

4 **EVALUATE THE PRESENTATION**

A good way to improve your speaking and listening skills is to evaluate each presentation you give and hear. Use this checklist to help you judge your TV sports report and the sports reports of your classmates.

- ☑ What was the speaker's topic?
- ☑ Did the speaker clearly tell the results and other details of the sports event?
- ☑ Did the speaker provide enough details that showed why the event was exciting, surprising, or special?
- ☑ Could you hear the speaker easily?
- ☑ Did the speaker use formal or informal language? Was it appropriate?
- ☑ What suggestions do you have for improving the presentation?

Speaking SKILLS

Always face the audience (or an imaginary TV camera) when you speak. Ask if people can hear you clearly.

Pronounce names and numbers carefully. Write these important details on your visuals so that the audience can both see and hear them.

Listening SKILLS

As you listen, identify the speaker's topic. Listen for the general meaning, main ideas, and important details. After each presentation, share this information with a partner to confirm that you have understood it correctly.

Take notes as you listen. Do you understand who played and what happened in this sports event? Do you know why it was exciting or special? If not, seek clarification.

STRENGTHEN YOUR SOCIAL LANGUAGE

Sharing information with others helps to expand your English vocabulary. Go to www.LongmanKeystone.com and do the activity for this unit. This activity will help you to retell simple stories and basic information that is represented or supported by pictures.

WRITING WORKSHOP
Expository Essay

Write an Expository Essay

In this lesson you'll use your skills to write an expository essay. An expository essay gives information and explanations about a specific topic. A good expository paragraph introduces the writer's topic in the first paragraph. Two or more body paragraphs develop and explain the topic with specificity and detail. A conclusion sums up the writer's ideas in a new and interesting way.

> **Writing Prompt**
> Write a five-paragraph expository essay about a topic that interests you. Focus on the theme of winning and losing. Use a method of organization that fits the topic. For example, you might compare and contrast information or explore cause-and-effect relationships. Remember to use a variety of sentence lengths and patterns.

1 PREWRITE Review your previous work in this unit. Now brainstorm ideas for a topic that interests you. After choosing your topic, answer these questions in your notebook:

Ongoing Writing Skills Practice

- What do my readers already know about my topic?
- What do I want them to learn from reading my essay?
- List your ideas in a graphic organizer that fits your topic.

Workbook Page 153

Here's a graphic organizer created by a student named Tamar. She plans to write about why certain bird species are extinct or endangered.

Cause	Effect
Passenger Pigeon 1. Food supply destroyed by people 2. Killed for food and to protect crops	Extinct
Great Auk 1. Climate change 2. Hunted for its valuable feathers	Extinct
Whooping Crane 1. Wetlands habitat destroyed 2. Hunted for food and sport	Endangered

2 DRAFT Use your graphic organizer and the model on page 294 to help you write a first draft.

- Keep your purpose in mind—to inform and explain.

- Remember to include an introduction and conclusion.

- Present information in an order that fits your topic.

3 REVISE Read over your draft. Think about how well you have addressed questions of purpose, audience, and form. Does your essay include an introduction and conclusion? Will your topic capture readers' attention? Does your essay include good information and clear explanations?

Keep these questions in mind as you revise your draft. Use the Writing Checklist below to help you identify additional issues that may need revision. Mark your changes on your draft using the editing and proofreading marks listed on page 456.

SIX TRAITS OF WRITING CHECKLIST

☑ **IDEAS:** Does my topic focus on winning and losing?

☑ **ORGANIZATION:** Do I present information in an order that readers can easily follow?

☑ **VOICE:** Does my writing show my knowledge of the topic?

☑ **WORD CHOICE:** Do I accurately use newly acquired and content-based vocabulary?

☑ **SENTENCE FLUENCY:** Do I use simple, compound, and complex sentences?

☑ **CONVENTIONS:** Do I use verb tenses correctly?

LEARNING STRATEGY

Monitor your written language production. Using a writing checklist will help you assess your work. Evaluate your essay to make sure that your message is clear and easy to understand.

Here are the revisions Tamar plans to make to her first draft.

Extinct and Endangered Birds

It may seem that there are plenty of birds in the world, but Several bird species are endangered, and others already have becomed extinct. It is important to realize that when a bird species dies out, it's gone forever In addition, we're always in danger of losing more birds.

Revised to correct an error in grammar and improve sentence fluency.

When european explorers first came comed to this continent, passenger pigeons were abundant. Today, this species no longer exists. One reason is that People chopped down forests. In doing so, they wiped out the passenger pigeon's food supply. Also, passenger pigeons were shot, because They were viewed as a threat to crops. Huge numbers were hunted for food as well. As a result, their population decreased. Eventually, none remained.

Revised to correct an error in grammar and clarify cause- and-effect relationships.

Another extinct bird is the great auk, a flightless bird that lived in the North Atlantic. Climate change may have helped cause the great auk's extinction. During a period known as "the little ice age, the climate turned colder, so Many birds died. However, one of the most important causes of the bird's disappearance is that people hunted the great auk for its valuable feathers and rare eggs. They killed as many birds and took as many eggs as they could. Mainly because of these human activities, the species did not survive.

Revised to clarify a cause-and-effect relationship and add details.

The whooping crane, the largest bird in North America, is endangered. It has been hunted for food and also shot for sport. Wetlands, which are its habitat, often have been turned into farmlands and towns. Some of the reasons it is endangered are familiar. Collisions with power lines have killed many birds. Fortunately, the whooping crane, although endangered, still exists.

These three bird species are just a few among the many that are extinct or in danger of becoming so. If people work hard, we may be able to help prevent more birds from becoming extinct. Once a bird species becomes extinct, it has been ~~losed~~ lost forever.
sadly

Revised to improve organization.

Revised to improve word choice and correct an error in grammar.

4 **EDIT** Check your work for errors in grammar, usage, mechanics, and spelling. Then trade stories with a partner and use the Peer Review Checklist below to give each other constructive feedback. Edit your final draft in response to feedback from your partner and your teacher.

Workbook
Page 153

PEER REVIEW CHECKLIST

- ☑ Does the essay have an introduction and conclusion?
- ☑ Does it include precise words and specific examples and details?
- ☑ Does the order of information fit the topic?
- ☑ Does the writing have energy?
- ☑ Are adverbs of manner used correctly?
- ☑ What changes could be made to improve the essay?

Look at the next page to see the changes Tamar decided to make to her final draft as a result of her peer review.

Tamar Honig

Extinct and Endangered Birds

It may seem that there are plenty of birds in the world, but several bird species are endangered, and others already have become extinct. It is important to realize that when a bird species dies out, it's gone forever. In addition, we're always in danger of losing more birds.

Revised to correct an error in mechanics.

When european explorers first came to this continent, passenger pigeons were abundant. Today, this species no longer exists. One reason is that people chopped down forests to build houses, towns, and farms. In doing so, they wiped out the passenger pigeon's food supply. Also, passenger pigeons were shot because they were viewed as a threat to crops. Huge numbers were hunted for food as well. As a result, their population decreased. Eventually, none remained.

Revised to correct errors in mechanics and add detail.

Another extinct bird is the great auk, a flightless bird that lived in the North Atlantic. Climate change may have helped cause the great auk's extinction. During a period known as "the little ice age," the climate turned colder, so many birds died. However, one of the most important causes of the bird's disappearance is that people hunted the great auk for its valuable feathers and rare eggs. They killed as many birds and took as many eggs as they could. Mainly because of these human activities, the species did not survive.

Revised to correct an error in mechanics.

The whooping crane, the largest bird in North America, is endangered. Some of the reasons it is endangered are familiar. It has been hunted for food and also shot for sport. Wetlands, which are its habitat, often have been turned into farmlands and towns. Collisions with power lines have killed many birds. Fortunately, the whooping crane, although endangered, still exists.

These three bird species are just a few among the many that are extinct or in danger of becoming so. If people work hard, we may be able to help prevent more birds from becoming extinct. Once a bird species becomes extinct, it sadly has been lost forever.

5 **PUBLISH** Prepare a clean copy of your final draft. Share your story with the class.

Workbook
Page 154

Test Preparation

PRACTICE

Read the following test sample. Study the tips in the boxes. Work with a partner to complete the statement or answer the question.

Taking Tests
You will often take tests that help show what you know. Study the tips below to help you improve your test-taking skills.

The Watchful Hikers

1   One day two friends decided to hike along the Tejas Trail in Dog Canyon. Juan packed water and food. Pete carried their map and other equipment. The experienced hikers checked in at the trailhead, then set off in the early light.

2   The sun sparkled through the large maples and pines that grew along the <u>well-worn</u> trail. Years of use had made the pathway easy to follow. The men moved along at an easy pace, careful not to step on the bluebells and cardinal flowers that grew on the forest floor. They were also on the lookout for the black-tailed rattlesnake, a beautiful but deadly critter commonly seen in the park.

3   As they came to a bend in the trail, Pete spotted three huge rocks. "This is a perfect spot to have lunch and rest our feet," he said.

4   Suddenly, Juan heard a sound near the rocks. All at once, the biggest boulder moved! It wasn't a rock at all, but a large black bear! Fortunately, the bear was just as startled as the hikers were. She took off into the bushes just as Juan and Pete ran back down the trail toward home.

Tip
You can tell that this passage is fiction. Your answer choice still has to make sense.

1 In paragraph 2, <u>well-worn</u> means —

   A   much appreciated
   B   nicely trimmed
   C   full of weeds
   D   much used

2 The hikers ran away from _____.

   F   a deadly rattlesnake
   G   a black bear
   H   sore feet
   J   a bend in the trail

Tip
The correct answer to Question 2 is not clearly stated in the passage. You must make an inference based on the information in the passage.

Workbook
Pages 155–158

Visual Literacy

Smithsonian American Art Museum

BASEBALL IN AMERICA

*A*mericans love to watch and play many different sports. Baseball, basketball, hockey, and football are all very popular. In these games, one team will win and another will lose. Everyone loves a winning team, but we don't always cheer for the winner. Sometimes the losing team has played a great game. Then we might cheer for the loser, too.

Mark Sfirri, *Rejects from the Bat Factory* (1996)

Artist Mark Sfirri's ten-year-old son wanted a new baseball bat. Sfirri agreed to make him one. As he worked, Sfirri realized that he could do a lot with the wood and shape of the bat as an artist. So he made his son a regular bat first. Then he made the five bats hanging in *Rejects from the Bat Factory.*

Sfirri made his bats out of different kinds of unusual wood. A wood called curly maple has a wavy pattern of red and yellow colors in it. Zebrawood has stripes. Sfirri used a method called turning to create the bats.

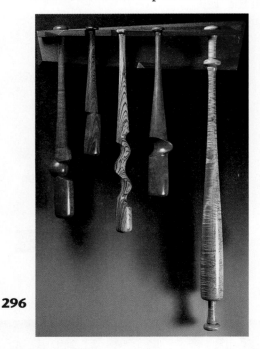

bats. Turning allows a woodworker to give pieces of wood a rounded shape by rotating them against a cutting tool. The bat on the far left still has a ball "stuck" in it. The bat fourth from the left has a dent!

Sfirri wanted to create a fun set of bats, but he also wanted to show how we often value things that aren't perfect. Sometimes a "loser" can be a real "winner."

◀ Mark Sfirri, *Rejects from the Bat Factory,* 1996, wood, 15⅜ × 36½ in., Smithsonian American Art Museum

▲ Morris Kantor, *Baseball at Night*, 1934, oil, 37 x 47¼ in., Smithsonian American Art Museum

Morris Kantor, *Baseball at Night* (1934)

Morris Kantor captures the charm of a small-town baseball game in *Baseball at Night*. The crowd fills the stands. The players in the field are ready for the next play. The pitcher steps toward the batter, and . . . .

The painting doesn't show what happens next, but you can use your imagination. Kantor puts all of the important elements in his painting: the players, the tall umpire dressed in black, the crowd, the lights that light up the field, and the warm lights from the house behind the stands. Night lights had just begun to be added to fields at this time. Now everyone is out to enjoy the game!

Both of these artists focus on the fun of team sports, where winning is just one part of a much larger story.

Discuss What You Learned

1 How do both of these artworks show the fun side of a sport like baseball?

2 What kind of artwork would you make to capture the feeling of another sport, such as basketball or soccer?

 Big Question
What would you show in a painting to illustrate the ideas of winning and losing?

Workbook
Pages 159–160

How are courage and imagination linked?

This unit is about courage and imagination. You'll read about an orphan who helps a grieving family and about a Native American who fought to keep his people free. You'll read about an effort to save burrowing owls from destruction and about a Kenyan woman who created a simple method of improving living conditions in her native country. As you read, you'll practice the literary and academic language you need to use in school.

Reading

1 Play

The Secret Garden by Frances Hodgson Burnett, adapted by David C. Jones

Reading Strategy:
Analyze text structure 1

2 Science

• "A Tree Grows in Kenya: The Story of Wangari Maathai"
• "How to Plant a Tree"

Reading Strategy:
Follow steps in a process

3 Novel

From *Hoot* by Carl Hiaasen

Reading Strategy:
Summarize

Listening and Speaking—Expository

At the end of this unit, you'll give a **how-to demonstration** that explains the steps involved in doing something.

Writing—Expository

In this unit you'll practice **expository writing**, or writing that explains a topic. You'll write four expository paragraphs and an expository essay at the end of the unit.

Quick Write

Write several sentences about a time when you used courage and imagination to solve a problem.

4 | **Social Studies**

"Between Two Worlds"

Reading Strategy:
Classify

DVD **VIEW AND RESPOND**
Watch the DVD for Unit 5 and answer the questions at
www.LongmanKeystone.com.

Prepare to Read

What You Will Learn

Reading
- Vocabulary building: *Literary terms, dictionary skills, word study*
- Reading strategy: *Analyze text structure 1*
- Text type: *Literature (play)*

Grammar
Be going to and *will*; Degrees of certainty about the future

Writing
Write a formal e-mail

► 🔍 THE BIG QUESTION

How are courage and imagination linked? Why does it take imagination to create a garden? You have to choose which plants to grow and where to plant them. You have to be able to imagine what the garden will look like after it grows and flowers.

Maybe you have seen photographs and drawings of gardens in books and magazines, or perhaps you have seen gardens in your own neighborhood. You might even have grown your own flowers, herbs, or vegetables.

Work with a partner. Use your prior knowledge to complete the chart below. Then share what you know with the class.

Why People Plant Gardens	What Plants I Like

► BUILD BACKGROUND

▲ A wild English garden

You will read an adapted version of the play **The Secret Garden**. The play is based on the novel *The Secret Garden*, written by Frances Hodgson Burnett. The book has been popular since it was first published in 1911. The story takes place in the early 1900s in the English countryside.

In the play, the actors tell the story through their dialogue and actions. When the play opens, the orphaned girl Mary Lennox has just arrived in England to live with Mr. Craven. Mary had been living in India with her parents. This is a difficult time for Mary because her parents died within days of each other. Mr. Craven was her father's best friend, so he agreed to take care of Mary. Mr. Craven has a very large house with many gardens. Mary is curious about the gardens.

► VOCABULARY

Learn Literary Words

Playwrights, or people who write plays, usually begin by setting the scene. They give important details about the time and place of each section of the play. This helps readers and actors to visualize each scene. Study this example from *The Secret Garden*. How has the writer helped you visualize the opening scene?

> Early 1900s. Bedroom in Misselthwaite Manor, England.
> Bed center; table next to it holds tray of food.

At the beginning of a play, you will also find a list of characters. Below is a list of characters from the *The Secret Garden*.

Characters		
Mary Lennox	Ben Weatherstaff	Mr. Archibald Craven
Martha Sowerby	Dickon Sowerby	Colin Craven

Stage directions are notes included in a play that tell how the play should be performed. These directions are in brackets and set in italics near the character's name. Stage directions tell actors what they should do and how they should look and act. They may also tell about the scenery and costumes. Study the stage directions below. How do they help you understand the characters and what is happening? How do they help you act out the dialogue?

> **Mary:** [*Puzzled*] How can a garden be locked?
> **Martha:** It can be if there's a high wall around it. [*She exits.*]
> **Mary:** [*Sighing*] How I wish I were back in India! [*Curtain*]

Practice

Workbook
Page 161

Take turns reading the lines above with a partner. Pay close attention to the stage directions. Act out each line, using the stage directions as your guide. Use a dictionary to look up any words that you don't know.

Listening and Speaking: Academic Words

Study the red words and their meanings. You will find these words useful when talking and writing about literature. Write each word and its meaning in your notebook, then say the words aloud with a partner. After you read *The Secret Garden*, try to use these words to respond to the text.

Academic Words
approach
convey
cooperate
drama

Audio

approach = move closer to someone or something	→	The girl wanted to **approach** the lamb, but she was afraid of coming too close to the animal.
convey = communicate a message or information, with or without using words	→	Birds **convey** their fear by flying away. Everyone understands their message.
cooperate = work with someone else to achieve something that you both want	→	When people **cooperate**, they get the job done faster.
drama = a play for the theater, television, radio, and so forth	→	The class **drama** was a big success. Everyone enjoyed watching the play.

Audio

Practice
Workbook Page 162

Work with a partner to answer the questions. Try to include the red word in your answer. Write the sentences in your notebook.

1. How would you approach a bird in a garden?
2. How do dogs and cats convey their feelings?
3. What happens when someone won't cooperate with you? What do you do?
4. What do you like about watching or acting in a drama?

Some students love to ▶
study drama and perform.

Word Study: Spelling Words with *oo*

In English, the letters *oo* can stand for either a short sound /o͝o/ or a long sound /o͞o/. For example, *The Secret Garden* has many words with the short sound of *oo*, such as *book*. It also contains words with the long sound of *oo*, such as *room*. Notice the /o͝o/ and /o͞o/ sounds and their spellings in the chart below.

oo as in *book*	*oo* as in *moon*
g**oo**d-bye	l**oo**se
t**oo**k	n**oo**n
underst**oo**d	ch**oo**se

Practice

Work with a partner. Copy the chart above into your notebook. Say a word from the chart, and ask your partner to spell it aloud. Then have your partner say the next word. Continue until you can spell all of the words correctly. Then work with your partner to spell the following words: *blooming, cook, afternoon, goodness, gloomy, wood, shook,* and *tools*. Add them to the chart under the correct heading.

READING STRATEGY | ANALYZE TEXT STRUCTURE 1

Analyzing text structure can help you understand what kind of text you're reading. It can also help you set a purpose for reading. Different kinds of writing, or genres, have different kinds of text structures. Read these descriptions to help you understand the various types of text structures:

- Stories and novels are written in sentences and paragraphs. Dialogue is enclosed within quotation marks.

- Poems are usually written in lines and groups of lines, called stanzas. The punctuation in poems may not follow the same rules as it does in other kinds of writing.

- Plays are mainly written in dialogue. The characters' names are given, followed by colons (:) and the words the speakers say. Stage directions are usually in brackets ([ ]) and set in italics. Many plays are divided into numbered scenes.

Preview the text structure of *The Secret Garden*. Describe it to a partner.

Set a purpose for reading How will certain characters' courage and imagination change life at Misselthwaite Manor? Read the play to find out.

The Secret Garden

Audio

Frances Hodgson Burnett,
adapted by David C. Jones

In this classic play, the orphaned girl Mary Lennox comes from India to live at Misselthwaite Manor, England. She finds the place gloomy until she hears about a long-lost garden. Then she has a wonderful idea.

> **CHARACTERS**
> **MARY LENNOX**
> **MARTHA SOWERBY**
> **BEN WEATHERSTAFF**
> **DICKON SOWERBY**
> **MR. ARCHIBALD CRAVEN**
> **COLIN CRAVEN**

Scene 1

Time: Early 1900s.

Setting: Bedroom in Misselthwaite Manor, England. Bed center; table next to it holds tray of food.

At rise: Mary is alone, looking around.

MARY: What a **dreary** place. I know I'm not going to like it here. [*Martha enters.*]

MARTHA: Good afternoon, miss.

MARY: [*Imperiously*] Good afternoon. Are you going to be my **servant**?

MARTHA: I'm to do a bit of cleaning up and bring you your food.

MARY: I don't like English food.

MARTHA: [*Sharply*] I've nine little brothers and sisters who would be glad to eat this food in a minute.

MARY: [*Surprised*] My goodness! You have nine brothers and sisters?

---

dreary, very dull and causing sadness
servant, someone paid to clean and cook for someone else

MARTHA: Yes. We have to take care of each other since Father died. Thank goodness for Dickon. He's a big help.

MARY: Who's Dickon?

MARTHA: My oldest brother. He's a rare boy. He talks to the animals, and when he plays his **pipes**, they all stop to listen. Everyone loves him. Well, I must be off now. I have a lot of work to do.

MARY: But what will I do?

MARTHA: You could go play in one of the gardens—except for the one that's locked.

MARY: [*Puzzled*] How can a garden be locked?

MARTHA: It can be if there's a high wall around it. [*She exits.*]

MARY: [*Sighing*] How I wish I were back in India! [*Curtain*]

Scene 2

Setting: *The **mansion** gardens. There are flowerbeds, bushes, etc., around the stage. Fence covered with ivy, **brambles**, etc., is **upright**.*

At rise: *Ben Weatherstaff is working with a hoe. Mary enters.*

BEN: [*Looking up*] Well, well. You must be Mistress Mary, quite **contrary**.

MARY: I am not contrary—and who are you?

BEN: I'm Ben Weatherstaff, the gardener. I've worked for Mr. Craven for many, many years.

MARY: And where's this locked garden I've heard about?

BEN: Why, you're standing next to it.

MARY: But where is the entrance?

BEN: Well, the gate is somewhere under all those brambles and ivy that have grown and covered it. It's been locked up so long.

MARY: But why was it ever locked? I never heard of such a thing.

BEN: Well, it was Mr. and Mrs. Craven's favorite spot, and they spent many a happy hour in it, reading and laughing together like two **lovebirds**. Mrs. Craven used to sit reading on a high branch of one of the big trees, but one day the branch broke and she fell to her death. After that, Mr. Craven had the gate locked, and he hasn't entered the garden since.

---

pipes, tube-shaped musical instruments, such as flutes
mansion, very large house
brambles, wild plants with thorns and berries
upright, straight up
contrary, deliberately doing or saying the opposite of what others want
lovebirds, people who show by their behavior that they love each other very much

»)) *Listening* SKILL

Follow along in your book as you listen to the Audio CD. Notice the bold words. To understand them, read the definitions at the bottom of the page. Knowing the meanings of these words will enhance and confirm your comprehension of the story.

✔ **LITERARY CHECK**
*Which two people on the **list of characters** are mentioned in the dialogue but have not yet appeared at the end of page 305?*

BEFORE YOU GO ON

1 What is Mary's first reaction to Misselthwaite Manor?

2 Who is Dickon?

On Your Own
How do most people feel when they are in an unfamiliar place far from home?

MARY: [**Resolutely**] Well, I shall find the entrance and go in there to play.

BEN: You won't be able to go in without the key.

MARY: [*Surprised*] There's a key? Where is it?

BEN: No one knows. Mr. Craven was so heartbroken he took the key one day and threw it as far as he could. No one has ever found it.

MARY: I'll find it. You'll see.

BEN: [*Wryly*] Well, good luck, Mistress Mary. You'll need it. [*Laughs and exits. After a moment, Dickon enters, carrying animals.*]

DICKON: Hello. You must be Miss Mary.

MARY: How did you know my name? And who are you?

DICKON: They call me Dickon. And I know about you because my sister, Martha, told me all about you.

MARY: Is it true you speak to animals?

DICKON: Aye. Say hello to my friends. This is Cert, the crow. [*Cawing sound is heard.*] The fox is Captain, and the lamb, Lady. [**Bleating** *is heard.*]

MARY: Those are strange names for animals.

DICKON: It's what they asked to be called.

MARY: [**Scoffing**] Animals and birds can't talk.

DICKON: Sure they can. You just have to know how to listen. [*Looks offstage*] Look! Here comes my friend, Robin. [*Robin enters.*]

ROBIN: Hello Dickon, Who is your friend?

MARY: [**Astonished**] Why, he does talk!

DICKON: See? You just have to want to listen to them. [*Curtain*]

Scene 3

Setting: *Colin's bedroom. There is a bed center, a large portrait covered with sheet, and a window.*

At rise: *Colin is in bed, covered completely with blankets. Mary wanders on stage, doesn't notice Colin.*

MARY: [*To herself*] I thought that the library was here somewhere. [*Notices bed*] Oh! [*Colin sits up.*]

COLIN: [*Frightened*] Are you a ghost?

MARY: Of course not. Do I look like a ghost? Who are you, and why are you in bed? It's two in the afternoon!

✔ LITERARY CHECK

*Why is **setting the scene** important at the beginning of Scene 3? What information does the playwright provide about the place? How does this help you visualize where Mary is now?*

---

resolutely, in a very determined way
bleating, the sound that a sheep or goat makes: "baa"
scoffing, laughing at or talking to in a scornful way
astonished, very surprised

COLIN: I'm Colin Craven. My father is the master of this manor.

MARY: Why didn't anyone tell me he had a son?

COLIN: Because no one is allowed to talk about me.

MARY: Why not?

COLIN: Because I'm going to have a hump on my back, just like my father.

MARY: Don't you ever leave this room?

COLIN: No. If people look at me, I get sick.

MARY: That's ridiculous! I'm looking at you and you're not getting sick.

COLIN: Well, I might.

MARY: Save yourself the trouble. I'm leaving.

COLIN: [*Pleading*] No, don't go! Tell me about India. I hear that's where you're from.

MARY: You can read about India in books.

COLIN: Reading gives me a headache.

MARY: Well, if I were your father I'd make you read so you can learn about things.

COLIN: [*Stubbornly*] No one can make me do anything I don't want to do.

MARY: Well, why not?

COLIN: Because I'm sick and I'm dying!

MARY: Well, do you want to live?

COLIN: Not if I have a hump on my back like my father. [*Cries*]

MARY: [*Disgusted*] I'm leaving. You cry too much! [*Mary exits. Quick curtain*]

---

pleading, begging

BEFORE YOU GO ON

1 Who are Dickon's friends?

2 What does Colin beg Mary to do?

On Your Own
Do you think that animals can communicate with people? Explain.

Reading 1 **307**

Scene 4

Setting: *Mr. Craven's library, with desk center, and bookshelves on walls.*

At rise: *Mary enters library where Mr. Craven is sitting.*

MARY: [*Timidly*] You sent for me, sir?

MR. CRAVEN: Yes. Come closer, my dear. Don't be afraid. I'm quite harmless.

MARY: [*Boldly*] You don't frighten me.

MR. CRAVEN: [*Kindly*] You look just like your father. He was my best friend, you know, and when he died, and I learned you had no living **relatives**, I felt it my duty to care for you.

MARY: Yes. And I'm truly thankful, sir.

MR. CRAVEN: I wish I could do more for you, but I have been ill, you know.

MARY: I'm sorry.

MR. CRAVEN: Are you being taken good care of?

MARY: Martha has been very kind to me.

MR. CRAVEN: But are you happy here? Is there anything you need or want?

MARY: I wonder if I could have a place to make a garden? I love gardens so.

MR. CRAVEN: [*Pleased*] You do? [*Distantly*] There was once someone very **dear to** me who loved gardens, too. Yes, of course. Choose any part of the garden you wish, and I will see that you get all the tools you need. Now, child, leave me—I wish to be alone.

MARY: Thank you, Mr. Craven. [*Nervously*] And . . . and try not to be so sad. [*Runs out. Curtain*]

Scene 5

Setting: *Same as Scene 2.*

At rise: *Mary and Dickon, holding Robin, are looking at fence covered with brambles.*

MARY: Oh, Dickon, if only we could find the entrance to this locked garden. Mr. Craven said I could have any garden I wish—and I want this one.

DICKON: But even if we found the door, we'd still need the key.

ROBIN: Key . . . Now, where did I see a key?

DICKON: You saw a key, Robin?

ROBIN: Yes. I was flying around the other day, and I spotted a rusty old key.

---

relatives, members of your family
dear to, much loved by

Sidebar:

✔ LITERARY CHECK

*Reread Scene 4, paying special attention to the **stage directions**. How does Mary behave at first with Mr. Craven? How does her attitude change?*

MARY: [*Excitedly*] Oh, Robin, think—please! Where was it?

ROBIN: [*Thinking*] Over there. Near that bush, I think. [*Mary and Dickon search.*]

DICKON: Look! Here it is! [*Holds up key*] Now if we only knew where the gate was.

ROBIN: Oh, I know that, too.

MARY: Well, why didn't you tell us?

ROBIN: You never asked me.

DICKON: Show us where it is, Robin.

ROBIN: It's over here, behind this ivy. [*They rush over to fence.*]

MARY: [*Finding door*] Yes, yes! Here it is. Quick, Dickon. Try the key!

DICKON: Very well. [*He tries the key.*] It's turning . . . but very slowly. It's very rusty. There! I think I've got it. Now, we'll just give a little push, and—[*Curtain goes up, revealing a dead garden.*]

MARY: [*Excited*] This is it! The locked garden! [*Disappointed*] Oh, but look! Nothing is growing. Everything is dead.

DICKON: It just needs some care, and lots of water. [*Gestures*] See, these rose bushes are alive. Soon they'll be blooming. [*Curtain*]

Scene 6

Setting: *Same as Scene 3.*

At rise: *Colin is in bed. Mary and Dickon enter, holding animals.*

MARY: Hello, Colin. This is my friend, Dickon. He brought his animals to show you.

COLIN: Where were you, Mary? I've missed you. Hello, Dickon. I've heard all about you.

DICKON: Hello! Want to hold Lady? She's a nice and gentle lamb. [*Baaing is heard.*]

COLIN: Oh, yes, thank you. [*Holds lamb*] I'm glad you came. I have so few visitors—only Mary and Martha. Not even Father comes to see me.

DICKON: Why not?

COLIN: Because he doesn't want to see the hump on my back.

MARY: Let me see. [*Looks at Colin's back*] Why, there's no hump there, Colin. Only a **knobby spine** like mine.

---

knobby spine, backbone with hard parts that stick out from under the surface

BEFORE YOU GO ON

1 Why does Mr. Craven decide to take care of Mary?

2 Who helps Mary and Dickon find the key to the garden?

On Your Own
What do you think Mary and Dickon will do next?

COLIN: [*Amazed*] You mean I don't have a hump, and I'm not dying?

MARY: Of course not! It's all in your mind.

DICKON: Roses won't grow where there are only **thistles**.

COLIN: What does that mean?

MARY: It means that you can't have happy thoughts if you always have **gloomy** ones.

COLIN: You're right. I must find something to do to keep me happy.

MARY: Dickon and I have a secret. I'll tell you if you promise not to tell anyone else!

COLIN: I promise.

MARY: We have found the garden that your mother and father used to love so much, and we're going to make it beautiful again—just the way it used to be.

COLIN: [*Excited*] Really? Oh, I wish I could help, but I can't walk.

DICKON: I could take you out into the garden in your wheelchair. You could sit on the ground and plant seeds and pull weeds.

COLIN: Do you really think I could?

MARY: Of course you could! In fact, you shall! We'll start tomorrow.

COLIN: [*Delighted*] That's wonderful!

MARY: We have to go now. We'll see you tomorrow. [*Dickon and Mary exit.*]

COLIN: [*Calling off*] Good-bye! Thanks for coming. [*He looks at the picture.*] Oh, Mother. Forgive me for covering you up. [*He gets out of bed and tries to walk toward the picture, but falls.*] If only I could walk . . . I will walk. I'll practice a little bit each day, and when Father comes home I'll show him I'm not an invalid anymore! [*Curtain*]

Scene 7

Time: *Two months later.*

Setting: *The mansion gardens. There are flowerbeds, bushes, etc., around the stage. Fence covered with ivy, brambles, etc., is upright.*

At rise: *Mr. Craven is on stage alone.*

BEN: [*Entering*] Mr. Craven! Welcome home. Mary wants to see you right away. She's in the locked garden, sir.

MR. CRAVEN: [*Amazed*] The garden? How is that? I thought the key was lost forever.

---

thistles, wild plants with purple flowers and leaves that have sharp points
gloomy, sad and hopeless

BEN: Come, I'll show you. The entrance is this way. [*Curtain goes up, reveals a beautiful garden. Mary, pushing Colin in a wheelchair, enters, followed by Dickon.*]

MARY AND COLIN: Surprise!

MR. CRAVEN: Why, it's beautiful! You've planted my favorite flowers!

BEN: Just the way it was when your wife was alive, sir. The children worked very hard.

MARY: Ben helped, too. He told us how it used to look and **pruned** all the dead wood.

MR. CRAVEN: And Colin! You have color in your cheeks, and you've gained weight.

COLIN: And that's not all, Father. [*He gets out of the wheelchair.*] I . . . can walk. [*He walks with difficulty to Mr. Craven, and they* **embrace**. *Ben and Dickon watch happily.*]

MR. CRAVEN: My son! [*Mary embraces them, too.*] My children. You have made me very happy! And you have brought love back into our garden.

COLIN: Our secret garden!

MARY: Yes, but now it needn't be a secret any longer. [*Curtain*]

---

pruned, cut back some of the branches of a tree or bush to make it grow better
embrace, hug; put their arms around each other in a caring way

ABOUT THE **AUTHOR** AND **PLAYWRIGHT**

Frances Hodgson Burnett was born in England in 1849. Her family moved to Knoxville, Tennessee, after her father's death. To help support her siblings, she began to write short stories for magazines. Later, she wrote many novels and children's books, including *Little Lord Fauntleroy* and *A Little Princess*.

David C. Jones has written more than a dozen plays for *PLAYS Magazine* with fellow-writer Lewis Mahlmann. He and Mahlmann also published several books through *PLAYS Magazine*, including *Puppet Plays from Favorite Stories* and *Folk Tales for Puppets*.

BEFORE YOU GO ON

1 What does Mary help Colin understand about his back?

2 What makes Mr. Craven happy at the end of the play?

On Your Own
Do you agree with Dickon that "roses won't grow where there are only thistles"? Why or why not?

Reading 1 **311**

▶ **READER'S THEATER**

Act out the following scene between Colin, Mary, and Mr. Craven.

Mary: Mr. Craven, Colin has a big surprise for you. [*Colin stands.*]

Mr. Craven: Colin, my boy! You are standing on your own!

Colin: Yes, I am, Father. It feels great to finally get out of my room and into the fresh air of this garden.

Mr. Craven: But how did you build your strength?

Colin: Mary and Dickon took me out to the garden. I practiced walking a little bit each day. I couldn't have done it without their help.

Mr. Craven: I'm so proud of you, son. [*Colin and Mr. Craven hug each other.*]

Mary: Congratulations, Colin. You worked very hard. I always knew you could do it.

Speaking SKILL

Vary the volume of your voice to keep your audience interested.

▶ **COMPREHENSION**

Workbook
Page 165

Recall

1. Which garden is the only one Mary is told that she can't play in?

2. Why does Dickon name the animals?

Comprehend

3. What causes Mr. Craven to toss away the key to the garden?

4. What do the children do to fix the garden?

Analyze

5. Why is the garden called "a secret garden"? Support your answer by evaluating information in the text.

6. What feelings about life does Colin **convey** through his words and behavior in the beginning of the play? How do they change by the end? Support your answer by evaluating information in the text.

Connect

7. Other authors write stories about characters who talk to animals. If you could talk to animals, which ones would you choose? Why?

8. Do you think that planting a beautiful garden can improve life in a city or town? Explain.

➤ DISCUSSION

*》∩ **Listening** SKILL*

Look at each speaker as he or she speaks to show that you are interested.

Discuss in pairs or small groups.

1. What part of *The Secret Garden* did you like best? Why?

2. Do you think the children should have restored the garden or left it as it was in memory of Mrs. Craven? Why?

3. This play is called *The Secret Garden*. What would be another good title for this drama? Why?

Q **How are courage and imagination linked?** Which character in *The Secret Garden* has the most imagination? Which character has the most courage? How does each character affect the other people in the play? How do the characters cooperate to bring about a happy ending?

➤ RESPONSE TO LITERATURE

Workbook
Page 165

Utilize Imagine that you are Mary Lennox. What was your life like in India? How do you feel about moving to England? Write a diary entry in which you describe your feelings about the changes in your life. You may want to use a graphic organizer like this one:

Life in India — How alike — Life in England

When you are done writing, share your diary entry with a classmate. Talk about the details in the play that helped you understand Mary's feelings.

Grammar

Be going to and will

You can use *be going to* or *will* to make predictions about the future. For *be going to*, use a form of *be* (*am, is, are*) and *going to* + the base form of the verb. Use *will* or the contraction *'ll* and the base form of the verb.

> Soon the rose bushes **are going to be** blooming.
> I **will walk**. **I'll practice** a little every day.

The negative form *will* is *will not* (*won't*). For questions, switch the subject and *will*. Form the negative of *be going to* with a negative form of *be* (*am not, isn't, aren't*). For questions, switch the subject and the *be* verb.

You **won't be able to** go in without a key.	**Will** you **tell** me your secret?
I know I**'m not going to like** it here.	**Are** you **going to be** my servant?

To express a plan, use *be going to*. To show a decision made at the moment of speaking, use *will*. Use either when predicting the future.

> We**'re going to make** the garden beautiful again. [a plan about the future]
> We**'ll start** tomorrow. [decision made when speaking]
> But what **will** I **do**?   OR   But what **am** I **going to do**? [asking about the future]

Practice

Workbook Page 166

Work with a partner. Copy the sentences below into your notebook. Then complete the sentences with the correct form of *will* or *be going to*.

Example: I <u>'ll</u> (will) arrive tonight.

1. Senad _____ (will) approach the angry dog.
2. Matt _____ (be going to) go to Spain this summer.
3. There _____ (be going to) be a storm. The sky is black.
4. Our teacher _____ (be going to) give us a test.
5. She said that she _____ (will) pick me up at the station.

Apply

Work with a partner. Find examples of *will* and *be going to* in the reading. Decide if they are used to predict the future, express a future plan, or express a decision made at the moment of speaking.

Degrees of Certainty about the Future

When you are 100% certain about the future, use *will* or *be going to*. When you are less certain, you can include the adverbs *probably*, *perhaps*, and *maybe*. Like many adverbs, they can appear in several places in a sentence.

> The roses **probably** will bloom soon.
> **Perhaps** the roses will bloom soon.
> **Maybe** the roses will bloom soon.

Grammar SKILL

The question form of *may* and *might* is used to make a polite request, not to express the future. *May / Might I borrow your pen?*

You can also use the modals *may* and *might* to show that you are not 100% certain about the future. Modals are auxiliary verbs. Auxiliary verbs have only one form and are used with the base form of the verb. *May* and *might* have the same meaning. Form the negative of *may* and *might* with *not*.

> Mr. Craven **may / might know** where the key is.
> He **may not / might not want** us in the garden.

Practice  Workbook Page 167

Work with a partner. Copy the sentences below into your notebook. Then complete the sentences with correct form of the verb and the words in parentheses. Remember to use *will* with the adverbs *probably*, *perhaps*, and *maybe*.

Example: She _might not be_ there today. (be, might not)

1. _____ we _____ early. (finish, perhaps)
2. Bob _____ to Germany. (go, may not)
3. Sandy _____ us later. (meet, probably)
4. Ralph _____ angry with you. (be, might)
5. _____ I _____ tickets tomorrow. (buy, maybe)

✔ GRAMMAR CHECK

What form of verb are the modals may *and* might *used with?*

Apply

Work with a partner. Take turns making predictions about the future based on how certain you are.

Example: Everyone will probably drive hybrid cars.

Writing

Write a Formal E-mail

You have been learning some of the skills used in expository writing.
In one type of expository writing, you present a problem and solution.
First you explain the situation, and why it is a problem. Then you
explain how the problem can be solved. Facts and details are presented
in a logical order to explain the solution.

> **Writing Prompt**
>
> Write a formal e-mail to your community's mayor. Tell about a
> problem in your community and suggest how the problem can be
> solved. Present facts and details to explain your solution. Be sure to
> include the topic of the e-mail in the subject line.

1 **PREWRITE** Begin by choosing a problem to write about.

- Think about something you want to change in your community.

- Ask yourself what a good solution to the problem would be.

- List your ideas in a graphic organizer.

Workbook Page 168

A student named Angelina used this graphic organizer to plan her
formal e-mail to her community's mayor.

Problem	Solution
The bare surroundings of the monument in Law Park don't express its importance.	Start a community garden to make a beautiful setting for the monument.

2 DRAFT Use your organizer to help you write a first draft.

- Remember to present a problem and its solution.

- Include specific facts and details to explain your solution.

- Be sure to include the topic of your e-mail in the subject line.

3 REVISE Read over your draft. Look for places where the writing is unclear or needs improvement. Use the Writing Checklist to help you identify problems. Then revise your draft, using the editing and proofreading marks listed on page 456.

4 EDIT Check your work for errors in grammar, usage, mechanics, and spelling. Trade papers with a partner to obtain feedback. Use the Peer Review Checklist on Workbook page 168. Edit your final draft in response to feedback from your partner and your teacher.

5 PUBLISH Prepare a clean copy of your final draft. Share your formal e-mail with the class. Save your work. You'll need to refer to it in the Writing Workshop at the end of the unit.

Here is Angelina's e-mail. Notice the format. Also note that she presents the problem first and then suggests a solution.

> **Writing Checklist**
>
> **IDEAS:**
> ☑ I presented a problem and its solution.
>
> **ORGANIZATION:**
> ☑ I included facts and details in a logical order.
>
> **CONVENTIONS:**
> ☑ I accurately used the future tense.

From: Angelina Xing <axing@coldmail.com>
Date: Tue, 6 Oct 2009 10:29:31
To: Mayor's Office <mayor@briarcliff.gov>
Subject: Law Park in Briarcliff Manor

Dear Mayor:

I am writing about a problem with Law Park. The park's main feature is a monument dedicated to the memory of World War II soldiers. However, the bare surroundings don't express the importance of the monument. I suggest starting a community garden in Law Park to make a beautiful setting for the monument. If only one percent of the population actively works on this project, there will be more than enough people to keep the garden alive all year long. The whole town could benefit from improving this special place. Thank you very much for taking the time to consider my idea.

Sincerely,
Angelina Xing

Prepare to Read

What You Will Learn

Reading

■ Vocabulary building: *Context, dictionary skills, word study*

■ Reading strategy: *Follow steps in a process*

■ Text type: *Informational texts (science) (instructions)*

Grammar
Imperatives; Sequence words and phrases

Writing
Write how-to instructions

🔍 THE BIG QUESTION

How are courage and imagination linked? Why might courage and imagination be needed to improve our environment? Do you think that one person really can make a difference? How might planting trees make a big difference to people throughout a country? Discuss with a partner.

▶ BUILD BACKGROUND

▲ A beech tree forest

"A Tree Grows in Kenya: The Story of Wangari Maathai" is a biographical science article about an environmentalist from Kenya. An environmentalist is someone who works to protect the natural world. The woman you will read about, Wangari Maathai, did a lot to improve the environment of Kenya, her home country. You will see how she used her imagination and courage to change the land around her.

Kenya is a country in eastern Africa. The southeastern part of the country borders the Indian Ocean. Kenya was once a colony ruled by the British. In 1963, Kenya won its independence from Britain. In 1964, Kenya became an independent republic.

► VOCABULARY

Listening and Speaking: Key Words

Read aloud and listen to the sentences with a partner. Use the context to figure out the meaning of the highlighted words. Use a dictionary to check your answers. Then write each word and its meaning in your notebook.

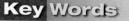

Key Words

campaign
committee
continent
democratic
natural
nutrition

1. The campaign to save the forest was successful. The series of actions helped to save the forest.

2. The committee has six members. The group is preparing a report on Kenya.

3. North America is a continent, one of the seven main areas of land in the world.

4. A democratic government is controlled by leaders who are elected by the people of the country.

5. Wood is a natural material. It is not man-made.

6. Fruit gives us the nutrition we need. It has many of the vitamins and minerals we need to stay healthy.

Practice

Workbook Page 169

Write the sentences in your notebook. Choose a key word from the box above to complete each sentence. Then take turns reading the sentences aloud with a partner.

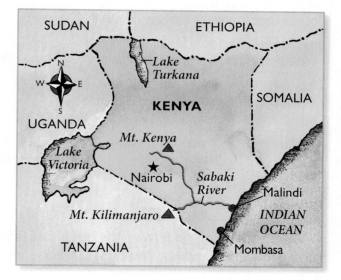

1. If you live in a _____ country, you elect leaders by voting for them.

2. Water is one important _____ resource. Others are minerals and land.

3. Trees get the _____ they need to grow from water, sun, and soil.

4. The girl started a _____ to save trees. She planned six events.

5. The planting _____ is in charge of planting trees.

6. Kenya and the United States are not located on the same _____.

Listening and Speaking: Academic Words

Study the red words and their meanings. You will find these words useful when talking and writing about informational texts. Write each word and its meaning in your notebook, then say the words aloud with a partner. After you read "A Tree Grows in Kenya: The Story of Wangari Maathai," try to use these words to respond to the text.

Academic Words

aspect
finance
resource
sustain
technology
welfare

Audio

aspect = one of the parts or features of a situation, idea, or problem	→	People try to think of every **aspect** of a problem and try to solve each part.
finance = provide money for something	→	The club needed to **finance** a trip, so they raised money with a bake sale.
resource = something such as land, minerals, or natural energy that exists in a country and can be used in order to increase its wealth	→	A waterfall is a natural **resource**. It makes power that can be turned into electricity.
sustain = make it possible for someone or something to continue to exist over time	→	Trees **sustain** life for many animals. They make life for these animals possible.
technology = a combination of all the knowledge, equipment, or methods used in scientific or industrial work		Computers and cars are examples of modern **technology**. We use these machines daily.
welfare = health, comfort, and happiness		Trees are good for our **welfare**. They add to our health and happiness.

Audio

Practice

Workbook Page 170

Work with a partner to answer the questions. Try to include the red word in your answer. Write the sentences in your notebook.

1. What **aspect** of nature would you like to photograph?
2. How might you **finance** a campaign to save a forest?
3. Which **resource** do you think helps a country become wealthier—gold or oil? Why?
4. How do forests help to **sustain** life?
5. What types of **technology** are used to communicate across continents?
6. How is a diet rich in fresh fruits and vegetables good for people's **welfare**?

Forests help to sustain life in many ways. ▶

Word Study: Suffixes *-ic*, *-ist*, *-able*

A suffix is a letter or group of letters placed at the end of a base word. It can change a word's part of speech and its meaning. If you know the meaning of a suffix, it can help you understand the meaning of the new word. Study the examples in the chart below. If a base word ends in *e*, remember to drop the *e* before adding the suffix.

Word	Suffix	New Word (Part of Speech and Meaning)
democrat (noun)	*-ic*	democratic (adjective) (having the characteristics of a democrat)
environmental (adjective)	*-ist*	environmentalist (noun) (person who works for the environment)
sustain (verb)	*-able*	sustainable (adjective) (capable of being sustained)

▲ Wind energy is a sustainable resource.

Practice
Workbook Page 171

Copy the chart above into your notebook. Work with a partner. Add these words and the suffixes to the chart to create new words:

poet + ic	art + ist	understand + able

Identify each new word's part of speech. Then define each word using what you know about suffixes. Check the dictionary to make sure that your answers are correct.

READING STRATEGY   FOLLOW STEPS IN A PROCESS

Learning how to follow steps in a process will help you read and understand instructions. The steps are usually arranged in chronological order, from first to last. The author often numbers the steps to make them easier to follow. When you read instructions, follow these steps:

- Look for numbers.
- Look for time-order words such as *first, second, then, next,* and *last.*
- Read the steps from first to last.
- Restate the steps to make sure that you can follow them in the correct order.

As you read "How to Plant a Tree," follow the steps above to understand the steps in the process.

Workbook Page 172

Set a purpose for reading Why might something as simple as planting a tree require courage and imagination? As you read this article, think about how a simple action can have a big effect. Then find out how to plant a tree yourself.

A Tree Grows in Kenya:
The Story of Wangari Maathai

Audio

In October 2004, Wangari Maathai (wan-GAH-ree mah-DHEYE), an environmentalist from Kenya, Africa, received an unexpected phone call. The person on the phone told her that she had won the Nobel Peace Prize. Each year, the Nobel committee chooses someone whose work for peace is judged to be the most important to the world. This was an incredible honor and an enormous surprise for Maathai. She was very excited. In an interview with *Time* magazine, she said, "I think what the Nobel committee is doing is going beyond war and looking at what **humanity** can do to prevent war. Sustainable management of our natural resources will promote peace." She was pleased that the judges had recognized the deep connection between environmentalism and peace. "If we conserved our resources better," she said, "fighting would not occur."

humanity, people in general

Maathai's love of the environment began when she was very young. She was born in the **highland** village of Nyeri in Kenya in 1940. As a child she enjoyed the lush, green forests around her. Her parents were farmers, so she grew up close to the natural world. In her Nobel prize speech, she said:

*I would visit a stream next to our home to fetch water for my mother. I would drink water straight from the stream. Playing among the arrowroot leaves, I tried in vain to pick up the strands of frogs' eggs, believing they were beads. But every time I put my little fingers under them they would break. Later, I saw thousands of **tadpoles**: black, energetic, and wriggling through the clear water against the background of the brown earth. This is the world I **inherited** from my parents.*

highland, mountain
tadpoles, small creatures with long tails that live in water and grow into frogs or toads
inherited, received

Maathai was an excellent student. She won a **scholarship** to attend a college in the United States. She studied hard and received a degree in biology. Then she worked toward more advanced degrees at the University of Pittsburgh and University of Nairobi in Kenya. In 1971, she earned a doctoral degree. She was honored to be the first woman in East and Central Africa to earn such an advanced degree.

At first, Maathai taught at the University of Nairobi. Soon she wanted to do more than teach. While in the United States, she had been deeply impressed by the democratic freedom that people enjoyed. She wanted the Kenyan people to enjoy similar freedom and a better quality of life.

Maathai was concerned that the **luxuriant** forests of her childhood were rapidly disappearing because of **excessive** logging and other practices. She wanted the people of her village, especially the women, to have more of a voice in government. Maathai decided that it was time for a change.

It is said that "a journey of a thousand miles begins with a single step." Maathai took one step to change the world around her: She planted nine trees in her backyard. With this simple act, she planted the seed of her campaign to save the forests of Africa!

In 1976, Maathai interviewed many farmers in the Kenyan countryside.

Most of them were women, and they often had the same concerns. They needed more firewood, which was their main source of energy. They needed clean water for drinking, cooking, and bathing. They needed to be able to grow their own food. In addition, they needed to be able to make more money so that they could become **self-sufficient**.

Maathai knew that the destruction of the forests was at the root of these problems. She decided to put her knowledge and creativity to work. Trees were needed to stop soil **erosion**. They were also important sources of firewood for cooking. Why not encourage farmers in Kenya to plant as many trees as possible? This would be a simple way to improve the farmers' living conditions. And this method wouldn't require expensive tools or large sums of money.

In 1977, Maathai founded the Green Belt Movement. A greenbelt is a band of farmland or parks surrounding a village. Maathai hoped to see belts of green trees again throughout Kenya. The goals of the Green Belt Movement were to encourage Kenyan farmers to plant trees and to conserve the environment. This, in turn, would help farmers, and women in particular, to improve their living conditions.

---

scholarship, money given to help pay for a person's education
luxuriant, healthy, thick, and strong
excessive, much more than reasonable or necessary

self-sufficient, able to provide for themselves
erosion, destruction and wearing away because of wind and rain

BEFORE YOU GO ON

1 Where in Kenya did Wangari Maathai grow up?

2 What did Maathai study in college?

On Your Own
Have you ever thought of a simple solution to a big problem? Explain.

Reading 2 **323**

At first, her idea wasn't very popular. As Maathai said, "It took me a lot of days and nights to convince people that women could improve their environment without much technology or . . . **financial resources**." Although it took a long time, the movement achieved its goal. Within thirty years, the women of Kenya had planted 30 million trees. The Green Belt Movement did other things to improve the quality of Kenyan life. Members also promoted better education and nutrition throughout the country.

When Maathai started her campaign to plant trees, she was working at the grass-roots level. This means that she worked directly with the local people. Sometimes, she also worked directly with the government to bring about change. For example, in the 1980s, Kenyan President Daniel arap Moi planned to build a sixty-two-story **skyscraper**. This plan would have destroyed Uhuru Park, a beautiful park in Nairobi, the nation's capital. Maathai had visited Uhuru Park many times. It was one of the only green spaces available in the city for public use. Families often went there on weekends to relax, play, and enjoy time together. To save this **precious** green space, she led protests against the government. President Moi called her "a threat to the order and security of the country." Maathai was arrested by the police and treated badly, but she never gave up the fight. Because of her courage and **persistence**, she eventually succeeded in preserving the park.

Wangari Maathai died in 2011, but her **legacy** lives on. She strongly believed that solutions to most of the world's problems come from the people themselves. She is a national hero in Kenya. If young Kenyan girls are **strong-willed** and **outspoken**, people say they are "like Wangari." "Like Wangari" has become an expression of **admiration** and affection.

Today, the members of the Green Belt Movement continue to plant trees throughout many countries in Africa, as well as in Haiti and the United States. They have educated thousands of people along the way. As the Nobel committee said, "Maathai is a strong voice speaking for the best forces in Africa to promote peace and good living conditions on the continent. She thinks globally and acts locally."

---

financial resources, money or
    access to money
skyscraper, very tall building
precious, valuable and important

persistence, determination
legacy, something that is received from
    someone
strong-willed, determined to achieve goals
outspoken, expressing opinions honestly
    and directly
admiration, approval and respect

▼ Uhuru Park

How to Plant a Tree

What You Need

- Something to dig with, like a shovel or spade.
- A tree! You can buy a tree at a garden center. In some places, state or community foresters have trees that they'll give to anyone who wants to plant them. When you buy your tree, you'll notice that all of its roots are wrapped up with fabric in a little ball. This is called the rootball.
- A watering can and some water.

What to Do

1. First, choose a site. Pick a place that gets enough sun, where your tree will be happy. Don't plant close to power or telephone wires.

2. Dig a hole as deep as the rootball and three times as wide.

3. Unwrap the rootball and spread out the roots. If they're tangled up, straighten them out.

4. Put the tree in the hole. The soil should come up as high on the tree as it was before you got it. Usually this will be to the top of the rootball. Be sure that the tree is straight.

5. Fill in the space around the rootball gently but firmly with soil. Pack down the soil with your hands and feet. Be sure that there are no air pockets.

6. Make a little dam around the base of the tree about as wide as the hole. This will keep the water close to the tree.

7. After it's planted, your tree will be very thirsty, so give it lots of water.

8. If you need more help, call your local garden store or contact a community park or forest agency.

Some Tips to Keep in Mind

- If you want to plant your tree in a park or other public place, make sure you ask for permission. Some places may have rules about what kind of trees can be planted there.

- Your tree is just a baby, and like any baby, you need to take care of it. You should water it every week. Most trees need 7.5 to 11 liters (2–3 gal.) of water per week.

BEFORE YOU GO ON

1. What did the Green Belt Movement promote besides planting trees?

2. What park did Maathai help to save in Kenya?

On Your Own
What do you think of Wangari Maathai? How did she show courage and imagination?

Reading 2 **325**

Review and Practice

► COMPREHENSION

Workbook
Page 173

Recall

1. What **resources** did Wangari Maathai protect through her actions?

2. What are the goals of the Green Belt Movement?

Comprehend

3. What education did Maathai receive? What degrees did she earn?

4. What concerns did the women farmers of Kenya have?

Analyze

5. How did Wangari's childhood teach her that it is important to **sustain** the natural world?

6. Why did the Nobel committee award her the peace prize?

Connect

7. Suppose that you could award the Nobel Prize. To whom would you give the prize and why?

8. How do parks contribute to the **welfare** of a city's inhabitants?

► IN YOUR OWN WORDS

Imagine that you are telling a small group of friends about this biographical article. Tell your friends three facts about Maathai's life and work. Use the chart below to help you list your facts and write a brief summary of the article's main points. Then share your summary with a classmate. Compare and contrast your summaries.

🔊 Speaking SKILL

Learning Strategy:
When you speak, decide if you will use formal or informal language. Use formal language in class. Use informal language with family and friends.

A Tree Grows in Kenya: The Story of Wangari Maathai
Fact 1:
Fact 2:
Fact 3:
Overall summary:

▶ DISCUSSION

Discuss in pairs or small groups.

1. In what ways was Wangari Maathai an admirable person?

2. Maathai spent time living and studying in the United States. How do you think this affected her life and her goals?

3. A Nobel Prize winner receives more than $1 million. How would you have advised Maathai to spend the money?

Q How are courage and imagination linked? What is the meaning of the saying, "A journey of a thousand miles begins with a single step"? What role does courage play in that journey? What role does imagination play?

▶ READ FOR FLUENCY

When we read aloud to communicate meaning, we group words into phrases, pause or slow down to make important points, and emphasize important words. Pause for a short time when you reach a comma and for a longer time when you reach a period. Pay attention to rising and falling intonation at the end of sentences.

Work with a partner. Choose a paragraph from the reading. Discuss which words seem important for communicating meaning. Practice pronouncing difficult words. Give each other feedback.

▲ Elie Wiesel

▶ EXTENSION 📖 Workbook Page 173

Utilize Learn more about other Nobel Peace Prize winners. Choose one recent winner and report on key **aspects** of his or her life and accomplishments. Here are some Nobel winners to choose from: Muhammad Yunus, Shirin Ebadi, Kim Dae Jung, Jody Williams, Nelson Mandela, F. W. de Klerk, Aung San Suu Kyi, and Elie Wiesel. Use encyclopedias, reference books, and reliable websites. Copy and complete the following diagram to organize your ideas. Report your findings to the class.

▲ Nelson Mandela

Grammar

Imperatives

You can use an imperative to make a request, give a command, give directions, or give instructions. The subject is *you*, but it is not stated. Often, with requests, the word *please* is used. It can come at the beginning or end of the sentence. When it is at the end, use a comma.

Make a Request Please **give** me the shovel. OR **Give** me the shovel, please.
Make a Command **Be** persistent!
Give Directions **Turn** left.
Give Instructions **Dig** a hole as deep as the rootball. **Put** the tree in the hole.

Grammar SKILL

An imperative is always in the simple present.

Form a negative imperative by adding *do not* or *don't* before the verb.

Don't plant close to power or telephone wires.

Practice **Workbook Page 174**

Work with a partner. Copy the sentences below into your notebook. Then use the words in the box to complete the imperatives.

give	help	put	slow	forget	wake

Example: _Wake_ up! We're going to be late!

1. Please _____ money to help finance the event.
2. _____ me, please. Otherwise I won't finish on time.
3. _____ the cheese on the bread.
4. Don't _____ to study for the test.
5. _____ down! You're driving too fast!

Apply

Work with a partner. Give each other commands by playing a game of "Simon Says."

Sequence Words and Phrases

It is important to know the sequence, or order, of events. Sequence words and phrases, also called transition words and phrases, will help your reader follow your thoughts better. Sequence words and phrases are often used with imperatives to give instructions.

Use a comma after all these sequence words except for *then*.

Practice

Workbook Page 175

Work with a partner. In your notebook, copy the instructions for frying an egg. Put the list in the correct sequence, or order.

_____ Then turn the egg over.

_____ Finally, remove the egg from the pan.

_2_ Then turn on the stove.

_____ Next, crack an egg in the pan.

_____ First, put butter or oil in a pan.

_____ After that, sprinkle salt and pepper on the egg.

Apply

Work with a partner. Using sequence words and imperatives, tell your partner how to do something you know how to do, for example, make a sandwich, brush your teeth, or hang a picture.

Example: First, put butter on the bread . . .

Writing

Write How-to Instructions

One type of expository writing gives step-by-step instructions explaining how to do something. When you tell how to do something, you present your instructions in time order from the first step to the last. Signal words such as *first*, *next*, and *last* clarify the sequence. Details help readers understand exactly what to do.

> **Writing Prompt**
>
> Write a paragraph explaining how to do something. Choose an activity that you enjoy doing. You might tell how to build a tree house or how to make a family recipe book. Give the instructions step-by-step in time order. Use imperatives in your instructions.

1 **PREWRITE** Choose an activity that you can explain clearly.

- Think about the steps involved in doing the activity.

- Ask yourself which step comes first. Which one comes last?

- List your ideas in a graphic organizer.

Workbook Page 176

A student named Danielle used this graphic organizer to plan her paragraph about caring for a tree.

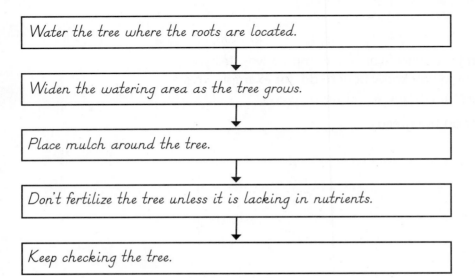

| Water the tree where the roots are located. |
| Widen the watering area as the tree grows. |
| Place mulch around the tree. |
| Don't fertilize the tree unless it is lacking in nutrients. |
| Keep checking the tree. |

2 DRAFT Use your organizer to help you write a first draft.

- Choose an activity you can explain clearly.
- Include enough details to help readers understand the task.
- Be sure to use imperatives correctly.

3 REVISE Read over your draft. Look for places where the writing is unclear or needs improvement. Use the Writing Checklist to help you identify problems. Then revise your draft, using the editing and proofreading marks listed on page 456.

4 EDIT Check your work for errors in grammar, usage, mechanics, and spelling. Trade papers with a partner to obtain feedback. Use the Peer Review Checklist on Workbook page 176. Edit your final draft in response to feedback from your partner and your teacher.

5 PUBLISH Prepare a clean copy of your final draft. Share your how-to paragraph with the class. Save your work. You'll need to refer to it in the Writing Workshop at the end of the unit.

Here is Danielle's paragraph of how-to instructions. Notice how she uses words such as *after* and *next* to clarify the sequence of steps.

Writing Checklist

ORGANIZATION:

☑ I presented each step in time order.

CONVENTIONS:

☑ I used imperatives correctly.

☑ I used English spelling rules accurately.

Danielle Christian

Caring for a Newly Planted Tree

After planting a new tree, the first thing you need to do is water it. Water the tree where the roots are located, just under the tree. Make sure that you widen the watering area as the tree grows. It is better to give regular deep soakings rather than water the tree lightly every day. Never water too little or too much! Next, make sure you place mulch, or decaying leaves, around the tree. Do not put a protective covering around the tree; that will prevent water and air from reaching the roots. Don't fertilize the tree unless it is lacking in nutrients. Finally, keep checking the tree to make sure that it is healthy and growing well. Check for any diseases or insects that might hurt the tree. If you think there are any problems, call a professional to come and check the tree immediately.

Prepare to Read

What You Will Learn

Reading

■ Vocabulary building: *Literary terms, dictionary skills, word study*

■ Reading strategy: *Summarize*

■ Text type: *Literature (novel excerpt)*

Grammar
Reported speech; Questions, imperatives, *told*

Writing
Write a plot summary

➤ 🔍 THE BIG QUESTION

How are courage and imagination linked? Why might people care enough about birds and animals to take risks to protect them? Why might courage and imagination be necessary to convince people that birds and animals have rights, too? Discuss with a partner.

The next reading involves efforts to save a unique type of owl. Work with a partner. Use your prior knowledge about owls to answer the following questions: Where do owls live? What do they eat? Why might it be important to protect their habitats? In your notebook, copy and fill in the first two columns of the K-W-L-H chart below.

K What do I **know**?	**W** What do I **want** to know?	**L** What did I **learn**?	**H** **How** did I learn it?

As you read the excerpt from *Hoot* and complete the activities after the reading, fill out the rest of the K-W-L-H chart with your partner.

➤ BUILD BACKGROUND

In the comic novel ***Hoot,*** burrowing owls play an important role. These tiny owls with big yellow eyes are quite different from most owls. Burrowing owls are very small, only 23 centimeters (9 in.) tall. They hunt throughout the day, not just at night, and they don't live in trees. They make their nests in underground holes, or burrows. They often use burrows made by prairie dogs or other animals. Burrowing owls eat mice, like other owls do, but they also eat beetles, moths, grasshoppers, frogs, and lizards. They even eat scorpions.

▲ Burrowing owls live in holes in the ground.

➤ VOCABULARY

Learn Literary Words

Everyone likes a funny story! **Humor** is anything that amuses people or makes them laugh. Writers create humor with the words they choose and the images these words create.

Sometimes writers exaggerate a scene or a character's traits to make something seem funny. Read these examples from *Hoot*. What is humorous about each sentence?

> Mr. Muckle's cheeks turned purple.
> The chamber-of-commerce guy looked like he'd swallowed a bar of soap.

Writers often use **colorful language**, such as idioms, hyperbole, and slang, to make their stories humorous. Slang is very informal language that certain people use. Colorful expressions can be used to create a silly character or to make the dialogue between characters amusing. Here are some examples of colorful language that you will read in *Hoot*.

dorky: silly-looking or strange-looking
hotshot: someone who is very successful and confident
twerp: an annoying or stupid person
noggin: head or brain

LEARNING STRATEGY

Earlier in this book you developed the ability to analyze expressions as you read (see Learn Literary Words on page 185). Expand your use of this strategy. Use context clues to analyze the meanings of colorful expressions. Later, try to use these expressions in your own writing.

Practice

Workbook Page 177

Write a funny paragraph about a "hotshot" who tries to convince a "dorky" friend of his to do something silly. You may want to use some of the words above in your paragraph and add some colorful expressions of your own. Share your paragraph with a partner.

Listening and Speaking: Academic Words

Study the **red** words and their meanings. You will find these words useful when talking and writing about literature. Write each word and its meaning in your notebook, then say the words aloud with a partner. After you read the excerpt from *Hoot*, try to use these words to respond to the text.

demonstrate = protest or support something in public with a lot of other people	➡	The students decided to **demonstrate** against the builders who were destroying the owls' habitat.
deny = say that something is not true	➡	The builders will **deny** that the burrowing owls live here. However, we know they're lying.
image = a picture that you can see through a camera, on television, or in a mirror; a picture that you have in your mind	➡	The protester drew the **image** of a burrowing owl on her poster. The picture looked real.
site = a place where something is being built or will be built	➡	The protest took place at the construction **site**, where the owls lived.

Audio

Practice

Workbook Page 178

Write the sentences in your notebook. Choose a **red** word from the box above to complete each sentence. Then take turns reading the sentences aloud with a partner.

1. What possible motive could the company have for constructing a restaurant on this _____?

   a. site   **b.** image

2. The boy is afraid of admitting the truth, so he will _____ what he did.

   a. demonstrate   **b.** deny

3. Roy's _____ of the owls was blurry.

   a. site   **b.** image

4. Many people plan to _____ against the new law, because they think that it is unfair.

   a. demonstrate   **b.** deny

▲ Anti-war protestors demonstrate in Washington, D.C.

Word Study: Prefixes *mega-, tele-, re-*

A prefix is a word part added to the beginning of a word that changes the word's meaning. Knowing the meanings of prefixes can help you figure out the meaning of many unfamiliar words. Study the chart.

Prefix	+ Base Word	= New Word
mega- (large; one million)	ton	megaton ("1 million tons")
tele- (distance; distant)	communication	telecommunication ("communication over a large distance by electronic means")
re- (again; backward)	capture	recapture ("capture again")

Practice

Work with a partner. Use what you have learned about prefixes to figure out the meanings of the words below. Copy the items below into your notebook. Write your own definitions for each word. Then check the meanings in a dictionary. Discuss how learning about prefixes can expand your vocabulary.

1. mega- + phone = _____

2. tele- + scope = _____

3. re- + viewing = _____

▲ A telescope

READING STRATEGY | SUMMARIZE

Summarizing helps you remember and understand a text. When you summarize fiction, you write a few sentences about what happened. You tell the goals of the characters, how they tried to reach their goals, and whether they succeeded. When you summarize nonfiction, you write a few sentences about the main ideas. To summarize, follow these steps:

- As you read, stop from time to time to summarize parts of the text.
- Write a sentence or two about the most important event or idea in that section. Leave out unimportant events, ideas, and details.
- After reading, summarize the most important points of the whole text.

As you read the excerpt from "Hoot," stop to summarize the plot. When you finish reading, summarize the entire excerpt in a short paragraph.

Set a purpose for reading What will happen when the Mother Paula Company starts to build a restaurant on a **site** inhabited by burrowing owls? Read to find out whether anyone will have the courage and imagination to help save the owls and their habitat.

from

HOOT

Carl Hiaasen

Chuck E. Muckle plans to build a new Mother Paula's restaurant on lands that are home to burrowing owls. The special groundbreaking ceremony is about to begin, and many people have gathered for the occasion. Three kids, Roy, Mullet Fingers, and his stepsister, Beatrice, are also on the scene. They are determined to save the tiny owls from the developers.

At a quarter past twelve, the door of the construction trailer swung open. First to emerge was a policeman whom Roy recognized as Officer Delinko; then the bald construction foreman with the rotten **temper**; then a snooty-looking guy with silver hair and dorky sunglasses.

The last to come out was the woman who played Mother Paula on the TV **commercials**. She wore a shiny gray wig, wire-rimmed glasses, and a **calico** apron. A few people clapped in recognition, and she waved **halfheartedly**.

The group marched to a rectangular clearing that had been roped off in the center of the construction site. A megaphone was handed to the silvery-haired guy, who said his name was Chuck E. Muckle, a vice-president from Mother Paula's company headquarters. He really thought he was hot snot, Roy could tell.

---

temper, tendency to become suddenly angry
commercials, advertisements
calico, light cotton cloth with a small pattern
halfheartedly, without interest or enthusiasm

Ignoring the **foreman** and the police officer, Mr. Muckle **proceeded** with great enthusiasm to introduce some local big shots—the mayor, a city councilman, and the head of the chamber of commerce.

"I can't tell you how proud and delighted we are to make Coconut Cove the home of our 469th family-style restaurant," Mr. Muckle said. "Mr. Mayor, Councilman Grandy, all of you terrific folks who've come out on this gorgeous Florida day . . . I'm here to promise you that Mother Paula will be a good citizen, a good friend, and a good neighbor to everybody!"

"Unless you're an owl," Roy said.

Mr. Muckle didn't hear it. . . . He **snickered** nervously. "Mother Paula, dearest, I think it's time. Shall we do the **deed**?"

They all posed side by side—the company V.P., the mayor, Mother Paula, Councilman Grandy, and the boss of the chamber of commerce—for the television crew and the news photographer.

Gold-painted shovels were handed out, and on Mr. Muckle's signal all the **dignitaries** smiled, leaned over, and dug up a scoopful of sand. . . .

As soon as the photo pose ended, Mr. Muckle tossed down his gold shovel and snatched up the megaphone. "Before the bulldozers and **backhoes** get rolling," he said, "Mother Paula herself wants to say a few words."

Mother Paula didn't look overjoyed to have the megaphone shoved in her hand. "You've got a real nice town," she said. "I'll see you next spring at the grand opening—"

"Oh no, you won't!"

This time the words came out of Roy's mouth as a shout, and nobody was more stunned than he. A **tremor** rippled through the audience and Beatrice edged closer, half expecting somebody to come after him.

The actress playing Mother Paula seemed miffed, peering over her cheap wire-rimmed glasses into the crowd.

"Now, who said that?"

Roy found himself raising his right arm. "I did, Mother Paula," he called out. "If you hurt a single one of our owls, I'm not eating any more of your stupid pancakes."

"What're you talking about? What owls?"

---

foreman, person who is in charge of a group of workers
proceeded, continued
snickered, laughed quietly in a way that is not nice at something that is not supposed to be funny
deed, action
dignitaries, people who have important official positions
backhoes, large digging machines
tremor, tense feeling or shudder

Reading Skill

Identify the words you don't understand *as you read* and ask your teacher or peers for help with those words.

BEFORE YOU GO ON

1 Which characters pose for the television crew and news photographer?

2 Who is playing Mother Paula at the ceremony?

On Your Own
Summarize the main events in the story so far.

Reading 3 **337**

Chuck Muckle **lunged for** the megaphone, but Mother Paula **threw an elbow** and caught him square in the gut. "Back off, Chuckie Cheeseball," she huffed.

"Go on, check it out for yourself," Roy said, gesturing around. "Wherever you see one of those holes, there's an owl den underneath. It's where they build their nests and lay their eggs. It's their home."

Mr. Muckle's cheeks turned purple. The mayor looked lost, Councilman Grandy looked like he was about to faint, and the chamber-of-commerce guy looked like he'd swallowed a bar of soap.

By now, the parents in the crowd were talking loudly and pointing at the den holes. A few of the schoolkids started chanting in support of Roy, and Beatrice's soccer teammates began waving their hand-lettered signs.

One said: MOTHER PAULA DOESN'T **GIVE A HOOT** ABOUT OWLS!

Another read: BIRD KILLERS GO HOME!

And still a third sign said: SAVE THE OWLS, BURY THE BUTTERMILKS!

As the news photographer snapped pictures of the protesters, Mother Paula pleaded, "But I don't want to hurt your owls! Really, I wouldn't hurt a flea!"

Chuck Muckle finally recaptured the megaphone and boomed a harsh **scolding** at Roy: "Young fellow, you'd better get your facts straight before making such outrageous and **slanderous** charges. There are no owls here, not one! Those old burrows have been **abandoned** for years."

> ✔ **LITERARY CHECK**
> *How do these sentences—"Back off, Chuckie Cheeseball" and "Mother Paula doesn't give a hoot about owls"—add to the **humor** of the story?*

---

lunged for, made a sudden forceful movement toward
threw an elbow, stuck out an elbow to stop someone
give a hoot, care
scolding, statement that someone has done something wrong
slanderous, untrue
abandoned, not used or taken care of

"Yeah?" Roy reached into his backpack and whipped out his mother's camera. "I've got proof!" he shouted. "Right here."

The kids in the crowd hooted and hurrahed. Chuck Muckle's face went gray and slack. He held out his arms and lurched toward Roy. "Lemme see that!"

Scooting out of reach, Roy switched on the digital camera and held his breath. He had no idea what he was about to see.

He pressed the button to display the first photograph that Mullet Fingers had taken. The instant that the blurred, crooked image appeared in the viewfinder, Roy knew he was in trouble.

It was a picture of a finger.

Anxiously he clicked to the second frame, what he saw was no less discouraging: a dirty bare foot. It appeared to be a boy's foot, and Roy knew whose it was.

Beatrice's stepbrother had many special talents, but nature photography obviously wasn't one of them. . . .

Roy was crushed—the pictures taken by Beatrice's stepbrother were worthless. The **authorities** in charge of protecting the burrowing owls would never block the construction of the pancake house based on such fuzzy evidence. . . .

Then a young voice rose up: "Wait, it ain't over! Not by a mile it ain't."

This time it wasn't Roy.

"Uh-oh," said Beatrice, lifting her eyes.

A girl in the rear of the crowd let out a shriek, and everybody wheeled at once to look. At first glance the object on the ground could have been mistaken for a kickball, but it was actually . . . a boy's head.

His matted hair was blond, his face was caramel-brown, and his eyes were wide and unblinking. A kite string led from his pursed lips to the handle of a large tin bucket a few feet away.

The big shots came hurrying out of the crowd, with Beatrice and Roy at their heels. They all stopped to **gape** at the head on the ground.

"What now?" moaned the construction foreman.

Chuck Muckle **thundered**: "Is this somebody's idea of a sick joke?"

"Good heavens," cried the mayor, "is he dead?"

The boy wasn't the least bit dead. He smiled up at his stepsister and winked slyly at Roy. Somehow he'd fit his entire skinny body down the opening of an owl burrow, so that only his noggin stuck out.

"Yo, Mother Paula," he said.

---

scooting, moving quickly
authorities, people or organization
gape, look at something for a long time, with their mouths open because they
  are shocked
thundered, yelled in a loud voice

✔ LITERARY CHECK
What is humorous about this scene in the story?

BEFORE YOU GO ON

1 Why does Chuck E. Muckle **deny** that any owls live in the burrows?

2 What is the **image** in the photo taken by Mullet Fingers?

💡 **On Your Own**
Summarize the most important events so far.

The actress stepped forward hesitantly. Her wig looked slightly crooked and her makeup was beginning to melt in the humidity.

"What is it?" she asked uneasily.

"You bury those birds," Mullet Fingers said, "you gotta bury me, too."

"But no, I love birds! All birds!"

"Officer Delinko? Where are you!" Chuck Muckle **motioned** for the policeman to come forward. "Arrest this **impertinent** little creep right now."

"For what?"

"Trespassing, obviously."

"But your company advertised this event as open to the public," Officer Delinko pointed out. "If I arrest the boy, I'll have to arrest everyone else on the property, too."

Roy watched as a vein in Mr. Muckle's neck swelled up and began to pulse like a garden hose. "I'll be speaking to Chief Deacon about you first thing tomorrow," Mr. Muckle hissed under his breath at the patrolman. "That gives you one whole night to work on your **sorry excuse** for a résumé."

Next he turned his **withering gaze** upon the **forlorn** foreman. "Mr. Branitt, please uproot this . . . this stringy *weed*."

"Wouldn't try that," Beatrice's stepbrother warned though clenched jaws.

"Really. And why not?" Chuck Muckle said.

The boy smiled. "Roy, do me a favor. Check out what's in the bucket."

Roy was happy to **oblige**.

"What do you see?" the boy asked.

"**Cottonmouth moccasins**," Roy replied.

"How many?"

"Nine or ten."

"They look happy, Roy?"

"Not really."

"What do you think's gonna happen if I tip that thing over?" With his tongue Mullet Fingers displayed the string that connected him to the bucket.

"Somebody could get hurt pretty bad," Roy said, playing along. He had been mildly surprised (though relieved) to see that the reptiles in the bucket were made of rubber.

---

motioned, gave directions using his hand(s)
impertinent, impolite, disrespectful
sorry excuse, worthless or poor excuse
withering gaze, look that makes someone feel stupid
    or embarrassed
forlorn, sad and lonely
oblige, do what he asked
cottonmouth moccasins, venomous water snakes
    that live in the southeastern United States

Mr. Muckle **stewed**. "This is ridiculous—Branitt, do what I told you. Get that kid outta my sight!"

The foreman backed away. "Not me. I don't much care for snakes."

"Really? Then you're fired." Once again the vice-president turned to confront Officer Delinko. "Make yourself useful. Shoot the damn things."

"No, sir, not around all these people. Too dangerous."

The policeman approached the boy and dropped to one knee.

"How'd you get here?" he asked.

"Hopped the fence last night. Then I hid under the backhoe," the boy said. . . . "Man, you don't understand. The owls got no chance against those machines."

"I do understand. I honestly do," Officer Delinko said. "One more question: You serious about the cottonmouths?"

"Serious as a heart attack."

"Can I have a look inside the bucket?"

The boy's eyes flickered. "It's your funeral," he said.

Roy whispered to Beatrice: "We've gotta do something quick. Those snakes aren't real."

"Oh, great."

As the policeman approached the tin bucket, Beatrice shouted, "Don't do it! You might get bit—"

Officer Delinko didn't flinch. He peeked over the rim for what seemed to Roy and Beatrice like an eternity.

Jig's up, Roy thought **glumly**. No way he won't notice they're fake.

Yet the patrolman didn't say a word as he backed away from the bucket.

"Well?" Mr. Muckle demanded. "What do we do?"

"Kid's for real. If I were you, I'd **negotiate**," said Officer Delinko.

"Ha! I don't negotiate with juvenile delinquents." With a **snarl**, Chuck Muckle snatched the gold-painted shovel from Councilman Grandy's hands and charged toward the bucket.

"Don't!" hollered the boy in the owl hole, spitting the string.

But the man from Mother Paula's was unstoppable. With a wild swing of the shovel he knocked over the bucket, and commenced **flailing** and hacking at the snakes in a blind, **slobbering fury**. He didn't stop until they were in pieces.

Little rubber pieces.

---

stewed, became angry because something bad has just happened
glumly, unhappily
negotiate, discuss something in order to reach an agreement
snarl, angry growl like an animal
flailing, waving his arms and legs in a fast but uncontrolled way
slobbering fury, state of extreme anger

BEFORE YOU GO ON

1 What does Chuck E. Muckle ask Officer Delinko to do to Mullet Fingers?

2 Why doesn't Officer Delinko flinch when he looks in the bucket?

On Your Own
What do you think will happen next?

Reading 3 **341**

Exhausted, Chuck Muckle leaned over and squinted at the **mutilated** toy snakes. His expression reflected both disbelief and humiliation. . . .

"Hey, them snakes're fake!" Curly piped. "They ain't even real."

Roy leaned toward Beatrice and whispered, "Another Einstein."

Chuck Muckle pivoted in slow motion. Ominously he pointed the blade of the shovel at the boy in the owl burrow.

"You!" he **bellowed**, stalking forward.

Roy jumped in front of him.

"Outta my way, kid," Chuck Muckle said. "I don't have time for any more of your nonsense. Move it *now*!"

It was clear that the Mother Paula's bigshot had totally lost his cool, and possibly his marbles.

"What're you doing?" Roy asked, knowing he probably wouldn't get a calm, patient answer.

"I said, *Get outta my way*! I'm gonna dig that little twerp out of the ground myself."

Beatrice Leep darted forward and stood next to Roy, taking his right hand. An anxious murmur swept through the crowd.

"Aw, that's real cute. Just like **Romeo and Juliet**," Chuck Muckle **taunted**. He dropped his voice and said, "Game over, kiddies. On the count of three, I'm going to start using this shovel—or better yet, how about I get Baldy over here to crank up the bulldozer?"

The foreman scowled. "Thought you said I was fired." . . .

Roy turned to see that Beatrice had been joined by the entire soccer team, linking arms in a silent chain. They were tall, strong girls who weren't the least bit intimidated by Chuck Muckle's **blustery** threats.

Chuck Muckle realized it, too. "Stop this foolishness right now!" he begged. "There's no need for an ugly mob scene."

Roy watched in wonderment as more and more kids slipped out of the crowd and began joining hands, forming a human barricade around Beatrice's self-buried stepbrother. None of the parents made a move to stop them.

The TV cameraman announced that the demonstration was being broadcast live on the noon news, while the photographer from the paper **swooped in** for a close-up of Mr. Muckle, looking drained, defeated, and suddenly very old. He braced himself on the ceremonial shovel as if it were a cane.

---

mutilated, severely damaged
bellowed, shouted loudly in a deep voice
Romeo and Juliet, two young lovers in a Shakespeare play
taunted, joked to anger or upset someone
blustery, loud and bullying
swooped in, moved in very quickly

"Didn't any of you people hear me?" he **rasped**. "This event is over! Done! You can all go home now." . . .

Roy was in an eerie yet **tranquil** daze.

Some girl started singing a famous old folk song called "This Land Is Your Land." It was Beatrice, of all people, and her voice was surprisingly lovely and soft. Before long, the other kids were singing along, too. Roy shut his eyes and felt like he was floating on the sunny slope of a cloud.

"Excuse me, hotshot. Got room for one more?"

Roy blinked open his eyes and broke into a grin.

"Yes, ma'am," he said.

Mother Paula stepped between him and Garrett to join the circle. Her voice was gravelly, but she could carry a tune just fine. . . .

Overhead, a small dusky-colored bird was flying in marvelous daring corkscrews. Roy and Beatrice watched in delight as it **banked** lower and lower, finishing with a **radical** dive toward the burrow at the center of the circle.

Everybody whirled to see where the bird had landed. All of a sudden the singing stopped.

There was Mullet Fingers, trying not to giggle, the **daredevil** owl perched calmly on the crown of his head.

"Don't worry, little guy," the boy said. "You're safe for now."

---

rasped, spoke in a rough, unpleasant way
tranquil, pleasantly calm
banked, sloped to one side while turning
radical, wonderful
daredevil, bold and not caring about danger

ABOUT THE **AUTHOR**

Carl Hiaasen is a best-selling author of young adult novels and a proud lifelong resident of Florida. After graduating from the University of Florida, Hiaasen began working at the *Miami Herald* as a reporter. He still contributes a weekly column to the paper today, in addition to writing novels. *Hoot*, one of Hiaasen's most popular novels, was a Newbery Honor book. It was so successful that it was made into a movie.

BEFORE YOU GO ON

1. What do Roy, Beatrice, and the other demonstrators do to protect Mullet Fingers?

2. How does Chuck E. Muckle look at the end?

On Your Own
How do Roy, Mullet Fingers, and Beatrice show courage and imagination?

Reading 3 **343**

► **READER'S THEATER**

Act out the following scene between Roy and Beatrice.

Roy: Bea, did you hear what just happened? Mother Paula's decided to build a new restaurant in our town!

Beatrice: Oh, that's cool.

Roy: No, it's not! They want to build it where the burrowing owls live over by Coconut Cove! They've got the mayor and the city council on their side.

Beatrice: Those poor little owls! We have to do something!

Roy: What can we do? They start building next week.

Beatrice: Hmm . . . I know! We have to get out and tell people. Once they know about the owls, they definitely won't want the restaurant there.

Roy: But how can we tell the whole town?

Beatrice: We'll bring signs and posters to the groundbreaking ceremony. The whole town will show up, and then we'll let them know what's *really* going on!

Audio

► **COMPREHENSION**   Workbook Page 181

Recall

1. Who is Chuck E. Muckle?
2. What kind of snakes does Roy say are in the bucket?

Comprehend

3. Roy wants to show that the owls still live in their burrows. What proof does he have? Why isn't it any good?
4. What kind of snakes does Mullet Fingers use to stop Chuck Muckle from breaking ground for the new restaurant? Why does this plan work?

Analyze

5. Do you think that the author agrees with Roy and Mullet Fingers or with Chuck Muckle? What makes you think so?

6. Why does Mother Paula decide to demonstrate with the kids and other community members at the end of the excerpt?

Connect

7. Is it a good idea for human beings to try to take care of wildlife? Why?

8. Have you or someone close to you ever felt so strongly about an issue that you decided to **demonstrate** about it? Explain.

➤ DISCUSSION

Discuss in pairs or small groups.

1. Which part of the excerpt from *Hoot* did you find the most humorous? Why?

2. In what ways can writers add humor to a story? Give some examples of humorous stories, television shows, and movies.

3. In what ways can builders be more careful when preparing to build on sites where birds and animals live?

Q How are courage and imagination linked? Do you think that it is important to fight for animals' rights? Would you be willing to work to preserve animals and their habitats? If so, how could you use your imagination to come up with ways to help animals?

➤ RESPONSE TO LITERATURE

Workbook
Page 181

Utilize *Hoot* is a humorous novel about saving burrowing owls. The author shows Chuck E. Muckle as a silly character with the wrong ideas and motives. But think about the problem of the burrowing owls from Chuck E. Muckle's point of view. After all, he can't open his new restaurant. He might even lose his job. Demonstrate your understanding of the story by retelling part of it from Chuck E. Muckle's point of view. Suggest how he might solve his problem. When you are finished writing, share your paragraph with a partner. Discuss how Chuck E. Muckle must feel about what is happening to him.

A burrowing owl ▶

Reading Skill

Questions are used routinely in speaking and in written classroom materials. Make sure you recognize the difference between information questions and *yes/no* questions so you can answer questions appropriately. *Yes/no* questions often begin with the words *do/did, is/are, was/were,* or *has/have.*

»)) *Listening* SKILL

In your mind, summarize what the speaker says.

Grammar

Reported Speech

Reported speech is used to tell someone what another person has said. There is a phrase with a reporting verb, such as *say*, and a noun clause that tells what the person has said. Verb tenses and pronouns usually change in reported speech. Be sure that all pronouns refer to their antecedents.

Verb Tense Change	Quoted Speech	Reported Speech
Simple present → simple past	"Then **you're** fired," Mr. Muckle said.	Mr. Muckle said **that he was** fired.
Simple past → past perfect	"Then **I hid** under the backhoe," the boy said.	The boy said **that he had hid** under the backhoe.
Simple future (*will*) → would	He said, "**I'll** have to arrest everybody."	He said **that he would** have to arrest everybody.

If the verb in the quoted speech is negative, use the negative form of the verb in the noun clause for reported speech.

> Mother Paula said, "I **don't want** to hurt your owls."
> Mother Paula said that she **didn't want** to hurt their owls.

Grammar SKILL

The word *that* is often used in the noun clause in reported speech.

Practice
Workbook Page 182

Work with a partner. Copy the quoted speech below into your notebook. Then change it to reported speech.

Example: She said, "I'm not coming home to dinner."
She said she wasn't coming to dinner.

1. Laura said, "She called me at noon."
2. "He will leave tomorrow," my mother said.
3. Roger said, "I'm not tired."
4. "We were there yesterday," the boys said.
5. She said, "They speak English well."

Apply
Work with a partner. In your notebook, write down five statements about yourself. Read them to your partner. Take turns changing each other's statements into reported speech.

Reported Speech: Questions, Imperatives, *told*

When reporting a question, you can use the reporting verb *ask*. Notice that the word order in reported speech is the same as in a statement.

> **Quoted Speech:** "What **is it**?" she asked.   "What **do you see**?" the boy asked.
> **Reported Speech:** She asked what **it was**.   The boy asked what **he saw**.

When reporting an imperative, change the imperative to an infinitive. If the imperative is negative, *not* comes before the infinitive. The auxiliary verb *do* is not used.

> **Quoted Speech:** "**Don't worry**, little guy," the boy said.
> **Reported Speech:** The boy said **not to worry**.

Grammar SKILL

Remember, an infinitive is *to* + the base form of the verb.

Another common reporting verb is *told*. Use *told* when you want to say who the person is speaking to. An object must always follow *told*.

> **Quoted Speech:** "There **are** no owls here," Chuck Muckle **said** (to Roy).
> **Reported Speech:** Chuck Muckle **told Roy** that there **were** no owls here.

Practice  Workbook Page 183

Work with a partner. Copy the quoted speech below into your notebook. Then change it to reported speech.

Example: "Which tie do you like?" my wife asked.
        My wife asked which tie I liked.

1. "How do we get there?" Mary asked.
2. Sidney said, "Stand over there."
3. My mother told me, "Don't be late."
4. "Where is the department store?" she asked.
5. "There will be a party tomorrow," our teacher said (to us).

Apply

Work with a partner. Find other quoted speech in the reading and take turns changing it into reported speech.

✔ **GRAMMAR CHECK**

How does an imperative change in reported speech?

Writing

Write a Plot Summary

In this lesson, you'll write a plot summary. As you know, the plot is what happens in a story. A plot usually focuses on a conflict and its outcome. In a plot summary, you briefly describe the story's setting, the main characters, their goals, the main events, and the outcome of the conflict.

Writing Prompt

Write a paragraph summarizing the plot of a story, novel, movie, or television show. Include only the most important events in your summary. Use reported and quoted speech correctly. Vary your sentence lengths and patterns to make your writing flow smoothly.

1 PREWRITE Choose a plot that you remember clearly.

- Think about the setting, the main characters, and their goals.
- Ask yourself how the characters achieved their goals.
- List your ideas in a graphic organizer.  **Workbook** Page 184

A student named Brandon used this graphic organizer.

Main characters and setting:
Roy, Beatrice, and Mullet Fingers
Coconut Grove, FL

Characters' goals:
Stop a restaurant chain from building on land that is home to burrowing owls

Main events:
1. Roy tries to stop the builders by speaking out.
2. Roy tries to convince the crowd by showing photos of the owls.
3. Mullet Fingers and Roy play a prank on Mr. Muckle.

Outcome:
The main characters save the burrowing owls.

2 **DRAFT** Use your organizer to help you write a first draft.

- Include only the most important events in your summary.
- Be sure to use reported and quoted speech correctly.
- Include content-based words and other newly-acquired words.

3 **REVISE** Read over your draft. Look for places where the writing is unclear or needs improvement. Use the Writing Checklist to help you identify problems. Then revise your draft, using the editing and proofreading marks listed on page 456.

4 **EDIT** Check your work for errors in grammar, usage, mechanics, and spelling. Trade papers with a partner to obtain feedback. Use the Peer Review Checklist on Workbook page 184. Edit your final draft in response to feedback from your partner and your teacher.

5 **PUBLISH** Prepare a clean copy of your final draft. Share your plot summary with the class. Save your work. You'll need to refer to it in the Writing Workshop at the end of the unit.

Here is Brandon's plot summary. Notice his accurate use of the word *site*. Also notice how he describes the outcome of the conflict.

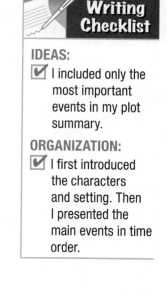

Writing Checklist

IDEAS:
☑ I included only the most important events in my plot summary.

ORGANIZATION:
☑ I first introduced the characters and setting. Then I presented the main events in time order.

Brandon Saiz

Hoot: A Summary of the Excerpt

Hoot is a funny novel set in Coconut Cove, Florida. The main characters are three teenagers: Roy, Beatrice, and her stepbrother, Mullet Fingers. They want to stop a pancake chain from building a new restaurant on a site that is home to burrowing owls. The excerpt begins at the groundbreaking ceremony for the new restaurant. Everyone in town is there, including the vice president of the chain, Chuck E. Muckle. First, Roy tries to stop the builders by speaking out. Mr. Muckle tries to shut Roy up, by saying that he'd better get his facts straight. Next, Roy tries to convince the crowd by showing photos of the owls, but the photos are unclear. Finally, Mullet Fingers appears. He has buried his body in an owl burrow. He and Roy play a prank on Mr. Muckle, who ends up looking foolish. Through their courage and creativity, the main characters save the burrowing owls.

Prepare to Read

THE BIG QUESTION

How are courage and imagination linked? Think of some situations in which you need to use your imagination to do something. These can be situations at school or at home with your family or friends, or when you are by yourself. Do you think it sometimes takes courage to have imagination? Why or why not? Use your prior experiences to discuss these questions with a partner.

BUILD BACKGROUND

In **"Between Two Worlds,"** you will learn about a great Native American leader—Quanah Parker, a Comanche chief. Quanah Parker led his people with courage. He used courage and imagination to live successfully among both whites and Native Americans.

In this article, you will learn another meaning for the word *imagination*. Quanah Parker was able to think creatively in dealing with the many problems he faced in his life.

Quanah Parker dressed as a Comanche chief ▶

► VOCABULARY

Listening and Speaking: Key Words

Read aloud and listen to the sentences with a partner. Use the context to figure out the meaning of the highlighted words. Use a dictionary to check your answers. Then write each word and its meaning in your notebook.

Key Words

armies
captured
gifted
nomads
tepees
reservation

1. None of his armies were ready for a war.
2. Cynthia Ann was just a child when she was captured by the Comanches.
3. The Comanches were gifted in languages; they spoke several.
4. Some tribes are nomads. They never settle in one place.
5. Some Native Americans lived in tepees, which made it easy to move from place to place.
6. The Comanches were forced to leave their lands and live on a reservation.

Practice  Workbook Page 185

Write the sentences in your notebook. Choose a key word from the box above to complete each sentence. Then take turns reading the sentences aloud with a partner.

1. Life on the _____ was often difficult for Native Americans.
2. The women took down the _____ and carefully packed the animal skins and wooden poles.
3. The young man was _____ and held prisoner.
4. Tribes that roam the desert are _____.
5. _____ were sent to protect the settlers and the forts.
6. Her voice was beautiful. She was considered a _____ singer.

Listening and Speaking: Academic Words

Study the red words and their meanings. You will find these words useful when talking and writing about informational texts. Write each word and its meaning in your notebook, then say the words aloud with a partner. After you read "Between Two Worlds," try to use these words to respond to the text.

Academic Words

circumstances
construct   Audio
react
region

circumstances = the facts or conditions that affect a situation, action, or event	Because of the difficult **circumstances**, Quanah Parker surrendered to the white armies.
construct = build something large such as a building, bridge, or sculpture	To **construct** a tepee, you need animal skin and wooden poles.
react = behave in a particular way because of what someone has done or said to you	Cynthia Ann's family did not **react** well when she didn't want to come back home.
region = a fairly large area of a state, country, and so on	The Comanches traveled the **region** of the Midwest looking for food.

Audio

Practice  Workbook Page 186

Work with a partner to answer these questions. Try to include the red word in your answer. Write the sentences in your notebook.

1. Under what circumstances can you leave school early?
2. What materials could you use to construct a tent?
3. How would you react if someone surprised you?
4. What region of the country do you live in?

Word Study: Spelling Words with -*ea*

Two vowels can work as a team to stand for one vowel sound. The vowel team *ea* often stands for the long vowel sound /ē/. The vowel team *ea* can also stand for the short vowel sound /e/. In a few words, *ea* stands for the long vowel sound /ā/. Study the chart.

Single and Multisyllabic Words with *ea*		
/ē/ spelled *ea*	/e/ spelled *ea*	/ā/ spelled *ea*
sp**ea**k	h**ea**d-wa-ters	gr**ea**t
tr**ea**t-ed	a-h**ea**d	br**ea**k

In multisyllabic words, or words with more than one syllable, the letters *ea* can also stand for two separate sounds because the letter *e* is part of one syllable and the letter *a* is part of another.

ar-**e-a**	cr**e**-**a**te	i-d**e**-**a**	Ko-r**e**-**a**

Practice

Work with a partner. Copy the chart above into your notebook. Say a word from the chart, and ask your partner to spell it aloud. Your partner says the next word. Continue until you have both spelled all of the words correctly. Then, practice spelling these words with your partner: *neat, dead, daybreak, breath,* and *breathe.* Add them to the chart under the correct headings.

READING STRATEGY ▏ CLASSIFY

Classifying helps you understand, organize, and remember what you read. To classify, you arrange things into groups with common characteristics. Classifying words helps you learn and remember their meanings. To classify words in a text, follow this example:

- In "Between Two Worlds" many words fall into one of two categories—Native Americans and whites.
- Ask yourself, "Which words relate to these categories?" Group the words.

As you read "Between Two Worlds," find words that relate to Native Americans and whites. Make a T-chart and copy the words into your notebook.

Set a purpose for reading How did Quanah Parker show courage when his people were starving? Do you think his mother, Cynthia Ann Parker, showed courage when she was captured by the Native Americans?

Between TWO Worlds

Audio

▲ Quanah Parker

One of the most famous Native American chiefs had an interesting **heritage.** His mother was a white woman, and his father was a great Comanche chief. Quanah Parker was the last chief of the Comanches. He was a fearless **warrior,** a brave leader, and a man who could **adapt** to any situation. His story is a fascinating one.

The Comanches were nomads who traveled from place to place. They lived in tepees, a kind of tent made from animal skins stretched over wooden poles. They were skilled horsemen and traders. The men hunted and the women gathered berries and other **edible** plants. When food became **scarce,** they packed up their tepees and traveled to a better spot. The women were responsible for taking down the tepees and putting them up again when they found a new place to settle. They were careful not to break the wooden poles or tear the animal skins.

The Comanches were very good traders. Many of them were gifted in languages. They could speak some of the European languages as well as a number of the Native American languages. Some people say many of the things they traded were stolen. They raided ranches to steal horses and cattle. They even captured women and children.

---

heritage, traditional beliefs, values, and customs
warrior, soldier or fighter
adapt, gradually change behavior to be successful
edible, safe to eat
scarce, low in supply

Quanah's mother was a young white woman named Cynthia Ann Parker. Her family settled in what is now central Texas along the **headwaters** of the Navasota River. The Parker family built a settlement with a **fort** for **protection.** Then in 1836, several Native American groups attacked the fort. Cynthia Ann was 11 or 12 years old when she was captured, or taken prisoner, during the raid. At first she was not treated well by her **captors.** They beat her and made her work very hard. After a while, she was given to a Comanche couple. They loved her and treated her like their own daughter. They taught her the Comanche language and customs.

As Cynthia Ann grew up, she learned to love the Native American ways. She married a young chief, Peta Nocoma. They had three children, two boys and a girl. Her oldest son was Quanah. Years later, when the white settlers tried to get her back, Cynthia Ann refused to go. She loved her family and loved the Native American ways. Eventually, when she was captured by white people, she was locked in a room to keep her from returning to her Native American family.

headwaters, streams that form a river
fort, strong building defended by soldiers
protection, a way of keeping someone or something safe
captors, those holding others prisoner

▲ The Parker family settled in the wilderness. They later built a fort for protection.

BEFORE YOU GO ON

1 How did Cynthia Parker become part of two worlds?

2 What work did the Comanche men do? What work did the women do?

On Your Own
How did the Comanches use imagination to adapt to a nomadic way of life? How do you use imagination to adapt to changes in your life?

Cynthia Ann's son, Quanah, grew up to become the chief. He was a wise leader and tried his best to **guide** his people. He was a **skilled** warrior. He was creative in the ways he defeated other Comanche **bands** and Native American tribes. He used this imagination to keep one step ahead of the white armies. These bands of soldiers wanted the Comanches to live on reservations. Reservations were areas of land that the white settlers didn't want. They forced the Native Americans to live on these plots of land so that they could settle the Native American lands themselves. The armies promised the Native Americans they would be well taken care of.

Quanah did not **trust** the armies. He had heard some of these **promises** before. He didn't trust them to keep their word. So he decided to go to war. He fought the armies to keep his people free.

---

guide, show the way
skilled, trained and experienced
bands, groups within a larger group
trust, believe in honesty and goodness of someone
    or something
promises, statements indicating that what is expected
    will definitely be done

Quanah Parker ▶

▲ Native Americans could pack tepees quickly for travel.

The battles continued until Quanah realized there was no hope of winning. His people were starving and his **braves** were tired of fighting. He realized that **surrender** was his only **option,** even though he had never lost a battle with the white settlers. It took a lot of courage on that June day in 1875 for Quanah and his warriors to surrender to the army at Fort Sill.

Quanah learned the ways of the white man, but he never gave up some of his Comanche customs. He still followed his Native American ways of worship. He became a **prosperous** rancher and eventually had a large herd of cattle. In his time he met many famous people. He even went hunting with President Theodore Roosevelt.

You could say that Quanah Parker lived between two worlds. Perhaps, at times, he was able to appreciate what was good in each of them.

---

braves, young Native American men
surrender, officially stop fighting; give up
option, choice
prosperous, well off; rich and successful

◀ **Though Quanah Parker was successful, he never gave up Comanche customs.**

BEFORE YOU GO ON

1 Why didn't Quanah trust the armies?

2 Why did Quanah decide to surrender?

On Your Own
Do you think Quanah was courageous? Why or why not?

> ### COMPREHENSION

Workbook
Page 189

Speaking SKILL

Be ready to answer questions and share your opinions with classmates.

Recall

1. What did the Parker family **construct** along the Navasota River?
2. Why did Cynthia Ann refuse to go back to the white settlers?

Comprehend

3. What **circumstances** caused Quanah to distrust the armies?
4. How did Quanah **react** to the promises of the white armies?

Analyze

5. Why do you think Cynthia Ann adapted so well to Comanche life?
6. Why do you think Quanah adapted so well to living among whites?

Connect

7. What would be your biggest challenge in adapting to a new **region** or another culture? Why?
8. How did imagination help Quanah to lead his people?

> ### IN YOUR OWN WORDS

Imagine that you are telling a classmate about "Between Two Worlds." You want to include all the main ideas and important details. Complete the chart below to help you organize your ideas. Then share your summary with a classmate.

Section	Main Idea	Important Details
Introduction (paragraph 1)		
Comanche Life (paragraphs 2 and 3)		
Cynthia Ann's life (paragraphs 4 and 5)		
Quanah's life (paragraphs 6–9)		

▶ DISCUSSION

Discuss in pairs or small groups.

1. How did having a white mother affect Quanah Parker?
2. What qualities did Quanah have that helped him prosper living among whites? Explain.

Q How are courage and imagination linked? Why are courage and imagination important traits in adapting to new situations? Think of an example when you showed courage and imagination in adapting to a new situation.

▶)) *Listening* SKILL
Do not interrupt your classmates when they are speaking. Save your questions until a speaker is finished.

▶ READ FOR FLUENCY

Reading with feeling helps make what you read more interesting. Work with a partner. Choose a paragraph from the reading. Read the paragraph to yourselves. Ask each other how you felt after reading the paragraph. Did you feel happy or sad?

Take turns reading the paragraph aloud to each other with a tone of voice that represents how you felt when you read it the first time. Give each other feedback.

▶ EXTENSION  Workbook Page 189

Utilize "Between Two Worlds" provides a lot of information about Comanche life. Now that you have read about this topic, go to www.LongmanKeystone.com for links to other types of media on this topic. Follow the online instructions to compare the social and cultural views presented in the different media with views presented in the reading.

◀ It takes courage to live in a new place.

Grammar

Active Voice and Passive Voice

The active voice is used when the focus is on the person or thing that performs the action, also called the performer. The passive voice is used when the focus is on the receiver of the action. A *by*-phrase is used to identify the performer.

> The white people **captured** Cynthia Ann. [focus is on the white people]
> Cynthia Ann **was captured** by the white people. [focus is on Cynthia Ann]

Form the passive voice with a form of *be* + the past participle. Form the negative with *not* or a contraction of *not* (*isn't, wasn't,* etc.).

> At first she **wasn't treated** well by her captors.

Grammar SKILL

Remember the simple present of *be* is *am, is,* or *are*; the simple past is *was* or *were*.

Form the past participle of regular verbs by adding *-d* or *-ed* to the base form of the verb. The past participles of irregular verbs must be memorized.

Irregular Past Participles								
be	→	been	do	→	did	give	→	given
become	→	become	drink	→	drunk	hit	→	hit
come	→	come	find	→	found	make	→	made

Practice  **Workbook** Page 190

Work with a partner. Write the sentences in your notebook. Identify which is active voice and which is passive voice.

Example: The stones were discovered by the scientists. *passive voice*

1. The document was signed by everyone. _____

2. Mice eat cheese. _____

3. Seeds are eaten by birds. _____

4. The flowers were grown by our neighbors. _____

5. Jack mailed the letter. _____

Apply

Work with a partner. Find and write down three active voice sentences and one passive voice sentence from the reading.

Passive Voice: Omitting the *by*-phrase

A *by*-phrase is used in passive voice sentences when it is important to know the performer of the action.

Many languages are spoken **by the Comanches**.
She was captured **by the Indians**.

Often the performer of the action is not known, or it is not important to know the performer. For these reasons, writers will use the passive, rather than the active, voice. When the performer of the action is unimportant or unknown, the *by*-phrase is omitted.

Cynthia Ann was eleven years old when she **was captured**. [The phrase *by the Indians* is omitted because it is not important.]
They **were** even **known** to steal or capture women and children. [The *by*-phrase is omitted because it is not known.]

Practice  **Workbook Page 191**

Work with a partner. Rewrite the sentences, changing them from active voice to passive voice. Include the *by*-phrase only if necessary.

Example: My father built that house.
That house was built by my father.

1. Someone built that house in 1999.
2. Shakespeare wrote *Romeo and Juliet* in 1597.
3. Someone published a new edition of *Romeo and Juliet* last year.
4. People reported a robbery on our street.
5. People speak Spanish in Peru.

Apply

Work with a partner. Find three active voice sentences in the reading and rewrite them in passive voice.

Writing

Write a Paragraph That Classifies

You have learned that expository writing gives information and explanations. When you classify information, you group similar ideas and details together by category. Classifying information is an effective way to organize a paragraph. First, you list the categories that your topic includes. Then you describe each category in detail.

Writing Prompt

Write a paragraph about three types or categories of art that you enjoy. First, introduce each type or category. Then explain the features of each category. Tell why you like each type of art. Remember to use the active and passive voice correctly.

---

1 **PREWRITE** Begin by choosing three types of art.

- Think about how these three types of art are different from each other. Is one type modern and another type ancient? Is one type sculpture and another type water-color paintings?

- Brainstorm similar features within each category.

- List your ideas in a graphic organizer.

**Workbook
Page 192**

Here's a graphic organizer created by a student named Koji. He decided to discuss three different types of art by the artist Picasso.

Paintings	Plates	Sculptures
most well-known	three dimensional	three dimensional
two dimensional	paintings and sculptural designs	made with wood, clay, metal, stone, or combination
wide range of realistic and abstract styles	images of people and birds	wide range of realistic and abstract subjects

2 **DRAFT** Use your organizer to help you write a first draft.

- Remember to list your categories at the beginning of your paragraph.
- Explain with specificity and detail each category's features.
- Vary your sentence lengths and patterns to make your writing flow smoothly.

3 **REVISE** Read over your draft. Look for places where the writing is unclear or needs improvement. Use the Writing Checklist to help you identify problems. Then revise your draft, using the editing and proofreading marks listed on page 456.

4 **EDIT** Check your work for errors in grammar, usage, mechanics, and spelling. Trade papers with a partner to obtain feedback. Use the Peer Review Checklist on Workbook page 192. Edit your final draft in response to feedback from your partner and your teacher.

5 **PUBLISH** Prepare a clean copy of your final draft. Share your classification paragraph with the class. Save your work. You'll need to refer to it in the Writing Workshop at the end of the unit.

Here is Koji's paragraph classifying different types of art by Picasso. Notice how clearly he describes the features of each category.

Writing Checklist

ORGANIZATION:
☑ I introduced my categories and then described the features of each one.

CONVENTIONS:
☑ I used the active and passive voice correctly.

Koji Mori

Picasso's Paintings, Plates, and Sculptures
I have seen and enjoyed three types of artwork by Picasso: his paintings, plates, and sculptures. His paintings on canvas are his most well-known works. Like all paintings, they are two dimensional. Picasso's come in a wide range of styles including realistic portraits and abstract works. Picasso did a second type of artwork that I like very much: paintings and sculpted designs on three-dimensional objects such as plates. The subjects of these paintings include images of people and birds. The third type of artwork, and my own personal favorite, are Picasso's sculptures. These three-dimensional artworks were made from all kinds of materials. Picasso used wood, clay, metal, stone, or a combination of materials. His sculptures exhibit a wide range of subjects, from realistic figures of people, animals, and birds to abstract works.

Link the Readings

Look back at the readings in this unit. Think about what they all have in common. They all have something to do with courage and imagination. Yet they do not all have the same purpose. The purpose of one reading might be to inform, while the purpose of another might be to entertain or persuade. In addition, the content of each reading relates to courage and imagination in different ways. Now copy the chart below into your notebook and complete it.

Title of Reading	Purpose	Big Question Link
From *The Secret Garden*	to entertain	
"A Tree Grows in Kenya" "How to Plant a Tree"		tells the story of an environmentalist who won the Nobel Peace Prize
From *Hoot*		
"Between Two Worlds"		

Discussion

Discuss in pairs or small groups.

- What conclusion can you draw about the imagination and courage of the people and characters in the readings? Do the real people and fictional characters share certain traits? Explain.

- **Q How are courage and imagination linked?** Think about the readings. In what ways do you think courage and imagination are linked? How do the people and situations in the readings demonstrate the link between the two traits?

Media Literacy & Projects

Work in pairs or small groups. Choose one of these projects.

1 Mary Lennox in *The Secret Garden* was born and raised in India. When her parents die, she moves to England. Create a poster showing all the countries controlled by Great Britain in the early 1900s when the story was written.

2 "A Tree Grows in Kenya: The Story of Wangari Maathai" is about the country of Kenya. Find out more about this country's history on the Internet. Make a fact file about Kenya with interesting facts about the country. Share your file with a partner.

3 You read only one chapter of *Hoot*. What do you think happens at the end of the novel? Write a plot summary of the ending. Then read the book to see if your prediction is correct.

4 You learned how to plant a tree. Now, grow some seeds. Save the seeds from the fruits you eat, such as apples and avocados. Plant different kinds of seeds in different containers. Write down when each type of seed starts to grow and how fast it grows.

Further Reading

Choose from these reading suggestions. Practice reading silently for longer periods with increased comprehension.

The Gift of the Magi and Other Stories, O. Henry
This Penguin Reader® adaptation includes the classic story of a poor couple who use their imaginations to buy each other a special holiday gift.

The Lotus Seed, Sherry Garland
Fleeing her war-torn country, a Vietnamese girl takes a lotus seed to remind her of her homeland. Later, when her grandson plants the seed, a pink lotus blossom grows.

Flash, Carl Hiaasen
This book, by the author of *Hoot*, also tackles environmental issues with a touch of humor.

Put It All Together

LISTENING & SPEAKING WORKSHOP
How-To Demonstration

With a group, you will tell and show the class how to do something.

1 **THINK ABOUT IT** Reread "A Tree Grows in Kenya: The Story of Wangari Maathai" and "How to Plant a Tree."

In small groups, discuss how Wangari Maathai helped the environment and the people of Kenya. Review the steps involved in planting a tree. Practice listing the steps you follow to perform another simple activity, such as making a sandwich or brushing your teeth.

Work together to develop a list of ideas for a how-to demonstration. Think of interesting activities your group could show the class, using props or pictures. For example:

- How to play the flute
- How to make an origami flower
- How to build a birdhouse
- How to wash a car

2 **GATHER AND ORGANIZE INFORMATION** As a group, choose a topic from your list. Write down what you already know about how to do the activity. Try to write step-by-step instructions. Also write down any questions you have.

Research Go to the library, search the Internet, or ask an adult for more information about how to perform the activity. Look for answers to your questions. Take notes on what you find.

Order Your Notes Organize your notes, using a sequence-of-events chart to show the order of the steps in your activity. Decide which step(s) each group member will present. Assign one person to give a short introduction that tells what activity your group will demonstrate.

Use Visuals Find or make props that you can use to show the key steps in the process that you will demonstrate. You may also want to create posters, models, or other visuals to help you explain the steps.

3 PRACTICE AND PRESENT Use your sequence-of-events chart as an outline for your how-to demonstration. As a group, practice your demonstration several times. Use your visuals to help explain each step in the activity. When possible, act out the steps with props. Work on making smooth transitions between speakers. If possible, ask a classmate or friend to listen and give your group suggestions about how to improve your demonstration. Listen to these directions and follow them.

Deliver Your How-to Demonstration Speak loudly enough so that everyone in the class can hear you. Make eye contact with people as you speak. Emphasize important points by changing your tone of voice, slowing down, and using actions or visuals to help show your meaning. At the end of the demonstration, give your audience a chance to ask questions.

4 EVALUATE THE PRESENTATION

A good way to improve your speaking and listening skills is to evaluate each presentation you give and hear. Use this checklist to help you judge your group's how-to demonstration and the demonstrations of your classmates.

- ☑ Did the group present each step in the how-to demonstration clearly?
- ☑ Were the steps presented in a logical order?
- ☑ Did the demonstration give you enough information to do the activity on your own?
- ☑ Did the group members use props and other visuals effectively?
- ☑ What suggestions do you have for improving the demonstration?

Speaking SKILL

Make note cards to remind yourself of important ideas and details in the step(s) you are presenting. Add words or symbols that tell you when to speak and what props or visuals to use.

Listening SKILLS

Listen and watch carefully. Use both verbal *and* nonverbal cues to interpret a speaker's message.

Monitor what you are hearing. Does it make sense? Would you be able to explain the steps to someone else? If not, seek clarification. Write down questions and ask them at the end of the demonstration. When responding, give your audience as much information as possible.

STRENGTHEN YOUR SOCIAL LANGUAGE

In your classes, you will need to be able to communicate with your teacher and classmates. Go to www.LongmanKeystone.com and do another activity for this unit. This activity will help you to learn and use routine language necessary for classroom communication.

WRITING WORKSHOP

Expository Essay

Write an Expository Essay

You have learned that an expository essay gives information about a topic. One type of expository essay explains how to solve a problem or do an activity. The essay begins with a paragraph that introduces the problem or activity. Body paragraphs provide suggested solutions to the problem or instructions for the activity. A conclusion summarizes what the writer has explained.

> **Writing Prompt**
>
> Write a five-paragraph expository essay that presents a problem you faced. Explain with specificity and detail how you solved this problem. Introduce the problem in the first paragraph. Include three body paragraphs with explanations, details, and examples to show how you solved the problem. Summarize your ideas in a conclusion.

1 **PREWRITE** Review your previous work in this unit. Now brainstorm ideas for a topic. Choose a problem that you were proud of solving. In your notebook, answer these questions:

Ongoing Writing Skills Practice

- What problem did I face that I wanted to solve?

- What steps did I take to meet this challenge?

- List your ideas in a graphic organizer.  **Workbook** Page 193

Here's a graphic organizer created by a student named Danielle.

Problem	Solution
Wanted to attract more wildlife to my yard	Figured out what lives in area, like butterflies and hummingbirds
	Found out facts about things they need for food and shelter
	Asked permission to add things like feeders
	Stopped doing things that might scare wildlife away
	Now, see hummingbirds in my yard

2 **DRAFT** Use your graphic organizer and the model on page 372 to help you write a first draft.

- Keep your purpose in mind—to explain how a problem was solved.

- Remember to include an introduction and conclusion.

- Be sure to use reported speech correctly.

3 **REVISE** Read over your draft. Think about how well you have addressed questions of purpose, audience, and form. Does your essay include an introduction and conclusion? Will your topic capture readers' attention? Does your essay provide details, examples, and explanations to help readers understand your solution?

Keep these questions in mind as you revise your draft. Use the Writing Checklist below to help you identify additional issues that may need revision. Mark your changes on your draft using the editing and proofreading marks listed on page 456.

SIX TRAITS OF WRITING CHECKLIST

- ☑ **IDEAS:** Does my topic focus on solving a problem?
- ☑ **ORGANIZATION:** Do I present details, examples, and explanations in an order that makes sense?
- ☑ **VOICE:** Does my writing show my knowledge of the topic?
- ☑ **WORD CHOICE:** Do I use sequence words to clarify the time order of events?
- ☑ **SENTENCE FLUENCY:** Do I include simple, compound, and complex sentences?
- ☑ **CONVENTIONS:** Do I use reported speech correctly?

Here are the revisions Danielle plans to make to her first draft.

Wildlife Report

Last year, my friend ~~digged~~ dug a hole in her backyard to plant a flower. Out of the hole jumped a big toad! When she excited ly told me, that a toad lived in her garden I decided to try to attract more birds and other animals to my yard. I ~~done~~ did it and you can do it, too.

First You need to know what appeals to the wildlife in your region. Which birds and animals can be found nearby? What food and shelter do they like? Books and websites can tell you these facts. Then ask permission to add some of these things to your yard. Once you have permission, you can create a little habitat. For example Hummingbirds visit my area every summer. I learned that they love nectar plants, so I planted a red hibiscus. A hummingbird feeder works, too. Birdbaths provide many birds with water and a place to splash and play. Some creatures are very private, so you can build hiding places for them with piles of dirt brush, or rocks.

There are some other general tips for attracting wildlife. Try not to use chemical pesticides. Don't place nests where barking dogs may scare the birds away. Don't put lots of food in bird feeders all at once. Predators may come and eat the leftovers. Instead, put in only a small amount of food every day.

Revised to correct errors in grammar and add detail.

Revised to clarify sequence, add details, and use connecting words for fluency.

Revised to improve organization.

Finally ∧
∧You don't need to live in the country to attract wildlife. I have a

little backyard in a town. If you don't have a yard, you may be able to

volunteer at a neighborhood park or community garden. you may have

a window large enough for a bird feeder. Maybe your schoolyard can

be turned into a garden!

Right now I'm looking at a yellow butterfly on a green bush. Have

you ever wanted to invite wildlife to visit you? If you learn the facts

and do some work, you will probably see lots of wildlife!

Revised to clarify sequence.

4 **EDIT** Check your work for errors in grammar, usage, mechanics, and spelling. Then trade stories with a partner and use the Peer Review Checklist below to give each other constructive feedback. Edit your final draft in response to feedback from your partner and your teacher.

Workbook
Page 193

PEER REVIEW CHECKLIST

☑ Does the essay hold my interest and attention?
☑ Does it include specific examples, details, and explanations?
☑ Does the order of information fit the topic?
☑ Does the writer use the active and passive voice correctly?
☑ Does the writer use imperatives correctly?
☑ What changes could be made to improve the essay?

Here are the changes Danielle decided to make to her final draft as a result of her peer review.

Danielle Christian

Wildlife Report

Last year, my friend dug a hole in her backyard to plant a flower. Out of the hole jumped a big toad! When she excitedly told me that a toad lived in her garden, I decided to try to attract more birds and other animals to my yard. I did it, and you can do it, too.

Revised to correct an error in mechanics.

First, you need to know what appeals to the wildlife in your region. Which birds and animals can be found nearby? What food and shelter do they like? Books and websites can tell you these facts. Then ask permission to add some of these things to your yard. Once you have permission, you can create a little habitat. For example, hummingbirds visit my area every summer. I learned that they love brightly colored nectar plants, so I planted a red hibiscus. A hummingbird feeder works, too. Birdbaths provide many birds with water and a place to splash and play. Some creatures are very private, so you can build hiding places for them with piles of dirt, brush, or rocks

Revised to add detail and correct an error in mechanics.

There are some other general tips for attracting wildlife. Try not to use chemical pesticides. Don't place nests where barking dogs may scare the birds away. Don't put lots of food in bird feeders all at once. Predators may come and eat the leftovers. Instead, put in only a small amount of food every day.

Finally, you don't need to live in the country to attract wildlife. I have a little backyard in a town. If you don't have a yard, you may be able to volunteer at a neighborhood park or community garden. you may have a window large enough for a bird feeder. Maybe your schoolyard can be turned into a garden! Remember to ask permission. Right now, I'm looking at a yellow butterfly on a green bush. Have you ever wanted to invite wildlife to visit you? If you learn the facts and do some work, you will probably see lots of wildlife!

Revised to correct errors in mechanics and add an imperative with important information.

5 PUBLISH Prepare a clean copy of your final draft. Share your expository essay with the class.

Workbook
Page 194

Test Preparation

PRACTICE

Read the following test sample. Study the tips in the boxes. Work with a partner to answer the questions.

The Fair Trade Movement

1   The fair trade movement began in the 1940s and 1950s. Groups tried to sell products made in poor countries to markets in rich countries. Most of the first products sold were craft items. Women made most of these items while they cared for their children.

2   There are now many fair trade products you can buy. Some of the products include coffee, cocoa, tea, chocolate, clothing, and cotton. People make or grow these products in groups called <u>cooperatives</u>.

3   Fair trade organizations must meet certain requirements. Buyers have to pay the farmers or producers a minimum price. The farmers and producers have to guarantee their workers a living wage and safe working conditions. Fair trade organizations have to invest some of the money they make in the community where they do business.

4   The fair trade movement has its supporters and critics. People who support it say it helps farmers and producers gain <u>access</u> to markets. Critics feel fair trade standards are too strict, or not strict enough. Whether we agree or disagree with the fair trade movement, we know it is here to stay.

1 A <u>cooperative</u> is _____.

    A   people or groups acting alone
    B   people or groups working together
    C   a very large company
    D   a place to buy organic food

2 If Maria wants to gain <u>access</u> to something, what does she want to gain?

    F   entry
    G   discounts
    H   promises
    K   profits

Taking Tests
You will often take tests that help show what you know. Study the tips below to help you improve your test-taking skills.

Tip
Some of the words in the passage have multiple meanings. Be sure you understand the context in which a word with multiple meanings is used.

Tip
In Question 2, you are being asked to apply the meaning of a word you learned to another context. Your answer must still make sense within the context of the passage.

Workbook Pages 195–198

Dignity Through Art

It takes courage to follow your imagination. You can't worry about what other people think. You have to follow where your imagination takes you. Some artists become famous because they follow their imaginations. They do things that most other people would not think about doing.

James Hampton, *The Throne of the Third Heaven of the Nations' Millennium General Assembly* (about 1950–64)

Gold and silver foil cover every object in James Hampton's *The Throne of the Third Heaven of the Nations' Millennium General Assembly*. When the light hits it, you feel as though you are looking at something from another world. This sculpture once filled an empty garage which became the artist's studio behind his small apartment in Washington, D.C. Art experts believe that Hampton started the piece in 1950 and worked on it for hours nearly every day for fourteen years. When Hampton finished it, the sculpture comprised dozens of parts, including a central unit that rose as high as 4.6 meters (15 ft.) and was 8.2 meters (27 ft.) across. The sculpture contains about 180 separate glittering objects!

Hampton had little money and was not trained as an artist. He could not afford to make a throne out of real gold and silver. But he wanted to celebrate his deep religious beliefs. He worked as a janitor at night. At his job, he picked up objects that he would later turn into parts of his artwork. He collected old lightbulbs, wood furniture, jelly glasses, pieces of a mirror, and many other objects. He carefully wrapped every single object in foil.

A throne that is 2.13 meters (7 ft.) high sits at the center of the sculpture. At the top of the throne, Hampton made a sign with the words FEAR NOT in foil. He added to his religious ideas by making altars and tablets with writings from the Bible. He also included many angels' wings. He made the wings from paper and cardboard covered with foil.

▲ James Hampton, *The Throne of the Third Heaven of the Nations' Millennium General Assembly*, about 1950–64, mixed media, 10½ x 27 x 14½ ft., Smithsonian American Art Museum

Hampton's artwork was virtually unknown until shortly after his death. However, he left behind a lot of his own writing in journals. He wrote in a code that only he understood, so no one knows what it says. Perhaps it's best that his feelings are kept private.

Hampton had the courage to follow his own artistic ideas, even though he was poor and had few resources to work with.

Discuss What You Learned

1 Why did James Hampton use found objects to make his artwork?

2 Why do you think that James Hampton used a secret code in his journals?

Big Question
How did James Hampton show courage, imagination, and dignity through his artwork?

Workbook
Pages 199–200

W hat is your vision of life in the future?

This unit is about life in the future. You will explore life in the years to come. You will read about how Earth and space look to an astronaut and how Earth might look to a visitor. You will read about a group of friends who travel to the year 2095, and you'll learn about NASA's facilities in Houston, Texas. As you read, you will practice the literary and academic language you need to use in school.

Reading

1 Social Studies

"Life in the Future"

Reading Strategy:
Take notes

2 Poems and Interview

- "Southbound on the Freeway," "Cardinal Ideograms" by May Swenson
- "Interview with an Astronaut: Dan Bursch"

Reading Strategy:
Analyze text structure

3 Novel

From *The Time Warp Trio: 2095* by Jon Scieszka

Reading Strategy:
Skim

Listening and Speaking—Expository

At the end of this unit, you will give a **speech** on life in the future.

Writing—Expository

In this unit you will practice writing parts of a **research report** (a kind of expository writing). You will choose a topic, do research, and write about it. At the end of the unit, you will develop one of your topics into a research report.

Quick Write

Write several sentences about a prediction you made in the past.

4   Science

"NASA and the U.S. Space Program"

Reading Strategy:
Employ analytical skills

DVD   VIEW AND RESPOND
Watch the DVD for Unit 6 and answer the questions at
www.LongmanKeystone.com.

What You Will Learn

Reading

- Vocabulary building: *Context, dictionary skills, word study*

- Reading strategy: *Take notes*

- Text type: *Informational text (social studies)*

Grammar
Transitions

Writing
Write an introductory paragraph

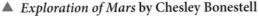

➤ THE BIG QUESTION

What is your vision of life in the future? What will our world be like one hundred years from now? What will travel, home life, medicine, and technology be like? Work in small groups. Study the picture below. Then create a word web with your ideas about life in the future. Share your ideas with other groups. Find out what your classmates think.

▲ *Exploration of Mars* by Chesley Bonestell

➤ BUILD BACKGROUND

"Life in the Future" is a nonfiction article that explores what life might be like ten, twenty, thirty, or more years from now. The article uses facts to describe inventions and advances that people are developing for the future. People have always tried to predict what will happen in the future. We sometimes call people who try to predict what will happen in years to come "futurists." In Italy, there was a futurist movement in the early 1900s. It inspired new forms of art, architecture, and writing. In the United States, organizations were formed to "think about" the future during the 1940s. As you read the selection, think about why people are fascinated by a time that hasn't come yet. Think also about the inventions you would like to see in your lifetime.

▲ A futurist sculpture by Umberto Boccioni

➤ VOCABULARY

Listening and Speaking: Key Words

Read aloud the sentences with a partner. Use the context to figure out the meaning of the highlighted words. Use a dictionary to check your answers. Then write each word and its meaning in your notebook.

Key Words

artificial
canyons
frontier
mass-produced
robots
volcanoes

1. In the future, doctors will use more artificial body parts to replace real body parts.

2. The airplane flew into the deep canyons. The pilot had to steer away from the steep cliffs surrounding the plane.

3. Space is called a frontier because it is far away from Earth. We have explored Earth, but we are just beginning to explore space.

4. Now many cars at a time are made in factories. They are mass-produced. The first cars were produced one at a time.

5. In the future, dangerous work will be done by machines called robots.

6. Scientists study active volcanoes and watch as they send out red-hot lava.

Practice
Workbook Page 201

Write the sentences in your notebook. Choose a key word from the box above to complete each sentence. Then take turns reading the sentences aloud with a partner.

1. The power of the erupting _____ surprised the movie audience.

2. In the United States in the 1800s, the area beyond the Appalachian Mountains was called the _____.

3. Car parts are _____ at factories.

4. Some people would like to have _____ do their housework.

5. Real plants need sunshine and water, but _____ plants do not.

6. The planet Mars has many deep _____ with steep rocky cliffs.

▲ Mount Etna is an active volcano in Sicily.

Listening and Speaking: Academic Words

Study the red words and their meanings. You will find these words useful when talking and writing about informational texts. Write each word and its meaning in your notebook, then say the words aloud with a partner. After you read "Life in the Future," try to use these words to respond to the text.

Academic Words

function
occupation
research
trend

Audio

function = the usual purpose of a thing, or the job that someone usually does	➡	The **function** of a brake is to stop a car. That's the brake's purpose.
occupation = job or profession	➡	An astronaut's **occupation** is exploring space.
research = serious study of a subject that is intended to discover new facts about it	➡	Scientists do **research** to predict the future. They study many books to gather information.
trend = the way a situation is generally developing or changing	➡	The **trend** is toward smaller cars. People want cars that use less gas.

Audio

Practice

Work with a partner to answer the questions. Try to include the red word in your answer. Write the sentences in your notebook.

1. What is a computer's function now? What might its purpose be in the future?

2. What occupation would you like to have twenty years from now? Why?

3. How would you research a topic like future inventions? What sources would you use to find factual information?

4. What trend do you predict for schools in the future? Would this be a good development or not?

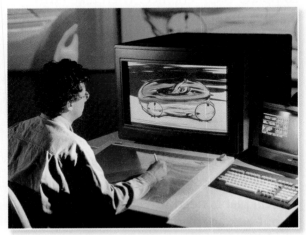

▲ Using computers to design cars is the current trend in the automotive world.

Word Study: Spelling the Diphthongs /oi/ and /ou/

Some English words, such as *boil* and *round* contain two vowel sounds that are said quickly so that the sounds glide into one another. Together the two sounds form a vowel sound called a diphthong. In the word *boil*, the letters *oi* stand for the diphthong /oi/. In the word *round*, the letters *ou* stand for the diphthong /ou/.

Below are some examples of words with the diphthongs /oi/ and /ou/. Sound out each word, saying the vowel sounds quickly, one after the other. Listen to how the two vowel sounds glide into one another in one syllable.

/oi/ as in *coin*	/oi/ as in *boy*	/ou/ as in *ground*	/ou/ as in *how*
boil	joy	found	now
voice	enjoy	shout	down
points	toy	our	downstage

Practice

Workbook Page 203

Work with a partner. Copy the chart above into your notebook. Say a word from the chart, and ask your partner to spell it aloud. Then have your partner say the next word. Continue until you can spell all of the words correctly. Now work with your partner to spell these words: *house, soil, destroy, mountain, royal, cow, noise, how, loyal, toil, brown, sound.* Add them to the chart under the correct headings.

READING STRATEGY   TAKE NOTES

Taking notes keeps you focused on what you are reading, and it helps you organize and remember new information. Notes are also a useful tool to refer back to when answering questions about a reading selection. To take notes, follow these steps:

- In your notebook, make two columns, one for main ideas and one for details.
- Think about your purpose for reading the text.
- Look for key dates, names, places, and events.
- Write short notes about the most important facts and details you may need to know.

As you read "Life in the Future," think about the information you want to remember. Take notes while you read. Review your notes and check that they are correct.

Workbook Page 204

Set a purpose for reading What will cities, travel, medicine, and other aspects of life be like in the future? As you read, contrast the writer's vision of the future with your own. Do you think that the writer's description of the future is accurate? Why?

Life in the Future

Imagine traveling in a time machine into the future. What do you think life will be like? This timeline shows some predictions about the future.

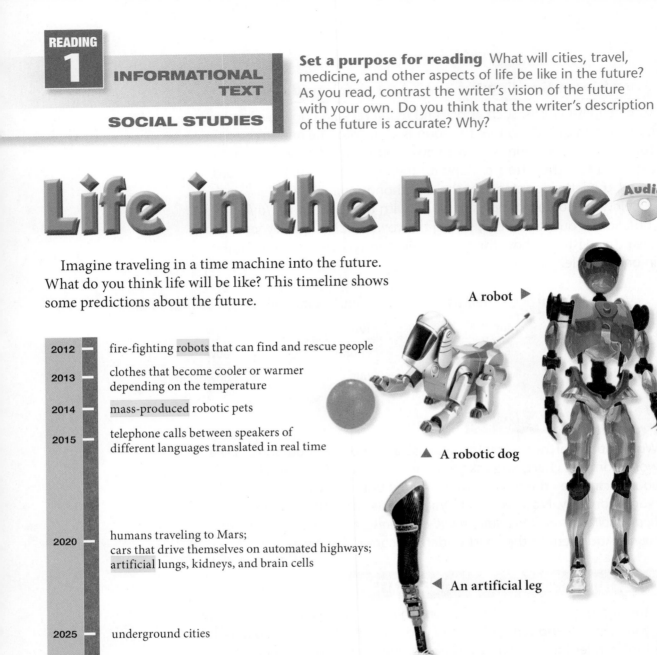

A robot ▶

2012	fire-fighting robots that can find and rescue people
2013	clothes that become cooler or warmer depending on the temperature
2014	mass-produced robotic pets
2015	telephone calls between speakers of different languages translated in real time
2020	humans traveling to Mars; cars that drive themselves on automated highways; artificial lungs, kidneys, and brain cells
2025	underground cities
2030	more robots than people in some countries
2035	fully functioning artificial eyes and legs; people **cured** of 98 percent of all cancers

▲ A robotic dog

◀ An artificial leg

▼ A robotic bug

---

cured, healed; restored to health

The Growing World

The world's population is growing very fast. In 1800, the population was about 1 billion. Now it is over 6.5 billion. One reason for this fast growth is that the birthrate is higher than the death rate. That is, there are more people being born than there are people dying. Also, medical advances and better living conditions help people live longer. Scientists predict that in the year 2100, the population will be 11 billion.

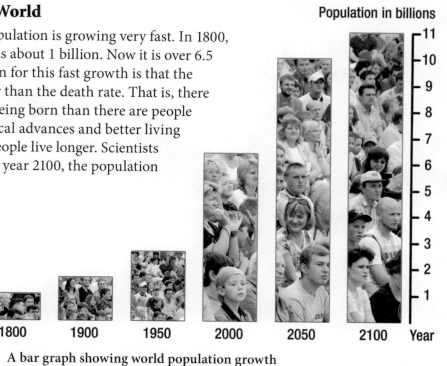

Population in billions

— 11
— 10
— 9
— 8
— 7
— 6
— 5
— 4
— 3
— 2
— 1

1800   1900   1950   2000   2050   2100   Year

▲ A bar graph showing world population growth

Future Cities

As the population grows, it will be necessary to rebuild existing cities and build new ones. Some apartment buildings will be like small cities. Architects have created a model for an apartment building in Tokyo. It will be 840 meters (2,750 ft.) high and will have 180 floors. A population of 60,000 will be able to live there. High-speed **elevators** will carry sixty people at a time. The building will have stores, restaurants, and cinemas. People won't ever have to leave!

---

elevators, machines in a building that carry people from one floor to another

A model for an apartment building in Tokyo ▶

Reading **Skill**

Take turns reading aloud with a partner. As you listen, use the visuals to help clarify words or ideas. Discuss these words or ideas with your partner to gain understanding.

BEFORE YOU GO ON

1 What new inventions do experts predict will be used in the future?

2 How large do experts think the population will be in 2100?

On Your Own
Do you think that life in the future will be more fun than it is today? Why?

▲ The X-43A will reach hypersonic speeds using an air-breathing engine.

Hypersonic Planes

The National Aeronautics and Space Administration (NASA) is developing a hypersonic plane that will be able to fly at least ten times faster than the speed of sound. It will be able to fly to outer space. NASA has produced a $230 million **prototype** plane, but it doesn't expect to use it for space travel until about 2020.

The X-43A prototype plane looks like a flying surfboard. It is thin and has a wingspan of 1.5 meters (5 ft.). It is 3.6 meters (12 ft.) long and weighs 1,270 kilograms (2,800 lbs.). This plane set a new world speed record by flying at nearly ten times the speed of sound. A fully functioning version of the X-43A will be about 60 meters (200 ft.) long.

---

prototype, model

»)🔊 *Listening* SKILL

As you listen to the Audio CD, look at the pictures on pages 382–387. Use these visuals to help explain new words or ideas. Discuss these words or concepts with a partner to gain understanding.

Cars of the Future

As more people own cars, the roads become more crowded. This causes more traffic jams and more accidents. The cost of traffic jams in the United States is about $78 billion per year—4.5 billion hours of travel time plus 26 billion liters (7 billion gal.) of fuel wasted sitting in traffic.

Car manufacturers are always looking for ways to make cars safer, faster, and more convenient. In the future, there may be automated highways. On these highways, cars will **steer** themselves. They will go faster and brake by themselves. Cars will have computers that pick up signals from **magnets** in the road.

▲ A model of a futuristic car

Jetpacks

People have always dreamed of flying. In the fifteenth century, the Italian artist Leonardo da Vinci drew many designs of flying machines. But a personal flying machine—or jetpack—has proved to be one of the most difficult inventions.

---

steer, guide
magnets, pieces of iron that attract other pieces of iron

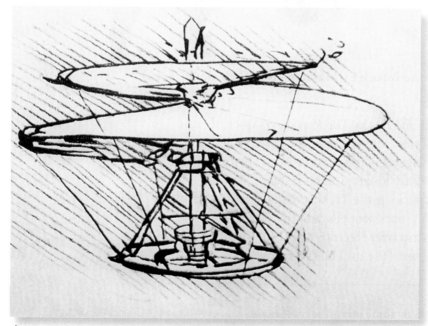

▲ One of Leonardo da Vinci's drawings of a flying machine

BEFORE YOU GO ON

1 What is a hypersonic plane?

2 Who is Leonardo da Vinci, and what kind of machines did he draw?

On Your Own
Would you like to fly in a personal flying machine? Why or why not?

Reading 1 **385**

▲ The Trek Aerospace Exoskeleton Flying Vehicle (EFV-4A)

Jetpacks have appeared in such movies as *The Rocketeer, Spy Kids*, and *Minority Report*. A "rocket man" flew into the opening ceremony of the 1984 summer Olympics in Los Angeles. Jetpacks today can fly for only a short time. In the future, they will fly longer and go faster.

One of the most successful jetpacks is the Trek Aerospace Exoskeleton Flying Vehicle (EFV-4A). The EFV uses propellers to lift you off the ground. Once in the air, you can **zip** over treetops at 181 kilometers (113 mi.) per hour for 296 kilometers (184 mi.) before **refueling**.

---

zip, move very fast
refueling, refilling with gasoline, oil, or some other fuel

Reading Skill

Using the chart, mention one similarity between Earth and Mars. Mention two differences. Understanding the differences shown in the chart will help you understand the problems described in the article that a traveler to Mars would experience.

▲ An artist's idea of a colony on Mars

New Frontiers

Throughout history, humans have loved to explore. Today, we have explored most of our planet. There are few new lands to explore, but there are new worlds, new planets, and new **galaxies**.

In the future, perhaps we will **colonize** other planets. The most likely planet will be Mars. NASA scientists have already sent probes—spacecraft without people—to explore Mars. But when will people be able to go there? Astronauts could travel to Mars by about 2020. However, it will be a difficult task! It will take six months to reach the red planet. (It takes only three days to reach the moon.) And Mars is not a friendly environment. Mars probably once had liquid water, but now it is a cold, rocky desert. It has the largest volcano in the solar system and the deepest canyons. Dust storms can cover the whole planet. There is no breathable **oxygen**.

For people to live on Mars, the cities will have to be protected from the **poisonous** air. Giant **domes** will have to be built to control the atmosphere. All food will have to be grown inside the domed cities.

Earth-Mars Comparison		
	Earth	**Mars**
Average distance from sun	150 million kilometers (93 million mi.)	228 million kilometers (142 million mi.)
Length of year	365.25 days	687 Earth days
Length of day	23 hours, 56 minutes	24 hours, 37 minutes
Temperature	average 14°C (57°F)	average −63°C (−81°F)
Atmosphere	nitrogen, oxygen, argon, others	mostly carbon dioxide, some water vapor
Number of moons	1	2

BEFORE YOU GO ON

1 What is an example of a new frontier that humans can explore?

2 Look at the Earth-Mars comparison chart. Which planet is farther away from the sun?

On Your Own
What other frontiers do you think will become important in the future?

galaxies, very large groups of stars
colonize, set up human communities on
oxygen, gas in the air that all plants and animals need in order to live
poisonous, deadly
domes, round roofs

Reading 1 **387**

Review and Practice

► **COMPREHENSION**
Workbook
Page 205

Recall

1. What is the cost of traffic jams in the United States per year?
2. According to the timeline, when will humans travel to Mars?

Comprehend

3. According to the article, what will cars be like in the future?
4. What will be the **function** of jetpacks?

Analyze

5. What would be the advantages of having everything you need in the building where you live?
6. What advantages does a hypersonic plane have over a rocket?

Connect

7. What **trends** do you think will be popular fifty years from now?
8. Would you rather live 100 years in the past or 100 years in the future? Explain your reasons.

▲ An artist's idea of future travel

► **IN YOUR OWN WORDS**

Imagine that a friend asked you to summarize the article "Life in the Future." Include the main ideas and important details and use the chart below to help you organize your ideas. Then share your summary of the article with your peers. Ask for their feedback and support to enhance and confirm your understanding of this article.

🔊 Speaking SKILL

Try to use content area vocabulary and use active, colorful verbs and adjectives as you summarize "Life in the Future."

Section	Main Idea	Important Details
The Growing World		
Future Cities		
Hypersonic Planes		
Cars of the Future		
Jetpacks		
New Frontiers		

➤ DISCUSSION

Discuss in pairs or small groups.

1. Does the article present a positive or negative view of the future? Give examples to support your conclusion.

2. Why is Mars the most likely planet to colonize? What would you need to live on Mars?

3. How are hypersonic planes and jetpacks similar? How are they different?

Q **What is your vision of life in the future?** How do you see life in twenty years? Fifty years? A hundred years?

»)) Listening SKILL

Give each speaker your attention. Make eye contact with the speaker.

➤ READ FOR FLUENCY

It is often easier to read a text if you understand the difficult words and phrases. Work with a partner. Choose a paragraph from the reading. Identify the words and phrases you do not know or have trouble pronouncing. Look up the difficult words in a dictionary.

Take turns pronouncing the words and phrases with your partner. If necessary, ask your teacher to model the correct pronunciation. Then take turns reading the paragraph aloud. Give each other feedback on your reading.

▲ An artist's idea of a future space colony

➤ EXTENSION

Workbook
Page 205

In "Life in the Future," you read about trends the author thinks we might see in the future. Pretend that you live in the future. Write a paragraph about a typical day in your life. Where do you live? What is your **occupation**? How do you travel? What kinds of clothing do you wear? What foods do you eat? You can use some of the inventions and trends described in "Life in the Future," or you can create your own inventions and trends. Try to use as much academic language as possible. Share your paragraph with a classmate.

LEARNING STRATEGY

To better acquire and understand new academic language, use and reuse these words in meaningful ways in your writing.

Grammar

Transitions

Transitions are words or phrases that connect two ideas. Transitions help your reader follow your line of thought. You can use transitions to add information, contrast ideas, or show cause and effect.

A transition usually connects two sentences or independent clauses. When it connects two sentences, use a period. When it connects two independent clauses, use a semicolon (;). When it begins a sentence or clause, use a comma after the transition.

You can use transitional words such as the conjunctive adverbs *also* and *furthermore* to add information to a statement.

> More people are being born than are dying. **Also**, people are living longer.
> The building will have 180 floors; **furthermore**, it will have stores and cinemas.

Like other adverbs, a conjunctive adverb can be used in different places in a sentence. When it is used midsentence, a comma is not used. However, there are exceptions. Note that a comma comes before and after *furthermore*.

> More people are being born than are dying. People are **also** living longer.
> The building will have 180 floors; it will, **furthermore**, have stores and cinemas.

You can also use the transitional phrases *in addition* and *as well* to add information to a statement. These can come at the beginning or end of a sentence or clause.

> Cars will go faster and brake by themselves. **In addition**, they will have computers.
> Mars is not a friendly environment; there is no breathable oxygen on it **as well**.

The following transitions contrast two ideas. Note that the transitional phrase *on the other hand* is often used with *on the one hand*.

> There are no fire-fighting robots yet. **Instead**, humans still fight fires.
> Mars isn't a friendly environment; **on the contrary**, it's very unfriendly.
> **On the one hand**, there are few new lands to explore. **On the other hand**, there are new worlds, new planets, and new galaxies.

Grammar SKILL

Don't confuse conjunctive adverbs with coordinating conjunctions. With coordinating conjunctions, a comma separates the two independent clauses.

You can use the following transitions to show cause and effect. Remember that transitions can begin a sentence or can be used after a semicolon.

> NASA has much more to discover about Mars. **As a result**, research continues.
> The air is poisonous on Mars; **therefore**, giant domes will have to be built.
> The domes will control the atmosphere. **Thus**, all food will have to be grown in them.
> NASA's hypersonic plane will be able to fly five times faster than the speed of sound. **Consequently**, it will be able to fly to outer space.

✔ GRAMMAR CHECK

*What punctuation follows **transitions** when they begin sentences?*

Practice

Workbook
Pages 206–207

Work with a partner. Copy the sentences below into your notebook. Circle the best transition to complete each sentence.

Example: He's going to Poland. ((Thus)/ Instead / Also), he's studying Polish.

1. He exercises a lot. (As well / Consequently / On the other hand), he's in great shape.

2. Mark doesn't speak Spanish. (Therefore / Furthermore / In addition), he couldn't understand the movie.

3. Will didn't study; (as a result / instead / thus), he went to the movies.

4. Don't forget to lock the door. (Thus / As well / Instead), remember to take your wallet.

5. It snowed a lot last week. (In addition / Consequently / Also), school was closed.

6. On the one hand, chocolate is fattening. (Thus / As well / On the other hand), it tastes so good!

7. Jim worked all night; (as a result / instead / in addition), he was tired.

8. I wanted another piece of cake. (Thus / Furthermore / Instead), I had some fruit.

Apply

Work with a partner. Look at the reading. Find sentences that you can combine with transitional words and phrases.

Writing

Write an Introductory Paragraph

One type of expository writing is a research report. In a research report, the writer explains a topic he or she has studied in depth. In this lesson, you'll learn how to narrow a topic for a research report. Then you'll do some research and write an introductory paragraph for a report.

> **Writing Prompt**
>
> Write an introductory paragraph about a topic related to life in the future. First, narrow your topic. Then, do research before writing. Your paragraph should state your topic clearly. Be sure to use transition words and phrases to connect your ideas and make your writing flow smoothly.

1 PREWRITE Begin by choosing a broad topic.

- Narrow your topic. Think about a particular area of the topic that interests or excites you.

- Ask yourself a specific question about this topic to narrow your focus even more.

- List your ideas in a graphic organizer like the one below.

Workbook Page 208

- Use the question in your organizer to guide your research.

Here's a graphic organizer created by a student named Anna.

Broad topic
Flight

Narrower topic
Flying Machines

Specific topic
Who designed early flying machines?

2 **DRAFT** Use your organizer and your research to write a first draft.

- Remember to state your topic clearly.
- Present facts and details in an order that makes sense.
- Use transitions to connect ideas and make your writing flow smoothly.

3 **REVISE** Read over your draft. Look for places where the writing is unclear or needs improvement. Use the Writing Checklist to help you identify problems. Then revise your draft, using the editing and proofreading marks listed on page 456.

4 **EDIT** Check your work for errors in grammar, usage, mechanics, and spelling. Trade papers with a partner to obtain feedback. Use the Peer Review Checklist on Workbook page 208. Edit your final draft in response to feedback from your partner and your teacher.

5 **PUBLISH** Prepare a clean copy of your final draft. Share your introductory paragraph with the class. Save your work. You'll need to refer to it in the Writing Workshop at the end of the unit.

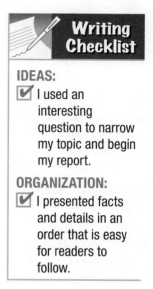

Writing Checklist

IDEAS:
☑ I used an interesting question to narrow my topic and begin my report.

ORGANIZATION:
☑ I presented facts and details in an order that is easy for readers to follow.

Here is Anna's introductory paragraph for a research report. Notice that early on she answers the question she asked in her organizer.

> *Anna Espínola*
>
> *Leonardo da Vinci's Flying Machines*
>
> *Why have humans always been fascinated with flight? The reason may be that flight has been beyond our reach for most of human history. Leonardo da Vinci, an artist, scientist, and engineer, wanted to create a way for humans to achieve flight. Therefore, he observed birds and studied how they flew. Then using his observations and scientific knowledge, he began to design flying machines for humans. In fact, many of da Vinci's concepts and designs are used in today's flying machines, such as helicopters and gliders. Other inventions that da Vinci envisioned and dreamed of may one day develop into new technology that will advance the human race and allow us to fly with the birds.*

Prepare to Read

What You Will Learn

Reading

- Vocabulary building: *Literary terms, dictionary skills, word study*

- Reading strategy: *Analyze text structure 2*

- Text type: *Literature (poetry and interview)*

Grammar

General rules of capitalization; Capitalization: abbreviations, initials, and special terms

Writing

Support a main idea with examples

▶ 🔵 THE BIG QUESTION

What is your vision of life in the future? Why are people fascinated by places beyond Earth? Work with a partner to explore the marvels and riddles of our universe. Discuss what Earth must look like from space. Talk about whether it is likely that humans will be able to travel to other planets or galaxies someday. Explore whether there might be life on other planets or in other galaxies. If so, how would it be different than life on Earth?

▶ BUILD BACKGROUND

You will read two poems about the universe: **"Southbound on the Freeway"** and **"Cardinal Ideograms."** They come from *Poems to Solve* by May Swenson. Swenson says that solving a poem can be like unwrapping a mysterious package. In a few short lines, a poem can express big ideas.

   "Interview with an Astronaut: Dan Bursch" follows the poems. Bursch answers questions about his three flights into space and his time spent living on the International Space Station. U.S. astronauts train at NASA (National Aeronautics and Space Administration). The first astronauts were all pilots. Today, scientists and other people can travel in space along with the astronauts who are trained to fly the aircraft.

The Andromeda Galaxy is the nearest galaxy to our own. ▶

◀ Astronaut Bruce McCandless II "space walking"

➤ VOCABULARY

Learn Literary Words

Poets often make imaginative comparisons to help you experience something ordinary in an extraordinary way. If a poet uses the word *like* or *as* to make the comparison, it is called a simile. May Swenson uses a simile in "Southbound on the Freeway" to describe the way cars on the highway might look from above to a visitor from outer space. What does she compare the cars to?

Literary Words
simile
metaphor
stanzas

> They all hiss as they glide, like inches, down the marked tapes.

The everyday expressions *"sly as a fox"* or *"fast as lightning"* are also similes, but they no longer call up an image in our minds. They are used too often. Poetic similes invent a new way of looking at something.

Sometimes a poet compares two things in a bolder way, without using the words *like* or *as*. For example, a poet might say that dreams are birds or the sea is a singer. A comparison like this is called a metaphor. In the poem "Cardinal Ideograms," Swenson uses metaphors that make you look at the cardinal numbers (1, 2, 3, etc.) in an unusual way. What does she compare the cardinal number 1 to?

> 1 A grass blade or a cut.
> 2 A question seated. And a proud bird's neck.

LEARNING STRATEGY

Use words that you already know to learn new and essential language, or words that you must know in order to understand your schoolwork.

Many poems are divided into groups of lines called stanzas. "Southbound on the Freeway" is divided into two-line stanzas called couplets. "Cardinal Ideograms" has stanzas of varying lengths.

Practice

Take turns reading the metaphor and simile below aloud with a partner. Identify the two things that are being compared.

> All the world's a stage . . .
> —*William Shakespeare*
>
> Mars glowed like a lone fire in the dark galaxy.

Create a metaphor and a simile of your own. You might compare time or a feeling to something in nature or space. Write your metaphor and simile in your notebook. Share them with a classmate.

▲ **Mars is known as the red planet.**

Listening and Speaking: Academic Words

Study the red words and their meanings. You will find these words useful when talking and writing about literature. Write each word and its meaning in your notebook, then say the words aloud with a partner. After you read "Southbound on the Freeway," "Cardinal Ideograms," and "Interview with an Astronaut: Dan Bursch," try to use these words to respond to the text.

complex = complicated	→	A computer is a **complex** tool because it is made of many parts. A wrench is a simple tool.
interpretation = an explanation	→	Everyone had a different **interpretation** of the poem. Each of us had a different reaction to the poet's metaphors.
published = printed and sold	→	A new book of poems was **published**. The poet was happy to see her poems in print in the bookstore.
section = a part of something	→	I looked in the nonfiction **section** of the library for a book about our space program.

Audio

Practice   **Workbook Page 210**

Work with a partner to answer the questions. Try to include the red word in your answer. Write the sentences in your notebook.

1. What kind of complex cars do you think you will see in the future?

2. Why might your interpretation of a poem be different from your friend's ideas?

3. What subject would you write about if you could have a book published?

4. In what section might a bookstore put up this sign: *Ages 3 to 5*?

▲ A wrench is a simple tool.

A race car is a complex machine. ▶

Word Study: Greek and Latin Roots

As you have learned, many English words come from Greek and Latin word parts called roots. Sometimes knowing and memorizing the meaning of a root word can help you figure out the meaning of a new word. Knowing and memorizing the meaning of a prefix can help, too.

Take, for example, the word *cycle*. It contains the root *cycl*, meaning "round." What happens when you add the following prefixes to *cycle*?

The prefix *uni-* means one.	A unicycle has **one** round wheel.
The prefix *bi-* means two.	A bicycle has **two** round wheels.
The prefix *tri-* means three.	A tricycle has **three** round wheels.

▲ A unicycle

Practice
Workbook Page 211

Work with a partner. Copy the chart below into your notebook. Memorize the meanings of the word parts. Discuss what the new words mean. Use a dictionary to check the meanings. List other words you know of that contain the roots *spec* and *verse* in your notebook. Add them to the chart.

LEARNING STRATEGY

To acquire grade-level vocabulary, actively memorize new root words and their meanings.
To help remember this information, be sure to review it often.

Prefix	+ Root	= New Word
re- ("again")	spec ("see")	respect
uni- ("one")	verse ("turn")	universe

READING STRATEGY | **ANALYZE TEXT STRUCTURE 2**

Analyzing text structure can help you identify what kind of text you're reading. Poems and interviews each have a special text structure.

To analyze the text structure of a poem, follow these steps:

- Look for rhyming patterns and stanzas.
- Look for punctuation that shows you where to pause, such as commas, periods, dashes, or line breaks.

To analyze the text structure of an interview, follow these steps:

- Find speakers' names; they will be bold and followed by a colon (:).
- Look for name changes that signal different speakers.

Preview the text structures of the poems and interview. Discuss them with a partner.

Workbook Page 212

Set a purpose for reading How does Earth look to a tourist from Orbitville or an astronaut on a space flight? In what ways does the number 8 seem like a model for the universe? Think about how the poems and interview affect your vision of time, space, and the future.

Southbound on the Freeway

May Swenson

A tourist came in from Orbitville,
parked in the air, and said:

The creatures of this star
are made of metal and glass.

Through the **transparent** parts
you can see their guts.

Their feet are round and roll
on diagrams—or long

measuring tapes—dark
with white lines.

They have four eyes.
The two in the back are red.

---

transparent, clear and easy to
see through

Sometimes you can see a 5-eyed
one, with a red eye turning

on the top of his head.
He must be special—

the others respect him,
and go slow,

when he passes, winding
among them from behind.

They all **hiss** as they glide,
like inches, down the marked

tapes. Those soft shapes
shadowy inside

the hard bodies—are they
their guts or their brains?

_____

hiss, make a sound like "ssss"

✔ **LITERARY CHECK**

_What **metaphor**
does the poet use
to describe the
light on top of a
police car?_

BEFORE YOU GO ON

1 Where is the
tourist from?

2 What puzzles the
tourist about the
scene on Earth?

💡 **On Your Own**
Would you like to be
a tourist on another
planet? Why or
why not?

Cardinal Ideograms*

May Swenson

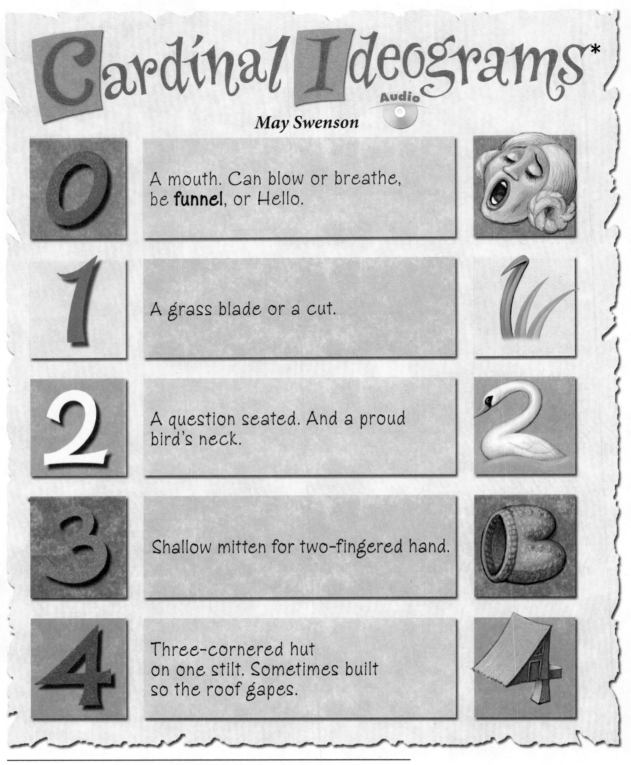

0 A mouth. Can blow or breathe, be **funnel**, or Hello.

1 A grass blade or a cut.

2 A question seated. And a proud bird's neck.

3 Shallow mitten for two-fingered hand.

4 Three-cornered hut on one stilt. Sometimes built so the roof gapes.

---

funnel, a tube with a wide top used for pouring things

* This excerpt from "Cardinal Ideograms" contains eight of the ten stanzas from the original poem. Cardinal numbers are any of the numbers 0, 1, 2, 3, and so on. Ideograms are written signs that stand for an idea or thing.

5
A policeman. Polite.
Wearing visored cap.

6
O unrolling,
tape of **ambiguous** length
on which is written the mystery
of everything curly.

7
A step,
detached from its stair.

8
The universe in diagram:
A cosmic hourglass.
(Note **enigmatic** shape,
absence of any **valve** of origin,
how end overlaps beginning.)
Unknotted like a shoelace
and whipped back and forth,
can serve as a model of time.

✔ **LITERARY CHECK**
*Which stanza
contains a simile?*

---

ambiguous, uncertain or hard to understand
enigmatic, mysterious and hard to explain
valve, part of a pipe that opens and closes to control the flow of liquid,
    air, or gas passing through it

ABOUT THE **POET**

May Swenson (1913–1989) was born in Utah.
She came from a very large family and was the
oldest of ten children. English was her second
language; Swedish was spoken at home. She
attended Utah State University and later taught
poetry there. Swenson also worked as an editor
and was the Chancellor of the Academy of
American Poets. Her poetry won many awards, including
the Bollingen Prize and the Shelley Memorial Award.

BEFORE YOU GO ON

1 What does the poem
compare the cardinal
number 3 to?

2 What reasons does
the poem give for
calling the cardinal
number 8 enigmatic,
or mysterious?

💡**On Your Own**
What does the
number 9 look like
to you? Create
your own cardinal
ideogram.

▲ The International
Space Station

Interview with
an Astronaut:

Dan Bursch

*Dan Bursch has made three space flights and has been in space for 746
hours. He lived on the International Space Station from December 5, 2001,
until June 19, 2002. Before this expedition, he **chatted** online with some
students on www.discovery.com.*

Dan Bursch: I would just like to say welcome to everyone tonight. Thank
you for spending your Sunday evening with me. . . .

Cody: I am ten years old, and I would like to know what the food is like.
I would also like for you to trade me just one day in the space station
and you can go to my school.

---

chatted, talked informally

▲ Astronaut Dan Bursch works in the weightless environment of space.

Dan Bursch: Food is very important for us up in space, as it is here on Earth. In fact, one of the things that I will be starting tomorrow . . . is food tasting. We are **selecting** our menu for the four- to six-month flight that I will have in space. What is different about my next mission on the space station is that we will have a mixture of American and Russian food, so that will certainly make it different. . . . Perhaps I can come to your school someday and perhaps in fifteen years or so you can go to space!

Gary TX: What kind of work do you do when you are at the space station?

Dan Bursch: We have a crew of three—myself, Carl Walz (another American astronaut), and Yuri. He is a Russian **cosmonaut**. He will be our **commander**. We divide up the work because there is a lot of work to be done. . . .

---

selecting, choosing
cosmonaut, Russian astronaut
commander, leader

BEFORE YOU GO ON

1 Who are the people interviewing Dan Bursch?

2 What is different about the menu on this trip?

💡**On Your Own**
Would you like to spend a day on the space station? Why or why not?

Reading 2 **403**

Galileo Guest: How do the astronauts deal with the effects of zero gravity on the space station?

Dan Bursch: Learning to work in space without feeling gravity is always a challenge. . . . Getting used to not feeling gravity usually takes a day or two.

International: What is it like working with scientists and other astronauts from all around the world? Do you all **get along**? Do you have fun?

The space shuttle *Discovery* blasts off into space.

Dan Bursch: This job is particularly interesting just because of that fact. . . . In the astronaut office, the range of different kinds of people is pretty wide. . . . But we all share one common goal, and that is to fly and live and work in space. . . .

Hollifeld: Can you see the lights of the world's cities from space?

Dan Bursch: Yes. We spend half of our time while **in orbit** on the dark side of the planet. If there is a thin cloud layer, you see kind of a glow like from a lampshade that dampens the light a little bit. But when it is clear—when there are no clouds—the lights are **spectacular**. . . .

Venus: What is the first time you go into space like? Is it hard to learn to use the tools or get used to things **floating around**?

Dan Bursch: I remember my first flight in 1993 on [the space shuttle]

---

get along, act friendly
in orbit, circling around Earth
spectacular, wonderful and exciting to see
floating around, moving around freely in the air

Discovery. . . . At lift-off, there is a lot of vibration and a lot of noise, and eight-and-a-half minutes later you are in orbit. When the engines turn off, instantly everything floats. . . . You have to make sure that you either strap something down or use **Velcro** because you will probably lose it otherwise.

AstroBob: Do you think that at some point ordinary people will get to go to the space station? Or will it always be **reserved for** scientists?

Dan Bursch: I think that is certainly a goal that we should try to reach. If it will be in my lifetime, I don't know. . . . When airplanes first came out, they were reserved at first for just the very **daring** or risk takers. And now anybody can fly on an airplane. So, I don't think it is a question of IF the opportunity will come . . . it is simply a matter of WHEN.

Sandy Fay: What kinds of things do they hope the space station will be good for once it is completed?

Dan Bursch: . . . I see the biggest challenge and the biggest thing that we are learning is two former enemies learning how to work together and build such a large and complex structure in space. And not just two former enemies, but all of the over one dozen countries that are working together . . .

Discovery.com: Thank you, Dan, for chatting with us tonight.

▲ Planet Earth, as seen from space

Velcro, a material that can stick to itself to fasten things together
reserved for, set aside for
daring, brave

BEFORE YOU GO ON

1 How do astronauts make sure that none of their things float away while in space?

2 For Dan Bursch, what is the biggest challenge of the space station?

 On Your Own
What question would you like to ask Dan Bursch about the future?

Review and Practice

▶ DRAMATIC READING

One of the best ways to understand a poem is to memorize it, or learn it by heart. First, work in groups of six to reread, discuss, and interpret "Southbound on the Freeway." Use suggestions and support from your peers and teacher to enhance and confirm your understanding of the poem. Describe what you visualize as you read the poem line by line. Identify any metaphors, similes, or vivid sensory words you find. Work together to interpret difficult words or phrasing. Use a dictionary or ask your teacher for help if necessary.

Next, have each member of your group memorize one or two of the poem's stanzas. Then recite the entire poem, with each student reciting the stanzas that he or she memorized. Comment on one another's oral reading and make suggestions for improvements. Practice reciting the poem with your group. Then hold a "poetry slam" with the whole class in which each group competes for the best oral reading.

> ♪» *Speaking* **SKILL**
>
> Face the audience when you say your lines. Speak clearly and loudly. If you turn away from the audience too much, people may not be able to hear or understand you.

▶ COMPREHENSION
Workbook
Page 213

▲ Astronauts cooperate with each other to repair the International Space Station.

Recall

1. Where does the tourist come from in "Southbound on the Freeway"?

2. How long does it take astronaut Dan Bursch to get used to not feeling gravity?

Comprehend

3. What two things does the poet compare to the number 2 in "Cardinal Ideograms"?

4. What does Earth look like from space according to Dan Bursch?

Analyze

5. What does the tourist think the people on Earth look like in "Southbound on the Freeway"? What is the tourist's **interpretation** of Earth's **complex** people?

6. Why would it be important for astronauts to cooperate with each other while they are in space?

Connect

7. What do you think the number 8 looks like? Compare the number 8 to different things.

8. What kinds of food would you choose for a six-month journey into space? Explain your reasons.

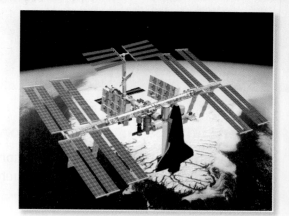

▲ The space shuttle, docked with the International Space Station

► DISCUSSION

Discuss in pairs or small groups.

1. How are "Southbound on the Freeway" and "Cardinal Ideograms" similar? How are they different?

2. Which of the metaphors in "Cardinal Ideograms" did you think was most interesting or accurate? Why?

3. Dan Bursch talks about the challenges of living on the space station, such as dealing with zero gravity and working with others. What would be your biggest challenge on the space station? Why?

Q **What is your vision of life in the future?** Imagine that you are going to the space station at some point in the future. What would you take with you? What do you think you would see?

»)) *Listening* SKILL

Listen to the verbs and adjectives your classmates use when they speak. Try to visualize, or picture in your mind, what each speaker is describing.

► RESPONSE TO LITERATURE

Workbook
Page 213

Utilize If you were a tourist from Orbitville visiting Earth, what aspects of Earth would you find most confusing? What aspects would you find most amazing? Write an e-mail to send to your home planet telling what strange and interesting things you discovered on Earth. When you have finished your e-mail, share it with a classmate.

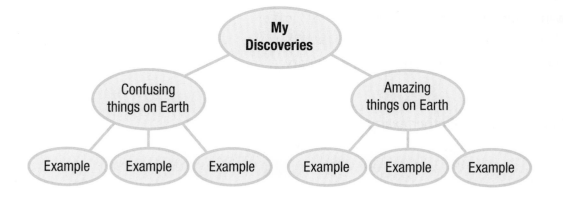

Grammar

General Rules of Capitalization

It is important to use capitalization correctly. Incorrect capitalization can be distracting to your reader. There are rules for capitalization.

Rule	Example
Capitalize the first word of a sentence.	We have a crew of three.
Capitalize proper nouns, such as names of people, including initials countries/states/cities languages/nationalities organizations	Cody, Yuri, Dan Bursch, H. G. Wells United States, Texas, Houston Russian, American United Nations Office for Outer Space Affairs
Capitalize certain dates, such as days of the week months of the year	Sunday June 19, 2002
Capitalize all words in a title, except for articles and shorter prepositions, unless they are the first or last word	Southbound on the Freeway Cardinal Ideograms Interview with an Astronaut: Dan Bursch

Practice  Workbook Page 214

Work with a partner. Copy the sentences into your notebook. Correct the capitalization mistakes.

Example: *H*e works for a **section** of the *E*uropean *C*ommission.

1. *the time warp trio: 2095* was last **published** in 2004.
2. are you leaving on friday or saturday?
3. her husband is lithuanian, but she is belgian.
4. will you give louis this book?
5. she and james are going to visit new york in january.

Apply

Work with a partner. Think of other examples for the rules in the chart.

✔ GRAMMAR CHECK

Which proper nouns are **capitalized**?

Capitalization: Abbreviations, Initials, and Special Terms

An abbreviation is a shortened version of a word or phrase and is often followed by a period. With abbreviations of street names, capitalize the first letter. With abbreviations of states or countries, capitalize all letters.

| Main **Street** → Main **St.** | **Vermont** → **VT** | **United States of America** → **USA** |

Grammar SKILL

No periods are used with abbreviations of states or countries or in acronyms.

An acronym is a type of abbreviation and is usually formed from the first letters of a multi-word term. All letters are capitalized.

| **I**nternational **S**pace **S**tation | **ISS** |
| **N**ational **A**eronautics and **S**pace Administration | **NASA** |

Some other terms that are capitalized include ship names (including spaceships), solar systems, and planets. Exceptions are *sun* and *moon*.

| **D**iscovery | the **M**ilky **W**ay **G**alaxy | **E**arth |

When a noun is a company trademark, it is also capitalized.

| **V**elcro | **M**c**D**onald's | **M**icrosoft | **D**isney |

Practice
Work with a partner. Copy the paragraph below into your notebook. Then add proper capitalization.

   If I lived on the international space station, the thing I would miss the most would be the food we have on earth. I can't live without hamburgers. Maybe one day, the united states will open a mcDonald's on mars!

Apply
Work with a partner. Think of some other abbreviations, including acronyms, that you know. Use a dictionary if necessary.

Writing

Support a Main Idea with Examples

Each paragraph of an expository essay or research report contains a main idea. The main idea is the paragraph's most important point. One way to explain an idea is by using examples. The examples in each paragraph need to support the main idea. Examples can include facts, dates, numbers, and descriptions of events. To find examples for a report, you can do research and take notes.

> **Writing Prompt**
>
> Write a paragraph about planets, space missions, or astronauts. Narrow your topic before doing research. Begin your paragraph with a question connected to your main idea. Support your main idea with three short examples (use different kinds).

1 **PREWRITE** Begin by narrowing your broad topic. Then ask yourself a question about your specific topic.

- Use your question to help you decide on your main idea.

- Do research. Take notes on facts, dates, events, and other examples that support your main idea.

- List your ideas in a graphic organizer.  **Workbook Page 216**

Here's a graphic organizer created by a student named Koji.

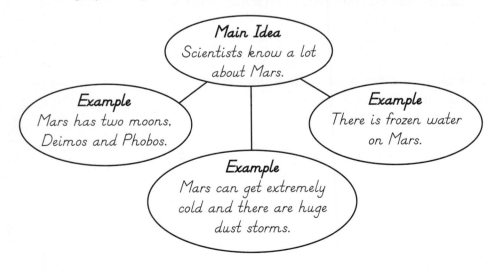

Main Idea
Scientists know a lot about Mars.

Example
Mars has two moons, Deimos and Phobos.

Example
There is frozen water on Mars.

Example
Mars can get extremely cold and there are huge dust storms.

410 Unit 6

2 **DRAFT** Use your organizer to help you write a first draft.

- Remember to state clearly your paragraph's main idea.

- Support the main idea with different types of examples.

- Be sure to use the rules of capitalization correctly.

3 **REVISE** Read over your draft. Look for places where the writing is unclear or needs improvement. Use the Writing Checklist to help you identify problems. Then revise your draft, using the editing and proofreading marks listed on page 456.

4 **EDIT** Check your work for errors in grammar, usage, mechanics, and spelling. Trade papers with a partner to obtain feedback. Use the Peer Review Checklist on Workbook page 216. Edit your final draft in response to feedback from your partner and your teacher.

5 **PUBLISH** Prepare a clean copy of your final draft. Share your paragraph with the class. Save your work. You'll need to refer to it in the Writing Workshop at the end of the unit.

Here is Koji's paragraph for a research report. Notice that he begins with a question connected to his main idea. He varies his examples.

Writing Checklist

ORGANIZATION:
☑ I included different types of examples to support my main idea.

CONVENTIONS:
☑ I edited my work for standard grammar and usage, including correct capitalization.

Koji Mori

Mars

What do scientists know about the red planet? Mars is the fourth planet from the sun and the seventh largest planet in our solar system. It has two moons, Deimos and Phobos. Temperatures on Mars can get extremely cold because of the planet's thin atmosphere. The temperature can drop to -133 degrees Celsius (-207 degrees Fahrenheit). Huge dust storms also take place on the planet. Despite the extreme weather, Mars is more like Earth than any other planet in our solar system. In fact, scientists have recently discovered that there is much more frozen water beneath the surface of Mars than previously thought. Also, ice was found near the equator of Mars. There may be enough ice to cover the entire planet.

Prepare to Read

What You Will Learn

Reading
- Vocabulary building: *Literary terms, dictionary skills, word study*
- Reading strategy: *Skim*
- Text type: *Literature (novel excerpt)*

Grammar
End punctuation, commas, and quotation marks; Parentheses, brackets, and ellipses

Writing
Include quotations and citations

➤ THE BIG QUESTION

What is your vision of life in the future? Some people think the future will be wonderful, thanks to machines that will save us time and effort. They think that there will be new ways to communicate and connect people all over the world. Others think that the future will not be so bright. They predict the world will be overcrowded and that wars will be fought over natural resources.

Work with a partner. Debate whether the future will be positive or negative. Decide whether the future holds great things or not-so-great things, or a combination of both. Put all of your ideas together and write a statement about the future. Share your statement with other pairs.

▲ An artist's idea of two future cities, with protective domes

➤ BUILD BACKGROUND

The Time Warp Trio: 2095 is a science fiction novel about traveling into the future. The novel takes place at two different times: 1995 and 2095. To create this science fiction story, author Jon Scieszka combined real things with imaginary, or fantastic, things. He made up the characters and their adventures. One part of the setting is real: the American Museum of Natural History. This famous museum is located in New York City opposite Central Park. And a statue of Theodore Roosevelt, the twenty-sixth president of the United States, really does stand outside the museum. Roosevelt loved nature and was a great friend of the museum. He was a strong believer in preserving the environment.

► VOCABULARY

Learn Literary Words

Writers of science fiction often imagine what life in the future might be like. They base their plots on ideas and predictions about science and technology. Science fiction usually takes place in the future or involves time travel. It may be about an ideal society or fantastic creatures, inventions, and places. For example, in *The War of the Worlds,* author H. G. Wells tells a story about visitors from Mars.

Setting is the time and place when an event or story occurs. Sometimes writers tell you the setting. Other times, you have to figure it out from clues such as the characters' speech, clothing, or ways of traveling.

Read this excerpt from *The Best New Thing,* by Isaac Asimov. How do you know that this selection is science fiction? Which paragraph reveals the setting?

<table>
<tr><td>

Rada lived on a little world, far out in space. Her father and her mother and her brother, Jonathan, lived there too. So did other men and women.

Rada was the only little girl on the little world. Jonny was the only little boy. They had lived there all their lives. Rada's father and other men worked on the spaceships. They made sure everything was all right before the spaceships went on their way back to Earth or to other planets.
</td></tr>
</table>

Literary Words
science fiction
setting

▲ *The War of the Worlds* is a classic science fiction novel about visitors from space.

Practice

With a partner, take turns reading aloud the descriptions below. Do you think that each is a setting for a science fiction novel? Explain your reasoning to your partner.

1. The story takes place on Mars in the year 2891. Humans live in a big dome. Martians live on the surface of the planet. The Martians and humans get along well but do not interact much.

2. The year is 1850. The place is Austin, Texas. The novel tells the real life story of a ranching family whose members are close and loving.

In your notebook, write a paragraph describing the setting for a science fiction story of your own. Share it with a partner.

Learn Academic Words

Study the red words and their meanings. You will find these words useful when talking and writing about literature. Write each word and its meaning in your notebook. After you read the excerpt from *The Time Warp Trio: 2095*, try to use these words to respond to the text.

shift = a change in the way most people think about something, or in the way something is done	There was a huge **shift** in their ideas about nature after their visit to the natural history museum.
specific = detailed and exact	Tell me more about your trip. You told me some general things, but I'd like to hear some **specific** details.
strategies = sets of plans and skills used in order to gain success or achieve an aim	Her **strategies** for preparing for an exam are to study with friends and get a good night's sleep.
techniques = special methods of doing something	There are many **techniques** that science fiction writers use to create believable stories.

Audio

Practice

Workbook
Page 218

Work with a partner to answer these questions. Try to include the red word in your answer. Write the sentences in your notebook.

1. Do you think that we will see a shift in how we use natural resources in the future? Explain.

2. What specific facts about the future would you like to know?

3. What strategies do you use to help you remember new words?

4. What techniques do you use to help you take good photographs?

▲ A popular study strategy is to have a friend quiz you on facts.

Word Study: Schwa spelled *a, e, i, o, u*

In many English words, the letters *a, e, i, o,* and *u* can stand for the sound you hear when you say "uh." The "uh" sound is called a schwa. The symbol for the schwa is the letter *e* turned upside down /ə/. In multisyllabic words, the schwa occurs only in an unstressed syllable. Recognizing and pronouncing /ə/ will help you spell many words correctly. Study the chart. As you read each word, say it aloud. Notice that the schwa occurs only in an unstressed syllable.

/ə/ spelled *a*	/ə/ spelled *e*	/ə/ spelled *i*	/ə/ spelled *o*	/ə/ spelled *u*
a-'maze	'tak-**e**n	'an-**i**-mal	'les-s**o**n	'care-f**u**l
'so-f**a**	'trav-**e**l	ex-'per-**i**-ment	'com-m**o**n	'Ve-n**u**s

Practice

Work with a partner to spell these words: *alike, museum, uniforms, lion, happen.* Write five headings in your notebook: *a, e, i, o, u.* Say a word from the list slowly and clearly, syllable by syllable. Listen for the schwa. Ask your partner to spell the word aloud. Then have your partner say the next word. Continue until you can spell all of the words correctly. Write the words under the correct headings in your notebook. If you have trouble finding the schwa, check the word's pronunciation in a dictionary.

READING STRATEGY | SKIM

Skimming helps you get an idea of what a text is about. Skimming will also help you make and confirm predictions and become an active reader. To skim a text, follow these steps:

- Glance at the title, text, and illustrations to see what the plot, characters, and setting will be like.
- Read through the first page quickly.
- Make predictions about what you think will happen in the selection.

Skim the excerpt from *The Time Warp Trio: 2095* and make predictions. Then read the selection carefully. Confirm or revise your predictions.

Set a purpose for reading What would it be like to travel into the future? Read to find out how Sam, Fred, and Joe travel to the year 2095. How did they get there? How will they get back home?

Audio

from

THE TIME WARP TRIO: 2095

Jon Scieszka

Sam, Fred, and Joe are three friends. They are visiting the American Museum of Natural History in New York City in the year 1995. Joe, the narrator, has The Book, *a time-travel guide given to him by his uncle, who is also named Joe. Without meaning to, Joe does something that transports him and his two friends into the year 2095. As this excerpt begins, the trio of friends is running away from a security robot called a Sellbot.*

We jumped over the twitching Sellbot and ran down a **flight of stairs**. We had almost made it to the lobby, when the sound of a buzzer filled the halls.

The museum doors opened. A **tidal wave of people** came flooding in, and we were right in its path.

We dodged the first bunch of teenagers. They had corkscrew, spike, and Mohawk hair in every color you can think of. But the most amazing thing was that no one was touching the ground.

"They're flying. People in the future have figured out how to fly," said Sam.

A solid river of people flowed past us. An old man in an aluminum suit. A woman with leopard-patterned skin. A class in shiny school uniforms. Everyone was floating about a foot above the floor.

"How do they do that?" I said.

"Look closely," said Sam. "Everyone has a small disk with a green triangle and a red square."

"Hey, you're right," I said.

"I'm always right," said Sam. "That is obviously the **antigravity disk** that kid was talking about. Now let's get out of here before another Sellbot **tracks us down**."

Fred grabbed my belt. Sam grabbed Fred's belt. And we fought our way outside. We stopped at the statue of Teddy Roosevelt sitting on his horse looking out over Central Park. We stood and looked out with him.

"Wow," said Fred. "I see it but I don't believe it."

The sidewalk was full of floating people of every shape and color. There were people with green skin, blue skin, purple skin, orange, striped, plaid, dotted, and **you-name-it skin**. The street was packed three high and three deep with floating bullet-shaped things that must have been antigravity cars. And all around the trees of Central Park, towering buildings spread up and out like gigantic mechanical trees taller than the clouds.

---

flight of stairs, group of steps from one floor to the next
tidal wave of people, large crowd of people
antigravity disk, small item that fights the force of gravity, allowing one to float above the ground
tracks us down, finds us
you-name-it skin, every kind of skin

✔ **LITERARY CHECK**
*What details confirm that this is a **science fiction** selection?*

BEFORE YOU GO ON

1 What do the people of the future look like? What **technique** do they use to travel?

2 What is the most amazing thing about people in the future?

💡 **On Your Own**
Imagine that you could travel to any time period. Which one would you choose?

Layers and layers of antigravity cars and lines of people snaked around a hundred stories above us. New York was bigger, busier, and noisier than ever. . . .

Now wearing antigravity disks, the boys fly through the streets of New York, still chased by the Sellbot and three futuristic girls who look strangely familiar. Joe's uncle has appeared out of nowhere to help. The girls catch up, and Joe is surprised to see that one of the girls looks very much like his sister.

"Come on," said the girl who looked like my sister. "Follow us."

Sam looked at Fred. Fred looked at me. I looked at Uncle Joe.

"Do we have any choice?" I asked.

We **took off** and followed the girls around the buildings, over crowds of crazily colored people, past streamlined **pods** and more talking, blinking, singing 3-D ads, until I had no idea where we were.

We finally stopped in front of a building too tall to believe.

"Here's my house," said the **lead girl**.

Fred, Sam, and I looked up and up and up at the building that disappeared in the clouds.

The girl led us through a triangle door that opened at her voice. She put her hand over a blinking red handprint on the wall. And in five seconds we were all transported to a room that must have been five miles above New York City.

The girls flopped down on cushions. "This is my room," said the girl who looked like my sister.

We stood nervously in one corner.

"So you're not **killer time cops**?" I said.

---

took off, left quickly
pods, long vehicles
lead girl, girl at the front of the others
killer time cops, secret police who catch time travelers

The three girls looked at me like I was crazy.

"Of course not," said one.

"Whatever gave you that idea?" said another.

Then we all started asking questions.

"Who are you guys?"

"How did you know we'd be at the museum?"

"Do you have anything to eat?"

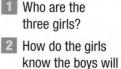

The girls laughed. The one who led us there pushed a green dot on a small table. A bowl of something looking like dried green dog food appeared with a pile of liquid filled plastic balls.

"Here's some **Vitagorp and Unicola**," said the girl who looked like my sister. "Now let me try to explain things from the beginning."

We copied the girls and sucked on the plastic ball things the same way they did. Fred ate a handful of the green dog food.

"I'm Joanie. This is Samantha. That's Frieda."

"But everybody calls me Freddi," said the girl with the baseball hat.

"And we have these names," Joanie continued, "because we were named after our great-grandfathers—Joe, Sam, and Fred."

"Or in other words—you," said Samantha.

Everything suddenly made sense. That's why they looked so much like us.

"Of course," said Uncle Joe, dusting off his **top hat**. "Your great-grandkids have to make sure you get back to 1995. Otherwise you won't have kids. Then your kids won't have kids. Then your kids' kids won't have—"

"Us," said Samantha. "Your great-grandkids. And we knew you would be at the museum because you wrote us a note." Samantha handed me a yellowed sheet of paper that had been sealed in plastic. It was our Museum Worksheet from 1995. On the back was a note in my handwriting that said:

Girls,

Meet us under Teddy Roosevelt's statue at the Museum of Natural History, September 28, 2095.

Sincerely,

Joe, Sam, Fred

"How did you get our worksheet from 1995?" asked Sam.

"I got it from my mom," said Joanie. "And she got it from her mom."

"But we didn't write that," I said.

"You will," said Samantha, "if we can get you back to 1995."

Vitagorp and Unicola, imaginary food and drink of the future
top hat, tall black hat

BEFORE YOU GO ON

1 Who are the three girls?

2 How do the girls know the boys will be at the museum?

On Your Own
Imagine that you are Joe. How do you feel at this point in the story?

"Saved by our own great-grandkids with a note we haven't written yet?" said Sam. "I told you something like this was going to happen. Now we're probably going to **blow up**."

"Wow," said Fred, eating more Vitagorp. "Our own great-grandkids. So what team is that on your hat? I've never seen that **logo**."

"That's the Yankees," said Freddi. "They changed it when Grandma was pitching."

"Your grandma? Fred's daughter?" I said. "A pitcher for the Yankees?"

"Not just a pitcher. She was a great pitcher," said Freddi. "2.79 lifetime ERA, 275 wins, 3 no-hitters, and the Cy Young award in '37."

"Forget your **granny's stats**," said Sam. "We could be genius inventors back in 1995 if we could reconstruct these **levitation devices**."

"What did he just say?" asked Freddi.

"He wants to know how the antigravity disks work," said Samantha. "A truly amazing discovery. More surprising than Charles Goodyear's accidental discovery of vulcanized rubber. More revolutionary than Alexander Graham Bell's first telephone. But all I can tell you is that the antigravity power comes from the chemical BHT. And it was discovered in a breakfast accident."

"What's a breakfast accident?" said Sam. "A **head-on collision** with a bowl of cornflakes? And who found out BHT could make things fly?"

"You did," said Samantha. "That's why we can't tell you more. You know the Time Warp Info-Speed Limit posted in *The Book*. Anyone traveling through time with too much information from another time blows up."

Sam's eyes nearly **bugged out** of his head. "I knew it. Don't tell me another word."

"Hey, wait a minute," I said. "Where did you say that info-speed limit was?"

Samantha looked at me like I was an insect.

"In *The Book*, of course."

"How do you know about *The Book*?"

"I got it for my birthday last year," said Joanie.

---

blow up, explode
logo, brand name or label
granny's stats, Grandma's *statistics*—facts about how well Grandma played
levitation devices, machines that let you float off the ground
head-on collision, violent crash
bugged out, popped out

»)) *Listening* SKILL

As you listen to the Audio CD, pay attention to the speaker's word choice and intonation. They are clues to the speaker's implicit ideas, or ideas that are not stated directly.

"And since then we've been all over time," said Freddi. "We've met cavewomen, Ann the Pirate, **Calamity Jane**. . . ."

"And don't forget **Cleopatra** and the underground cities of Venus," said Samantha.

"But if you have *The Book*, that means we're saved," said Sam.

Samantha gave Sam her look. "If you remember the Time Warpers' Tips, you know nothing can be in two places at once. Of course our *Book* disappeared as soon as your *Book* appeared."

"So now we have to help you get *The Book* back to the past," said Freddi, "so we can have it in the future."

"Of course," said Sam.

"We knew that," said Fred.

"Uh, right . . ." I said, trying to talk my way out of this mess. "We knew that would happen, but we uh . . . " I looked around at Sam, Fred, Samantha, Freddi, and Joanie. Then I **spotted** Uncle Joe. "We thought we could really learn some tricks about finding *The Book* from Uncle Joe!"

Uncle Joe looked up from something he was **fiddling with** in his lap. "*The Book*? Oh, I never could get it to work the way your mother did. That's why I gave it to you for your birthday."

"Oh, great," said Sam. "We're **doomed**."

"But that's also why I put this together." Uncle Joe held up the thing he had been fiddling with in his lap. It was an old-fashioned pocket watch. "My Time Warp Watch."

"We're saved!" yelled Sam.

Calamity Jane, an American frontier woman from the 1800s famous for her
  unconventional behavior and courage
Cleopatra, an ancient Egyptian queen
spotted, saw
fiddling with, playing with
doomed, in a hopeless situation

ABOUT THE **AUTHOR**

Jon Scieszka has written many books for kids. Other books in the Time Warp Trio series include *The Good, the Bad, and the Goofy; Knights of the Kitchen Table; The Not-So-Jolly Roger;* and *Your Mother Was a Neanderthal.*

BEFORE YOU GO ON

1 Which character discovers the antigravity disk but doesn't know it?

2 What will happen to the boys if they learn too much information while visiting the future?

On Your Own
Do you think that any of the inventions described in this selection will really exist in the future? Explain.

Reading 3 **421**

▶ READER'S THEATER

Act out the following scene between Joe and Joanie.

Joe: You look so much like my sister. This is very strange, Joanie.

Joanie: Well, I was named after my great-grandfather Joe. Samantha, Frieda, and I were named after our great-grandfathers.

Joe: Well, that explains why you look like you are part of my family. You are! I am your great-grandfather!

Joanie: This means that all three of you—Sam, Fred, and you, Joe—must get back to your own time, 1995.

Joe: Why does that matter so much?

Joanie: If you don't get back, you won't be able to have kids when you grow up. Then your kids won't have kids, and . . .

Joe: I understand now! If we don't get back, you, Samantha, and Frieda won't be born. If we don't get back, we will change the future.

Joanie: We must find a way to get all of you back to 1995—and fast!

▶ COMPREHENSION

Workbook Page 221

Recall

1. Under what statue do the boys meet the girls at the American Museum of Natural History?

2. Where does the antigravity power come from?

Comprehend

3. Who are some of the people the girls have visited?

4. What are the Sellbots?

Analyze

5. Describe the tone of this story. For example, is it serious or funny? Support your answer by evaluating information in the story.

6. Do you think the author's view of the future is positive or negative? Support your answer by evaluating information in the story.

Connect

7. What **specific strategies** would you use to write a believable story about the future? How would you make your story realistic and futuristic at the same time?

8. Imagine that you could travel in time. Would you go ahead to the future or back to the past? Why?

▶ DISCUSSION

Discuss in pairs or small groups.

1. Why do the girls—Frieda, Joanie, and Samantha—help the boys?

2. How is the year 2095 different from the year 1995? How is it similar?

3. Describe the skin of people in the future. Why do you think the author included this detail in the novel?

Q **What is your vision of life in the future?** Is Jon Scieszka's vision of the future realistic and believable? Why or why not? Did this excerpt from his novel cause a **shift** in your own vision of the future? Explain.

▶ RESPONSE TO LITERATURE  Workbook Page 221

Utilize *The Book* has directions for time travel. But nothing can be in two places at the same time. As a result, the girls' copy of *The Book* disappeared as soon as the boys' copy of *The Book* appeared. Help the boys get back to 1995. Write directions for time travel. When you have finished writing, share your instructions with a classmate. Talk about the steps in the process.

Listening SKILL

When your classmates speak, listen for supporting details and reasons. Ask yourself, "Did the speaker explain why these ideas are important?"

LEARNING STRATEGY

Monitor your written language production. Ask a classmate for feedback. If necessary, use different words, place them in a different order, or reorganize your sentences to make your message clear.

Grammar

End Punctuation, Commas, and Quotation Marks

The three kinds of end punctuation are periods (.), question marks (?), and exclamation points (!). Use a period to end a statement or an imperative; use a question mark to end a question; use an exclamation point to end a sentence that expresses strong feeling.

> The girls flopped down on cushions.
> Look closely.
> What do you know about wormholes, or space-time warps?
> We're saved!

A comma (,) sets off certain words or phrases in a sentence. Use commas to separate nouns or phrases in a series, to separate introductory words or phrases, and to set off a speaker's quoted words in a sentence. Quotation marks (" ") are used to set off a speaker's exact words.

> I looked around at Sam, Fred, Samantha, Freddi, and Jane.
> Hey, wait a minute.
> "Of course not," said one.

Practice  **Workbook Page 222**

Work with a partner. Copy the sentences below into your notebook. Then add proper punctuation to each

Example: Su, Mae, and Kim are coming.

1. Nora said She missed the bus
2. Leave right now
3. Rick asked Have you finished your homework
4. Oh no That's terrible
5. I'll have the salad the fish and water please

Apply

Work with a partner. Look at the reading. Take turns naming some of the punctuation.

Parentheses, Brackets, and Ellipses

Parentheses (( )) are marks that go around words and phrases. They are mainly used to show additional ideas.

> A bowl of crackers **(which looked like green dog food)** appeared.

Grammar SKILL

When the parenthetical information comes at the end of a sentence, the period comes after the closing parenthesis.

Brackets ([ ]) are used to show changes made to someone else's writing. This is useful when more information is needed to make the statement understood.

> **Original: It** was our Museum Worksheet from 1995.
> **Changed: [The yellowed sheet of paper]** was our Museum Worksheet from 1995.

Ellipses (. . .) are used when a word or phrase is missing from a statement. This is useful when quoting from a text and not all the information is necessary. Ellipses can also be used when a statement is interrupted.

> We . . . followed the girls around the building. [missing phrase]
> We knew that would happen, but we uh . . . we thought we could learn some tricks from Uncle Joe! [interrupted statement]

Practice  **Workbook** Page 223

✔ **GRAMMAR CHECK**

When do you use ellipses?

Work with a partner. Copy the sentences below into your notebook. Read the instructions in parentheses and use parentheses, brackets, or ellipses.

Example: She left before we did and went to the park. (Delete "before we did.")
  She left . . . and went to the park.

1. Jan, who was at work, called. (Show "who was at work" is extra information.)
2. She was crying. (Change "she" to "the baby.")
3. It rained all day and night. (Delete "day and.")
4. The cat, who was big and fat, was hungry. (Show "who was big and fat" is extra information.)
5. He stayed in the car. (Change "he" to "Harry.")

Apply

Work with a partner. Look back at the reading. Take turns marking the new sentences with parentheses, brackets, and ellipses.

Writing

Include Quotations and Citations

When you write a research report, you'll often want to use quotations to support your main ideas. For example, you might want to quote an expert in your topic. When you use another person's exact words, you place them in quotation marks. You also provide a citation, or information about the source of the quote.

> **Writing Prompt**
>
> Write a paragraph about time travel or science fiction. Be sure your paragraph includes at least one quotation to support the main idea. Punctuate the quotation correctly. Also, remember to include a citation that tells the source of the quote. (See www.LongmanKeystone.com for a guide to creating citations for various sources.)

1 **PREWRITE** Choose a broad topic and narrow it.

- Do research. Take notes on quotations you might want to include in your paragraph.

- Think about your paragraph's main idea and details.

- List your ideas in a graphic organizer.

Workbook Page 224

Here's a graphic organizer created by a student named Andrew. Now that he knows his main idea and important details, he can choose the best quotation to include in his paragraph.

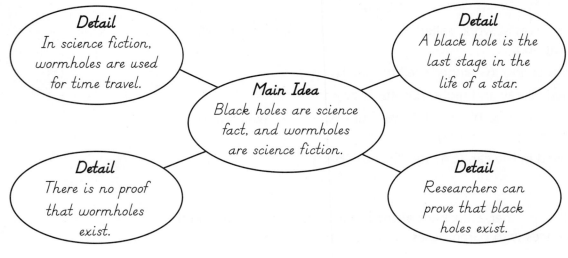

Detail
In science fiction, wormholes are used for time travel.

Detail
A black hole is the last stage in the life of a star.

Main Idea
Black holes are science fact, and wormholes are science fiction.

Detail
There is no proof that wormholes exist.

Detail
Researchers can prove that black holes exist.

2 **DRAFT** Use your organizer to help you write a first draft.

- Remember to state clearly your paragraph's main idea.
- Choose an interesting quote that supports your main idea.
- Include an accurate citation for the quote.

3 **REVISE** Read over your draft. Look for places where the writing is unclear or needs improvement. Use the Writing Checklist to help you identify problems. Then revise your draft, using the editing and proofreading marks listed on page 456.

4 **EDIT** Check your work for errors in grammar, usage, mechanics, and spelling. Trade papers with a partner to obtain feedback. Use the Peer Review Checklist on Workbook page 224. Edit your final draft in response to feedback from your partner and your teacher.

5 **PUBLISH** Prepare a clean copy of your final draft. Share your paragraph with the class. Save your work. You'll need to refer to it in the Writing Workshop at the end of the unit.

Writing Checklist

IDEAS:
☑ I included at least one quotation that supported my main idea.

CONVENTIONS:
☑ I punctuated quotations and citations correctly.

Here is Andrew's paragraph with a quotation and citation. Notice that he includes the full citation at the end of his work.

Andrew C. Dubin

Wormholes and Black Holes

Time travel is a popular topic in science fiction. Authors sometimes have their characters use wormholes as a way to travel through time. Wormholes are two black holes that are connected. Researchers say that wormholes "are more science fiction than they are science fact" (NASA). Wormholes are popular in science fiction, but there is no proof that they even exist. Researchers can prove that black holes exist, though. A black hole is the last stage in the life of a star. The force of gravity in black holes is very strong. Black holes and wormholes are related, but black holes are science fact, and wormholes are science fiction.

Works Consulted List

"Black Holes." NASA Goddard Space Flight Center. September 2006. 28 March 2009 <http://imagine.gsfc.nasa.gov/docs/science/know_12/black_holes.html>.

Prepare to Read

What You Will Learn

Reading
- Vocabulary building: *Context, dictionary skills, word study*
- Reading strategy: *Employ analytical skills*
- Text type: *Informational text (science)*

Grammar
Using quotation marks for exact words; Quotation marks: terms, expressions, and titles

Writing
Include paraphrases and citations

➤ 🔵 THE BIG QUESTION

What is your vision of life in the future? Do you ever wonder what travel will be like in the future? Do you ever think about traveling to other planets in our solar system? You can get an idea of what places you can visit and how you will get there by learning about our country's space program.

➤ BUILD BACKGROUND

"NASA and the U.S. Space Program" is a science article about the National Aeronautics and Space Administration (NASA) and its space program. NASA's headquarters is in Washington, D.C., and it has centers and facilities around the country. The Lyndon B. Johnson Space Center (JSC) in Houston, Texas, is NASA's center for spaceflight training, research, and flight control. The JSC is a large facility with over 100 buildings on 1,620 acres. Houston has good weather most of the year, and it is close to water. Therefore, the Johnson Space Center is in an ideal location for tracking spacecraft and training astronauts.

Since the formation of NASA in 1958, the space program has been the subject of controversy. Some people think that the money used for space exploration would be better spent here on Earth. In this article, you will learn how NASA research provides benefits that go beyond our knowledge of space.

▼ Aerial view of the Johnson Space Center in Houston, Texas

Learn Key Words

Read aloud and listen to the sentences with a partner. Use the context to figure out the meaning of the highlighted words. Use a dictionary to check your answers. Then write each word and its meaning in your notebook.

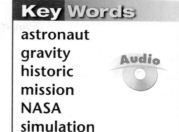
1. An astronaut trains hard for a trip into space.
2. Astronauts have to learn to move around in low gravity.
3. The White House is a historic building.
4. Her mission in life was to become an astronaut.
5. Scientists and engineers at NASA direct the space program.
6. Astronauts use a simulation to train for a flight into space.

Practice

Write these sentences in your notebook. Complete each sentence with a phrase that includes the key word shown in parentheses. Then take turns reading the sentences aloud with a partner.

1. She made it her _____. (mission)
2. For a successful launch, a rocket _____. (gravity)
3. The pilot of a spacecraft _____. (astronaut)
4. The Civil War is _____. (historic)
5. His new video game _____. (simulation)
6. Spacecraft send pictures _____. (NASA)

Listening and Speaking: Academic Words

Study the red words and their meanings. You will find these words useful when talking and writing about informational texts. Write each word and its meaning in your notebook, then say the words aloud with a partner. After you read "NASA and the U.S. Space Program," try to use these words to respond to the text.

challenge = something that tests your skill or ability	⇨	Completing the task on time was a **challenge.**
contact = communication with a person, organization, or place	⇨	The people at Mission Control keep in **contact** with the astronauts.
controversy = a serious argument about something involving many people over a long time	⇨	Text messaging while driving is the subject of **controversy.**
crucial = extremely important	⇨	Many scientists think space exploration is **crucial** to understanding life on Earth.
function = work properly	⇨	The electrical panel in the spacecraft did not **function.**
professional = well trained and good at a job	⇨	Some astronauts are **professional** airplane pilots.

Audio

Practice

Workbook
Page 226

Write the sentences in your notebook. Choose a red word from the box above to complete each sentence. Then, take turns reading the sentences aloud to a partner.

1. She could not lock the door because the lock did not _____.
2. When talking to the parents, his manner was very _____.
3. The way the mayor handled the emergency was the subject of _____.
4. Her role was _____ in solving the problems facing the city.
5. Completing the project on time was a _____.
6. Her mother was worried because she could not _____ her sister.

▲ An astronaut

Word Study: Identifying Cognates

Some words in English look and sound almost the same as the word in Spanish. They also have the same meaning. We call these words cognates. Compare and contrast the cognates in the chart below. How are these words the same? How are they different? What other cognates can you add to this list?

English	Spanish
atmosphere	atmósfera
cafeteria	cafetería
music	música
air	aire
explosion	explósion

Practice  Workbook Page 227

Use each English word above in a sentence. Write the sentences in your notebook. Read your sentences to a partner. Be sure to use the English pronunciation of the word.

READING STRATEGY | EMPLOY ANALYTICAL SKILLS

Employing analytical skills is the process you use to evaluate a writer's argument for an issue. You can perfect these skills by asking yourself the following questions while you read:

- What was the writer's purpose for writing this text? What issue or controversy is presented?
- What are the most important ideas in this text?
- Which of these ideas are opinions? Which are facts supported by evidence?
- Does the writer provide enough evidence to convince you? Why or why not?

As you read "NASA and the U.S. Space Program," stop from time to time to ask yourself whether you agree with the writer's position.

 Workbook Page 228

LEARNING STRATEGY

Compare and contrast grade-level vocabulary and cognates. You will better remember new words by identifying how they are similar to and different from others.

Set a purpose for reading What do you know about space travel? Would you like to go to the moon someday? Some people feel strongly that space exploration is important to our future. Do you?

NASA *and the U.S. Space Program*

Audio

Problem Solving at Its Best

There's a famous scene in the Hollywood movie *Apollo 13*. Tom Hanks, playing the astronaut James Lovell, says, "Houston, we have a problem!" This has become a popular **expression.** People now say it when joking about a problem. During the real Apollo 13 mission, this line was not a joke. It was one of many scary moments the space program experienced at the Johnson Space Center in Houston, Texas.

An explosion on board the *Apollo 13* spacecraft caused an electrical failure. Many systems in the spacecraft were affected. The astronauts had to change their mission. They had a lunar module, which was a vehicle designed to explore the moon. Instead of landing on the moon, they had to use their lunar module for power and life support until they could make the journey back to Earth.

Though they were alone in space, the astronauts had help on the ground. A professional team in Houston worked hard to solve the problem. The challenge they faced was how to get the astronauts home.

NASA is the National Aeronautics and Space Administration. This **agency** directs the U.S. space program. The Johnson Space Center is one of 11 NASA **facilities.** Here, hundreds of astronauts have been trained. NASA made the United States the world leader in space exploration.

---

expression, phrase
agency, organization
facilities, places or buildings

> **Reading Skill**
>
> To help you understand the reading, study the title and headings. This will help you identify the most important ideas.

The Space Program Controversy

Missions into space are very expensive. All of the equipment for a mission is designed for the **harsh** conditions in space. A rocket must be able to **overcome** the force of Earth's gravity to reach its destination.

Fortunately, the Space Shuttle program enables NASA to reuse spacecraft. But the cost of a new mission is still high. Each shuttle mission averages about 450 million dollars. The space shuttle *Endeavor* cost 1.7 billion dollars to build. You can understand why some people feel that the space program is too expensive. They would like to see its funding greatly reduced or cut off completely.

Their argument that this money could be used to solve other problems seems to make sense. However, NASA and the Johnson Space Center provide much more to the **public** than the exploration of space.

Spin-Offs

Does anyone in your family have a cell phone? Maybe your family has satellite TV. Have you been in a car that has a GPS (Global Positioning System)? All of these common technologies have their **roots** in the space program.

A visit to any hospital also shows NASA **creativity** in action. New technology is used to image and monitor patients. Some of the devices are **spin-offs** that were originally developed to monitor the astronauts during training and spaceflight. Researchers have learned much about the human body by studying the effects of low gravity on bones and muscles. The Johnson Space Center is home to the Space Environment Simulation Lab, which is used for this purpose.

---

harsh, severe or difficult
overcome, break free of
public, people in a society
roots, starting points
creativity, imagination
spin-offs, things based on the design of something else

BEFORE YOU GO ON

1 What caused some systems in the *Apollo 13* spacecraft to no longer **function**?

2 How did the *Apollo 13* astronauts' vision of the future change after the explosion?

On Your Own
What did you learn about the space program that you did not know?

Life in space is not possible without protection. There is no air to breathe. Temperatures are extreme. The need to create a comfortable space suit resulted in the development of new fabrics. These spin-offs have improved the suits firefighters wear to protect them from high temperatures. Clothing and bedding are now made of new fabrics designed to keep you comfortable in all different temperatures.

The most famous facility at the Johnson Space Center is Mission Control. The new Mission Control building is the **"heart"** of NASA during a space mission. Mission control **specialists** are in contact with the astronauts from before the **launch** until they are safely home. They even play music to wake the astronauts each morning. This new building has state of the art equipment.

The old Mission Control building has been preserved as a historic site. It shows what things were like in the early days of the space program, when a mission to the moon was only a dream. The vision of many great scientists made that dream a reality.

Advances in Communication

It was NASA that made wireless communication happen. By the early 1960s, NASA was able to put **satellites** into **orbit.** This achievement started a **revolution** in communications. Private companies understood how life could change. With a satellite, signals could be sent and received in all parts of the world. We could see what was happening "live" anywhere in the world. Communications satellites now bring us live TV from all parts of the world. We can talk to people almost anywhere at any time with cell phones. Satellite pictures help in predicting severe weather. We can watch weather patterns as they form. We can warn people to take shelter before a storm hits. None of this would have been possible without the space program.

---

heart, center of
specialists, people that are very skilled in something
launch, time when a spacecraft is sent into the sky
satellites, objects that orbit Earth
orbit, path traveled by an object around a larger object
revolution, major change

▲ The space progam created the demand for wireless technology.

What's Next?

The Space Shuttle program ended in 2011 after thirty years. But NASA says this is not the end of sending humans into space. NASA has many plans for the future, including deep-space exploration. The **unmanned** Mars Science Laboratory is scheduled to land on Mars in 2012. A new rover called Curiosity will explore Mars to determine whether it is **habitable.** Eventually, NASA plans to send astronauts to Mars, but doing this safely remains a huge challenge.

In 2012, NASA plans to launch the Nuclear Spectroscopic Telescope Array to search for black holes, map supernova explosions, and study distant galaxies. Another unmanned spacecraft, Juno, was launched in 2011 and is scheduled to arrive on Jupiter in 2016. The International Space Station (ISS) and its programs have been extended through 2020. The ISS will continue to conduct experiments in biology, physics, astronomy, and meteorology. NASA is committed to using this **unique** resource for scientific research.

---

unmanned, without humans on board
habitable, suitable for people to live on
unique, special; one-of-a-kind

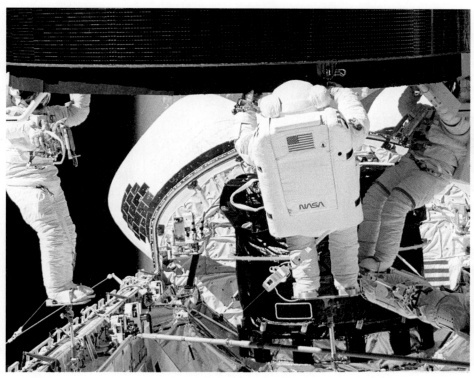

▲ NASA astronauts working in space

BEFORE YOU GO ON

1 How does Mission Control help the astronauts while they are on a mission?

2 What are some of NASA's spin-offs?

On Your Own
What NASA discoveries have changed your life?

Review and Practice

► **COMPREHENSION** 📖 **Workbook** Page 229

Recall

1. What facility at the Johnson Space Center stays in constant contact with astronauts during a mission?

2. How did people at the Johnson Space Center help the *Apollo 13* astronauts?

Comprehend

3. What is meant by saying Mission Control is the "heart" of NASA?

4. How has the space program helped medical research?

Analyze

5. What controversy surrounds the space program?

6. What do people mean when they say "Houston, we have a problem"?

Connect

7. In your opinion, what professional qualities should someone have to be in the space program?

8. In your opinion, what crucial role does NASA have?

► **IN YOUR OWN WORDS**

Summarize "NASA and the U.S. Space Program" for a friend. Find six important ideas to include in your summary. Copy the graphic organizer below in your notebook to help you organize your ideas. Then share your summary with a classmate.

LEARNING STRATEGY

If you can't remember a specific word you want to use, try to define it, use other words to describe it, or use a synonym.

Six Important Arguments for Funding the Space Program

▶ DISCUSSION

Discuss in pairs or small groups.

»)) *Listening* SKILL

Listen carefully to other people's ideas so that you understand what they are saying.

1. Do you think space travel is important? Why or why not?
2. Being an astronaut can be dangerous. Why do you think so many children want to be **professional** astronauts when they grow up?

Q **What is your vision of life in the future?** Do you think that in your lifetime you will travel in space? Do you think that someday people will live on other planets? Explain.

▶ READ FOR FLUENCY

It is often easier to read a text if you understand the difficult words and phrases. Work with a partner. Choose a paragraph from the reading. Identify the words and phrases you do not know or have trouble pronouncing. Look up the difficult words in the dictionary.

Take turns pronouncing the words and phrases with your partner. If necessary, ask your teacher to model the correct pronunciation. Then take turns reading the paragraph aloud. Give each other feedback on your reading.

▶ EXTENSION **Workbook Page 229**

Utilize In small groups, visit the NASA website. Analyze how similar information is conveyed in different media. Study the effect that visual and sound techniques have on your experience. Do they change your reaction to the information? If so, explain how.

◀ The United States was the first country to land a man on the moon.

Grammar

Using Quotation Marks for Exact Words

Knowing how to use quotation marks correctly will help you write better and more clearly. When writing dialogue, or a conversation, in a narrative, enclose a character's exact words or thoughts in quotation marks.

> "Have you ever visited the Johnson Space Center?" I asked.
> "No, I haven't. Have you?" he responded.
> "Yes, I was there last year," I said.

In expository writing, place quotation marks around a person's exact words when you are quoting them.

> Tom Hanks, playing the astronaut James Lovell, says, "Houston, we have a problem!"

For long quotations, use a block quotation. A block quotation is indented, single-spaced, and not enclosed in quotation marks.

> According to the author,
>
> > People at NASA have learned from their successes as well as their mistakes. The Johnson Space Center is one of eleven NASA facilities. Here, hundreds of astronauts have been successfully trained. NASA made the United States the world leader in space exploration.

Practice Workbook Page 230

Work with a partner. Write the sentences in your notebook. Add quotation marks where they are needed.

Example: He said, "This is an interesting article."

1. I have read this book before, she said.
2. Can we go? I asked. Yes, any time, he said.
3. The author writes, Life in space is not possible without protection.
4. The Johnson Space Center knows how to solve problems, the author concludes.
5. She said, I might work for NASA one day.

Apply

Work with a partner. Talk about your opinion of the reading. Then write down three quotations from your conversation.

Quotation Marks: Terms, Expressions, and Titles

Use quotation marks to enclose special or unfamiliar terms and any other unusual expressions.

> Test your skills at the "Space Shuttle Flight Simulator Experience" at the Johnson Space Center.
> This area is the "heart" of NASA during a space mission.

Use quotation marks to set off a word or phrase that defines another word or phrase.

> *Simulation* means "creating special conditions to test something."

Use quotation marks to set off a title of a short written work such as articles, poems, and short stories.

> "NASA and the U.S. Space Program" is a short article about NASA and the Johnson Space Center.

Practice  Workbook Page 231

Work with a partner. Write the sentences in your notebook. Add quotation marks where they are needed.

Example: I read a short article called "A Family History."

1. The word *legislation* means a law or set of laws.
2. He's written an article called Becoming an Astronaut.
3. Crystals somehow know which shape to grow into.
4. Have you read the poem Cosmonauts?
5. The Johnson Space Center describes its tours as intelligent fun.

Apply

Work with a partner. Think of examples for the different uses of quotation marks presented here. Write them in your notebook.

Writing

Include Paraphrases and Citations

To support your ideas in a research report, you can quote information from a source, or you can restate the information in your own words. When you put other people's ideas into your own words, you are *paraphrasing*. Whether you quote or paraphrase, you must provide a citation that tells the source of the information.

> **Writing Prompt**
>
> Write a paragraph about a science topic that includes a paraphrase and a citation. Use reliable sources of information such as recent science books, encyclopedias, and government or university websites. Remember to use quotation marks to enclose special or technical terms or another person's exact words.

1 **PREWRITE** Choose and narrow a topic.

- Ask yourself a question about your specific topic. What do you most want to know about it?
- Use your question to guide your research.
- Think about the main idea of your paragraph. Ask yourself which details from your research support this main idea.
- List your ideas in a graphic organizer.

Workbook Page 232

Here's a graphic organizer created by a student named Angelina, who chose the topic of DNA, which is a chemical set of instructions unique in every person except identical twins.

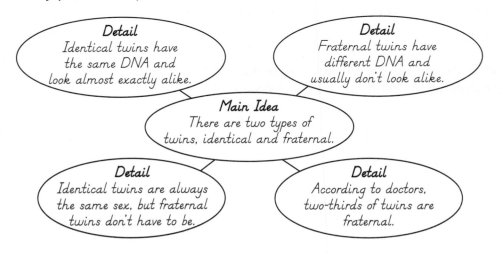

Detail
Identical twins have the same DNA and look almost exactly alike.

Detail
Fraternal twins have different DNA and usually don't look alike.

Main Idea
There are two types of twins, identical and fraternal.

Detail
Identical twins are always the same sex, but fraternal twins don't have to be.

Detail
According to doctors, two-thirds of twins are fraternal.

2 DRAFT Use your organizer to help you write a first draft.

- Remember your purpose—to inform and explain.
- State your main idea clearly.
- Remember to include a citation when you paraphrase information, and quotation marks when quoting exact words.

3 REVISE Read over your draft. Look for places where the writing is unclear or needs improvement. Use the Writing Checklist to help you identify problems. Then revise your draft, using the editing and proofreading marks listed on page 456.

4 EDIT Check your work for errors in grammar, usage, mechanics, and spelling. Trade papers with a partner to obtain feedback. Use the Peer Review Checklist on Workbook page 232. Edit your final draft in response to feedback from your partner and your teacher.

5 PUBLISH Prepare a clean copy of your final draft. Share your paragraph with the class. Save your work. You'll need to refer to it in the Writing Workshop at the end of the unit.

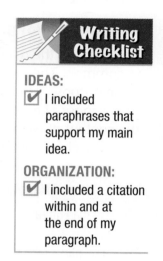

Writing Checklist

IDEAS:
☑ I included paraphrases that support my main idea.

ORGANIZATION:
☑ I included a citation within and at the end of my paragraph.

Here is Angelina's paragraph that includes a paraphrase and a citation. Notice how she uses negatives and contractions correctly.

Angelina Xing

Fraternal and Identical Twins

There are two types of twins, identical and fraternal. The word <u>identical</u> means "exactly the same." Identical twins have the same DNA and look almost exactly alike. Identical twins are also always the same sex. Giving birth to identical twins occurs less frequently than giving birth to fraternal twins. According to doctors, approximately two-thirds of twin pregnancies are fraternal (Iannelli). Fraternal twins are actually quite different from each other. Most of the time, they don't look alike at all. Fraternal twins are sometimes the same sex, and other times, they're not. They also have different blood types and different DNA.

Works Consulted List

Iannelli, Vincent. "Facts about Twins." <u>Keep Kids Healthy</u>. May 2003. 15 March 2009 <http://www.keepkidshealthy.com/twins/expecting_twins.html>.

Link the Readings

Critical Thinking

Look back at the readings in this unit. Think about what they all have in common. They all tell about the future. Yet they do not all have the same purpose. The purpose of one reading might be to inform, while the purpose of another might be to entertain or persuade. In addition, the content of each reading relates to the future in different ways. Now copy the chart below into your notebook and complete it.

Title of Reading	Purpose	Big Question Link
"Life in the Future"		*tells about life in the future*
"Southbound on the Freeway" "Cardinal Ideograms" "Interview with Dan Bursch"		
From *The Time Warp Trio: 2095*	*to entertain*	
"NASA and the U.S. Space Program"		

Discussion

Discuss in pairs or small groups.

- How does the purpose of "Life in the Future" differ from the purpose of *The Time Warp Trio: 2095*?

- **Q** **What is your vision of life in the future?** Think about the readings in this unit. What picture of the future does each one show? Is the picture positive or negative? What's your opinion? Does life in the future look positive, negative, or both? Explain.

Media Literacy & Projects

1 You have read a lot about the future. What do you think the future will look like? Paint a picture of your town or city 100 years from now.

2 You read an interview with an astronaut. What training do astronauts need? Go to the NASA website to find out the requirements for being a U.S. astronaut. Share your findings in an oral report. Include handouts or other visuals.

3 *The Time Warp Trio: 2095* is part of a series of books about the travels of Sam, Fred, and Joe. Read another book in the series, such as *Tut Tut* or *It's All Greek to Me*. Then give a brief book report to the class. You might want to read the entire series!

4 Working with some classmates, adapt *The Time Warp Trio: 2095* as a brief play. Choose any part of the novel you like, rewrite it as a script, and act it out for the class. Include some costumes and simple props, too.

Further Reading

Choose from these reading suggestions. Practice reading silently for longer periods with increased comprehension.

The Time Machine, H. G. Wells
This Penguin Reader® adaptation tells the story of a man who uses his time machine to travel to the year 802,701, where he finds the world inhabited by the Eloi and their enemies, the Morlocks. What will he find when he travels even farther into the future? Will he ever be able to return?

Tomorrowland: Ten Stories About the Future, Michael Cart
This collection of short stories, written by current writers, explores many aspects of life in the future.

Tuck Everlasting, Natalie Babbitt
The Tuck family discovers a spring with "unusual" properties. A conflict arises when others learn the spring's secret.

Put It All Together

LISTENING & SPEAKING WORKSHOP

Speech

You will give a speech that expresses your vision of life in the future.

1 **THINK ABOUT IT** In small groups, discuss the texts you read in this unit. Did any influence your vision of life in the future? Discuss your own predictions about life in the future. For instance, discuss what you think future schools will be like. Work together to develop a list of topics for a speech about the future. Here are some examples:

- space tourism
- new technology for communications
- homes of the future
- environmental issues in the future

2 **GATHER AND ORGANIZE INFORMATION** Choose a topic from your group's list. Write down what you already know about the topic. Look at an encyclopedia or a website to find out more about it. Decide what the focus of your speech will be.

Research Use the library or the Internet to find more information about your topic. Look for interesting facts, examples, and details that support your main idea or prediction about the topic. Take notes on what you find. Be sure to write down the sources of the information you wish to include.

Order Your Notes Decide on the main idea or prediction for your speech; for example: *In the future, people will live in "smart houses." Computers will turn the lights on and off, lock the doors, and water the plants.* Arrange your note cards in logical order and prepare an outline for your speech. Your outline should include your main idea and the facts, examples, and details that you will use to support it. Think of an interesting way to begin your speech. Plan a conclusion that summarizes your findings.

Prepare a Script Use your outline and note cards to write a script for your speech.

Use Visuals To make your speech more interesting and effective, find or make visuals such as posters and models that illustrate your ideas and predictions. Your visuals should be big enough for everyone to see easily. Decide when to show your visuals, and mark reminders in your speech.

3 PRACTICE AND PRESENT

Practice reading your speech aloud until you know it very well. Keep practicing until you can speak smoothly and at a natural rate, looking just occasionally at your script. To make your speech richer, use a variety of grammatical structures, sentence lengths and types, and connecting words. Then have a friend or family member listen as you practice giving your speech. Ask whether your words and ideas are understandable. Keep practicing until you feel comfortable and confident saying your speech while looking at your audience.

Deliver Your Speech Remember that a speech is a formal presentation. Be sure to use appropriate language. Speak clearly and loudly enough so that everyone in the class can hear you. Glance at your script as needed, but remember to look up and make eye contact with your listeners. Use natural hand and body movements, too. At the end of your speech, ask the audience members whether they have any questions.

4 EVALUATE THE PRESENTATION

A good way to improve your speaking and listening skills is by evaluating each presentation you give and hear. Use this checklist to help you judge your speech and the speeches of your classmates.

- ☑ What was the speaker's topic?
- ☑ Was the speaker's main idea or prediction clear?
- ☑ Do you agree with the speaker's main idea or prediction? Why or why not?
- ☑ Did the speaker include interesting facts, examples, and details that supported the main idea or prediction?
- ☑ Did the speaker use formal or informal language? Was it appropriate?
- ☑ What suggestions do you have for improving the speech?

Speaking SKILL

Use words such as *may, might, will, could, would, perhaps,* and *probably* to explain your predictions for the future.

Listening SKILLS

As you listen, identify the speaker's topic. Listen for the general meaning, main ideas, and important details. After each presentation, share this information with a partner to confirm that you have understood it correctly.

Listen for the implicit ideas in a speaker's presentation. You can infer what the speaker means by associating *what* he or she says with *how* he or she says it. Also, pay attention to facial expressions and body language.

STRENGTHEN YOUR SOCIAL LANGUAGE

In social contexts as well as in some of your content-area classes, you will need to ask for and give information. Go to www.LongmanKeystone.com and do the activity for this unit. This activity will help you acquire key structures, expressions, and words needed during extended speaking assignments and in everyday academic and social contexts.

WRITING WORKSHOP

Research Report

Write a Research Report

In a research report, you explain with specificity and detail a topic you have studied in depth. You use research gathered from different sources and include a list of sources. The report begins by introducing the writer's topic and controlling idea or focus. Each body paragraph presents a main idea that develops the topic. Facts, details, examples, and quotations support the main ideas. A conclusion sums up the information.

> **Writing Prompt**
>
> Write a five-paragraph research report about a topic related to life in the future. You might write about medicine, education, transportation, or any other area of human life that might be different in the future from the way it is now. Use a variety of reliable sources for research such as encyclopedias, newspapers, and university or government websites.

1 PREWRITE Review your previous work in this unit. Now choose and narrow a topic for your report. In your notebook, answer the following:

Ongoing Writing Skills Practice

- What do I want to know about my topic?

- What resources can I use to find the answer to this question?

As you research, take notes. Then use a question-and answer outline to organize your ideas for your research report.

Workbook Page 233

Here's an outline created by a student named Brandon. He decided to write about transportation in the future.

I. Introduction
    A. Huge advances made in the last 200 years
    B. More advances coming in the future
II. Hybrid cars
    A. Already have better gas mileage than before
    B. Stronger batteries needed to become main
        energy source
III. Faster and more fuel-efficient airplane
    A. Flying wing
    B. Shaped like triangle
IV. Other flying vehicles
    A. SoloTrek EFV
    B. Urban Aeronautics X-Hawk
V. Safer, faster, more fuel-efficient modern vehicles
    A. Will be even better in the future
    B. Designed for environment-friendly society

2 **DRAFT** Use your graphic organizer and the model on page 451 to help you write a first draft.

- Begin with a paragraph that states your topic and focus.

- Use your own words when your write the report.

- If you use exact words from a source, punctuate the quotation correctly.

Citing Sources Look at the style, punctuation, and order of information in the following sources. Use the examples on the next page as models.

Book

Stanchak, John. Civil War. New York: Dorling Kindersley, 2000.

Magazine article

Kirn, Walter. "Lewis and Clark: The Journey That Changed America Forever." Time 8 July 2002: 36–41.

Internet website

Smith, Gene. "The Structure of the Milky Way." Gene Smith's Astronomy Tutorial. 28 April 1999. Center for Astrophysics & Space Sciences, University of California, San Diego. 20 July 2009 <http://casswww.ucsd.edu/public/tutorial/MW.html>.

Encyclopedia article

Siple, Paul A. "Antarctica." World Book Encyclopedia. 1991 ed.

3 **REVISE** Read over your draft. Think about how well you have addressed questions of purpose, audience, and form. Your purpose is to inform and explain. Is your topic one that will interest your audience? Does your research report begin with an introduction? Does your report develop your topic in body paragraphs and end with a conclusion?

Keep these questions in mind as you revise your draft. Use the Writing Checklist below to help you identify additional issues that may need revision. Mark your changes on your draft using the editing and proofreading marks listed on page 456.

SIX TRAITS OF WRITING CHECKLIST

- ☑ **IDEAS:** Does my first paragraph introduce my topic and focus?
- ☑ **ORGANIZATION:** Do I include a main idea supported by facts and details in each paragraph?
- ☑ **VOICE:** Does my writing show my knowledge of the topic?
- ☑ **WORD CHOICE:** Do I correctly use content-based words and other newly acquired vocabulary words that fit my topic?
- ☑ **SENTENCE FLUENCY:** Do I vary my use of simple, compound, and complex sentences in order to achieve sentence fluency?
- ☑ **CONVENTIONS:** Do I punctuate quotations correctly?

LEARNING STRATEGY

Monitor your written language production. Using a writing checklist will help you assess your work. Evaluate your essay to make sure that your message is clear and easy to understand.

Here are the revisions Brandon plans to make to his first draft.

Transportation of the Future

In the last 200 years, transportation technology has made ∧ astonishing advances. Steamships replaced sailing ships. Railroads were created. ∧ Automobiles were invented⊙ The Wright brothers made the first airplane flight. Astronauts traveled to the moon! What ~~can~~ will transportation be like in the future. ? Transportation technology ~~may~~ will continue to advance, perhaps more than we can imagine today. We will see improvements in hybrid and electric cars, airplanes, and personal jetpacks.

Car companies are already making hybrid or fuel efficient cars that have improved gas mileage. However, Batteries must become stronger and cheaper in order to become the main energy source for cars. electric cars today (must use gasoline power as a backup.) They can go only 50 to 100 miles between charges. so they According to scientist Joshua Cunningham, "Gasoline will remain a dominant fuel until at least 2050" (Layton, Nice).

Many airlines are trying to make their jets faster and more fuel efficient. A group called Greener By design predicts that a new kind of plane, the flying wing, will be carrying passengers by 2025. These planes made of plastic and will be shaped like a triangle. Passengers will sit in rows of up to 40 seats across.

Several new flying vehicles ~~will~~ may be in the sky. in the next few decades Inventors are close to creating a jetpack that can go as high as a plane and maneuver

Revised to correct errors in grammar, improve word choice, and add detail.

Revised to add connecting words and improve organization.

Revised to add details.

better than a helicopter. The SoloTrek EFV is one example. According to its inventor, Michael Moshier, it one day will "fly at altitudes of nearly 8,000 feet . . . and reach speeds of up to 80 mph" (Sieberg). An emergency vehicle by Urban Aeronautics, known as the X-Hawk, will go places that cannot be reached by helicopters. or other emergency vehicles

Modern vehicles are becoming safer, faster, and more fuel-efficient. In the future, people will have access to even better transportation. This new technology will be specially designed to work in a fast-paced society.

Revised to correct errors in grammar, add details, and improve organization.

Works Consulted List

"Future Planes Might Be 'Flying Wings'." Future Planes. 5 April 2007. 23 March 2009 <http://futureplanes.blogspot.com/>.

Layton, Julia, and Karim Nice. "How Hybrid Cars Work." How Stuff Works. 23 March 2009 <http://auto.howstuffworks.com/hybrid-car.htm>.

Sieberg, Daniel. "Personal 'Jetpack' Gets off the Ground." CNN Sci-Tech. 6 February 2002. 24 March 2009 <http://archives.cnn.com/2002/TECH/ptech/02/06/solotrek.jetpack/index.html>.

Stearns, Peter N., general editor. "The Modern Period: Transportation and Communication." The Encyclopedia of World History. 2001 ed.

4 **EDIT** Check your work for errors in grammar, usage, mechanics, and spelling. Then trade research reports with a partner and use the Peer Review Checklist below to give each other constructive feedback. Edit your final draft in response to feedback from your partner and your teacher.

Workbook
Page 233

PEER REVIEW CHECKLIST

- ☑ Does the report provide good information and explanations?
- ☑ Does it use strong quotations to support some of the main ideas?
- ☑ Was the organization of facts and details easy to follow?
- ☑ Does the writer spell words correctly?
- ☑ Is there a complete list of sources at the end of the report?
- ☑ What changes could be made to improve the essay?

Here are the changes Brandon decided to make to his final draft as a result of his peer review

Brandon Saiz

Transportation of the Future

In the last 200 years, transportation technology has made astonishing advances. Steamships replaced sailing ships. Railroads were created. Automobiles were invented. The Wright brothers made the first airplane flight. Astronauts traveled to the moon! What will transportation be like in the future? Transportation technology will continue to advance, perhaps more than we can imagine today. We will see improvements in hybrid and electric cars, airplanes, and personal jetpacks.

Car companies are already making hybrid or fuel efficient cars that have improved gas mileage. However, batteries must become stronger and cheaper in order to become the main energy source for cars. electric cars today can go only 50 to 100 miles between charges, so they must use gasoline power as a backup. According to scientist Joshua Cunningham, "Gasoline will remain a dominant fuel until at least 2050" (Layton, Nice).

Many airlines are trying to make their jets faster and more fuel efficient. A group called Greener By design predicts that a new kind of plane, the flying wing, will be carrying passengers by 2025. These planes will be made of plastic and shaped like a triangle. Passengers will sit in rows of up to 40 seats across.

Revised to correct errors in mechanics.

Several new flying vehicles may be in the sky in the next few decades. Inventors are close to creating a jetpack that can go as high as a plane and maneuver better than a helicopter. The SoloTrek EFV is one example. According to its inventor, Michael Moshier, one day it will "fly at altitudes of nearly 8,000 feet . . . and reach speeds of up to 80 mph" (Sieberg). An emergency vehicle by Urban Aeronautics, known as the X-Hawk, will go places that cannot be reached by helicopters or other emergency vehicles.

Modern vehicles are becoming safer, faster, and more fuel-efficient. In the future, people will have access to even better transportation. This new technology will be specially designed to work in a
∧ environment-friendly
fast-paced ∧ society.

Revised to add detail.

5 **PUBLISH** Prepare a clean copy of your final draft. Share your research report with the class.

Test Preparation

PRACTICE

Read the following test sample. Study the tips in the boxes. Work with a partner to complete the statement and answer the question.

Telephones Then and Now

1   Telephones have changed a lot in recent years. The first telephone my family had was connected to a wall in the house. Wires in the house connected to telephone wires outside. The sound was carried over the wires until it finally made it to my friend's house. Even if you had a long cord, it was still difficult to move around the room while you were talking.

2   The next telephone we had was still connected to the wall. But the receiver had a battery, and you could walk around the house while you called your friend. You could dial the number, speak, and listen using the mobile receiver. You still had to put the receiver in its base when you were finished talking so that it could be charged.

3   My mom recently bought a new phone. This phone does just about everything! She can use it to surf the Internet and send e-mails. She can even check her social networking page. She doesn't even need to use the number keys any more. Mom can just touch the application on the screen with her finger, and the phone does the rest. Most importantly, the phone isn't connected to anything unless it is time to charge it. You can take it almost anywhere.

1 Today's telephones are _____.
- **A** able to do many things
- **B** connected to a wire
- **C** only available to the rich
- **D** available in many styles

2 What is one thing Mom <u>cannot</u> do with her new phone?
- **F** Send e-mail
- **G** Surf the Internet
- **H** Check her social networking page
- **J** Mail a package

Taking Tests
You will often take tests that help show what you know. Study the tips below to help you improve your test-taking skills.

Tip
You don't have to know what earlier telephones were like in order to answer the questions. Just make sure your answer choices are supported by evidence from the selection.

Tip
In Question 2, pay attention to the word <u>cannot</u>. You are looking for something Mom is not able to do with her new phone.

Workbook
Pages 235–238

IMAGINING THE FUTURE

*N*o one can see into the future, but most of us can imagine it. Artists often show the future in their work. Sometimes they show people zooming around in flying jackets across strange-looking cities. Other times, they just try to capture a futuristic mood.

Alexander A. Maldonado, *San Francisco to New York in One Hour* (1969)

In Alexander A. Maldonado's vision of the future, people are able to travel thousands of miles quickly. In *San Francisco to New York in One Hour*, vehicles zip through underground tubes. The tops of these tunnels are round. The overall image looks like a big stadium with a parking lot packed with cars and buses. The artist surrounded his brightly colored painting with a wooden frame. This makes you feel as though you are looking through a window into the future.

A Mexican American who lived in California for most of his adult life, Maldonado continued to have strong ties to his native Mexico. One of the tunnel stations in the painting travels from the United States to Mexico (notice the Mexican flag on the upper right building), a speedy route between the artist's past as a child and where he built his future.

▲ Alexander A. Maldonado, *San Francisco to New York in One Hour*, 1969, oil, 18 × 24 in., Smithsonian American Art Museum

▲ Harry Bertoia, *Sculpture Group Symbolizing World's Communication in the Atomic Age*, 1959, brass and bronze, 142¼ × 231¼ × 81 in., Smithsonian American Art Museum

Harry Bertoia, *Sculpture Group Symbolizing World's Communication in the Atomic Age* (1959)

Harry Bertoia's *Sculpture Group Symbolizing World's Communication in the Atomic Age* is made up of one large 2.4-meter (8-ft.) sculpture and three smaller sculptures. Bertoia worked with metals such as brass and copper. Then he added light so that the objects seem to glow like the planets and stars. In the larger piece to the left, he put together squares of metal attached to poles, which formed a circle shaped like the sun.

Even though Bertoia lived at a time when computers and television were new, he felt that electronics and atomic energy already dominated American culture. When you look at his bright sculpture, it's easy to imagine that you're in outer space or inside a TV.

Any future that someone can imagine is always based on what we find in our present. Both of these artists used images we understand today to imagine a different world tomorrow.

Discuss What You Learned

1 What is similar in the way each of these artists views the future? In what way are their artworks different?

2 What do you think Alexander Maldonado wanted to express in his painting?

Big Question
If you were asked to imagine the future in an artwork, what would you create?

Workbook
Pages 239–240

455

Editing and Proofreading Marks

To:	Use This Mark	Example:
add something	∧	We ate rice, bean, and corn.
delete something	ℨ	We ate rice, beans, and corns.
close space	⌣	We ⌣ ate rice, beans, and corn.
start a new paragraph	¶	¶ We ate rice, beans, and corn.
add a comma	⋏	We ate rice, beans and corn.
add a period	⊙	We ate rice, beans, and corn⊙
switch letters or words	∼	We ate rice, baehs, and corn.
change to a capital letter	a̲	we ate rice, beans, and corn.
change to a lowercase letter	⫽	WE ate rice, beans, and corn.
let the marked text stand	(stet)	We ate rice, beans, and corn. (stet)

Glossary

accurate correct or exact

achieve succeed in doing or getting something as a result of your actions

affect do something that produces a change in someone or something

alter change in some way

ancient very old

approach move closer to someone or something

appropriate suitable for a particular time, situation, or purpose

archaeologist someone who studies very old things and buildings made by people who lived a long time ago

architecture the shape and style of buildings

armies the soldiers of countries that fight on land

arrangement a plan or agreement that something will happen

artificial not natural, but made by people

aspect one of the parts or features of a situation, idea, or problem

assassinated murdered, especially for political reasons

assist help someone do something

astronaut someone who travels in space

attitude the opinions and feelings that you usually have about someone or something

average calculated by adding several amounts together and dividing by the total number of amounts

aware realizing that something is true, exists, or is happening

benefit something that gives you an advantage, that helps you, or that has a good effect

bond a feeling or interest that unites two or more people or groups

brief continuing for a short time

campaign a series of actions done to get a result, especially in business or politics

cancer a serious illness which causes a growth to spread in the body

canyons deep valleys with very steep sides

captured taken as a prisoner

category a group of people or things that have related characteristics

ceremony group of special actions done and special words spoken at an important public or religious event

challenge something that tests your skill and ability

character traits special qualities or features that someone or something has that make that person or thing different from others

characters people or animals in a novel, story, movie, or play

chemotherapy treatment for cancer

circumstances the facts or conditions that affect a situation, action, or event

citizen a person who lives in a particular country or city and has special rights there

classical belonging to the culture of ancient Greece or ancient Rome

clues things that help you find the answer to a difficult problem

colorful language words an author uses to make a story, play, or movie sound and look more fun

comment a stated opinion made about someone or something

committee a group of people chosen to do something, make decisions, etc.

communicate express your thoughts and feelings so that others understand them

complex complicated

concept an idea of how something is or how something should be done

conflict disagreement

conservationists people who protect natural things such as animals, plants, or forests

consist be made up of or contain particular things or people

constant happening regularly or all the time

construct build something large such as a building, bridge, or sculpture

contact the act of talking to someone

continent one of the large areas of land on earth, such as Africa, Europe, Australia, etc.

controversy a serious argument about something involving many people over a long time

conversion the art or process of changing from one form, purpose, or system to a different one

convey communicate a message or information, with or without using words

cooperate to work together with someone else to achieve something that you both want

create make something exist

creature an animal

crucial extremely important

cultural relating to a particular society and its way of life

cycling the act of riding a bike

damage harm that has been done to something

define show or describe what something is or means

democratic organized by a system in which everyone has the same right to vote, speak, etc.

demonstrate protest or support something in public with a lot of other people

deny say that something is not true

destruction the act of breaking or damaging something completely

device a way of achieving a particular purpose or effect

dialect a form of language that is spoken in one area in a different way than it is in another area

dialogue a conversation by two or more characters in a book, play, or movie

disappeared was lost or stopped existing

document record information about something by writing about it, photographing it, etc.

drama a play for the theater, television, radio, etc.

education teaching and learning

effect the way in which an event, action, or person changes someone or something

element part of a plan, system, piece of writing, etc.

enormous extremely large in size or amount

environment the land, water, and air in which people, animals, and plants live

establish create

estimate judge the value or size of something

evidence facts, objects, or signs that make you believe that something exists or is true

extinct no longer existing or living

extraordinary very special

fable a story that teaches a lesson

factors several things that influence or cause a situation

fantasy an imagined situation or thing that is not real

feature quality, element, or characteristic of something that seems important, interesting, or typical

figure of speech a word or expression that is used in a different way from the usual one, to give you a picture in your mind

final last in a series of actions, events, or parts of something

finance provide money for something

focus attention to a particular person or thing

founders people who establish a business, organization, school, etc.

frontier the area where people are just beginning to explore or live

function the usual purpose of a thing, or the job that someone usually does; work properly

gifted having a special ability to do something

gigantic very big

gradual happening or changing slowly

gravity the force that makes objects fall to the ground

grueling very tiring and difficult

height how tall or how far from the ground something is

historic important as a part of history

humor something that amuses people or makes them laugh

hyperbole a way of describing something by saying that it is much bigger, smaller, heavier, etc., than it really is

identify recognize and name someone or something

idioms groups of words that have special meaning when they are used together

illustrate explain or make something clear by giving examples

image a picture that you can see through a camera, on television, or in a mirror; a picture that you have in your mind

impact the effect that something or someone has on someone or something

individual a person, not a group

infinity a space or distance without limits or an end

instruct teach someone or show him or her how to do something

intelligent having a high ability to learn, understand, and think about things

interpretation an explanation

intruder someone or something that enters a building or area where they are not supposed to be

length the distance from one end of something to the other; how long something is

list of characters a set of names that identify the characters of a play to the reader

lunar module a vehicle designed to explore the moon

mass-produced produced in large numbers using machinery so that each object is the same and can be sold cheaply

metaphor a way of describing something by comparing it to something else that has similar qualities, without using the words *like* or *as*. "A river of tears" is a metaphor.

method a planned way of doing something

mission an important job someone is asked to do

mood the way you feel at a particular time

moral a lesson about what is right and wrong that you learn from a story or an event

motive the reason that makes someone do something, especially when this reason is kept hidden

myth an ancient story, especially one that explains cultural beliefs or a natural or historic event

narrator someone who tells the story in a movie, book, etc.

NASA National Aeronautics and Space Administration, a government agency that explores space

natural found in nature, not made by people or machines

nomads people who travel from place to place, especially as a tribe

numerals written signs that represent numbers

nutrition the process of giving or getting the right kinds of food in order to be healthy

objective something that you are working hard to achieve

occupation job or profession

occur happen

ornithology the scientific study of birds

percent equal to a particular amount in every hundred

period a particular length of time in history or in a person's life

personification a literary device in which nonhuman characters are given human traits

perspective a way of thinking about something that is influenced by the type of person you are or by your experiences

philosophy the study of what it means to exist, what good and evil are, what knowledge is, or how people should live

physical relating to the body or to other things you can see, touch, smell, feel, or taste

plot the main events that make up the story of a book, movie, or play

point of view the position from which a story is told

positive good or useful

precise exact and correct in every detail

predator an animal that kills and eats other animals

prestigious highly respected and admired

process a series of actions that someone does in order to achieve a particular result

professional relating to a job for which you need special education or training

published printed and sold

puns amusing uses of a word or phrase that has two meanings, or of words with the same sound but different meanings

pursue chase or follow someone or something to catch him, her, or it

rate the number of times or the speed at which something happens

react behave in a particular way because of what someone has done or said to you

region a fairly large area of a state, country, etc.

rely on trust or depend on someone or something

repetition the act of doing or saying something again

require need something

research serious study of a subject that is intended to discover new facts about it

reservation an area of land that is kept separate for Native Americans to live on

resistance refusal to give in to someone or something

resource something such as land, minerals, or natural energy that exists in a country and can be used in order to increase wealth

respond react to something that has been said or done

rhyme scheme a pattern of end rhymes in poems or song lyrics

rhythm a regular pattern of sounds, or beats

rights what things are or should be allowed by the law

rituals ceremonies or sets of actions that are always done in the same way

robots machines that can move and do some of the work

role the position, job, or function someone or something has in a particular situation or activity

sacred relating to a god or religion; extremely important and greatly respected

science fiction a type of writing that describes imaginary future developments in science and their effect on life, for example, time travel

section a part of something

sequence a series of related events, actions, or numbers that have a particular order

setting where or when a story or real-life event takes place

setting the scene an author's details about the time and place in a book or play

shift a change in the way people think about something or in the way something is done

simile an expression in which you compare two things using the words *like* or *as*, for example, "Her face was as pale as the moon."

simulation something you do or make in order to practice what would happen in a real situation

site a place where something is being built or will be built

specific detailed and exact

sphere something in the shape of a ball

spirals shapes that go around and around as they go up

stage directions notes in a play that tell actors what they should do and how they should act

stanzas groups of lines that form part of a poem

statistics a collection of numbers that represents facts or measurements

steep having a slope that is high and difficult to go up

strategies sets of plans and skills used in order to gain success or achieve an aim

stress continuous feelings of worry caused by difficulties in your life

structure the way in which the parts of something connect with each other to form a whole

style a way of doing, making, or painting, something that is typical of a particular period

superintendent a person who is responsible for a place, job, activity, etc.

survive continue to live or exist

suspense a feeling of not knowing what is going to happen next

sustain make it possible for someone or something to continue to exist over time

techniques special methods of doing something

technology a combination of all the knowledge, equipment, or methods used in scientific or industrial work

tepees tents made from animal skins

theory an explanation that may or may not be true

tolerance willingness to allow people to do, say, or believe what they want

tram a small, open-sided train

trend the way that a situation is generally developing or changing

triathlon a sports competition with three parts: swimming, cycling, and running

tsunami a very large, forceful wave that causes a lot of damage when it hits the land

unique the only one of its type

vehicle something such as a bicycle, car, or bus that is used for carrying people or goods

volcanoes mountains with holes at the top from which ash, lava, and hot gases come out

weight how heavy something is

welfare health, comfort, and happiness

462

Index of Skills

465

Index of Authors, Titles, Art, and Artists

Acknowledgments

UNIT 1

"Fact or Fiction?" Copyright © Pearson Longman, One Lake Street, Upper Saddle River, NY 07458.

Teenage Detectives: "The Case of the Defaced Sidewalk" by Carol Farley and "The Case of the Disappearing Signs" by Hy Conrad. Originally appeared on MysteryNet.com. Copyright © 1998, 2005 by Newfront Productions, Inc. Reprinted by permission.

Excerpt from *G Is for Googol: A Math Alphabet Book* by David M. Schwartz. Copyright © 1998 by David M. Schwartz, Tricycle Press, Berkeley, CA, www.tenspeed.com. Reprinted with permission.

"The Haunted Yacht Club" by Ellen Fusz. Copyright © Pearson Longman, One Lake Street, Upper Saddle River, NY 07458.

UNIT 2

"Ancient Kids." Copyright © Pearson Longman, One Lake Street, Upper Saddle River, NY 07458.

"A Cry of Hounds" and "Soap Carving" from *Becoming Namoi León* by Pam Muñoz Ryan. Copyright © 2004 by Pam Muñoz Ryan. Reprinted by permission of Scholastic Inc.

"Amazing Growth Facts." Adapted from *Incredible Comparisons* by Russell Ash, Dorling Kindersley.

"The Old Grandfather and His Little Grandson," an adapted folktale by Leo Tolstoy. Public domain.

"Thirty Dollars" by Alan Govenar. Copyright © Pearson Longman, One Lake Street, Upper Saddle River, NY 07458.

UNIT 3

Excerpt from *Run Away Home* by Patricia C. McKissack. Scholastic Inc./Scholastic Press. Copyright © 1997 by Patricia C. McKissack. Reprinted by permission.

"Extraordinary People: Serving Others." Copyright © Pearson Longman, One Lake Street, Upper Saddle River, NY 07458.

Excerpt from *Zlata's Diary: A Child's Life in Sarajevo* by Zlata Filipović, translated by Christina Pribichevich-Zoric. Translation copyright © 1994 Editions Robert Laffont/Fixot. Used by permission of Viking Penguin, a Division of Penguin Group (U.S.A.) Inc. First published in France as *Le Journal de Zlata* by Fixot et Editions Robert Laffont 1993. Copyright © Fixot et Editions Robert Laffont, 1993. Reproduced by permission of Penguin Books Ltd. and by permission of Editions Robert Laffont.

"Friendship and Cooperation in the Animal Kingdom." Copyright © Pearson Longman, One Lake Street, Upper Saddle River, NY 07458.

UNIT 4

"Casey at the Bat" by Ernest Lawrence Thayer, 1888. Public domain.

"Swift Things Are Beautiful" from *Away Goes Sally* by Elizabeth Coatsworth. Copyright © 1934 by Macmillan Publishing Company, renewed 1962 by Elizabeth Coatsworth Beston. By permission of Paterson Marsh Ltd on behalf of the Estate of Elizabeth Coatsworth.

"Buffalo Dusk" from *Smoke and Steel* by Carl Sandburg. Copyright © 1920 by Harcourt, Inc. and renewed 1948 by Carl Sandburg. Reprinted by permission of the publisher.

"Going, Going, Gone?" Adapted from *Time for Kids*, January 22, 2002. © 2002 Time for Kids. Reprinted by permission.

"Ivory-Billed Woodpeckers Make Some Noise" by Jill Egan. Adapted from *Time for Kids*, August 5, 2005. © 2005 Time for Kids. Reprinted by permission.

"The Hare and the Tortoise" by Aesop. Public domain.

"The Biggest Winner of All." Copyright © Pearson Longman, One Lake Street, Upper Saddle River, NY 07458.

UNIT 5

Excerpt from *The Secret Garden* by Frances Hodgson Burnett and adapted by David C. Jones, from *Plays, The Drama Magazine for Young People*, © 2005. Reprinted with the permission of the publisher PLAYS/Sterling Partners, Inc., PO Box 600160, Newton, MA 02460.

"A Tree Grows in Kenya: The Story of Wangari Maathai" and "How to Plant a Tree." Copyright © Pearson Longman, One Lake Street, Upper Saddle River, NY 07458.

Excerpt from *Hoot* by Carl Hiaasen. Copyright © 2002 by Carl Hiaasen. Used by permission of Alfred A. Knopf, an Imprint of Random House Children's Books, a Division of Random House, Inc., and by permission of the author c/o Rogers, Coleridge & White Ltd., 20 Powis Mews, London, W11 1JN.

"Between Two Worlds." Copyright © Pearson Longman, One Lake Street, Upper Saddle River, NY 07458.

UNIT 6

"Life in the Future." Copyright © Pearson Longman, One Lake Street, Upper Saddle River, NY 07458.

"Southbound on the Freeway" and "Cardinal Ideograms" from *The Complete Poems to Solve* by May Swenson. Copyright © 1993. Used with permission of The Literary Estate of May Swenson.

"Interview with an Astronaut: Dan Bursch." Copyright © 2000 Discovery Communications, Inc. All rights reserved. Reprinted by permission of Discovery Kids.

Excerpt from *The Best New Thing* by Isaac Asimov. Copyright © The World Publishing Company, New York, 1971.

Excerpt from *2095: Time Warp Trio* by Jon Scieszka. Copyright © 1995 by Jon Scieszka. Used by permission of Viking Penguin, a Division of Penguin Young Readers Group, a member of Penguin Group (U.S.A.) Inc., 345 Hudson Street, New York, NY 10014. All rights reserved.

"NASA and the U.S. Space Program." Copyright © Pearson Longman, One Lake Street, Upper Saddle River, NY 07458.

Credits

of Congress; 170 center-right, Martin McEbilly/© New York Daily News, L. P. Reprinted with permission; 170 bottom-left, Bettmann/CORBIS; 171 bottom-right, JP Laffont/Sygma/CORBIS; 172 bottom-right, Adam Smith/Taxi/Getty Images; 174 center-right, ©LC-USZ62-7875/Prints and Photographs Division/Library of Congress; 175 top-right, Bettmann/CORBIS; 175 bottom-right, Hulton-Deutsch Collection/Bettmann/CORBIS; 176 top-right, Bettmann/CORBIS; 176 bottom-right, AP/Wide World Photos; 177 top-right, Francesco Zizola/Magnum Photos, Inc.; 179 center-right, Bettmann/CORBIS; 179 bottom-right, Jean Claude Francolon; 183 center-right, Bettmann/CORBIS; 186 bottom-left, Ian Shaw/Stone Allstock/Getty Images; 187 top-right, Michael Dinges/Photodisc/ Getty Images; 188 bottom-right, Alexandra Boulat/Sipa; 189 bottom-right, Alexandra Boulat/Sipa; 190 bottom-right, Francoise de Mulder/CORBIS; 191 top-right, Alexandra Boulat/Sipa; 192 center-right, Alexandra Boulat/Sipa; 193 top-left, Otto Lang/ CORBIS; 193 bottom-right, Les Stone/Sygma/CORBIS; 194 top-right, Nigel Chandler/Sygma/CORBIS; 194 bottom-right, ©Orhan Cam/Shutterstock; 195 bottom, Alexandra Boulat/Sipa; 199 center-right, Courtesy of the Library of Congress; 200 Bryan Reese/iStockphoto; 201 Josef78/Shutterstock; 202 Joshua Haviv/iStockphoto; 204 Wendell Franks/iStockphoto; 205 Jason Lugo/iStockphoto; 206 Amy Walters/iStockphoto; 207 Shutterstock; 208 Nuno Santos Photography/iStockphoto; 209 Monika Wisniewska/iStockphoto; 216 center-right, Bettmann/CORBIS.

UNIT 4: 226–227 background, Bob Thomas/Stone Allstock/Getty Images; 226 bottom-left, Doran Milich/Allsport Photography/Getty Images; 226 center-bottom, Arthur A. Allen/Cornell Laboratory of Ornithology; 226 bottom-right, Hart, G. K. & Vikki/Image Bank/Getty Images; 227 bottom, Kati Molin/iStockphoto; 228 bottom-left, The Bridgeman Art Library International/A Bison, c.1832 (coloured engraving) by George Catlin (1794–1872) © Bibliotheque Nationale, Paris, France/Lauros/Giraudon/The Bridgeman Art Library; 229 top-right, Hopkins, Edith (fl.1879–98)/The Bridgeman Art Library International/Private Collection/The Bridgeman Art Library; 230 bottom-right, Karl Weatherly/Photodisc/Getty Images; 231 center-right, Tony Freeman/ PhotoEdit; 235 bottom-right, Bettmann/CORBIS; 236 top-right, R. C. Frampton/Pearson Education/PH College; 237 top-right, ©LC-USZ62-115064/Prints and Photographs Division/Library of Congress; 239 bottom, Tom Leeson/Mira; 243 center-right, Joe Sohm/Chromosohm/Stock Connection; 244 top-right, Schafer and Hill/Peter Arnold, Inc.; 244 center-right, Terry Andrewartha/Nature Picture Library; 244 bottom-right, Doug Gardner/Mira; 245 bottom-right, David Tipling/Nature Picture Library; 246 bottom-right, ©Maksym Deliyergiev/Shutterstock; 247 top-right, Jorg Greuel/Image Bank/Getty Images; 248 background, Peter Anderson/Dorling Kindersley; 248 center, © Academy of Natural Sciences of Philadelphia/CORBIS; 249 background, Peter Anderson/Dorling Kindersley; 249 top-left, Dorling Kindersley; 249 center-right, © Academy of Natural Sciences of Philadelphia/CORBIS; 249 center-bottom © Academy of Natural Sciences of Philadelphia/ CORBIS; 250 background, Peter Anderson/Dorling Kindersley; 250 bottom, Arthur A. Allen/Cornell Laboratory of Ornithology;

251 background, Peter Anderson/Dorling Kindersley; 251 top-right, © Academy of Natural Sciences of Philadelphia/CORBIS; 252 top-right, David Peart/Dorling Kindersley; 252 center-right, John Cancalosi/Nature Picture Library; 252 bottom-right, Theo Allofs/Danita Delimont Photography/DanitaDelimont.com; 253 center-right, Prentice Hall School Division; 257 center-right, Joel Sartore/National Geographic Image Collection; 258 bottom-left, Stockbyte/Getty Images; 259 top-right, Noble, John Edwin (1876–1961)/The Bridgeman Art Library International/Private Collection/The Bridgeman Art Library; 260 bottom, © Craig Ellenwood/Alamy; 261 top-right, Cal Vornberger/Peter Arnold, Inc.; 262 full page, Noble, John Edwin (1876–1961)/The Bridgeman Art Library International/Private Collection/The Bridgeman Art Library; 263 bottom-right, Mary Evans Picture Library; 264 top, Fine Art Photographic Library, Ltd.; 265 top-right, The Bridgeman Art Library International/Roger-Viollet, Paris/ The Bridgeman Art Library, London/New York; 266 center-right, Hart, G. K. & Vikki/Image Bank/Getty Images; 267 bottom-right, The Bridgeman Art Library International/Louvre, Paris, France/ The Bridgeman Art Library; 271 center-right, © Ancient Art & Architecture/ Danita Delimont Photography/DanitaDelimont.com; 272 Michele Princigalli/iStockphoto; 273 wsfurlan/iStockphoto; 274 robograf/iStockphoto; 276 Shutterstock; 277 Kati Molin/iStockphoto; 278 Marc Pagani Photography/Shutterstock; 279 Rixie/Dreamstime; 281 Tyroneras/Dreamstime.

UNIT 5: 298–299 background, Jeff Hunter/Stone Allstock/Getty Images; 298 bottom-left, Richard Hutchings/PhotoEdit; 298 center-bottom, William Campbell/Peter Arnold, Inc.; 298 bottom-right, Tom Vezo/Nature Picture Library; 299 bottom, Bettmann/CORBIS; 300 bottom-left, Jacqui Hurst/Dorling Kindersley; 302 bottom-right, Richard Hutchings/PhotoEdit; 311 center-right, Bettmann/CORBIS; 311 bottom-right, Plays Magazine; 313 bottom-right, Comstock Images/Alamy Images; 317 center-right, Peter J. Robinson/Photolibrary.com; 318 top-right, Christop Burki/Stone Allstock/Getty Images; 318 bottom, Skip Brown/National Geographic Image Collection; 320 bottom-right, Shutterstock; 321 top-right, Simon Harris/Robert Harding World Imagery; 322 background, Charlotte Thege/Das Fotoarchiv/Peter Arnold, Inc.; 322 center, Terje Bendiksby/Agence France Presse/Getty Images; 323 background, Charlotte Thege/Das Fotoarchiv/Peter Arnold, Inc.; 323 center-bottom, William Campbell/Peter Arnold, Inc.; 324 background, Charlotte Thege/Das Fotoarchiv/Peter Arnold, Inc.; 324 bottom, ©Friedrich Stark/Alamy Images; 325 background, Charlotte Thege/Das Fotoarchiv/Peter Arnold, Inc.; 325 top-right, Mark Winwood/Dorling Kindersley; 326 top-right, © Marc Romanelli/Alamy Images; 327 top-right, Agence France Presse/Getty Images; 327 bottom-right, David Turnley/CORBIS; 331 center-right, Dorling Kindersley; 332 bottom-left, © Jim Parkin/Shutterstock; 333 bottom-right, Mark Richards/PhotoEdit; 334 bottom-right, ©ES James/Shutterstock; 335 center-right, Larry Landolfi/Photo Researchers, Inc.; 343 bottom-right, Jeffery Allan Salter/SABA Press Photos, Inc./CORBIS; 345 bottom-right, Klaus Nigge/National Geographic Image Collection; 349 center-right, Tom Vezo/Nature Picture Library; 350 Bettmann/CORBIS; 351 Philip Lange/iStockphoto; 352 Ann Taylor-Hughes/iStockphoto; 354 CORBIS; 355 Harry Thomas/iStockphoto; 356 bottom-left,

Smithsonian American Art Museum List of Artworks

UNIT 1 Solving the Puzzle of Letters and Numbers
Page 74
Mike Wilkins
Preamble, 1987
painted metal on vinyl and wood
96 x 96 in.
Smithsonian American Art Museum, Gift of Nissan Motor Corporation in U.S.A.
© 1987 Mike Wilkins

Page 75
Robert Indiana
Five, 1984
wood and metal
69⅛ x 26¾ x 18½ in.
Smithsonian American Art Museum, Gift of the artist
© 1984 Robert Indiana

UNIT 2 Capturing Childhood
Page 150
Albert Bisbee
Child on a Rocking Horse, about 1855
daguerreotype
4¼ x 4½ in.
Smithsonian American Art Museum, Museum purchase from the Charles Isaacs Collection
made possible in part by the Luisita L. and Franz H. Denghausen Endowment

Page 151
William Holbrook Beard
The Lost Balloon, 1882
oil on canvas
47¾ x 33¾ in.
Smithsonian American Art Museum, Museum purchase

UNIT 3 Respect
Page 224
Jesse Treviño
Mis Hermanos, 1976
acrylic on canvas
48 x 70 in.
Smithsonian American Art Museum, Gift of Lionel Sosa, Ernest Bromley,
Adolfo Aguilar of Sosa, Bromley, Aguilar and Associates
© Smithsonian American Art Museum

Page 225
Jacob Lawrence
"Men exist for the sake of one another. Teach them then or bear with them."—Marcus Aurelius
Antoninus, Meditations, VIII: 59. From the series Great Ideas of Western Man., 1958
oil on fiberboard
20¾ x 16¾ in.
Smithsonian American Art Museum, Gift of Container Corporation of America

472

UNIT 4 Baseball in America
Page 296
Mark Sfirri
Rejects from the Bat Factory, 1996
various woods
15⅜ x 36½ in.
Smithsonian American Art Museum, Gift of Fleur and Charles Bresler in honor of
Kenneth R. Trapp, curator-in-charge of the Renwick Gallery (1995–2003)
© 1996 Mark Sfirri

Page 297
Morris Kantor
Baseball at Night, 1934
oil on linen
37 x 47¼ in.
Smithsonian American Art Museum, Gift of Mrs. Morris Kantor

UNIT 5 Dignity Through Art
Page 375
James Hampton
The Throne of the Third Heaven of the Nations' Millennium General Assembly, about 1950–64
gold and silver aluminum foil, Kraft paper, and plastic
180 pieces: 10½ x 27 x 14½ ft.
Smithsonian American Art Museum, Gift of anonymous donors

UNIT 6 Imaging the Future
Page 454
Alexander A. Maldonado
San Francisco to New York in One Hour, 1969
oil on canvas and wood
18 x 24 in.
Smithsonian American Art Museum, Gift of Herbert Waide Hemphill Jr.
and museum purchase made possible by Ralph Cross Johnson
© Smithsonian American Art Museum

Page 455
Harry Bertoia
Sculpture Group Symbolizing World's Communication in the Atomic Age, 1959
braised and welded brass and bronze
142¼ x 231¼ x 81 in.
Smithsonian American Art Museum, Gift of the Zenith Corporation